Argumentation in Dispute Mediation

Argumentation in Context (AIC)

This new bookseries highlights the variety of argumentative practices that have become established in modern society by focusing on the study of context-dependent characteristics of argumentative discourse that vary according to the demands of the more or less institutionalized communicative activity type in which the discourse takes place. Examples of such activity types are parliamentary debates and political interviews, medical consultations and health brochures, legal annotations and judicial sentences, editorials and advertorials in newspapers, and scholarly reviews and essays.

Volume 3

Argumentation in Dispute Mediation. A reasonable way to handle conflict
by Sara Greco Morasso

Argumentation in Dispute Mediation

A reasonable way to handle conflict

Sara Greco Morasso
USI - University of Lugano

John Benjamins Publishing Company
Amsterdam / Philadelphia

™ The paper used in this publication meets the minimum requirements of American National Standard for Information Sciences – Permanence of Paper for Printed Library Materials, ANSI Z39.48-1984.

Library of Congress Cataloging-in-Publication Data

Greco Morasso, Sara.

Argumentation in dispute mediation : a reasonable way to handle conflict / Sara Greco Morasso.

p. cm. (Argumentation in Context, ISSN 1877-6884 ; v. 3)

Includes bibliographical references and index.

1. Persuasion (Rhetoric) 2. Mediation. 3. Discourse analysis. I. Title.

P301.5.P47M665 2011

303.6'9014--dc22 2010045327

ISBN 978 90 272 1120 0 (Hb ; alk. paper)

ISBN 978 90 272 8727 4 (Eb)

John Benjamins Publishing Co. · P.O. Box 36224 · 1020 ME Amsterdam · The Netherlands

John Benjamins North America · P.O. Box 27519 · Philadelphia PA 19118-0519 · USA

To my family

Table of contents

Acknowledgements

Throughout the journey of writing this book, I have had many encouraging and challenging encounters with many persons whom I wish to thank.

The origin of the journey coincides with my doctorate, conducted at USI-University of Lugano (Switzerland) under the supervision of Eddo Rigotti; yet its itinerary includes a long phase of re-discussion, re-elaboration and revision that I have done after my Ph.D, both at USI[1] and at the University of Neuchâtel.

I feel honoured and grateful for having been supported by so many and so rich dialogical exchanges. First, I am indebted to Eddo Rigotti and to the jury members of my Ph.D dissertation defence, Frans van Eemeren and Anne-Nelly Perret-Clermont. Their support was precious in all phases of my work. In the writing of this volume, I enormously benefited from the comments of two anonymous reviewers, whose remarks have been decisive for the results that I am presenting.

I am grateful to my colleagues at the Institute of linguistics and semiotics for their argumentative and friendly support, and to the colleagues at the Institute for Psychology and education at the University of Neuchâtel for their interest in interdisciplinary confrontation and for having welcomed me in their research group.

Many other colleagues from different backgrounds and institutions have accompanied me along this journey. Among them, particularly, several colleagues at USI and in the larger networks of the projects Argumentum and Argupolis; I would also like to mention the colleagues at the Department of foreign languages and literatures at the Catholic University of Milan and the participants to the Amsterdam-Lugano Colloquia on Argumentation (2004–2009).

My work has benefited equally from advice by several professional mediators, particularly in Ticino. I would like to thank Marianne Galli-Widmer, whose experience and passion have been so important to me, the other colleagues of the Comitee of the Associazione Ticinese per la Mediazione and of the SUPSI professional mediation training program.

1. In June 2009, I received a one-month grant from the USI/SUPSI Gender Service, which allowed me to delegate my administrative duties and devote my time entirely to scientific research, including the revision of the present book. I am grateful for this precious support.

Last but not least, I am indebted to Mrs. Kathryn Clements for her valuable language revision of my manuscript; and to the John Benjamins publishing staff for their technical support.

***

It is difficult to find words to thank my family, because their support has been so important to me that this work is, in many regards, their merit. I am certainly thinking of Carlo, Giacomo and Ilaria; but I am also referring to the larger (Greco-Morasso) family.

As any academic mother knows, sitting in front of a computer and writing is the tip of the iceberg of a complex organization system. A very special mention in this relation goes to the grandparents, who regularly looked after my children while I was working. In relation to childcare, many thanks go also to my great au pairs.

I would also like to thank several friends in Lugano, Milan and London who have been very important to me and helped me in this work much more than they think. I shall not list their names here, because of space reasons; yet I hope that each of them will feel personally quoted.

CHAPTER 1

Argumentation in mediation

"There are enough human problems to go around; what is needed are more problem solvers who care, not just about winning, but about really solving the problems".
(Carrie Menkel-Meadow)

1.1 Mediation as a reasonable way out of conflict

"Man hat nur die Wahl zwischen Vernunft und Gewalt" (we can only choose between reason and violence): Karl Popper's well-known remark is particularly appropriate to identify the two extreme poles in the paradigm of responses to conflict available to humankind. Disagreements, disputes and conflicts touch everyone's experience, and violence is sometimes the response chosen to resolve such problems; in extreme situations, people may become adversaries or enemies, occasionally with fatal consequences.

Yet, as Popper suggests, there is a less brutal alternative to tackling problems, facing disagreements, and solving conflicts: the use of human reason in dialogue, namely, the adoption of an *argumentative* attitude. In relation to this, human societies have elaborated different civil practices to cope with conflict, from juridical systems to alternative approaches. All of these approaches are based on the ideal principle of finding reasoned solutions while satisfying the disputants' desire for justice and legitimacy (see Section 2.1.).

Among these different practices, mediation emerges as particularly relevant from the point of view of the parties' argumentative engagement in the process of conflict resolution. Mediation is based on the intervention of a third neutral party who can help those in conflict discuss their problem without removing responsibility for the solution from the individuals concerned. The very structure of mediation ensures that the resolution of the conflict must emerge from the *reasonable discussion of the disputants themselves*, rather than from a solution imposed by some external authority. The third neutral intervenor in this framework is someone who helps the development of the discussion without assuming the task of making the final decision. In this sense, mediation is clearly based on an optimistic view: it is assumed that human beings are able to reach a reasonable agreement by using reason in dialogue.

A peculiar trait of mediation is the *movement from conflict to consent* that this practice allows, through which two parties that have been in conflict restart communication and become confident that they can engage in an argumentative discussion and agree on a mutually satisfying solution to their problem. Counter-intuitively, conflicting individuals may abandon their adversarial and hostile attitude and come to regard their counterpart as a reasonable interlocutor, someone with whom they might co-construct a satisfactory solution. This change in the parties' attitude, which in mediation represents a true turning point towards the resolution of the conflict, is made possible by the help of the mediator who, discreetly but decisively, makes it possible for parties to speak to one another and discuss a reasonable solution.

The success of mediation as a conflict resolution professional practice, with a wide range of applications and the enthusiasm of practitioners and parties who have experienced it, can be considered as a sign that this practice offers disputants the possibility to restore jeopardized relationships by using reason in dialogue.

A significant event that has witnessed the growing interest in mediation is the decision of the Nobel foundation to award the 2008 Nobel Peace Prize to Martti Ahtisaari "For his important efforts, on several continents and over more than three decades, to resolve international conflicts". This decision is surely to be understood within the framework of Ahtisaari's personal merits in relation to his interventions in difficult conflicts.[1] Not less importantly, however, his nomination signals a progressive societal interest in mediation, which allows intervention in extremely delicate situations thanks to its structure based on the parties' argumentative co-construction of the solution.

Indeed, since its original establishment in North America in the 1970s, mediation has been part of a social movement demanding swift and tailor-made justice processes in response to the involved parties' requirement for just treatment, a resolution that meets their needs, interests and desires (Menkel-Meadow 2001: 922). The potential for mediation has frequently been

1. See http://nobelprize.org/ for the motivation of this award. The choice of Ahtisaari as a Nobel laureate has provoked political and cultural controversy. However, without discussing here the appropriateness of his nomination, it is important to consider that the motivation of awarding the prize clearly shows an increasing social awareness of the crucial topic of conflict and its resolution.

identified as a possible way for the parties' to control the outcome of the resolution process. In other words, parties are recognized as competent and responsible for making decisions on the settlement of their conflict. It has often been pointed out that consequently mediation offers the possibility of reaching a *win-win solution*, namely a solution based on integrative justice in which all the parties can benefit (Princen 1992a). Such solutions, being co-constructed by the parties themselves, can ideally meet their true interests and allow them to maintain their relationship, or even reconstruct it on a new and more solid basis. Frequently, mediators themselves, especially if they are former lawyers, testify to this possibility offered by mediation; sometimes it becomes the reason for their personal and professional "conversion" from adversarial litigation to mediation (see Menkel-Meadow 2001 and Friedman 1993, whose remarks on this topic are reported in Chapter 2, Footnote 42).

However, many of the individuals and groups who initially fostered mediation within the Alternative Dispute Resolution (ADR) methods (see Section 2.1.2 for a brief historical survey of their establishment) may not have been completely aware of the *argumentative difference* implied by this practice; namely of the extent to which a reasonable exchange of arguments taking place in a constructive mediation process can contribute to the settlement of the conflict. Indeed, the study of mediation, considered within the perspective of an evaluation of real-life practices in today's society, shows the relevance of its communicative component. In mediation, communication plays an essential role, as the whole process is managed by means of a discussion between the mediator and the parties (Folger & Jones 1994: ix). Even more specifically, argumentative dynamics (i.e. the effort to find a decision that resolves the conflict on a reasonable basis) constitute the very kernel of the communicative exchange in mediation (van Eemeren et al. 1993). Interestingly, mediation is configured as a practice with a high "argumentation rate"; its voluntary nature,[2] which could be interpreted as its weak point, turns out to be its real strength, because parties become protagonists of the rational foundation of their decision, which is not the case with several other methods and practices of conflict resolution. In fact, as already mentioned, only in the case of mediation do conflicting parties make a shared decision about their own conflict, by communicating about their problem and, specifically, by arguing with each other in order to establish the best possible

2. Even in those cases in which mediation is established by law as a mandatory process in order to resolve a conflict, it is not mandatory to arrive at a solution through the mediation. See Chapter 2 for some examples of actual practices.

solution. They are thus engaged in a process of weighing arguments in favour of one or the other solution and discussing them together, and of trying to understand each other's reasons with the help of the mediator in an ideally reasonable fashion (Herrman, Hollett & Gale 2006: 22).

1.2 From disputants to co-arguers: A change in attitude raising complex research questions

Mediation has for long been studied from the argumentative point of view, in light of the interest that the parties' self-determination can have and for the consequent potential relevance of argumentation in this specific context. It can be very difficult for conflicting parties, who are entrenched in conflict and have been quarrelling for a long time before entering mediation, to engage in an ideally sound argumentative discussion. However, mediation can succeed, sometimes quite unexpectedly, and parties can learn to manage their problem themselves by means of argumentation.

In such successful cases, during the course of the parties' communicative interaction, their respective attitudes evidently change. If we compare the discussion of two parties at the beginning and at the end of a mediation session, a difference can be detected in the communication style; for example, in the parties' capacity to concentrate on the issue of resolving their conflict, on talking directly to each other, while at the same time leaving space for the other party to express their reasons. The brief excerpts presented in Table 1.1, taken from one of the cases that will be analysed in Chapter 6,[3] represent a paradigmatic example of the parties' change in attitude. The involved parties are, beside the mediator (M), a university professor, Philip (P), who has been accused of harassment by a student, Ann (A), who is enrolled in an academic programme for which (P) is responsible. The first column reports the parties' discussion at the very beginning of the case, while the second column refers to a more advanced stage, coinciding with the final minutes of the session.

Even at first sight, it is clear that, in column A, the conflict is still in its salient phase and the parties' statements fuel it (see turns 11 and 13 in particular). By the end of the session (column B) the parties show mutual understanding and respect

3. This case is analysed in Section 6.2.

Table 1.1. Example of a comparison between the parties' discussion style at the beginning and at the end of a mediation session

(A) Parties at the beginning of the session			**(B) Parties at the end of the session**		
6	P	Well I really don't know what the basis of the whole thing is a:: (.) bunch of UNFOUNDED nonsense ah:: (.) I really (.) [don't know why we are here	338	A	= I mean I want to forget it Professor Ford I I
7	A	[Well that's a bit strange =	339	P	[( )
8	P	= putting me in just an AWFUL situation some WILD allegations being made =	340	A	[I'm not going to go around looking for things↓
9	A	= Ya	341	P	Okay well that's what it seemed to me that you were sort of out to get me I must say that's how I perceived it at the (.) start of
10	P	A:nd (.) [and so ( ) past coming and:: (.) I really don't know what	342 I	M	Does it seem that now↑
11	A	[So I'm just (.) one of those CRAZY women/ (.) you're a victim of (.) some loony single mom	343	P	Well I (.) no I've got a bit more understanding (.) no
12	M	Ann (.) tell me (.) what's the basis for the allegation =	344	M	All right
13	P	= Well paranoia ( ) a lot of [paranoia	345	P	Eh: (.) no I had thought she was a nice student and she's a good student and (.) now I have a lot of regret that this took place but (.) eh (.)
			346	A	[I still am nice/
			347	P	[I understand now that (.) what she's saying has a lot more genuineness to it than I perceived it I thought that they were a lot of wild allegations and she was trying to get me for some reason and I didn't know why (.) so I understand now this (.) this (.) boundary business that it's a
			348	M	Okay all right
			349	P	That it has been a ( ) trouble (.) but hopefully she understands (1.5) that (.) that there was nothing (.) more intended by it than than than eh (3)

(turn 347), while the conflict is conceived as a past event that will not affect their relationship in the future (see turn 345 in particular).

Quite clearly, the parties have experienced a change in attitude, moving from disputants to interlocutors involved in what could almost be defined as a problem-solving discussion (van Rees 2003), where all the parties contribute to the resolution of a common problem. This change in attitude progresses at the same time as the process of conflict resolution, which is ultimately the pragmatic goal of mediation. In pragma-dialectical terms, as van Eemeren (2010) suggests, this change in attitude turns out to fulfil an important *second order condition*[4] necessary for the parties to resolve their difference of opinion by means of argumentation.

The excerpt considered in the second column of Table 1.1 is taken from the end of the process, and so there is seemingly no proper exchange of *arguments* in the parties' communicative exchange. Indeed, by taking into account larger portions of co-text, this passage represents a particularly happy case of a concluding stage of a critical discussion, in which the parties in conflict have agreed on a solution, setting the basis for mutual trust and for the continuation of their discussion. In this sense, this passage suggests that the parties have changed their communicative style by means of their engagement as co-arguers.

Within this framework, the *mediator* role emerges as fundamental. Mediators, in fact, being the facilitators of the parties' communicative interaction, act as the architects of their argumentative discussion. The parties' change in attitude can only happen because of the mediator's continuous interventions, which aim at establishing a reasonable setting for the parties' argumentative discussion (van Eemeren et al. 1993: 19). It is clear that the progressive constitution of the parties' argumentative attitude brings an essential contribution to the resolution of the conflict. Argumentation indeed, is oriented towards the reasonable resolution of *differences of opinion* (van Eemeren & Grootendorst 2004), namely of disagreements and conflicts of opinion.

The change in attitude that the parties experience also seems to reflect a change in their relationship, which is progressively re-established and somehow renewed on the basis of their argumentative exchange, which guarantees the possibility that problems in the future can be discussed reasonably.

Yet, as has already been pointed out in the literature, the mediator role presents a *paradoxical* situation in this relation (see Aakhus 2003 in particular and the other argumentative studies presented in Section 2.2.1). In other words, although mediators are crucial in defining the parties' argumentative discussion, they are far removed from corresponding to the traits of canonical arguers. In fact, mediators are expected to contribute to the discussion without expressing a personal standpoint about any specific resolution, and without advancing any arguments in

4. See van Eemeren and Grootendorst (2004: 36): "The 'internal' mental states that are a precondition to a reasonable discussion attitude can be regarded as 'second order' condition for a critical discussion".

support of given standpoints.[5] This is their paradox: *they express no standpoint and no argument, yet they are essential for the argumentative discussion in mediation to be fruitfully conducted.*

Such a paradox brings to light the relevance of the *context* (Rigotti & Rocci 2006) and, in particular, of the *activity type* in relation to the development of the argumentative discussion (van Eemeren & Houtlosser 2005). Indeed, the paradox in which the mediator is entangled, as well as the constraints and opportunities deriving from it, are a direct consequence of the context in which the argumentative discussion is embedded.[6] It is therefore particularly important to understand the nature of the mediation process, its goals and phases, in order to elicit the role that argumentation plays in it. This will also make clear that argumentation is not extrinsic to the mediation process; it is actually essential for the achievement of the pragmatic goal of mediation, namely conflict resolution.

It is important to remark that the parties' change in attitude can be said to have a direct influence on the fulfilment of the mediation process goals. In fact, parties learn to become co-arguers by discussing the resolution of their conflict; and, as soon as they learn to engage in a sound argumentative discussion, they simultaneously acquire the means to reasonably solve their problem. Thus, in a successful mediation process, the achievement of an argumentative attitude coincides with the possibility that the disputing parties can solve the conflict. Although this coincidence is well known, its dynamics have scarcely been investigated. What does it mean *concretely* to manage an argumentative discussion, to help parties

5. This paradox might also have hidden the relevance of argumentation in this practice. Significantly, to my knowledge argumentation is not introduced in the training of mediators. Some interest seems to be present only in the domain of Online Dispute Resolution practices (see Lodder & Vreeswijk 2004).

6. The mediator's argumentative paradox is strictly bound to the nature of mediation. In fact, it appears to be entailed by the mediator's mandate as an agent in the *agency relationship* he/she is involved in with the parties. The concept of agency relationship, first introduced in finance (Ross 1973) and later in economics and other social sciences, proves to be an excellent conceptual instrument to explain the crossing of commitments deriving from institutional roles and individuals' desires in organizations. Agency theory, in fact, analyses the interpersonal relationship between a *principal* – someone who has a goal, and delegates its realization to someone else – and an *agent* – who is in charge of realizing the principal's goal in exchange for some form of remuneration. This theory offers a realistic view on a usual form of human relationship bound to various interactions that is typically institutionalized by a form of *contract* (Eisenhardt 1989). In mediation, the mediator is hired in order to help parties find a reasoned and reasonable solution but, at the same time, is expected not to actively engage in the discussion.

create an argumentative space, without being a co-arguer? How does this happen? And how does this contribute to the resolution of the process?

The role that argumentation plays in mediation must be investigated by analysing how the argumentative discussion is structured, whether and to what extent it corresponds to the ideal standard of a *critical discussion*, and which roles the parties and the mediator play (van Eemeren & Grootendorst 2004). Within this framework, particular attention must be devoted to the mediator's argumentative intervention, which, as already mentioned, is at the same time paradoxical and decisive. Therefore, the mediators' contribution to the setting up of the parties' argumentative discussion will be considered, by verifying in particular whether and how they help the parties to structure argumentative discussions, and whether and how they help parties construct sound argumentations both at the level of their logical validity as well as at the level of their correct and effective link to shared premises (Rigotti 2006; see Chapter 5).

Answering these questions will entail a grasp of the specific role that argumentation can play in the development of human interaction in a social practice such as mediation.

1.3 Structure of the volume

Analysing how argumentation is generated in the context of dispute mediation requires a complex research structure. This book is organized into three main parts, corresponding to the conceptual blocks that are necessary to carry out this research.

In order to analyse argumentation in the context of dispute mediation, it is first necessary to become familiar with this specific context of human interaction. This observation may seem redundant or even trivial but it is not. I maintain that, in order to understand how argumentation works in a process of conflict resolution and how it is possible to lead the parties to become co-arguers, it is not sufficient to have only general notions about mediation. A rich understanding of dispute resolution practice is necessary, including its goals, the mediator's and parties' expectations, and the ideal script that constitutes a successful mediation process. I shall give a characterization of mediation that comes from an internal perspective, trying to look at the meaning of mediation as professionals do. I believe that this rich understanding of context is the key for a relevant argumentative analysis; namely an argumentative analysis able to grasp the constitutive dynamics of a certain context and point to the relevance of argumentation to these dynamics.

Thus the first conceptual block will be constituted by a progressive definition of mediation as a context for argumentative interactions. This conceptual block corresponds to Chapters 2 and 3 of the present volume.

Chapter 2 will have the function of exploring the context and showing its significance for argumentative studies. After briefly delineating the history and present institutional status of mediation (2.1), I shall address the issue of why mediation matters to argumentative studies (2.2). In this regard, I shall first report on state-of-the-art argumentation studies in mediation, and then elaborate on the different reasons why this practice may be viewed as a benchmark for the study of argumentation in context. It is not just its international relevance and the wide spectrum of applications of mediation that make it an interesting social phenomenon for analysis; the communicative structure of mediation and the particular type of "thirdness" embodied by mediators make this practice unique as for its argumentative dynamics.

Chapter 3 will more specifically map the context of mediation, by analysing contemporary studies in conflict resolution. Currently many different disciplinary perspectives and approaches tackle mediation; the result is a very fragmentary picture of this practice. This chapter aims to reconstruct as far as possible a consistent map of mediation. Of course, as in any synthesis, this chapter includes a selection and re-orientation. The selection is determined by the goal of the present study in which mediation is understood as a context of argumentative interaction. The primary interest is in the role that argumentation plays in this practice, and how it determines communication between the mediator and the involved parties. In order to reach this goal, it is important to clarify the interagents involved in a communicative-argumentative process in mediation; how they interact, why they come to mediation, what type of relationship they may have, and how the communication process in mediation develops. Bearing these questions in mind, I shall re-read the different approaches to mediation and categorize and re-orient them according to two main aspects that together form a mediation model: the mediation *scenario* (3.1) and *script* (3.2).

The resulting mediation map, however integrated it may be, still does not provide a comprehensive overview of mediation as an argumentative context (3.3). For this reason, a second conceptual block is required for the goals of the present research; namely an analytical, concept-building part that, building on the results of the previous synthesis, allows drawing an *ontology-oriented conceptual framework of mediation* including its relation to argumentation. What is meant under the term "ontology-oriented framework" will be explained in greater detail in Chapter 4. For the moment, it is important to highlight that this framework aims at capturing the defining traits of mediation at the level of involved interagents and of their relationships; namely those traits that are essential to the definition of a mediation process as such (hence "ontology-oriented"). Such a representation of the defining characteristics of mediation, building on the interconnected notions of scenario and script, is necessary in order to understand the role that argumentation plays in the mediation process. This second conceptual block is discussed in two chapters – Chapters 4 and 5 – which have very different functions.

Chapter 4 will complete the picture emerging from the literature review presented in Chapter 3 by introducing two interdisciplinary integrations to the current accounts of mediation provided by conflict resolution studies. These integrations concern two concepts that are universally acknowledged as crucial nodes for a mediation intervention, but are surprisingly underinvestigated: the *context* of the communicative interaction occurring in mediation, constituted by the parties' relationships; and *conflict,* namely the trigger of any mediation process. In order to reconstruct the parties' relationship as a possible context for the argumentative discussion in mediation (4.1), I shall introduce a model of context drawn from communication research (Rigotti & Rocci 2006) that is suitable for providing a general basis for the research on argumentation in the context of dispute mediation. As for the notion of *conflict*, I shall introduce a semantic analysis of this term (4.2; see also Greco Morasso 2008). Clarification of the notions of context and conflict will constitute the basis on which to sum up the results of the previous literature review and sketch an ontology-oriented conceptual framework of mediation (4.3).

The task of integrating the argumentative perspective in this conceptual framework is then the purpose of Chapter 5. After having briefly presented the argumentation models that are assumed in the present work (5.1), I shall provide some cues to this integration (5.2).

At this stage, argumentation is integrated into the framework of dispute mediation at the conceptual level. However, this does not thoroughly answer the questions posed initially in the present work. To do this, we still need an empirical analysis of how argumentation is actually developed in successful mediation processes. For this purpose, I shall introduce a third and final conceptual block constituted by the argumentative analysis and discussion of a sample of successful mediation cases. The goals of this section are to understand how argumentation is set up in mediation. More specifically, I shall go through the communicative interaction and verify how an argumentative discussion can be established in an interpersonal conflict; and what role mediators play in the parties' change in attitude that leads them to become co-arguers. I shall look for any prominent and recurring argumentative patterns that characterize argumentation in the context of dispute mediation and reconstruct how the context affects the argumentative discussion and, in particular, the mediator's *strategic manoeuvring* (van Eemeren & Houtlosser 2002). I shall also consider to what extent argumentation allows the goals of dispute mediation, namely the resolution of the parties' conflict, to be achieved.

After the presentation of the empirical corpus (6.1), Chapter 6 is entirely devoted to the discussion of the results of the argumentative analysis (6.2 and 6.3). Chapter 7 will elaborate on the significance of the present research, making explicit some of the limits to the research and suggesting further research perspectives. In this final chapter, I shall draw some general conclusions about the study of argumentation in context.

CHAPTER 2

Mediation as a context of argumentative interactions

Methodologically, the interpretation of any text and the choice of relevant context can only be done by starting from the text itself.[1] Context, in fact, is virtually infinite; and understanding what is relevant to the interpretation of a text cannot be done in advance. However, in the case of contexts that are to some extent institutionalized, such as the legal context, the financial context, as well as practices such as teaching, doctor–patient consultation, or mediation itself, starting a textual analysis without a definition of the main characteristics of the concerned context or practice would be unwise. In fact, as van Eemeren and Grootendorst (2004: 12) put it, specific knowledge of the context in which the argumentative interaction takes place is relevant to the *analytical reconstruction* of argumentation. Context often sets up expectations and conventions which may justify a specific reconstruction. Thus, knowledge of the specific context in terms of institutional and interpersonal relations becomes a source for an accurate analytical reconstruction. For this reason, in the block constituted by Chapters 2 and 3, the main features of mediation as a conflict resolution practice will be illustrated. Grasping the basic features and the "spirit" behind current applications of mediation is necessary to reach the goal of the present study; namely to understand how argumentation is subservient to the pragmatic goals of mediation. Moreover, a brief illustration of the uses of mediation in society will be useful to picture its current significance, which constitutes a reason to focus on this particular context of argumentative discourse.

More specifically, the goal of this chapter is to introduce mediation as a context of argumentative analysis by showing its characterizing features and making its relevance to argumentation explicit. In Chapter 3, building on these acquisitions, I shall focus in greater detail on the structure and goals of dispute mediation.

---

1. I owe this remark to Marcelo Dascal, who discussed this topic during his course "From difference of opinion to conflict", held in Lugano in February 2010 in the framework of the Argupolis doctoral program (www.argupolis.net [July 13, 2010]).

I shall now briefly illustrate the contents of the present chapter. In Section 2.1, “Exploring the context”, a first approach to mediation will be proposed, starting from a diachronical perspective that takes into account the origin and current institutional status of dispute mediation. Section 2.2 elaborates on the reasons why mediation matters to argumentation studies. After discussing state-of-the-art literature on argumentation in mediation (2.2.1), I suggest that mediation is a particularly important object of study in relation to contextualized argumentation for two sets of reasons. A first set, intrinsic reasons of interest, is bound to the unique communicative structure of mediation, which boosts the role of argumentation in conflict resolution practice (2.2.2). A second set of reasons, more extrinsic in nature, is bound to the importance of mediation in our society. Section 2.2.3.1 describes the various domains in which mediation is currently applied. Section 2.2.3.2 explains how this wide range of applications has made mediation an object of scientific study from different disciplinary angles.

This overview represents a first exploration of the territory of mediation in terms of its argumentative relevance. Chapter 3 will more systematically elicit the characterizing features of mediation as they are emerging from the literature on conflict resolution.

2.1 Exploring the context

2.1.1 From conflict to conflict resolution practices

“Like it or not, you are a negotiator” (Fisher, Ury & Patton 1991: xvii). The opening statement of this volume on negotiation and conflict resolution, which has had and is still having an enormous impact for its groundbreaking implications, highlights the ubiquity of negotiation in an individual’s life. Negotiation needs to be entered into so frequently because disagreements, conflicts of interest, interpersonal disputes, and other forms of conflict are equally frequent in human interaction, and human beings have to face and settle them as productively as possible. Conflict is a *problematic* event, and, as such, it needs to be managed. Also, it is natural to look for ways to resolve conflict, because it undermines and endangers existing relationships. It triggers alliances and oppositions which polarize the parties’ positions; it creates a situation of precarious rapport that may block any constructive initiative; and it focuses attention and energy on the parties’ reciprocal endeavour to hinder the realization of each other’s desires.

Whether it is an interpersonal dispute or an international conflict over the recognition of the independence of a new state, conflict throws the human subjects involved in it into a state of uncertainty, including the fear of losing every positive value that characterized the pre-conflictual phase and of being forced to surrender one's deeply-held interest or desire – in the extreme case, to be annihilated. Such fear, which has a rational origin insofar as it derives from a realistic consideration of possible outcomes of the conflict, clearly encompasses a strong emotional component (Deutsch 2006: 29).

For all the implications that conflict may have, it is natural, as mentioned above, to try to resolve it and re-establish the situation of a durable and peaceful relationship, where constructive initiatives are possible, and in which trust and hope are established. Thus, ingeniously, human beings have elaborated different ways to cope with conflict. Before tackling these ways, however, it is worth considering that the event of conflict can touch and endanger people's relationships on different levels. For the moment, the feature of conflict that has been highlighted above – its nature as an event capable of jeopardizing the existing network of human rapport – will suffice as a rough approximation of its definition. The genesis and dynamics of the conflictual event, however, requires further investigatation in order to fully understand mediation (in relation to this, see the semantic analysis presented in Chapter 4).

Not all approaches to conflict are argumentative in nature. At one extreme, the solution to conflict is war and other forms of physical elimination of the adversary party, which thereby becomes an *enemy*. These forms can constitute a way out of conflict as, by physically eliminating adversaries, one can actually manage to eradicate a problem. Needless to say, eliminating the people involved in a problem may prove effective, but is a brutal method of resolving the problem itself.[2]

Yet human beings strongly desire not only to close conflict but also to have the possibility of saving valuable relationships and to live in a stable and friendly environment. Not every way out of conflict is considered to be equally fair and satisfying. In this relation, the authors referring to the research centre named Program on Negotiation (PON) based at Harvard University have elaborated a model of conflict resolution (which will be discussed in Chapter 3) in which they identify the notion of *legitimacy* as constitutive of the disputants' interests or "one of the most powerful human motivations" (Patton 2005: 281). In this use of the term, legitimacy is defined as the need to receive fair treatment in conflict resolution and to achieve a fair outcome (ibid.). It can arguably be interpreted not only as the wish for an equitable distributive solution, but also as encompassing the desire that the solution can be the basis of stable, well-ordered and durable relationships, based on mutual trust and respect.

2. I shall not discuss here whether war is always avoidable or not. Its brutal nature remains evident in all cases.

It could be argued that war and violence in general are opposed to those methods of conflict resolution that take into consideration legitimacy as an interest of all the subjects involved in the conflict. The latter approaches more or less directly rely on argumentation as a means to solve the conflict. They are at the origin of peaceful relationships and dispute resolution systems in all civil societies (see Grossi 2003),[3] the most important and well known of which is the juridical system. However, the juridical systems organized and managed by the State are not the unique instruments that societies have at their disposal to resolve disputes (Grossi 2003: 36–37 and *passim*). Various interventions on conflict, more or less formalized, are admitted and fostered, among which a particularly significant position is occupied by those practices that, as mediation, foresee the intervention of a third neutral subject who is in charge of re-establishing a legitimate and possibly peaceful order. Interestingly, the dispute resolution instruments developed by civil societies are all based on communication and, more specifically, on the reasonable weighing of arguments that ideally results in a sound persuasion. Indeed, *reasonableness* is the key to understanding societies' civil answer to conflict, and it is the reason why argumentation plays a fundamental role in these practices (see Chapter 5).

Mediation is historically attested as one of the practices of conflict resolution that complement the function of a juridical system in a civil society. Mediation is present as an informal practice employed privately to resolve conflicts of an

3. Grossi discusses an interesting analogy between *law* and *language*, which are both considered to be institutions that regulate the social dimension of the individual subject; the former being a means to allow effective communicative activities, and the latter being a means for peaceful coexistence in society (Grossi 2003: 27). The fact that law (and all the forms that the juridical system may assume) is to be considered as an institution, the author argues, highlights its embeddedness in society. Law is an institution whose "natural realm" is society; it is a necessarily history-bound experience, guided by the goal of the individuals' peaceful co-operation and of the mutual respect of their freedom in their communal coexistence: "Vogliamo cioè sottolineare [...] che il diritto [...] appartiene alla società e quindi alla vita, esprime la società più che lo Stato, è il tessuto invisibile che rende ordinata la nostra esperienza quotidiana, consentendo la convivenza pacifica delle reciproche libertà. È, insomma, identificabile in un vero autosalvataggio della società" (Grossi 2007: 6). However, Grossi also warns against the possible risks of absolutizing positive law imposed by the State; law, in this case, becomes almost autonomous from its goal of being a legal *order* of society. Grossi's interpretation of law is particularly illuminating for the study of mediation and other forms of dispute resolution like ADR practices. Indeed, if the subject of law is society rather than the State, it is possible to acknowledge the various and manifold sources of law that are present in civil society; such "private" forms of law are established by communities that want to preserve some relevant value by means of rules or even proper codes (see Grossi 2007: pp. 36–37 in particular).

interpersonal nature in families, small communities, between friends, and so on. But the crucial importance that mediation may have is becoming increasingly acknowledged in more formalized contexts. Nowadays, indeed, we look to a progressive institutionalization of the mediation practice as a juridically valid and recognized alternative to court in a variety of contexts, from interpersonal disputes in all sectors of social life, to inter-group and international conflicts concerning, for example, commercial transactions or inter-state relations. It is worth briefly examining the historical development of mediation and the progressive social awareness of its validity as a form of dispute resolution on many levels of human relationships.

2.1.2 A concise history of formal and informal practices of mediation

The story of mediation is certainly longer than that of the ADR movement. The rationale for the practice coincides with the discovery of the fact that, often, when conflicts are particularly exacerbated and prolonged over time, the parties in conflict become no longer able to talk to each other directly and need help in solving their problem and, possibly, in restoring their relationship. The intervention of a third party who is not personally involved in the issue provides a way for the disputants to start seeing things in a more detached and reasonable way. Such awareness arose a long time before the origin of the ADR movement (Duss-von Werdt 2005). Knowing the history of formal and informal practices of mediation means understanding how powerful an argumentative intervention can be at the level of the construction of human societies.

In European history in particular, two institutions have successively been involved in mediation processes between nations and other political institutions: the Venetian Republic and the Vatican (Princen 1992b). Vatican diplomacy already had a strategic function in the first centuries after Christ. Later on, both the Vatican and the Venetian Republic were asked to send their ambassadors to help in international disputes. Today, papal diplomacy still fulfils a significant mediatory function on an international level (along with a few other institutions, such as the U.N.). For instance, a relatively recent case, the Beagle Channel conflict between Argentina and Chile, is often quoted as a particularly successful example of international mediation overseen by the Vatican in the years between 1978 and 1984.[4]

4. The success of this mediation is proven by its durability through time. Benadava (1989: 50) who was one of the Chilean negotiators at the time, has observed that the parties accepted the final agreement (the *Tractado de Paz y Amistad*) giving the islands to Chile, but maritime

Outside European history, mediation is attested as an informal practice that has developed into formal dispute resolution systems in other traditions too. In particular, James Wall and his colleagues have devoted a series of studies to mediation in some non-Western contexts, which aim to connect the modern mediators' techniques now applied in different countries with the respective ancient cultural and religious roots that are present in these countries. In particular, a first study (Wall & Blum 1991) surveyed community mediation in China; the study was then repeated in South Korea (Kim, Wall, Sohn & Kim 1993), Hawaii (Wall & Callister 1995), Japan (Callister & Wall 1997), Malaysia (Wall & Callister 1999) and Thailand (Callister & Wall 2004).

Mediation has been and is applied also *beyond* the framework of institutionalized ADR practices. Nowadays, informal mediation is practised in multiple social contexts and realities. In this sense, mediators are much more widespread in our society than one may think: relatives who help to solve family conflicts, friends who intervene to restore relationships at risk of being damaged, and so on, are clear examples of informal mediators. Sometimes being a mediator is part of a differently denominated job. For example, team leaders, school directors, social workers, sometimes even police officers, can all be examples of informal mediators. This is worth signalling because there is an underworld of

rights to Argentina, as the definitive solution to their issues ("la solución completa y definitiva de las cuestiones a quel él se refiere"), and have committed themselves to not putting forward incompatible interpretations later. The agreement ended a long controversy concerning the Beagle Channel, a small strait separating the islands of the Tierra del Fuego archipelago in extreme southern South America. The channel in itself only hosts three little islands of no value; but, of course, its strategic positioning was of interest for both Argentina and Chile, who both wanted access respectively to the Pacific and Atlantic oceans. Rights over who the channel belonged to and its navigation rights were left ambiguous after Spain divided the land into two countries. In 1971, Argentina and Chile requested arbitration from the International Court at Le Hague, under the auspices of Britain's Queen Elisabeth II. When, in 1977, the arbitration award arrived, Argentina refused to accept it, considering it an invasion of state sovereignity. Such a reaction was the origin of a period of tension between the two countries, which brought them close to a real war in December 1978. The Argentinian army would have invaded the islands on December 22, but due to unfavourable weather, the invasion was delayed for two days. Meanwhile, the Vatican, which had previously been contacted for possible help in resolving the conflict, sent its envoy to South America. This allowed the climate of the crisis to be mitigated; finally, from March 4, 1979, proper mediation was started, overseen by Pope John Paul II, who sent his envoys, Cardinal Antonio Samoré until 1983 and, after his death, Cardinal Agostino Casaroli, there. The mediation process was long and complex; the final treaty was signed on November 29, 1984 in the Reggia Hall, next to the Sistine Chapel, in Vatican City. The most extensive and detailed studies on this mediation were conducted by Thomas Princen (see in particular Princen 1992a: 133–185).

informal mediation practices that is highly beneficial to the construction of society, but which cannot be labelled as part of the ADR movement, and in which the mediators involved probably do not define themselves as such.

Surely, those who work as informal mediators must be authoritative persons whom both parties trust enough to allow them to intervene in the conflict. Indeed, trust plays a huge role in formal mediation; in informal cases, it is only bound to the mediator's personal qualities and does not normally depend on formal training. A person's authority, of course, depends on the surrounding and personal relationship; thus, informal mediators normally "work" for a specific community, such as an office or other working place, a family, a small town, or a cultural community. The stronger the community ties are, the more this form of self-regulation of conflict is possible. For example, there is much evidence of mediation in religious communities. Folberg and Milne (1988: 4) quote, for instance, a passage from one of St. Paul's letters inviting Christians to solve their disputes within the community rather than by addressing the external juridical system.[5] The case of the Swiss Confederation is particularly representative and interesting, as its patron saint, Nicholas of Flüe, is well known for his mediation interventions at the civil and political level. In particular, he is well known for having prevented a civil war and having resolved the endless discussions of the Cantons meeting at the Diet of Stans in 1481 (Journet 1980). Since, after that moment, the first Latin Canton (Fribourg) was united to Switzerland, Saint Nicholas may also be interpreted as having helped foster the mediative attitude of multicultural Switzerland.[6] Similarly, in other religious traditions, the mediative role of religious figures is

5. In Corinthians 1.6, Paul's reproach seems to be a hymn for responsibility in conflict resolution, as he condemns those Christians who refuse to assume the burden of handling disputes and entrust external judges to handle the situation on their behalf: "3 Do you not realise that we shall be the judges of angels? – then quite certainly over matters of this life. [...] 7 No; it is a fault in you, by itself, that one of you should go to law against another at all: why do you not prefer to suffer injustice, why not prefer to be defrauded?"

6. In this relation, Durrer (1917–1921: xxix, quoted by Journet 1980: 205–206), describes Saint Nicholas as *the first confederate patriot*: "On peut affirmer que frère Nicolas fut *le premier patriote confédéré*, en ce sens qu'il fit prévaloir pratiquement et théoriquement l'idée d'une commune patrie suisse, indivisée et débordant les préoccupations des intérêts cantonaux". The author remarks that such a kernel of a free confederation can be assumed as the basis for a pacific alliance between the European peoples: "L'œuvre de paix du Convenant de Stans, en permettant concrètement la création d'une libre confédération d'Etats souverains, qui n'ont d'autres limites que celles que leur impose la conservation de la paix, ouvrait de lointaines perspectives sur la possibilité d'une alliance pacifique des peoples de l'Europe, fondée sur des bases analogues".

reported; see for instance Wall and Callister (1999) regarding the role of imams as mediators in Malaysia.[7]

In general, in relation to disputing parties, the mediator represents the community itself and thus guarantees the support and help of the community to the parties in order to restore a reasonable attitude towards each other. Here, an example taken from a novel will be of use in understanding the kind of relationship that can be established in a cultural community between an informal mediator of this kind and conflicting parties. The well-known novelist Chaim Potok movingly describes a dispute resolution intervention in one of his works, *My Name is Asher Lev*, published in 1972. The dispute occurs within the Hasidim community in New York (Brooklyn) between Asher, a Hasidim boy with a prodigious aptitude for painting, and his father, who has devoted his entire life to the spreading of Orthodox Judaism among Jews and is a political advisor to the Rebbe, the spiritual leader of the community. Asher's father, together with many members of the community, considers art a waste of time or, worse, a manifestation of the "Other Side", the realm of the demonic. Asher is in overt conflict with his father because he refuses to abandon painting; in fact, though being very young, he already feels his artistic creativity to be a gift from God, which should not be

7. The role of the imam is generally that of a mediator for the interpersonal conflicts occurring in the community that refers to him, in particular in relation to family conflicts. As witnessed in an interview which the author had with Radouan Jelassi (July 2008), an imam active in Lugano (Switzerland), probably the most interesting challenge an imam is faced with in present society is mediating intercultural conflicts, particularly if the community he is responsible for is placed in a non-Muslim country. In this case, Jelassi says, the most important principle that an imam should follow is that of finding a reasonable adaptation of the cultural implications of the Islamic religion to the different cultural context that one faces in a foreign country. In particular, as an imam, he devotes much attention to three categories of mediative interventions. First, he carefully prepares and follows the progress of couples engaged in mixed marriages, either constituted by a Muslim man and a Swiss woman, or by two Muslims coming from different countries. In these cases, even minor cultural differences (concerning, for instance, cuisine) can escalate into conflicts. Second, misunderstandings and conflicts can arise from the inability of one party to understand the other party's reasons because of either linguistic differences or ignorance of local customs and rules. In this case, the imam serves as an interpreter; for instance, between the local institutions (schools, hospitals, the police, and so on) and his followers, thus helping to prevent violent conflictual situations. Finally, some conflicts, which could indeed also affect monocultural communities, concern the very implications of the Islamic faith to the facts of real life. In this relation, Jelassi reports the very delicate case of a man wanting to separate from his wife because she was abused during the war in the former Yugoslavia. In this case, Jelassi maintains, it is part of an imam's task as a mediator to explain to the husband that his wife cannot be considered guilty from a religious point of view and, in any case, she "would not deserve to be punished twice".

wasted. At a certain point, the Rebbe himself wants to meet Asher personally. In a concise yet intense conversation, the Rebbe "mediates" between Asher's family and the young painter by showing that Asher's and his father's ways of living can be reconciled and that their conflict does not cancel the love that they feel for each other (Potok 1973: 168):

> 'Asher.'
> 'Yes, Rebbe.'
> 'A life should be lived for the sake of heaven. One man is not better than another because he is a doctor while the other is a shoemaker. One man is not better than another because he is a lawyer while the other is a painter. A life is measured by how it is lived for the sake of heaven. Do you understand me, Asher Lev?'
> 'Yes, Rebbe.'
> 'But there are those who do not understand this.'
> I was quiet.
> 'There are those you love and who love you who do not accept this. Asher, to honour your father is one of the Ten Commandments.'
> 'Yes, Rebbe.'
> 'I give you my blessings, Asher Lev son of Reb Aryeh Lev.'

Then the Rebbe, as a practical follow-up to his intervention, finds a master for Asher, who will teach him the fundamentals of painting. In this way, he legitimates Asher's professional decision in front of his father.

Now, of course, the Rebbe could not be hired in a modern mediation centre because of his undoubtfully interventionist way of proceeding. What it is important to point out, however, is the deep mediative attitude underlying this whole passage: the Rebbe interprets the controversy between Asher and his father, which has already escalated, as an unreal conflict in God's eyes. He also recalls the deepest interests of the parties, who are both suffering in this conflict, by restating (and, thus, putting to the fore) their reciprocal love, which is not hindered by the conflict: "those you *love* and who *love* you". Finally, the Rebbe suggests a reasonable solution to the struggle. The Rebbe's role, however, is not that of a judge,[8] because the final decision on the parties' relationship is up to them – as the rest of the story demonstrates.

8. Even the fact that the Rebbe reminds Asher of the Ten Commandments is not to be interpreted as the imposition of a rule to be followed regardless of a person's feelings, but as a way of recalling the common belonging to a community which is a larger family for both Asher and his father, and in which both of them are respected.

2.1.3 1976: The "Big Bang" of Alternative Dispute Resolution practices

Mediation, today, is more than an informal practice and a non-institutionalized way of peacefully handling conflicts by means of interpersonal communication. It is attested as a professional practice of conflict resolution applied in various contexts. This acknowledgement has given rise to the category of Alternative Dispute Resolution (ADR) techniques. These techniques are defined as *alternative* in relation to the ordinary juridical system. Under this label, techniques such as negotiation, arbitration, mediation itself, and "hybrids" such as med-arb, are included (Moffitt & Bordone 2005). In mediation, in particular, a third party (the mediator) intervenes in a conflict in order to facilitate a reasonable discussion between the opposing parties because, although they are no longer capable of negotiating directly, they are nevertheless committed to trying to find a solution.

The establishment of ADR practices is relatively recent, having begun in the 1970s. In general, these practices have had a positive response from society,[9] and some governments have started to foster their introduction. The origin of the ADR movement is located in North America (U.S. and Canada), but the establishment of ADR practices has also spread to Europe and other continents (Alexander 2003). In order to understand the relevance of ADR in Europe, it is worth considering that the European Commission, after having launched studies in this topic at the end of the 1990s, published the *Green Paper on ADR in Civil and Commercial Law* in 2002; in 2004, the *European Code of Conduct for Mediators* was presented while, in 2008, a new directive on this topic was adopted. In the United States, the Uniform Mediation Act was established in 2001 in order "to draft proposed legislation and/or court rules on various aspects of mediation that states may consider adopting to help bring more clarity and uniformity to the mediation process, while at the same time improving the quality and practice of mediation in the United States".[10]

When considering the historical development of ADR practices, a milestone is found in the lecture of a Harvard legal scholar, Frank Sander, in 1976, "Varieties of dispute processing" (republished in Sander 1979; see also Menkel-Meadow 2005: 19). Sander is credited with introducing the idea that a just process of dispute

9. Significantly, as mentioned in the introduction, the Nobel Prize 2008 was awarded to Martti Ahtisaari with a motivation that witnesses the increasing social awareness of the importance of dispute resolution practices: "For his important efforts, on several continents and over more than three decades, to resolve international conflicts" (see http://nobelprize.org/nobel_prizes/peace/laureates/2008).

10. See respectively http://ec.europa.eu/civiljustice/adr/adr_ec_en.htm and http://www.pon.harvard.edu/guests/uma/.

resolution was not limited to the state-governed juridical system. He suggested that a variety of alternative dispute resolution processes (such as arbitration and mediation)[11] could be used according to the different specific goals of the settlement and the characteristics of the dispute (Sander 1979: 83–84; Sander & Goldberg 1994). The introduction of the concept of a paradigm of dispute resolution processes to the academic world is probably Sander's most important contribution; Sander pointed out that the instrumental nature of the juridical system is in all cases subordinated to its goals of being a dispute resolution system. Thus, when the juridical system turns out to be inadequate to reach its aim, finding *alternative* means for obtaining the same goal -in this case, alternative dispute resolution methods – turns out to be a reasonable possibility.[12] Sander's 1976 lecture has thus been considered "a Big Bang of modern dispute resolution theory and practice" (Menkel-Meadow 2005: 19)[13] and has become a foundational text for research on alternative dispute resolution practices.[14]

On a professional level, the ADR challenge was taken up very seriously by two main groups of stakeholders. One group was made up of judges who, at the time, were questioning the ability of the legal system to process all cases in a reasonable

11. Some applications of arbitration and mediation were already present in the U.S., especially in the field of labour disputes (Menkel-Meadow 2005: 21).

12. See Sander (1979: 67): "By and large we lawyers and law teachers have been far too single-minded when it comes to dispute resolution. Of course, as pointed out earlier, good lawyers have always tried to prevent disputes from coming about, but when that was not possible, we have tended to assume that the courts are the natural and obvious dispute resolvers. In point of fact there is a rich variety of different processes, which, I would submit, singly or in combination, may provide far more "effective" conflict resolution".

13. Recently, a special section of *Negotiation Journal* 22 (4) has been devoted to "Frank Sander and his legacy as an ADR Pioneer". See in particular Moffitt (2006).

14. It happens sometimes that a programmatic discourse becomes the inspiration for the foundation of an entire branch of study. This happened, for instance, in the field of research in *nanotechnologies*, which still recognizes as its foundational text the lecture that Richard P. Feynman gave on December 29, 1959, at the annual meeting of the *American Physical Society*, significantly titled "There's plenty of room at the bottom". (I thank Carlo Morasso for having suggested this example of a foundational text in a scientific community.) Something very similar happened to Sander's lecture, which proposed the powerful image of a "Dispute Resolution Center, where the grievant would first be channeled through a screening clerk who would then direct him to the process (or sequence of processes) most appropriate to his type of case" (Sander 1979: 84). This idea inspired the metaphor of a "multi-door courthouse", where different approaches to dispute resolution could be practised; such a metaphor, being based on the relation between goals (resolving disputes) and means (various dispute resolution practices), has stimulated scientific research on alternative dispute resolution.

amount of time and within reasonable monetary expenditures. The other set of stakeholders was "a more amorphous social movement" whose members "sought greater party control and participation in dispute resolution" (Menkel-Meadow 2005: 19). The reasons for adopting the ADR challenge varied. First, in comparison to the ordinary juridical system, each person's deep interests and desires are specifically considered. In the case of mediation, this is particularly relevant, given the fact that the parties remain responsible for their decisions. Moreover, a mediated solution is often a win-win solution, whereas a judge's decision tends to create winners and losers, and, in this sense, blocks the conflict without resolving it. Second, in several countries, "traditional" juridical systems are overwhelmed by an excessive number of procedures, which usually impose an extremely high economic burden on involved parties.[15]

2.2 Why mediation matters to argumentative studies

Mediation has already been approached in different argumentation studies (Section 2.2.1). Much however remains to do in order to understand how argumentation is structured in this practice. The reasons for the choice of mediation as a context of study of argumentation are twofold. On the one hand, as I shall show in Section 2.2.2, there are intrinsic reasons to choose mediation, because the very nature of this practice has the potential to show the significance that argumentation may have in conflict resolution. On the other hand, mediation is also becoming a more and more significant context because of the pervasiveness of this practice in a number of different institutional domains (2.2.3). This is testified by the growing scientific interest reflected in the various disciplinary approaches to mediation currently present. This societal and scientific importance constitutes a somewhat extrinsic reason for focusing the interest of our argumentative research on the context of mediation.

2.2.1 The argumentative approach to mediation

The argumentative approach to mediation can surely be considered a field in development, whose foundational studies, however, have shown promising

15. See also Breidenbach (1995: 30): "Die Attraktion des (Grund-)Gedankens einer gütlichen Verständigung und die (unterstellte) Überlastung der Gerichte sowie die dadurch verursachte zunehmende Dauer und Kostenbelastung gerichtlicher Verfahren sind universale Gründe für eine Alternativen-Diskussion".

insights to the understanding of the core dynamics of mediation (see in particular van Eemeren et al. 1993). The argumentative interest in mediation arises from an awareness of the significance of argumentation in the context of the communicative interaction giving shape to the mediation process.[16] Indeed, the parties' task – that is, making a decision on the resolution of their conflict – necessarily involves critical reflection and evaluation of each other's arguments. The final decision, however, does not only depend on a rational weighing of arguments, but must also take into account the parties' emotional and interpersonal involvement in order to guarantee that the solution is made in the context of a discussion characterized by *reasonableness* (van Eemeren & Grootendorst 1994, 2004; see also Section 5.1). The communicative process in mediation is thus oriented towards a typically argumentative task, and largely constitutes an argumentative discussion.

Not coincidentally, a series of studies in argumentation have considered mediation as a relevant field of study (van Eemeren et al. 1993; Jacobs 2002; Jacobs & Aakhus 2002a and 2002b; Aakhus 2003; van Eemeren & Houtlosser 2005; Walton & Godden 2005; Walton & Lodder 2005; Greco 2005a; Greco Morasso 2007).[17]

16. Aakhus (2003: 270) observes that "the dispute mediator is just one example of an important class of work in society organized around the practical art of creating and maintaining forums for argumentative discourse, especially as realized in professional roles, institutions, organizational routines, and technology".

17. The communicative dynamics of mediation have not been extensively and systematically tackled except for this stream of study on argumentation. A relevant exception coming from the linguistic field is represented by a German project held at the *Institut für deutsche Sprache* (IDS) in Mannheim in the years between 1983 and 1988. This project was devoted to the empirical analysis of conversations labelled as *Konfliktschlichtung* (conflict settlement) interpreted as complex patterns of actions and texts (Nothdurft 1995b: 5). The results of this project were based on about 30 conversations taken from different conflict resolution practices bound to various institutional contexts (family, business, work relationships, and so on, see Nothdurft 1997: 4–5; Schröder 1997). The conflict resolution practices involved are, in general, quite similar to mediation, insofar as they involve the intervention of a third neutral with the aim of helping parties find a solution. The rights and duties of this third neutral vary according to the institutions concerned. Remarkable features of this project are the thorough description of the institutional context in which the selected conversations take place (see in particular Nothdurft 1995a); a careful analysis of the mediator's moves at the level of *elocutio* (see in particular Nothdurft 1997); and the elicitation of typical moves that can be said to constitute the pragmatic structure of the conflictual discussion in institutional settings, at least in its initial constitution (in particular the accusation made by one party, and the justification of the opposite position presented by the other party; see ibid.). Some observations are also made on the parties' argumentation (ibid., pp. 149 ff.) but, in general, the project does not take into account the argumentative dynamics promoted by the third neutral in order to help parties find a solution to their conflict. Moreover, the analysis seems to be more complete and

More specifically, the majority of argumentation studies devoted to mediation until now have focused on the specific mediator's contribution to the argumentative discussion.[18] Definitely, the mediator's role can be interpreted as an argumentative one – or, more precisely, as a co-argumentative one – as he/she assumes the delicate task of helping parties engage in a critical discussion that they could not manage alone, in order to find a reasonable solution for a difference of opinion that they could not solve by themselves. In fact, the mediator "triggers" an argumentative discussion (hence the often employed metaphor of the mediator as a *catalyst*) in a context in which it would be blocked or, at least, made extremely difficult because of the previous dynamics of the conflict.

In this relation, van Eemeren et al. (1993: 119), in a study that can be considered to be the first investigation specifically focused on the argumentative nature of mediation, noticed that the mediator is involved in argumentative interaction because he/she is in charge of helping parties reasonably discuss their issues in order to find the most reasonable solution for them. In this sense, the mediator's role precisely respects the fundamental aim of any argumentative discussion, which can be defined, in pragma-dialectical terms, as reasonably resolving a difference of opinion (van Eemeren & Grootendorst 1992, 2004). In particular, van Eemeren et al. (1993: 19) remark that the mediator's intervention is crucial for the correct development of the critical discussion because parties would be unable to conduct a critical discussion by themselves:

> "They [mediators] must remain impartial with respect to competing positions and uninvolved in the advocacy of those positions, but the resolution of differences may be seemingly blocked by unjustifiable proposals, evasion of issues, bogus objections, and the like. If one of the disputants persists in these practices, the mediator may be faced with the choice of "taking sides" or letting the process become a mere contest of wills [...]. And while mediators must be substantively neutral and leave the disputants to identify issues relevant to their dispute, if left unrestricted, disputants may get lost in squabbles, personal recriminations, and irresolvable differences of opinion that sidetrack discussion and block progress".

results appear more generalizable concerning the first phase of the conflictual discussion (the confrontation between the parties, and the presentation of the problem), while the development of the discussion towards a resolution of the conflict is less clear. Despite these possible limitations, however, this project is certainly remarkable for the specificity of the linguistic analysis. However, it is relatively unknown to conflict resolution scholars. Sadly one is tempted to think that its publication in German has undermined its fortune.

18. Only a few analyses constitute an exception, focusing on the parties' argumentation (Cisterna Rojas 2007).

The situation of mediation as a realm of argumentative discussion may be defined as "non canonical" (Greco Morasso 2007) and paradoxical (see Chapter 1). Such a situation (see also van Eemeren et al. 1993: 119; Jacobs 2002: 1405) arises from different concomitant causes. On the one hand, as noted above, the mediator, differently from the canonical arguer, cannot have a personal standpoint in support of the arguments, but must remain neutral with respect to the decisions made by the parties (on the central role attributed to neutrality see Jacobs 2002: 1405–1407), while engaging in the enhancement of the discussion's reasonableness.[19]

On the other hand, the parties also have a peculiar status in relation to their role as participants to the argumentative discussion. If they are pre-committed to resolving the dispute, as demonstrated by their willingness to engage in the mediation process,[20] and prepared to engage in a discussion in which they will be responsible for making the final decision, they may nevertheless refuse to behave in a reasonable way or be able to set up a discussion in line with standards of reasonableness (van Eemeren et al. 1993; Aakhus 2003). In relation to this, van Eemeren et al. (1993) and Aakhus (2003: 267) speak of mediation as a field where it is possible to test the model of critical discussion under "less-than-ideal conditions", thus integrating the theoretical model with insights from argumentative reality.[21]

Yet the study of the argumentative dynamics characterizing mediation has not merely originated as a test bench for theoretical models of argumentation. It primarily aims at improving the understanding of the mediation practice. In this relation, the argumentative studies of mediation have developed into two distinct but related directions.

The first direction is centred on the *quality* of the mediator's intervention (Jacobs & Aakhus 2002a: 30; Walton & Lodder 2005: 75). Quality is defined against the backdrop of a theoretical model of argumentation that can be specified

19. In this relation, Aakhus (2003: 269) speaks of an "ironic position" of mediators, which makes mediation exemplary of a class of interactions where parties to argumentation work under less-than-ideal conditions (van Eemeren et al. 1993: 174).

20. Mandatory mediation may create even more problems, because disputants, albeit compelled to show up at the (first) mediation sessions, may refuse to assume a communicative behaviour consistent with the aim of this practice.

21. Some studies which interpret critical discussion in narrower terms (as a type of communicative practice rather than an ideal model of the argumentative discussion), claim that the mediator's chief goal is to find a practical settlement of the conflict, and, therefore, he or she intervenes in a general framework of bargaining, which often does not match the ideal model of argumentation; it has been noticed that critical discussion, however, plays a subservient role also within this framework as a means for critically testing parties' standpoints and arguments (Jacobs & Aakhus 2002a; Walton & Lodder 2005).

by taking into account the specific contextual conditions imposed by the activity of mediation. A first essential condition of argumentation in mediation is, as has already been pointed out in discussing the positioning of mediation in relation to other ADR practices, the fact that the parties remain the legitimated decision-makers of the argumentative discussion and, thus, they should be the protagonists of argumentation and be persuaded of the reasonableness of the final solution, which should not be imposed on them by the mediator.

The model of a critical discussion may work as a normative grid for analysing the reasonableness of the moves and, thus, overall, the quality of the argumentative management of the practice in question. As Aakhus (2003: 285) puts it, critical discussion is "a blueprint for the dialogue to be realized". A similar function of the argumentative model of a critical discussion has been implemented for the evaluation and improvement of problem-solving discussions (van Rees 2003) and also of legal argumentation (Feteris 1999, 2005) in relation to the special role of the third neutral assumed by judges (Feteris 1987, 1993).

As mediation is an argumentative activity that is performed under less-than-ideal conditions (van Eemeren et al. 1993), the evaluation process must take into account the implementation and embeddedness of the ideal model in real-life contexts, which shape the opportunities of argumentation (van Eeemeren & Houtlosser 2005; Rigotti & Rocci 2006; Rigotti 2006). Evaluating the reasonableness of mediators' moves is thus a delicate process involving a consideration of the aims of a proper critical discussion in the concerned contexts. Some of the observations made by Aakhus (2003: 282–283) on the "puzzle" of mediators' moves is to be interpreted in this sense as specifying that some apparently uncritical and irrational moves may, on closer inspection, be interpreted as reasonable in regard to the final aim defined by their professional task.

In considering the topic of quality, a further research tradition also deserves to be mentioned, inaugurated by Walton and Lodder (2005) and Walton and Godden (2005). These studies, focusing in particular on Online Dispute Resolution,[22] aim to identify the various dialogue types (Walton 1998) occurring in the practice of mediation and other conflict resolution practices, and discuss their implications at the argumentative level.

A second direction of research has focused on different communicative strategies and techniques that mediators may exploit to fulfil their task within the boundaries imposed by the practice. This concern derives directly from the

22. ODR studies, in particular those stemming from the juridical perspective, appear to be a particular receptive field for the integration of the argumentative component into the study of conflict resolution practices (Lodder & Vreeswijk 2004).

consideration that the paradoxical argumentative role that the mediator's contribution is expected to fulfil entails the necessity of performing it through an appropriate communicative instrumentation. Indeed, the complexity of the paradoxical task that mediators assume is inevitably mirrored in the use of complex communicative strategies (Jacobs 2002: 1404, 1407 and *passim*). In this relation, mediators' reflection on the discourse strategies at their disposal still needs further development (van Eemeren et al. 1993: 119).

In regard to the different techniques mediators may employ, much of the analysis has focused on the specific role that certain speech acts (Austin 1962; Searle 1969; van Eemeren & Grootendorst 1984) play at the level of the argumentative reconstruction of the mediator's activity. The most interesting results are derived from studying the activity of asking *questions* (van Eemeren et al. 1993; Jacobs 2002; Greco Morasso 2007); the importance of questions is acknowledged also by renowned professionals of mediation involved in the reflection on their practice (Duss-von Werdt 2005: 223; Fong 2005).

A comprehensive study of the value of questions in mediation is a delicate task, as the speech act *question* – which does not necessarily coincide with the interrogative linguistic form – may fulfil different pragmatic and argumentative functions (Gobber 1999; Gobber 2007). Although further research on this topic is still required, a fundamental aspect of questions has been identified by Jacobs (2002: 1411, 1413) as a specific way to contribute to the argumentative discussion without contradicting the mediator's function and, in particular, his/her commitment to neutrality.[23] More specifically, Jacobs points out that certain questions "may get the respondent to commit to answers that could serve as common premises for arriving at some conclusion" (ibid., p. 1411). Similarly, Greco Morasso (2007) has shown how the mediator, by asking questions, may suggest specific arguments to the parties for resolving their conflict. As such arguments must in any case be verified and accepted by the disputants themselves, the mediator's contribution emerging from this kind of questioning can be interpreted as that of a "heuristic advisor" (ibid.).[24]

23. See Jacobs (2002: 1411): "But questions are also a common means whereby mediators perform many of the tasks that could have been accomplished more directly by just making arguments, giving directions, or otherwise rejecting or accepting disputant standpoints. [...] The advantage of this technique is that, through their answers, the disputants are the ones who make the assertions so that the mediator has not publicly advocated any standpoint or committed himself to any particular argument" (van Eemeren et al. 1993; Jacobs 1989).

24. The analyses performed indicate the main traits of the mediator's questioning and their argumentative implications without, however, analysing in detail all the possible functions of questions. Particularly interesting would be the communicative and argumentative study

Beyond questions, which are also quantitatively predominant in the mediator's way of talking (ibid.), other techniques have also been identified, such as *reformulations* (van Eemeren et al. 1993). Reformulations may fulfil different communicative and argumentative tasks, including *summarizing* and *equivocal advocacy* (Jacobs 2002: 1414 ff.).

The analysis of mediators' recurrent speech acts does not only take into account the linguistic and communicative levels but, more specifically, considers the argumentative implications of the presentational devices within the mediator's strategic manoeuvring (van Eemeren & Houtlosser 2005); in other words, these analyses aim to highlight the argumentative impact of the mediator's linguistic choices.

Still with an eye on the argumentative relevance of communicative moves, some authors have begun to study not only specific speech acts, but also the level of management of the argumentative discussion, in particular in relation to the management of issues. Aakhus (2003) describes some argumentative strategies by which mediators can help parties exit situations of *impasse* at particularly critical moments of the mediation discussion. In fact, impasse moments constitute real breakpoints in the argumentative discussion, as "the impasse moves contradict the fundamental values of critical discussion" (ibid., p. 282). Thus, mediators must find ways to re-trigger the disputants' involvement in the argumentative discussion or accept that it is unhappily concluded. In relation to this kind of situation, mediators' creativity in continuously reopening argumentative spaces emerges as crucial. Aakhus identifies and focuses on three main strategies: *redirection* (to other issues), *temporizing*, and *relativizing* (the importance the parties give to the issues and arguments, which may turn out to be misleading with regard to the aim of conflict resolution). From the examples analysed by Aakhus, it emerges that strategies reflect complex sets of moves that the mediator may perform in trying to resolve the impasse. A similar perspective is also assumed by Jacobs (2002), who also touches on the level of issue management while analysing the implications of questions and reformulations.

However, these studies do not explicitly tackle the problem of how argumentation can arise and an argumentative discussion be set up in mediation (see Chapter 1). How is it possible for the conflicting parties to become co-arguers? How is their argumentative discussion constructed, if the origin of their encounter is far from being a reasonable confrontation? What is the role of the mediator in this process? These questions remain open; they show that it is necessary to go

of so-called "circular questions" (Fong 2005), which are one of the tools taught in numerous mediation professional courses.

further along the path indicated by the first studies of argumentation to show how argumentation in mediation is structured.

This type of questioning requires particularly careful contextual analysis, because in order to understand how argumentation contributes to fulfil the pragmatic (contextual) goals of mediation, it is necessary to outline the characteristics of the context itself in a more detailed fashion than has previously occurred in mediation studies. Before starting the reconstruction of an ontology-oriented model of mediation, however, it is worth looking in more detail into the reasons why it is worth choosing mediation as a field for the study of argumentation in context. Mediation, in fact, is in some aspects paradigmatic, because it shows how and to what point a well-conducted argumentation can contribute to the development of an orderly society and to the resolution of conflicts (cf. Rigotti & Greco 2005). Moreover, the social significance of the practice of mediation, which is steadily increasing, is a reason to understand how this practice works from the argumentative point of view.

2.2.2 A special argumentative "thirdness" (intrinsic reasons of interest)

In the expression Alternative Dispute Resolution, the term *alternative* is employed to signal opposition to the ordinary juridical system, *litigation* or *adjudication*.[25]

In contrast to other ADR practices, mediation is distinguished by the *specificity of its argumentative dynamics*. The key for understanding the role that argumentation plays in mediation can be found in the apparently controversial figure of the mediator. A mediator is hired by the parties to help them reason together in order to find a solution to their conflict. Mediators should not be seen to actively participate in such reasoning, since their role as a neutral facilitator hinders them from suggesting any concrete proposals for resolving the dispute. In what follows, a concise overview of the fundamental characteristics of ADR techniques will be presented, with the aim of eliciting the specific role that argumentation plays in this practice.[26]

25. Litigation (or adjudication) involves two or more parties each represented by a lawyer who tries to persuade a third neutral. Both terms refer to the court-based dispute resolution process. The term *adjudication* refers to the judge's perspective, whereas *litigation* refers to that of the parties.

26. In relation to the study of argumentation in mediation, it is worth mentioning some recent research on the significant role of argumentation to construct effective Online Dispute Resolution tools (Walton & Lodder 2005; Walton & Godden 2006; and Lodder & Vreeswijk 2004). Recently, some alternative dispute resolution methods, in particular arbitration and

Particularly tied to the business environment (commercial disputes, construction issues, etc.), and especially widespread in the U.S., the so-called *mini-trial* consists in a sort of simulation of a court process. The parties agree to perform in this because it offers them the opportunity to see how their case might be resolved if they decide to opt for litigation and go to court (Sander & Goldberg 1994). As for argumentative dynamics, the mini-trial, being a representation of a court, maintains its organizational and decisional structure: the case is presented by the parties' representatives and then evaluated by a judging authority. Being a theatrical representation in which the judgment is not legally binding, the mini-trial works as a presentation of a possible world, part of a paradigm of the potential ways of handling the parties' conflict. The underlying argumentative principle is bound to a principle of opposition and, in particular, to a logical rule that may be formulated as follows: *within a paradigm of alternatives, it is convenient to choose the one that best suits one's interests*. In other words, according to the advantages and disadvantages that the foreseen solution has for the parties, they can decide whether this possible world is positive for them or if finding another solution through negotiation or mediation would be better. The practice of a mini-trial can turn into mediation if this is the parties' wish. In fact, it is clear that ADR practices are not necessarily mutually exclusive, but can be combined if parties feel that their initial choice did not work with their case. In this respect, some hybrid forms have been introduced, such as *arb-med* and *med-arb* (Ross & Conlon 2000).[27]

Arbitration is probably the most well-known and widespread ADR practice, and often the strongest alternative to mediation in a number of fields, including contract arbitration, labour arbitration, and international arbitration.[28] Arbitration

mediation, have developed in an online mode, based on the use of e-mail, phone and videoconferencing (Conley Tyler & Bornstein 2006: 334); these practices are commonly indicated with the acronym of ODR (Online Dispute Resolution). The spreading of this distance approach to conflict resolution had its origin in the context of business (Syme 2006: 346), in which it is still most widely employed, even though some applications in other fields have also been tried (Conley Tyler & Raines 2006). Interestingly, some of the developers of these software applications acknowledge the importance of a sound argumentative conceptuality in order to develop tools that can effectively support a reasonable discussion.

27. Med-arb, probably the most common hybrid form of ADR, consists of a first mediation phase followed by arbitration if mediation fails to secure an agreement by a predetermined deadline (Ross & Conlon 2000: 417). Arb-med is opened by an arbitration hearing. The arbitrator's award is not disclosed to the parties unless they cannot reach an autonomous agreement through mediation (ibid., p. 418).

28. Arbitration is also the first ADR practice that was established in the U.S. In 1920, the first modern contract arbitration law was passed in New York, and was followed in the next

"is a process by which a private third-party neutral renders a binding determination of an issue in dispute" (Cole & Blankley 2005: 318). Arbitration is considered alternative because it is outside the institutional juridical system and it allows a certain flexibility in the identification of the arbitrators and in the setting up of the process. However, from the point of view of the reconstruction of the argumentative dynamics between the involved participants, it may be said that no difference can be found between a judge and an arbitrator. The arbitrator, in fact, listens to and reconstructs the parties' stories in order to make a final binding decision (the arbitrator's *award*) on how to resolve the dispute.

Negotiation is the only ADR practice that in principle does not foresee external interventions in the conflict, but which the parties try to manage themselves. Differently from all other dispute resolution practices, negotiation is normally applied when the dispute has not yet become an extreme conflict because it presupposes that the parties are able to autonomously engage in an argumentative discussion.[29]

In *mediation* a third-party neutral, the mediator, intervenes in the conflict in order to help disputing parties reach a mutually agreeable resolution (see Kovach 2005). The process of mediation, in its institutional form, is normally concluded with a written agreement that is legally binding. Differently from negotiation, mediation involves the presence of a third party who does not

---

five years by fifteen other analogous laws in as many states. By that time, Congress enacted the U.S. Arbitration Law, "which remains the basic commercial and maritime arbitration law" (Barrett & Barrett 2004: 81). In 1926, the American Arbitration Association (AAA, see www.adr.org) was founded.

29. The most prominent studies on negotiation have originated from the research group called *Project of Negotiation* (PON, www.pon.harvard.edu), founded in 1980 by Roger Fisher, officially recognized by Harvard University in 1983 and now based at Harvard Law School and involving numerous schools and departments in the Boston area. The Harvard model of negotiation is currently considered to be one of the fundamentals of the study of conflict resolution practices. This model was first introduced in the foundational work called *Getting to Yes* by Roger Fisher and William Ury in 1981 and was further elaborated on in the updated version of this research (Fisher, Ury & Patton 1991) as well as in a number of other publications (see in particular Susskind, Mnookin, Fuller & Rozdeiczer 2003; Patton 2005). The strength of the Harvard approach lies in its introduction of a concept of negotiation, called *principled negotiation*, which presupposes the possibility of finding an agreement that truly respects the parties' interests through direct communication between the parties themselves. In other words, the hypothesis underlying the model is that human beings are able to express their interests, work in order to realize them and, when possible, find options that constitute mutual gains. Negotiation (including bargaining) is thus deprived of any negative moral judgement, and becomes the practice enabling such an encounter of desires.

assume the constituency of one of the conflicting parties, but works as a third neutral. The mediator is thus equally distant from – or, as is sometimes said by mediators themselves, *equally close to* – each party. In contrast to arbitration, the mediator does not have the power to impose a conflict resolution outcome on the parties and does not suggest any decision. For this reason, the mediator's role has often been described as the role of a "facilitator" of a resolution process that is co-constructed by parties who know their conflict and are responsible for the content of their discussion; the mediator has only to guarantee its form (Haynes & Haynes 1989: 3). The mediator, however, is not less involved in the process than a negotiator. Being responsible for the process, the mediator must guarantee that the *quality* of the parties' discussion is good (Greco 2005a). He/she helps the opposing parties to verbalize "individual positions and stories [which] provides the speaker and listener with an opportunity to develop a greater understanding of underlying needs and to stimulate higher-level reasoning" (Herrman, Hollett & Gale 2006: 22).

In any negotiation, the resolution of a conflict is expected to emerge from the parties' discussion. However, in cases that are handled by means of mediation, the conflict will already have escalated so that it is impossible for the parties to handle it without external help. Hence the intervention of a third neutral, whose function is intrinsically paradoxical (see Chapter 1): though being the catalyst (possibly) allowing the resolution of the conflict, the mediator will not personally contribute to the co-construction of a given resolution. His/her role is limited to helping parties find their own way to a reasonable discussion and resolution of the conflict. Within this narrow manoeuvring space, the huge value of the mediator's work appears to be that of allowing blocked communication and common reasoning to restart, and offering the possibility of re-establishing endangered relationships.

The services of *ombudsman* precede the ADR movement and have been incorporated in it in the last decades. The origin of the ombudsman service is to be found in the Swedish constitution dated 1809, where it was conceived as a service to citizens to enable them to pursue grievances against the executive and administrative offices of government. The ombudsman model then migrated to other Scandinavian countries and, in the 1960s, to the U.S. (Stieber 2000: 50–52). Like arbitrators, ombudsmen are third parties who are asked to intervene in conflicts that cannot be managed directly by the parties involved. They listen to the parties' views on the conflict, try to interpret their needs and, finally give a recommendation for conflict resolution that is similar to the arbitral award, except for the fact that parties may not be compelled to follow it. In contrast to mediators, however, ombudsmen tend to be based *inside* an organization (an institution or a company) and provide their services to people working in it. Therefore, the ombudsman's service has been defined as an "*internal* dispute resolution mechanism" (Harrison 2004: 313, emphasis added). This possibility is largely exploited by big organizations, such as universities,[30] states or other political institutions,[31] and large companies and institutions, such as banks[32] or newspapers.[33]

From the point of view of argumentation, the ombudsman's recommendation is thus an argumentative text that presents a solution and tries to support it with reasons based on evidence from the case at hand. The final decision on the conflict depends on how much the parties have been persuaded by this recommendation.

All in all, mediation shows to have, in relation to the other ADR practices, some specific features that, taken together, make it a unique approach to conflict resolution. Indeed, the positioning of mediation within the realm of ADR practices is important for the definition of this practice, and has therefore been tackled by theoretical studies (in relation to this, see the different proposals presented in Section 2.2.1). As a first approximation, it can be said that mediation, differently from negotiation, allows the intervention of a third neutral in the parties' process of conflict resolution. Differently from arbitration and ombudsman, however, the third neutral has no power to impose a decision; therefore, the parties remain the principal interlocutors in the communication process that may bring a resolution to the conflict, while the mediator assumes the delicate and discreet role of facilitator. A successful mediator opens the way for reflection on the power of communication and argumentation for, by means of pure discursive instruments, he or she is able to catalyse a change in the parties' attitudes, allowing resentful disputants to become co-operators involved in a communicative discussion oriented towards the resolution of their conflict. In this discussion, the arguments for resolving the conflict are oriented towards the parties themselves, who need to be persuaded and accept a shared solution. This makes communication and, in particular, argumentation, a privileged perspective for understanding mediation.

---

30. Stieber (2000: 51) reports that the number of ombudsmen in U.S. and Canadian universities exceeds 150 units.

31. The European Union provides an ombudsman service to which all European citizens and residents in member states can directly address a complaint (see www.ombudsman.europa.eu).

32. Since 1993, a Swiss banking ombudsman has been established by the Swiss Banking Association for all complaints raised against banks in Switzerland. In an interview given in 2007 and reported on the Swiss banking ombudsman website (www.bankingombudsman.ch), the current ombudsman Hanspeter Häni declares that "The number of cases has in fact risen continually over the last five years", which indicates the success of this service.

33. See the website of the Organization of News Ombudsmen: http://www.newsombudsmen.org/. An analysis of newspaper ombudsmen nowadays in different geographical and cultural areas is presented in Elia (2007).

2.2.3 The social significance of mediation (extrinsic reasons of interest)

A second, less substantial reason why mediation deserves attention in argumentative study – though one equally worthy of notice – is its broad social importance. Formal and informal mediation practices are used more and more as a conflict resolution method, which, as previously seen, is founded on a particular communicative structure that makes argumentation central to the achievement of its goals. This shows that a well-conducted mediation can have a significant impact at the societal level. If only for this reason, it is worth considering the role that argumentation plays in mediation.

In this section, I shall argue for the current societal significance of mediation in two different ways: first, I shall show the ubiquitous presence of mediation in a broad spectrum of application domains (2.2.3.1); second, the increasing multidisciplinary scientific interest in mediation will be illustrated (2.2.3.2).

2.2.3.1 *A widespread practice with a broad spectrum of applications*

Albeit the underworld of informal mediation practices (see Section 2.1) is a flourishing and dynamic environment that would constitute an interesting object of study, the majority of present-day studies concerning mediation are focused on *formal* (juridically institutionalized) practices, in particular as applied to *interpersonal*[34] conflicts (Herrman, Hollett & Gale 2006: 21). In part, the relative lack of information about informal practices of mediation certainly makes it difficult to approach them scientifically. Some of them inevitably pass unnoticed. Others, like processes of mediation in international contexts, are kept as secret as possible for the sake of their very success (Princen 1992a). However, the focus on ADR techniques and, within this context, on formal practices of mediation is primarily due to the increasing importance of the alternative dispute resolution methods in various social contexts and at different levels.

Although there are several studies devoted to single application fields of mediation, a complete and systematic overview of the whole panorama of mediation experiences is still lacking. Such an overview is nevertheless necessary in order to figure out the social relevance of this conflict resolution practice; thus here, I shall sketch a typology of conflicts of a different nature in which mediation is currently used. The typology is summarized in Figure 2.1. A more comprehensive description of the contexts as well as a more detailed justification of the typology is presented in Greco Morasso (2009a).

34. These studies on mediation and other ADR techniques do not exclude the application of international mediation in principle, although the most common field of application chosen in these studies is interpersonal conflict.

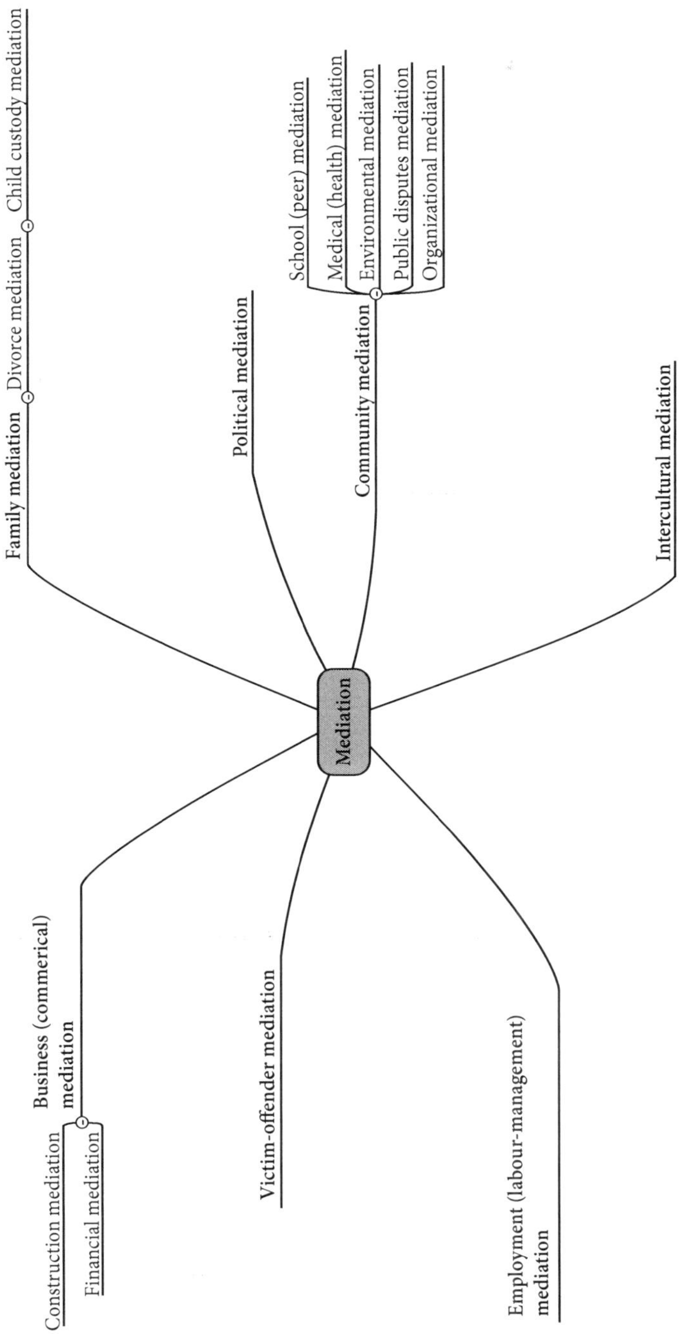

Figure 2.1. Current applications of dispute mediation: towards a reasoned typology

The list of application fields described below follows the terminology that has emerged from practice and from studies in mediation. Such terms, taken as a whole, do not constitute a homogeneous taxonomy; the categorization tends to privilege those areas in which mediation has been more successfully established. In general, the names tend to highlight either the major issue that has given rise to conflict (as in *business mediation* or *environmental mediation*), or the context where mediation is applied (as in *family mediation* or *community mediation*).

Generally, in all fields, mediation services can either be offered by individuals (who are frequently lawyers or psychologists) in the form of a private consultation service,[35] or they can be completely or partially funded by public institutions, which often support mediation centres offering services free of charge or at an affordable price.

Family mediation is probably the most affirmed field of application of mediation (Jones 2005; Kelly 2004). This label refers both to saveable marriages and to divorce and separation issues (Parkinson 1997: 48), thus enabling family mediation to work as a way to deal constructively with conflict within a family[36] as well as to manage divorce and post-divorce arrangements. In practice, however, most family mediation cases refer to *divorce mediation* and *child custody mediation* (which normally takes place some time after the post-separation agreement).[37] In comparison to the juridical system, family mediation offers swifter solutions and, most importantly, the parties' empowerment, as they are allowed to manage the outcome of their dispute by themselves (Bailey & Robbins 2005). Empowerment is often a very delicate question in divorce mediation, since parties, although they have broken their marital relationship, want to discuss the best solu-

35. Private mediation services are sometimes very expensive, though they vary a lot according to the location of services. For example, in 2008 the American Arbitration Association reported hourly mediation rates varying from $ 125 to $ 800 depending on the mediator selected, with a four-hour minimum charge for a mediation conference (see www.adr.org/sp.asp?id=33581). Such rates are charged in the U.S. where mediation is relatively widespread and well known. It must be remembered, however, that even if some mediators cost as much as lawyers, if two parties decide to go to a mediator together instead of individually seeing separate lawyers, the final consultation cost is cut in half, as parties normally share it.

36. Interestingly, the well-known conflict resolution scholar Jeffrey Z. Rubin wrote, together with his wife Carol Rubin, a book entitled: *When families fight: how to handle conflict with those you love*, aimed at preventing and managing conflict within a family (see Rubin & Rubin 1989).

37. Folberg and Milne (1998) and Folberg, Milne and Stalem (2004) present collections of studies on divorce mediation from different disciplinary points of view, and tackling different issues. Haynes and Haynes (1989) and Kressel (1994) report on actual cases of divorce mediation.

tion possible for the future of their relationship, especially if they have children (Cigoli & Scabini 2004; Marzotto & Tamanza 2004).

An equally important category is represented by *business* or *commercial mediation*. Barrett and Barrett (2004) claim that the origin of ADR in business in the United States was due to the anti-Federalist stream and, in particular, to Thomas Jefferson, who believed that "the American experiment in self-governance required creative solutions to difficult issues and selfless compromises to bridge differences and discover common ground" (ibid., p. 49). Important evidence on business mediation in Europe is presented in Singer (2004) and Filler (2006). The introduction of ADR procedures into European business disputes was fostered by the European Commission in 2002.[38] In Switzerland, official rules for commercial mediation were introduced by the Chambers of Commerce in April 2007; these rules, in turn, refer to the European Code of Conduct for Mediators.

The so-called *construction mediation* can be considered a specific case of business mediation concerning construction work contracts. Another specific field is within economics and is constituted by *finance*, whereby the economic exchange is oriented towards the creation of new value rather than to the distribution of given amounts of resources (Barone-Adesi 2002). Given such specificity, the category of *financial mediation* should be introduced. In fact, although this type of mediation is not sufficiently recognized in its uniqueness, mediation is *de facto* applied in financial disputes (Krivis 2006: 175–184; Cohen et al. 2006).

Employment mediation, or *labour-management mediation* in the U.S., has developed quite autonomously since the early twentieth century (Barrett & Barrett 2004). Originally, it was typical for labour-management mediation to be applied in the coal mines and railroad construction (Brett & Goldberg 1983; Ury, Brett & Goldberg 1998a; Goldberg 1989; Barrett & Barrett 2004); today, however, this type of mediation is also applied to a number of other areas of work (Bingham 2004). This category only concerns disputes between employers and employees, while mediation of workplace conflicts normally goes under the category of community mediation (in particular, organizational mediation).[39]

38. See the Green Paper on alternative dispute resolution in civil and commercial law, http://europa.eu/eur-lex/en/com/gpr/2002/com2002_0196en01.pdf.

39. In relation to labour disputes, it is worth mentioning the Swiss example as a unique way of handling conflict in the international panorama. The *Peace of Work* agreement was introduced in 1937 (initially in the machine and metalwork industries), which nowadays regulates labour–management relationships in almost all industrial sectors – a negotiation-based co-operative style (Broussolle 2006). The spirit of this agreement should focus on the parties' common values which must in any case be preserved despite any union or management opposition (I owe to Mauro Martinoni – interview with the author, August 27, 2008 – this

In North America and in the UK, the label *community mediation* indicates the mediative handling of disputes within a community, for example, a neighbourhood, small town, workplace, association, and so on. Different kinds of conflict can thus be included in this category, which are normally covered by civil law. These include, for instance, disputes between private individuals over property rights, such as the boundaries of front- and back-yards (as in the example discussed by Honeyman, Goh & Kelly 2004), the use of a path, or over noise or other forms of harassment conflicts between friends or colleagues, struggles between different groups of stakeholders and so on, which amount to an estimated number of 100,000 mediated conflicts per year in the United States (Hedeen 2004: 101). Some of these conflicts are dealt with by professional mediators offering private services; more often, especially in the United States, these conflicts are dealt with in public centres, usually managed by volunteer mediators, or in specific "community projects" (Nowell & Salem 2004: 400) whose goal is to make justice accessible to everybody (Hedeen 2004).

Community mediation is a very broad term, which only indicates that the conflict treated through mediation had its origin in a context that can be considered to be a community: a group of persons bound by some cultural tie or common goal. In this sense, particular forms of mediation, such as *school mediation*, *organizational mediation*, *health (medical) mediation*, *environmental mediation* and *public disputes mediation* are considered in the typology illustrated in Figure 2.1 as subcategories of community mediation.

Mediation in school institutions has been established in the last two decades in the U.S. as part of a larger programme in conflict resolution education (CRE). Conflict resolution education programmes "have educated children about constructive approaches to managing conflict in their schools and communities" (Jones 2004), among which are problem-solving and *peer mediation* (Compton 2002; Bickmore 2003; Jones 2004; Guy-Ecabert 2002; Martello 2006).

interpretation of the *Peace of Work* agreement). In other words, parties are committed to actively search for a co-operative win-win solution to their problems, while avoiding violent or hostile behaviour (including strikes). Collective labour agreements, sometimes including peace clauses, are a typical Swiss instrument for the maintenance of peace in the workplace. Collective agreements have "a binding power close to a real contract". They do not represent an unstable truce in the framework of labour negotiations. Instead, they represent "a true commitment for a definite period" (Broussolle 2006: 4). Some examples of collective labour agreements are reported in Schweingruber (1979: 14–73). In this way, "within the OECD, Switzerland turned out to be the country with the lowest labour conflict rate" (ibid., p. 3).

Organizational mediation is a form of intervention within enterprises or institutions in which the mediator is called upon to intervene in interpersonal conflicts between the collaborators. This type of intervention may require subsequent steps, whereby mediation is preceded and followed by one-to-one conversations or other forms of colloquia; mediation practitioners sometimes borrow the systemic intervention concept of *Interventionsarchitektur* (intervention architecture) to indicate the delicate phase of planning that precedes the intervention (Königswieser & Exner 1998; Königswieser & Hillebrand 2008: 54–67). A context where this kind of mediation is often required is represented by those enterprises – very widespread – that are managed and owned on a family basis (Marinoni 2001; Canyameres I Sanahuja 2002).

Health or *medical* mediation is a form of community mediation that refers to mediation processes that take place in hospitals and analogous institutions. It concentrates on conflicts related to cases of medical malpractice (Dauer & Marcus 1997; Brown 1998; Liebman & Hyman 2004; Hyman & Schechter 2006).

Environmental mediation is applicable to disputes tied to the preservation of the environment (Orr, Emerson & Keyes 2008). Often, environmental concerns conflict with urban development or industrial plans, so that the same territory turns out to be sought after for different purposes (see the prototypical cases illustrated in Vraneski & Richter 2003 and Levine 2005). Some environmental mediators, such as Lawrence Susskind, contend that the expression *environmental mediation* narrows the scope of their interventions too much, and they prefer to use the expression *public dispute mediation*, which not only covers strictly environmental issues (like pollution, preservation of natural areas, and so on), but also conflicts over the allocation of scarce resources, policy priorities on environmental standards, quality-of-life standards (health, security, freedom) and so on (Forester 1994: 311). The boundaries of public dispute mediation, however, are fairly undefined; sometimes, they overlap with political and international mediation, with community mediation, or even with business mediation; arguably, the interpretation most likely depends on how much the conflict becomes a public issue for a community.

Political conflicts can also be handled through mediative instruments, thus giving rise to the category of *political mediation*. These conflicts can be internal (intranational) conflicts, such as civil wars (Collier & Hoeffler 1998, 2005; Reuveny & Maxwell 2001). More often they are international conflicts (Lall 1966; Bercovitch & Rubin 1992; Bercovitch 2002; Touval & Zartman 1985a and 1985b); in these cases, mediation takes on the tradition of international diplomacy.

Victim–offender mediation (commonly referred to as VOM) originates from the U.S. victim–offender reconciliation programs (VORP) which took place in the mid-1970s and 1980s (Umbreit, Coates & Vos 2004: 279) as part of the so-called *restorative justice* approach[40] (Umbreit 2001). The main reason for the introduction of VOM is the belief that "traditionally, victims were left out of the justice process" (Umbreit, Coates & Vos 2004: 287) and that "the offender seldom noticed that his/her actions had an impact on real, live people" (ibid.). Indeed, the "power of encounter" (Zehr 2004: 305) between victims and offenders allowed by VOM enhances satisfaction with the judicial outcome (Umbreit, Coates & Vos 2004).

Intercultural mediation is a broad category including those conflicts – sometimes denominated *ethnic* conflicts – that, though they may be included into at least one other application field, are characterized by the strong presence of an intercultural dimension between the parties and/or the mediator and the parties, whereby the mediation process is significantly affected (Broome & Murray 2002; Lowry & Littlejohn 2006; Herrman, Hollett, Gale & Foster 2001: 145; Honeyman, Goh & Kelly 2004; Greco 2005b). It has been remarked (Avruch 2003: 352) that cultural factors in mediation have only just received the necessary attention;[41] today, some studies on culture and mediation are available, particularly based on case studies and lessons learned. Indeed, often in the case of protracted intercultural conflict, the mediation experience is a long process involving steps and techniques that are not used in other fields. For example, the organization of *workshops* where representatives of the parties in conflict are invited to talk to each other is

40. Restorative justice moves on from the idea that justice is about defining who is right and who is wrong, but also tries to restore, as much as possible, human relationships; it tends to focus on individuals' stories and reasons (see Umbreit 2001 for a discussion of this topic).

41. This observation seems to be confirmed by the caution with which some international programmes dealing with conflict tackle the issue of culture. Consider, for example, the Development Assistance Committee (DAC) Guidelines "Helping prevent violent conflict" published in 1996 and updated in 2001 by the international Organization for Economic Cooperation and Development (OECD). This organization is vocationally devoted to the promotion of economic expansion and world trade in member and non-member countries (see Article 1 of the convention signed in Paris on December 14, 1960, which came into force on September 30, 1961). The DAC is a specialized committee within OECD having to deal in particular with "past, current and potential violent conflict" (OECD 2001: 3). It is stressed that the guidelines primarily focus on collective conflicts among groups within or across nations and, to some extent, they also cover state violence against groups and individuals (ibid., p. 13). Such situations are quite likely to involve cultural issues. Indeed, the "promotion of multiculturalism" (ibid., p. 19) is included in the recommendations of the guidelines. However, a marginal role is given to this variable in comparison to others, such as the economic or institutional environment. In OECD (2001: 88) it is said that "ethnic, religious and cultural differences, in themselves, seldom cause conflict", but they can "offer fertile ground for political exploitation" in cases of "heightened tensions resulting from socio-political conflicts". This view on cultural identity as subordinate to other (socio-political) factors seems to need a more in-depth exploration.

frequently used (see the examples presented in Lowry & Littlejohn 2006; Noel, Torfin Shoemake & Hale 2006; and Desivilya & Gal 2003).

Intercultural mediation in a proper sense must be distinguished from the so-called linguistic-cultural mediation, which is a practice of conflict prevention established, especially in Europe, mostly in the health and educational domains (see Castiglioni 1997 and Martello 2006 respectively). Linguistic-cultural mediation is conceived of as an enrichment of an interpreter's work, whereby the interpreter is not only requested to translate from one language to another, but also to bridge the two cultures whose corresponding languages he/she is translating.

2.2.3.2 *Scientific relevance and disciplinary perspectives*

The ADR practice of mediation as an object of scientific investigation is increasingly receiving attention from a variety of disciplinary perspectives. Scholars from different disciplines have varying reasons for being interested in conflict resolution and different issues on which to focus. In general, a connection between the theory of mediation and its practical spin-offs can be envisaged in the majority of disciplinary areas.

In introducing their *Handbook of dispute resolution*, Moffitt and Bordone (2005: 5–6) quote the following disciplinary fields as relevant to mediation: law, psychology, ethics, economy, mathematics (in particular, game theory), anthropology, sociology, history, journalism, political science and theology. Menkel-Meadow (2005: 13) adds international relations and peace studies to this list. Journalism is included, in Moffitt and Bordone's view (2005: 6), because of "the important role(s) of the media in shaping the views of those in disputes".

Juridical studies have been primarily interested in mediation as an Alternative Resolution Practice. As already stated, many of the ADR pioneers, such as Fuller, saw ADR as a real *alternative* to overwhelmed and, sometimes, unjust justice systems. Consequently, the fields of application that have much interested law scholars are those in which mediation offers a real improvement to the court system. First and foremost among these is divorce and child-custody mediation, where a number of lawyers felt frustrated from their involvement in a process that seemed only to produce unhappy outcomes (Breidenbach 1995; Friedman 1993).[42]

42. In this relation, see the narration of Gary J. Friedman, a former adversary lawyer who then "converted" to mediation (Friedman 1993: 4–5): "After practicing successfully in this [adversarial] mode for five years in the early seventies, I began to grow increasingly disheartened, particularly when I saw the human costs of the litigation process – relationships seemed only to be worsened by the adversary experience. I often felt estranged from my clients, even after what was clearly a 'win'. Though the results were usually what I considered good, the clients often felt dissatisfied. Something was missing – for both of us. I wanted

Commercial and business mediation (Bühring-Uhle, Kirkhoff & Scherer 2006) and employment mediation (Brett & Goldberg 1983; Ury, Brett & Goldberg 1998a; Goldberg 1989) are other areas that can benefit from the swiftness and manageability that mediation offers. Because the role played by interpersonal relationships is of primary importance in family conflicts which are difficult to resolve without taking into account the whole set of desires and concerns of the individuals involved, family mediation has raised the interest of psychologists (Haynes & Haynes 1989; Parkinson 1997; Kelly 2004; Cigoli & Scabini 2004; Marzotto & Tamanza 2004; Saposnek 2004). For analogous reasons, community mediation (Bertoluzzo 2006; Nowell & Salem 2004), in particular in the education domain (Jones 2004), has also been approached from the psychological perspective. The focus on the relationship between the parties, approaches such as *transformative mediation* (Bush & Folger 1994), and the adaptation of therapeutic techniques based on the systemic approach, is typical of psychologists tackling mediation. More generally, social psychologists have contributed to shedding light on the dynamics of interpersonal conflict (Deutsch 2002; Zittoun, Perret-Clermont & Carugati 1997; Grossen & Perret-Clermont 1994; Light and Perret-Clermont 1989; Perret-Clermont, Carugati & Oates 2004; Arcidiacono 2007).

Commercial and business mediation, together with their "indoor" application in organizational mediation, also benefits from studies in the organizational and business fields. Economic studies tackle, in particular, the advantages of mediation in comparison to litigation (Cutler & Summers 1988); they also provide accurate reviews of the present situation of business mediation in different countries (Singer 2004; Filler 2006). Moreover, studies in economics have helped to develop theories of negotiation based on mathematical accounts, such as game theory, which contribute to a quantitative study of decision-making practices under conditions of uncertainty. These studies have sometimes been integrated in the study of international disputes (Hopmann 1996).

Sociologists take alternative dispute resolution methods into account when they concern social dynamics (such as restorative justice, see Zehr 2004), as is

to be interrelating with clients on a level of mutual respect, but I began to see that the more wholeheartedly I acted on their behalf the more disempowered they became. [...] Another thing that disturbed me about the litigator's life was the high value placed on negative human qualities. Fear of losing face, of just plain losing, or of being sued by the client often seemed to be at least as powerful a motivator as the search for justice. But even worse, aggression, defensiveness, and blame were the main currency I dealt with as a lawyer, both in the way I approached opposing lawyers and in my interactions with my clients. And truth – which in my personal life I valued above all – was often considered irrelevant".

often the case in, for example, community mediation, environmental mediation and public policy mediation (Volpe & Philips 2003; Volpe & Strobl 2005).

As already mentioned, scholars in political sciences address the application of mediation in the field of international relations in its various forms (Lall 1966; Bercovitch & Rubin 1992; Bercovitch 2002; Princen 1992a and 1992b; Touval & Zartman 1985a and 1985b).

The communicative dynamics of the mediation activity have been deepened in particular by argumentative studies (see Section 2.2.1) Argumentation, indeed, is seen to be at the core of the parties' decision making in resolving their conflict. From the point of view of the contextual interest, argumentative studies are transversally oriented, in that they are not interested in the dynamics of single fields of application of mediation, but rather tend to focus on the general communicative dynamics of this practice.

The following synoptic table lists the disciplines studying mediation in relation to their specific fields of application and the specific issues on which they elaborate.

Table 2.1. Disciplines that study mediation, typical application contexts and main issues tackled

	Most "typical" application contexts	*Main issues tackled*
Juridical studies	Family mediation; penal mediation; commercial and business mediation	Alternativeness (juridical status of the ADR practices), advantages of mediation in comparison to other forms of dispute resolution, educational background of mediators
(Social) psychology	Family mediation; community mediation (school mediation), VOM	Conflict, restoring relationships
Economics and finance	Commercial and business mediation, financial mediation.	Economic advantages for individuals, corporations and other institutions; conflict in corporations, mergers, etc; rationality of economic agents in conflictual situations
Sociology	Community mediation, social dispute mediation	Restorative justice, social effects of mediation
Political sciences	International mediation, political mediation, social dispute mediation	Conflict, negotiation, role and personality of third parties in international processes, power issues
Argumentation	Family mediation (divorce mediation), community mediation, business mediation. Virtually all fields	Quality of argumentation and quality of mediation. Mediators' communicative instrumentation for fulfilling their task.

Recently, the various approaches to conflict resolution illustrated above have begun to converge into a more systematized multidisciplinary – if not yet truly interdisciplinary[43] – paradigm of studies of the conflict phenomenon and of the different ways of handling it. Such a multidisciplinary effort has produced outcomes both at the scientific and at the educational level. In the former, different scientific journals, such as the *Negotiation Journal*, the *Journal of Conflict Resolution* and the *Conflict Resolution Quarterly* (formerly *Mediation Quarterly*), feature contributions from different disciplinary areas. In addition, they encourage a dialogue between the academic and the practitioners' worlds. Furthermore, some online providers have steadily increased their reliability as sources of information on conflict and conflict management; generally speaking, they collect materials (case-studies, articles, etc.) from various disciplinary areas. Prime examples are the website of the already-mentioned PON consortium (http://www.pon.harvard.edu) and the *Conflict Resolution Information Source* (CRInfo, to be read as "See our info", http://www.crinfo.org/), which is provided by the *Conflict Information Consortium* based at the University of Colorado at Boulder (see http://conflict.colorado.edu/). Other websites offer gateways to specific conflicts; for instance, resources on the Northern Ireland conflict can be found on the website of the *International Conflict Research* project of the United Nations University and the University of Ulster (INCORE, http://www.incore.ulst.ac.uk/), or at *Conflict Archive on the INternet* (CAIN, http://cain.ulst.ac.uk/), also based within the University of Ulster.

At the educational level, as Moffitt and Bordone (2005: 7) observe, the interdisciplinary perspective on conflict is very productive: "students can now study the disputing process in programs explicitly aimed at dispute and conflict resolution at both the undergraduate and graduate level at a number of institutions". This is particularly evident in North America, where courses on conflict resolution are now numerous. The first institution that established a major in this field in 1982 was George Mason University in Virginia, which currently offers an undergraduate programme, two graduate certificates, a master of science and a doctoral title in the subject. To mention another significant case, the schools participating in the PON consortium, all located in the greater Boston area, offered a total of

43. Rigotti and Rocci (2006: 156) distinguish between *multidisciplinary* approaches, which offer "an interesting aggregate of different points of view", and *interdisciplinary* approaches, which aim "at building up and realising an epistemological design, ideally corresponding to the deep nature of the object". Ideally, the multidisciplinary orientation that conflict resolution studies are assuming today can be viewed as an intermediary step towards the establishment of a well-thought-out interdisciplinary approach.

99 courses on conflict resolution at the undergraduate, graduate, and continuing education levels for the 2007–2008 academic year. Moreover, three of the member schools (the University of Massachusetts Boston, the Cambridge College and the Brandeis University) offer interdisciplinary degrees or certificates in conflict resolution. These examples are not rarities; in fact, degrees in dispute resolution and conflict management are nowadays offered by numerous universities not only in the United States and Canada, but also in Europe and, increasingly, in other areas of the world.

CHAPTER 3

Mapping mediation

A necessary prerequisite to the argumentative analysis

The previous chapter explored the main features of dispute mediation and presented the reasons why mediation is particularly relevant to the study of argumentation in context. I have argued that mediation could constitute a basis for the study of argumentation in context for different reasons; in this relation, some notions, such as the quality of the interaction and some communicative tools have been extensively explored in past studies (see Section 2.2.1). However, the problem of the structuring of the argumentative discussion and how it allows the parties' to change their attitude – from disputants to co-arguers – has not been the subject of much focus. Moreover, the possible connection between the parties' change in attitude and the mediator's intervention has not been studied.

In order to tackle these issues, it is now necessary to develop a thorough analysis of the context of mediation. In other words, a conceptual framework of mediation must be sketched, by mapping the essential factors that constitute this practice. This will allow us to understand how the successful structuring of an argumentative discussion can achieve the pragmatic goals of mediation.

As for any research truly focused on *argumentation in context*, the reconstruction of the specific features of mediation calls for interdisciplinary integrations. In order to reconstruct how mediation is in fact structured, it is wise to rely on the different disciplines that have approached this topic. In particular, I shall select those studies that have conceptually analysed mediation and, thus, can help an understanding of the main features of this practice. For this purpose, I shall rely mainly on the literature on mediation and, more generally, on conflict resolution studies. Some integration has been necessary in relation to the concept of dispute or *conflict*, which tended to be underanalysed in these studies; thus, I have integrated insights from organization theory, economics, social psychology and argumentation. The selection of the approaches presented in this chapter is by no means exhaustive of the studies on mediation. For a comprehensive overview, see Greco Morasso (2009a).

In considering models of mediation, a main problem comes to light: single contributions rarely present an endeavour to construct a comprehensive framework of mediation. Often, such models analyse in detail some specific aspects and thus they can be considered to be partial accounts of this practice. Furthermore, the different theoretical proposals are put forward without, in the majority of cases, engaging in a real scientific confrontation.[1] In this sense, examining the various proposals requires the effort of comparing and organizing them into a framework of mediation that is as comprehensive as possible, by focusing in particular on their commonalities and complementarities. Critical points will be advanced, but the general aim is that of finding clues to reconstruct what is essential to mediation in its constituency, relations and process. By adopting such an approach to the literature, the present chapter will lay the foundations of the required framework of mediation. This framework will then be presented in the following Chapters (4 and 5).

In general, if we consider all the approaches of mediation globally, they describe the characterizing features of this practice from two different yet complementary perspectives. First, some approaches elicit the constituency of mediation by identifying the relevant interagents and institutions involved. In general, the description of interagents is made in combination with the elicitation of their reciprocal relations. The approaches that make explicit the constituency and relations of mediation model this practice by presenting its *scenario* (see Section 3.1). Second, to the modelling level of the scenario, a *script* dimension is also added by some approaches (see Section 3.2), which focus, in particular, on the pragmatic structure and on the communicative dynamics of the mediation process. Both perspectives need to be adopted and integrated in order to understand what factors mediation includes and what constitutes a successful mediation process. Bearing these results in mind, it will then be possible to map argumentation onto it and see how it contributes to this practice.

3.1 The scenario perspective

The approaches that will be considered now aim at constructing a *scenario* of mediation. I have identified two different approaches to the mediation scenario

1. Herrman, Hollett and Gale (2006:19) remark that: "The literature unfortunately lacks consensus with respect to definitions of key concepts and variables. A panoply of conceptual and operational definitions acts as a rich resource and a source of confusion for scholars and mediation practitioners. The array of scholars and practitioners writing about conflict resolution and mediation from so many disciplinary backgrounds and experiences produces a sense of fragmentation".

that correspond to two levels of zooming. The first level (see Section 3.1.1) approaches mediation from the outside, by comparing it to other practices of conflict resolution. The other approaches (Sections 3.1.2ff.) consider specific points of the scenario of mediation. These studies also provide a picture of the preceding factors determining the choice of mediation and of the possible outcomes of this process. Some crucial concepts, such as *conflict*, *relationship* and *interests*, emerge as determinants of mediation.

3.1.1 Mediation within the ADR practices: A definition by opposition

A first stream of theoretical reflections on mediation aims at positioning this practice among its "relatives", i.e. the other ADR methods. Various categorizations and taxonomies of ADR practices are proposed (sometimes only *presupposed*) in the theoretical approaches to mediation. Indeed, specifying mediation's characteristics means defining it; namely, outlining the proper traits distinguishing it from other functionally close practices. For this reason, it is useful to reconstruct taxonomies that reflect the major approaches to this topic. Such taxonomies will be constructed here through the tool of the *Arbor porphyriana* (Porphyrian tree),[2] a tree-structured way of defining the constituency of notions by means of eliciting their genus and specific difference. The arbor porphyriana is thus a tool for the conceptual clarification of notions that allows inserting each concept in the network of its relations with other close concepts. In view of a positioning of mediation within other ADR practices, this way of proceeding appears particularly suited.

A very common way to categorize methods of dispute resolution is based on the consideration of the parties' *control over the outcome* that they allow. In this perspective, albeit slightly different focuses are possible, all approaches recognize negotiation as the pure case of self-settlement based on the parties' complete control over the process and the outcome or solution of their dispute.

Here, it is imperative to start with the very well-known approach proposed by the Program on Negotiation (PON) based at Harvard (see also Chapter 2). The name *Program on Negotiation* would seem to suggest that the focus of this research programme is limited to negotiation as an ADR practice. Indeed, PON scholars consider negotiation not only as one of the dispute resolution practices, but also, with a slightly different meaning, as a basic process that is present also in other conflict resolution practices. Mediation, in this sense, would be a species of the genus of negotiation, involving a third person who has the special role of

2. Porphyry (c. 232 AD – c. 304) is known in particular for his commentary on Aristotle's *Categories*. His representation of the definition of concepts has also been reported and commented in Petri Hispani Summulae logicales 2.10 (see Bochenski 1947: 18).

facilitating the parties' interaction.[3] This offers a first characterization at least of some of the ADR practices, namely negotiation and mediation, which is considered as a form of facilitated negotiation (see Figure 3.1). The negotiation-based processes are opposed to the adjudicative processes, which can be more flexible, like arbitration (Rudolph Cole & Blankley 2005) or more structured, like litigation (Seul 2005):

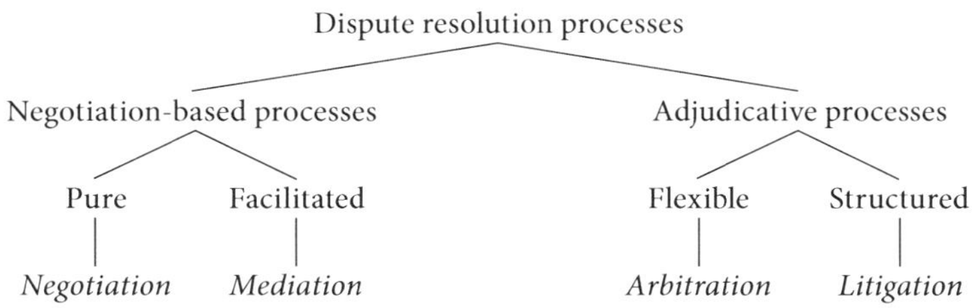

Figure 3.1. Categorization of conflict resolution processes according to the Harvard (PON) model

A limpid categorization of ADR practices, which adopts a similar conceptualization, is offered in Uzqueda and Frediani (2002: 4). In the authors' view, a crucial concept is represented by the dichotomy *negotiated-imposed*, which constitutes the first important distinction between dispute resolution methods. As mentioned in Chapter 2, this difference bears important consequences at the level of the argumentative structuring of ADR practices, in particular concerning the decision makers to whom argumentation is addressed. In a negotiated (self-settling, non-adversarial) order, one can have a practice, like mediation, in which conflicting parties are assisted by a third neutral, or a pure form of self-settlement represented by negotiation itself. In an imposed (hetero-settling or adversarial) order, we find the pure form exclusively represented by court settlement and other more numerous mixed forms, of which the authors only mention the case of arbitration.[4] This taxonomy could be represented as in Figure 3.2:

3. See Patton (2005: 279): "Negotiation can be defined as back-and-forth communication designed to reach an agreement between two or more parties with some interests that are shared and others that may conflict or simply be different".

4. Why arbitration is considered a mixed form is not specified. We might argue that it depends on the fact that parties can choose their arbitrator(s) and thus maintain some control over the process.

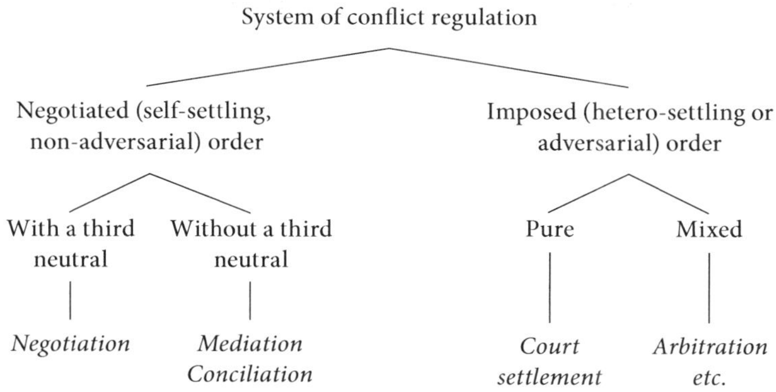

Figure 3.2. Categorization of conflict resolution practices according to Uzqueda and Frediani (2002)

A slightly different interpretation is proposed by Goldberg et al. (2007: 3). In this case, negotiation is also considered the only practice that allows the parties' control of both the process and the solution of their dispute, while the introduction of a third neutral entrusts him/her with control of the process (as in the case of mediation) or of both the process and the solution. In the latter case, one can have a private form of settlement like arbitration[5] or a court-based form like adjudication.[6] The definition of mediation does not substantially deviate from that of Uzqueda and Frediani, although in this approach its difference from negotiation is more explicitly marked, being identified in the parties' lack of control over the process.

Yet, as Goldberg et al. (2007: 6) remark, the focus on the parties' control of the dispute resolution method is not the only possible way to distinguish it among the various practices of conflict resolution. They refer to the proposal by Ury, Brett and Goldberg (1988b), based on the *goal* of resolution practices, which these authors categorize as reconciling the disputants' underlying interests, determining who is right, or determining who is more powerful. The three criteria are not equivalent in that, as the authors remark, in general, reconciling interests "costs less and yields more satisfactory results" than the other two choices (ibid., p. 4).[7]

5. Here, arbitration is considered for its nature of hetero-based settlement, while the fact that it allows the parties some control over the process is not focused on.

6. Adjudication is here considered together with ADR practices for its functional value as a conflict resolution method.

7. Determining who is right, in turns, costs less and yields more satisfactory results than determining who is powerful (ibid.).

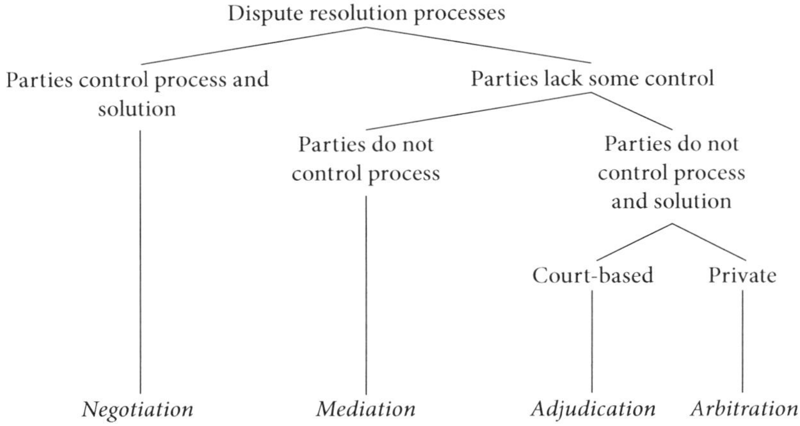

Figure 3.3. Categorization of conflict resolution processes according to Goldberg et al. (2007)

Thus, a hierarchy of selection criteria is established which helps to determine a corresponding classification of dispute resolution practices. In particular, disputes are resolved on the basis of *power* in violent approaches such as fights, strikes, and so on. They are resolved by *establishing who is right*, typically, in the procedure of adjudication. Negotiation and mediation are oriented towards offering the possibility to settle conflicts *by reconciling interests*, namely those "needs, desires, concerns, fears – the things one cares about or wants" and which "underlie peoples' positions – the tangible items they *say* they want" (ibid., p. 5).

Indeed, such a remark is particularly interesting because it suggests that the constituency of mediation does not need to be confined to its feature of allowing parties to maintain control over the outcome of their dispute, although this is certainly a relevant aspect of this practice. On a closer look, maintaining the control over the results of the dispute may be interpreted as the possibility to ensure that the parties' real interests are met. This appears as a relevant feature of mediation in particular, which makes it an interesting terrain in which to test the possibilities of argumentation.

Beyond the characterizations explicitly found in literature and illustrated above, and on the basis of the overview of dispute resolution practices presented in Chapter 2, at least two other variables can be added that are particularly relevant to characterising the specific difference of mediation from other practices, and the significant role that communication plays in it.

The first variable is the *escalation of the conflict*. It should be considered, in fact, that the choice of an ADR practice also depends on the type of conflict to be faced and, in particular, on its escalation. In fact, it is not always possible to handle a conflict by direct negotiations when the parties have reached a degree of such interpersonal hostility that communication is difficult or impossible. Thus, ADR practices can be distinguished in two categories,[8] defined by the type of conflict they are tackling: those practices that intervene when the conflict has already escalated and parties are no longer able to treat it by themselves (mediation, arbitration, ombudsman, mini-trial) versus practices used to handle more manageable conflicts (negotiation).

The second variable, which directly refers to the argumentative process, is the parties' *participation in the reasoning supporting a certain decision on the resolution of the conflict*. Here, we consider the *subjects* involved in the argumentative process and, in particular, those who are responsible for making a final decision and, thus, become the addressees of the persuasive process encompassed in argumentation. In negotiation and mediation, parties are co-arguers, because they are directly involved in an argumentative discussion oriented towards the resolution of their problem. In arbitration, ombudsman, and in the non-alternative dispute resolution called adjudication, on the other hand, parties (or their attorneys) direct their argumentative discourses towards the persuasion of the person who will make the decision (be it an arbitrator, ombudsman, judge or jury). Let us imagine an arbor porphyriana of ADR practices based on argumentative dynamics:

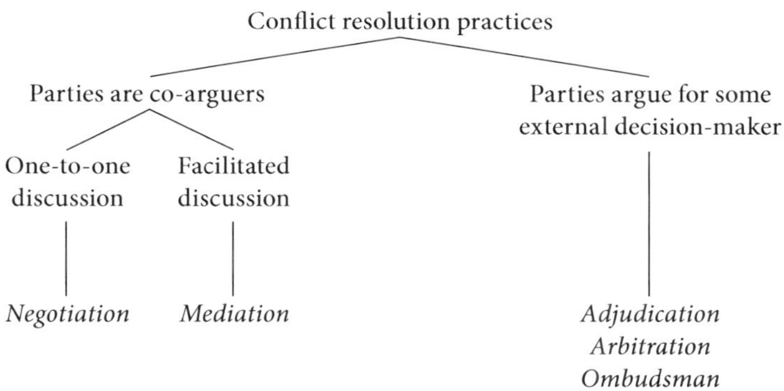

Figure 3.4. Categorization of conflict resolution processes according to their argumentative dynamics

8. The intervention of a third neutral defines a precise distinction between these two categories and signals a certain degree of conflict escalation. However, the degree of escalation of conflict can vary even between, for instance, mediation and arbitration. In fact, some conflicts escalate too far to be treated by mediation, whereas the decision of an arbitrator can be accepted as a solution. In this sense, one could imagine a continuum ranging from easily manageable conflicts to intractable conflicts and categorize ADR practices along this continuum.

The approaches considered here tackle mediation by trying to categorize it among the ADR practices, thus outlining its characterizing traits. Such traits bear important consequences at the level of the argumentative dynamics.

However, in order to understand the structure of mediation internally, it is important to consider those approaches to its scenario that can either elaborate on one or the other aspect of this practice (see Sections 3.1.2 and 3.1.3) or attempt to propose comprehensive scenarios of mediation (Sections 3.1.4. and 3.1.5).

3.1.2 Negotiation as the core of mediation: The Harvard model

In the previous section, we have seen how negotiation can be considered a basic form of dispute resolution that can be implemented in mediation through the help of a third neutral. Now it becomes relevant to understand some of the features of negotiation that are useful to understand the ontological constituency of mediation. For this purpose, I will refer to the Harvard *model of principled negotiation*, which has already been mentioned for its merits in defining basic principles of conflict resolution (such as the notion of *legitimacy*, see Section 2.1) and for its current relevance in research and education (Susskind, Mnookin, Fuller & Rozdeiczer 2003).[9]

The model lists seven basic elements of any negotiation interaction: interests, legitimacy, relationship, alternatives and BATNA (Best Alternative to a Negotiated Agreement), options, commitments, and communication (Patton 2005: 279–285).

1. *Interests* are the underlying desires of people involved in negotiation. The model highlights that interests do not always coincide with positions, i.e. with the parties' standpoints concerning what they want. Thus, at the level of

9. Some authors, starting from Bush and Folger (1994), have criticized the applicability of the Harvard model to mediation, labelling it as "the problem-solving approach", and contrasting it with the "transformative approach" or "narrative approach" (derived from narrative therapy) to mediation (Winslade & Monk 2001). The transformative approach starts from an anti-realist stance, and is not interested in the content of the dispute, but in its reconstruction by the parties. Indeed, from the study of the event of conflict (see Chapter 4), it is clear that the real content of the conflict and the parties' personal reconstructions should not be opposed, but must be tackled together for conflict resolution. Moreover, the description of the Harvard model given by these authors is quite simplistic, and, thus, not complete, since it does not consider attempts to consider the parties' relationship, and the role of interests in the construction of the individuals' identity. However, transformative approaches to mediation have the merit of focusing on the restoration of the parties' relationship, which is; indeed, one of the challenges of mediation in comparison with adjudication but also with other ADR techniques such as arbitration. Furthermore, the emphasis on the narrative aspects has brought scholars belonging to this approach to study communicative aspects of mediation (Folger & Bush 1994).

strategies a negotiator must be able to "focus on interests, not positions" (Fisher, Ury & Patton 1991: 4–5), in order to get a solution that can satisfy the parties. It might be added that interests are the drive that makes people take a position within a negotiation and, more or less directly, motivates them to get involved in a dispute. The goal of negotiation is to meet the parties' interests as far as possible.
2. *Legitimacy* has already been introduced (Section 2.1) as a crucial notion characterizing civil approaches to conflict resolution. Legitimacy is focused on as a "special category of interests" (Patton 2005: 281), mirroring "one of the most powerful human motivations" (ibid.): the need for justice –, the wish to receive fair treatment and a fair outcome. This is a general concern presupposed by all dispute resolution practices, including, ideally, litigation.
3. *Relationship* reminds negotiators that no agreement can be abstracted from the reality of the human relationship established by the parties (and their negotiators).
4. *Alternatives and BATNA*. Negotiators must be aware of parties' alternatives to a negotiated solution to the dispute; namely, of the possibilities if they do not reach a mediated agreement. In particular, the BATNA defines the boundary that makes the resolution of the dispute meaningful for each party. In fact, if a party is sure that he/she will win the case in court, he/she may not be interested in alternative dispute resolution methods.
5. *Options* are the possible alternative outcomes of the dispute that emerge during the process of negotiation, i.e. the alternative possibilities that can be activated by one or the other solution of the conflict. For the Harvard model, only those "positive" outcomes that emerge in the communicative process are considered options; in other words, alternatives (like the BATNA itself) that lead to a non-negotiated solution, or possible solutions that do not emerge in the process, are not considered options.
6. *Commitments* are decisions on options. They might be interpreted as commissive speech acts performed by the parties, which constitute the progressively increasing basis for agreement.
7. *Communication*. In the Harvard model, communication is "the process by which parties discuss and deal with the preceding six elements of negotiation" (ibid., p. 284). Interestingly, according to this model, communication is an overarching activity encompassing all other elements and making them possible.

Although the seven elements listed here emerge as relevant to the process of negotiation, a critical remark on the list as a whole is still necessary. In fact, it seems to lack a common *principium divisionis*, insofar as the seven elements have different relations to one another. This leads to the question of whether this account can really be considered a comprehensive and justified model. In order to enhance the explanatory force of the model, the respective relations between the seven elements might be reconstructed as follows (this representation does not mirror the one given in Patton 2005, see in particular the scheme on p. 295):

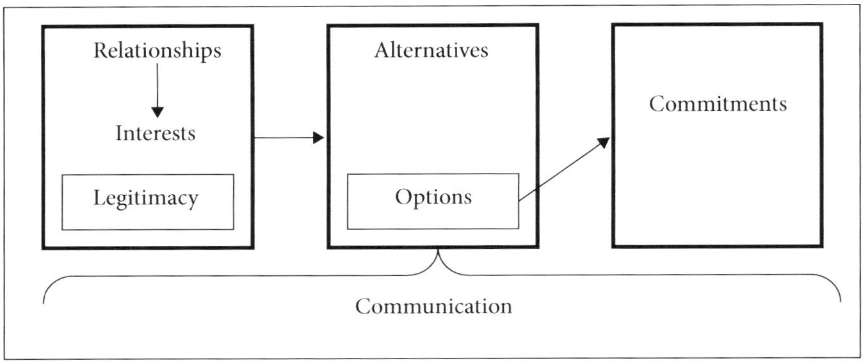

Figure 3.5. The Harvard seven elements model of negotiation revisited

As anticipated above, legitimacy is one of the most important interests, whereas options can be interpreted as possible alternatives at the parties' disposal. Interests, which are bound to the parties' relationships, lead them to seek alternatives to conflict; options are those alternatives that go in the direction of conflict resolution and emerge during the communication process in negotiation. Together, alternatives and options constitute the parties' reasoning on alternative possible outcomes at their disposal and on their correspondence to their interests. Options bring the parties to commit themselves to proposals and counterproposals. Relationships and, in particular, relationships between the parties, define their interests, by setting the values that they want to preserve. At the same time, relationships are built through the negotiation process; in particular, commitments specify changes in the parties' (and mediator's) relationships. The whole negotiation process is enabled by communication. However, not much is said about how communication should be managed; it seems to be a natural process inspired by the negotiators' innate skills.

3.1.3 Defining conflict

In the field of mediation and other conflict (or dispute) resolution practices, conflict is assumed as an unavoidable presupposition of any intervention. Most studies in conflict resolution identify the existence of a conflict as a general precondition of the resolution intervention (Moffitt & Bordone 2005: 2–3), and often remark that the analysis of conflict is necessary in order to effectively intervene and manage it. There is no mediation without conflict; for this reason, conflict is clearly a pivotal notion. Unexpectedly, however, the term *conflict* contains a certain amount of ambiguity and confusion. Such ambiguity probably derives from the fact that conflict is assumed to be a term in everyday language whose meaning is clear; only rarely are efforts made to specify its constituency.

In this section, the different meanings bound up in this term in different scientific approaches will be tackled briefly.[10] Reference is made first of all to studies in mediation and other conflict resolution practices that explicitly focus on conflict; useful insights to the nature of conflict in various other areas of research, such as organization theory, agency theory, and social psychology are also considered. Through this overview, it emerges that the term *conflict* is used in the literature to refer to two distinct and apparently unrelated events. The *Dictionary of Conflict Resolution*, edited by Yarn (1999), highlights these two distinct meanings: *disagreement* and *incompatibility* (p. 113). This text proposes a series of definitions of conflict extracted from previous studies whereby the prevailing meaning is surely that of a disagreement that involves overt hostility between two or more parties. However, it also emerges that such a state of hostility is generated by an incompatibility perceived by the involved parties. According to this second definition, conflict should be considered as "the broader state of incompatibility that may or may not give rise to a dispute" (ibid., p. 120); that is, as an incompatibility between two parties' goals or perceptions. In some cases, such an incompatibility degenerates into a full dispute, which involves "hostile action and the potential destruction of people and institutions" (Burton 1969: 2, quoted by Yarn 1999: 114). According to this more limited sense, which is at the origin of conflict resolution initiatives, conflict becomes an antagonistic struggle between human subjects. It is clear, thus, that conflict as incompatibility and conflict as struggle are two distinct meanings, which are separately assumed in different scientific approaches. In this section, I shall review studies that focus on both meanings. A possible connection between these two interpretations will be given while constructing the mediation framework in Chapter 4.

Conflict as a difference of opinion. The meaning of conflict as an incompatibility of positions is acknowledged in some studies, where its positive contribution in the development of knowledge and identity through communication is highlighted. This is the notion of *conflict of opinion* introduced by Barth and Krabbe (1982: 56)

10. The overview of the literature on conflict presented in Section 3.1.3 was first proposed in a paper published in the journal *Pragmatics & Cognition* (Greco Morasso 2008). I am grateful to the editor, Marcelo Dascal and to John Benjamins for permission to reproduce large portions of that text.

to indicate a perceived incongruity of judgements about the acceptability of a certain statement between different (individual or collective) subjects. This expression turns out to be consistent with the use of *difference of opinion* in the pragma-dialectical theory of argumentation. Van Eemeren and Grootendorst (2004: 21) consider argumentation "as part of an explicit or implicit discussion between parties who try to resolve a difference of opinion (that may be implicit) by testing the acceptability of the standpoints concerned". In the normative account of the critical discussion proposed by pragma-dialectics, the *confrontation stage* is defined as the moment in which a party puts forward a standpoint and the opponent either casts doubt on it, or proposes an alternative standpoint (see Section 5.1.2). The term *confrontation* refers to the viewpoints that give origin to a difference of opinion. More specifically, a difference of opinion, which is at the origin of the confrontation stage, can be defined as the emergence of the fact that a standpoint has not been accepted "because it runs against doubt or contradiction" (ibid., p. 60). A difference of opinion, thus, is clearly to be interpreted as an incompatibility between different worldviews.

If conflict is understood in the "weaker" sense as an incompatibility of positions, it can be regarded as a category including differences of opinion, but also differences in the parties' desires, goals, etc. However, if conflict is taken in its meaning of overt interpersonal hostility, the relation between this notion and that of difference of opinion is much more complex. A difference of opinion, in fact, does not per se imply hostility between the carriers of the difference. Indeed, differences of opinion can be handled in various ways; and *resolving* a difference of opinion properly means, in pragma-dialectical terms, that parties involved in the discussion "reach an agreement on the question of whether the standpoints at issue are acceptable or not" (ibid., pp. 58–59). In other words, one of the parties may realize that the other's position is more reasonable, and consequently change his or her mind. This does not conclude a settlement of the difference based on compromise, but rather on the parties' real persuasion achieved through discussion. However, the pragma-dialectical account also acknowledges the possibility that a difference of opinion may turn into open conflict. In these cases, one or more differences of opinion might be involved, and the conflict might be handled in different ways; the solution may be non-communicative – an adversary may be physically eliminated without assuming the burden of a communicative solution – but it can also be achieved by communicative means.[11] In the latter case,

11. Indeed, one of the problems faced in third parties' interventions is to find a right time for intervening (Princen 1992: 51–54); the conflict should not have escalated so much that it has degenerated into a sort of communicative epilepsy (Greco 2005a).

an argumentative discussion may be implemented in a variety of activity types (e.g. mediation, arbitration or adjudication; see van Eemeren & Houtlosser 2005) properly pertaining to conflict resolution interventions.

In the following, I will focus on some major interpretations of conflict, in an attempt to understand the type of event that conflict – conceived as interpersonal or inter-group hostility – represents.

Organization theory and other macro-approaches. Several studies adopt a "macro" approach for studying the genesis of interpersonal and group conflict. Such an approach is not based upon the analysis of the specific interactional event in which conflict occurs; rather it aims at identifying the structural causes that might generate hostility and conflict. It has the advantage of searching for those variables that it is possible to work upon in order to regulate or prevent conflicts. On the other hand, it is poor in the *esprit de finesse* with which the actual conflict is considered, and tends to neglect the reasons and motivations of single individuals, and the role of specific communication moves in the genesis of the conflictual event. It is also not focused on the possible relations between the presence of an incompatibility and the insurgence of a proper conflict.

Organization theory is probably the most productive of these macro-approaches in terms of the study of conflict, considered in particular in organizational settings (Hatch 1997; March & Simon 1958). In this view, conflicts of interest among individual or collective interagents are generally (more or less explicitly) considered as leading to distributive situations, i.e. to situations in which one agent wins and the other loses (Lawrence & Lorsch 1967: 12; Knight, 1992: 14). Generally, however, the process through which diverging interests may lead to overt conflict is neither explained nor even explicitly focused on in these studies. This can be said also of the *economic theory of conflict* (Collier & Hoeffler 1998; Mansfield & Pollins 2001; Reuveny & Maxwell 2001; Sørli, Petter Gleditsch, & Strand 2005; Collier & Hoeffler 2005), which focuses particularly on hostility and conflict in the presence of scarce economic resources (Collier & Hoeffler 1998: 571) and on the economic interdependence of nations. Some other accounts, drawing on Marxist philosophy and other *coercion theories* (Wehr 1979: 3), lead the economic theory of conflict to its extreme, claiming that conflict is necessarily present in society because it is intrinsically connected to the societal structure. The situation of a "fixed pie" of resources is always presupposed in these accounts, whereby the mere presence of different interests necessarily creates conflictual relations (Knight 1992: 8).

Agency relationship and conflict. Agency theory, developed in the economic/financial field (Ross 1973; Mann 1997) but largely adopted in other fields, like the theory of organizations, political sciences and sociology, assumes a more specific view on conflict, focusing on a particular kind of human relationship that may give origin to conflict. Agency theory, in fact, analyses the interpersonal relationship between a *principal* – someone who has a goal, and delegates its realization to someone else – and an *agent* – who is in charge of realizing the principal's goal in exchange for some form of remuneration. This theory offers a realistic view on a very usual human relationship bound to various interactions that is typically institutionalized by a form of *contract*. The principal and the agent are both considered as human subjects having their own desires, interests and goals, and behaving accordingly. This approach does not see two persons' desires or interests as necessarily opposite to each other, but takes into account the complexity of the relation between institutional roles and the human subjects who implement those roles. Within this framework, the *agency problem* is singled out. This originates from the non-alignment of the principal's and the agent's goals, which might induce the agent to behave in a way that is not correspondent with the principal's goal. The agency problem (Eisenhardt 1989: 58), in fact, arises when "(a) the desires or goals of the principal and agent conflict and (b) it is difficult or expensive for the principal to verify what the agent is actually doing". The origin of this problem, thus, lies in conflict conceived of as an incompatibility of goals, which might turn into an overt opposition between the principal and the agent.

The agency relationship is not the only form of relationship that can be established among human beings. First, the category of contract is broader than that of agency relationship. There are contracts that cannot be interpreted as forms of agency: selling or buying a house puts both interagents on the same level, and it is unnatural to interpret one as the agent of the other. Even more clearly, marriage includes a contract signed by a husband and wife; but it would be odd to regard one as the principal and the other as the agent. Furthermore, not all human relationships are regulated by contracts: in some relationships, the reciprocal commitments are not made explicit or enforced by an external authority. Consider, for instance, friendship, or the ties linking members of the same linguistic or, more generally, cultural community, which are forms of communal identity somehow "inherited" by the individual. Indeed, agency is a very specific form of relationship, characterized by a particular type of asymmetry: only the principal enjoys and is interested in the proper aim of the interaction, whereas the agent assumes the principal's goal in exchange for remuneration. Remuneration is a subservient goal for the agent in order to reach his or her specific goals. The asymmetry between principal and agent in relation to the goals of the interaction is also not mirrored in other kinds of contracts, such as the selling and buying of a house, or in other forms of complex relationships, like that binding two friends or two members of the same family. In agency theory, by contrast, such asymmetry is a characterizing feature: for example, in a doctor–patient relationship it is the patient who, as the principal, is affected and cares about the goal of the interaction. Such a characterizing feature of agency relationships may become, as already noted, a source of conflict given the different nature of interest for the goals of the interaction.

Moreover, in analysing conflicts bound to agency relationships, the principal–agent asymmetry, which defines the parties' institutionalized relationship, is often intertwined with other relationships that are not agency based. To quote an example, a doctor may become the best friend of a patient, thus assuming the goal of his or her health as a personal concern. Empathy is not part of the agency relationship, but these two dimensions can affect each other. For example, someone can decide to change their doctor because they do not feel comfortable with the doctor's character or ethical views, or a problem may occur within the doctor–patient agency because the patient may suspect that the doctor is inadequately experienced, and this can affect the doctor–patient interpersonal relationship. Even a long-lasting friendship can be damaged by such problems, which can turn into open conflicts (see the example discussed in Greco Morasso 2007).

In sum, even though agency theory does not cover all possible forms of human relationship, and therefore it does not cover all possible contexts for the insurgence of conflicts, it does provide a reasonable framework for understanding how differences in people's interests can lead to real conflicts, and how such conflicts can be prevented.

From difference of opinion to interpersonal hostility: the notion of socio-cognitive conflict. Conflict resolution studies in the psychological domain have pointed out that human beings feel that their identities are being threatened when their positions are incompatible with those of others (Cigoli & Scabini 2004; Hicks 2001). In such studies, the notion of *socio-cognitive conflict*, introduced in studies in social psychology (Light & Perret-Clermont 1989; Grossen & Perret-Clermont 1994; Perret-Clermont, Carugati & Oates 2004; Zittoun, Perret-Clermont & Carugati 1997), turns out to be particularly illuminating. This term was introduced to explain how children may, under certain conditions, make use of situations involving conflicts to make progress in their development. In some cases, as different points of view come into the discussion and a communicative difference of opinion needs to be managed, a joint cognitive construction may be developed. However, cognitive conflicts do not always bring to more mature knowledge constructions, precisely because the cognitive dimension is associated to the social dimension. Empirical research into how children resolve conflicts leads to a consideration that it is impossible to find an intellectual solution to the problem without taking into account the social implications of the fact of being in conflict. Any contraposition (child–child but, even more clearly, child–teacher), in fact, implies a psycho-social challenge for the subject, who feels questioned or even attacked on his or her personal position and, in some cases, on him- and herself too. The notion of *socio-cognitive conflict* thus helps us to understand how sometimes differences and incompatibilities between individuals' views may degenerate into interpersonal hostility because a *social* component is always present also in a *cognitive* conflict.

3.1.4 A first proposal of a scenario: Wall

I shall now turn to consider two approaches that try to consider mediation globally in all those aspects that constitute its scenario (Sections 3.1.4 and and 3.1.5).

The first of these approaches is James Wall's account of mediation. This is based on a comprehensive literature review, published in three phases, two of which include collaboration with other authors (Wall 1981; Wall & Lynn 1993; Wall, Stark & Standifer 2001). Such work is remarkable from two points of view. First, it is certainly, together with the important proposal by Herrman, Hollett and Gale (2006, see Section 3.1.5), one of the most extensive reviews of the literature on mediation currently available. In fact, in a scientific stream of research in which several approaches are largely auto-referential, these two proposals are distinguishable for their focus on theoretical confrontation. Second, it represents a first attempt to provide an ontology-based comprehensive account of mediation, ideally encompassing all its factors.

More specifically, Wall's model is intended to be a "structure for a systematic categorization of the current mediation techniques" (Wall 1981: 158), limited to the consideration of studies dealing with strategies and techniques of mediation. As such, this survey explicitly tries to answer the problem of how to situate the huge set of strategies and techniques listed by the literature[12] in a mediation

12. In Wall and Lynn (1993) about 100 techniques are identified and listed. The selection of these techniques appears to be based on very broad criteria; more precisely, the notion of *technique* is never directly defined within this review, and seems to have a quite uncertain meaning. Indeed, Wall lists, among the mediator techniques, communicative acts such as in "claims to be a source of information" (Wall 1981: 171), "highlights negotiators' common interests" (ibid., p. 172), together with activities such as in "acts as a sounding board for negotiators' tactics" (ibid., p. 173), non-communicative actions as in "allows no communication" (ibid., p. 171), inference processes at the cognitive level as "interprets the complexity of issues" (ibid.), and even events such as "creates an audience effect with his presence" (ibid., p. 173).

scenario. The goal of this model is intended to be "the underpinning to a framework for future mediation research" (ibid.).

Indeed, the scenario of mediation, which is proposed in Wall (1981) and Wall and Lynn (1993), and updated in Wall, Stark and Standifer (2001), consists of two different models. The first, called *mediation's paradigm*, is a static picture, focusing, in particular, on the most relevant interagents involved in the process of mediation (see Figure 3.6). In particular, the parties (*negotiators' constituents*) and the subjects willing to mediate the dispute (*mediator's constituents*) are imagined to be respectively represented by two negotiators (as is often the case in processes of international mediation) and an individual working as a mediator. Therefore, the narrow "mediation system" is constituted by the mediator himself and the two negotiators. Third parties are also considered as possible determinants of the process. The mediation techniques taken from the literature are associated with each of the relationships between these interagents.

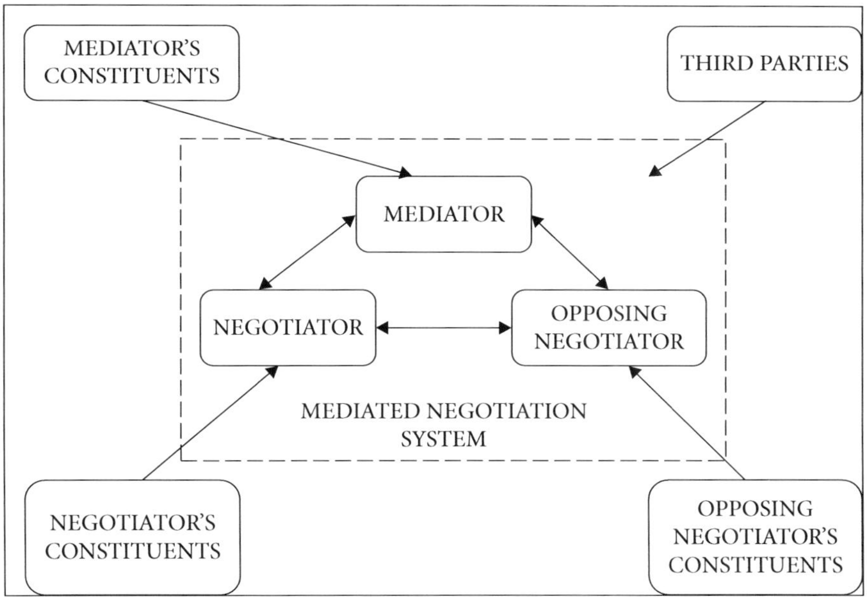

Figure 3.6. Mediation's paradigm, Wall (1981: 159)

In the following works (Wall & Lynn 1993; Wall, Stark & Standifer 2001), Wall and his colleagues propose a sequential model of mediation, called the *mediation framework*, which to some extent presupposes the representation of the main interagents presented in Figure 3.6. This more recent model shows the development of the mediation process and the factors influencing it, as represented in Figure 3.7:[13]

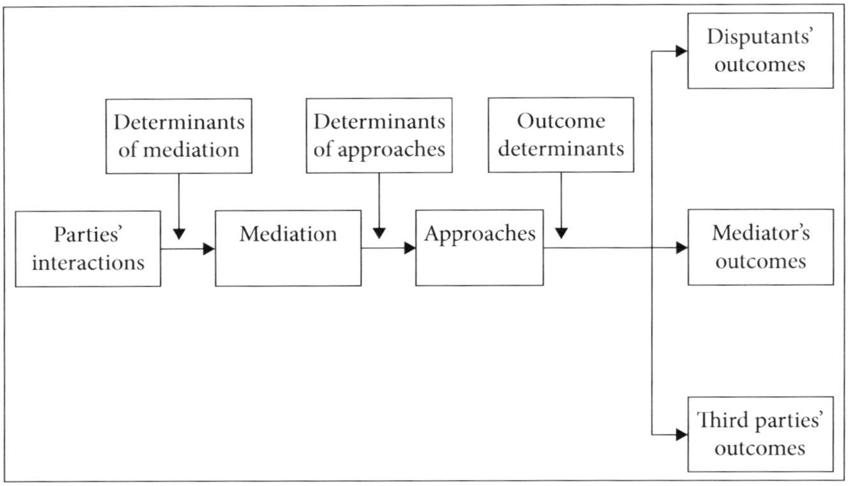

Figure 3.7. "The mediation framework" proposed by Wall, Stark and Standifer (2001: 372)

What is particularly worth noticing is the collocation of the mediation process proper and of the *approaches* (conceived of as sets of techniques) in a more comprehensive framework that takes into account both the *situation preceding mediation* (the parties' interactions and the determinants of mediation) and the *outcomes of the process. Parties' interactions* is a category referring to the relationship pre-existing the mediation intervention, which can be more or less co-operative. According to the level of their previous co-operation, parties may decide not to use mediation, either because their conflict has not escalated, or because they prefer to fight rather than to resolve their conflict (Wall & Lynn 1993: 164). Between these extremes, a range of possible interactions that allow for a mediative solution is available. With *determinants of mediation* the authors refer more specifically to the parties' and the mediator's decisions to enter the mediation process. *Mediation* and *approaches* are strictly bound; the former concerns the specific kind of mediation domain (community, marital, and so on, see Wall, Stark & Standifer 2001: 374), while *approaches* refers to the techniques adopted by the mediators during the process, in turn influenced by different *determinants of approaches.* The process of mediation is then expected to produce outcomes respectively concerning all the essential interagents: the mediator, the parties

13. Here, the latest version of the model, which presents some refinements, has been adopted (Wall, Stark & Standifer 2001: 372).

and third parties who are indirectly affected by the dispute (like children in relation to conflicting parents, or neighbour states or countries at war).

Two aspects are of particular relevance in this framework. First, the *focus on outcomes*, which Wall, Stark and Standifer (2001: 380) describe as "the most bountiful arena for the past decade"; and, second, the relation between mediators' approaches (techniques and strategies) and the context in which these are employed.

The problem of outcomes, indeed, is currently an open issue in research on mediation. In comparison with other ways of dealing with conflict, defining what a successful mediation is represents a delicate task (Pearson d'Estrée et al. 2001). First of all, as conflict threatens human relationships, the implications of conflict and the results of conflict resolution are usually delicate and difficult to measure,[14] as measuring the "health condition" of a human relationship is not simple. What can be measured, at least in standard cases of formal mediation of interpersonal conflicts, is the parties' compliance with the signed agreement (Long 2003; Kelly 2004; Li 2001).[15] However, such data could turn out to be poor or at least insufficient to grasp the value that restoring an endangered human relationship can have.[16] Even if limiting the problem to this restricted measurement, however, a problem arises over the evaluation of the *durability* of the agreements stipulated within mediation. Some studies have tackled this point by contacting parties some time after their mediated agreement to ask them whether it is still functioning (Meierding 1993). In the case of child-custody mediation, in particular, accessing data on the durability of agreements is relatively easier, because even successful agreements often need to be rediscussed after some time, for example, as children grow up, or other factors intervene (like one of the parents plans to move to another city, see Haynes & Haynes 1989). In other fields, however, critics argue that too few efforts have been made to study the effects of mediation after a relevant period of time (Malhotra & Liyanage 2005: 911). In the specific context of conflict resolution education, some research has been made about the effects of mediation

14. Given this difficulty, some scholars prefer to speak of *conflict management* and avoid the term *solution*.

15. Li (2001) also takes into account the cost-effectiveness advantage provided by mediation, in particular applied to the business field.

16. Many mediators would agree that their intervention can be defined as successful when parties who have not been able to reach an agreement within the process, find a personal solution out of the formal boundaries of the practice (Tamara Erez, interview with the author, June 24, 2004); the same is true in the case of divorcing couples entering a child-custody mediation process and then discovering that they want to try to continue their marriage. In such cases, however, gaining measurable information on the resolution process outcomes becomes difficult even for the mediators involved.

programmes on the parties' acquisition of instruments allowing them to deal with future conflicts (Bickmore 2003; Burrell, Zirbel & Allen 2003; Compton 2002).

The second significant aspect highlighted in this model concerns the relationship between the *context* of the dispute and the mediators' *choice of techniques*. In other words, techniques, also at the communicative and argumentative level, must fit the context of the dispute. Wall, Stark and Standifer (2001: 377) describe the context in terms of (1) the environment and the interested parties within such an environment, (2) the mediator and (3) the disputants. Such a description elaborates on a proposal already presented in Wall (1981), where the author, in line with his effort of providing a framework for further research, also considers the importance of studying the specific contingent effectiveness of each technique, i.e. its effectiveness in the context of the specific case where it is employed. As Wall explains (ibid., p. 177):

> "Crossing the techniques with the contextual factors provides a matrix of potential hypotheses as to whether or not each mediation technique is effective within the delineated negotiation contexts".

To this purpose, Wall proposes a matrix in which all techniques are correlated to various possible contextual factors (negotiation context, nature of negotiation); see the following table:

Table 3.1. Wall's mediation technique-negotiation context matrix (Wall 1981: 176)

Mediation technique – Negotiation context Matrix			
	Negotiation context		
	Relative experience of the negotiators (equal vs. unequal)	**Whom negotiators represent (constituents vs. no constituents)**	**Nature of negotiations etc. (One shot, repeated, sequential, serial, multiple, or linked)**
Mediation techniques			
Clarifies situation			
Misrepresents situation			
Establishes protocol			
Lays out perceptions			
Interprets complexity of issues			
Informs negotiators of how similar problems have been handled previously			
Makes negotiators aware of relevant information			
Finds and supplies relevant information			

However, a fundamental problem affects Wall and colleagues' approach, which is related to an attitude of uncritical eclecticism. In other words, mediator strategies and techniques are elicited without taking into account their *quality* and their intrinsic validity. Thus, as demonstrated in the limited extract of the list presented in Table 3.1, mediator techniques such as in "distorts information" and in "clarifies situation" (ibid., p. 171) are considered as equal, despite their clear imbalance from the point of view of communication and social quality. Therefore, a problem arises as to the meaning of "effectiveness", because one might ask in which sense a manipulative technique like distorting information should lead to an outcome that is really in line with the goal of the mediation practice and with the parties' desires and concerns.

3.1.5 The "comprehensive mediation model": Herrman, Hollett and Gale

One of the most recent models proposed in the literature, and probably the most comprehensive in terms of the identification of the constitutive factors and relationships that give origin to the mediation scenario, is that put forward by Herrman, Hollett and Gale (2006). This model, as that proposed by Wall and his colleagues, derives from a comprehensive synthesis of the literature on mediation.[17] It delineates the essential factors of its scenario, aiming at specifying variables that can be used in further research at the empirical level. More specifically, it aims to offer a basis on which different hypotheses can be tested by scholars of mediation and, at the same time, which can serve practitioners in understanding the process they work with (ibid., p. 20).

Differently from Wall and colleagues, however, these authors not only consider the literature on mediator strategies and techniques, but aim to take into account all relevant factors of the mediation process mentioned by studies in conflict resolution. Indeed, the wide scope of this literature review and the strong systematization effort turns out to constitute the strength of this approach – which has been named by the authors the *comprehensive* mediation model. However, as noticed for the approach by Wall and colleagues, the attitude underlying the model is eclectic and not critically founded, as it lacks criteria for a systematic and precise assessment of the reliability of the sources found in literature.[18]

17. The authors explicitly mention their intention to follow Wall's steps concerning the level of specificity of their model in the description of mediation (Herrman, Hollett & Gale 2006: 22).

18. Moreover, as the authors themselves point out, the model is *testable* but it has not yet been *tested*; in fact, it appears that both the relations between the different factors and their relative weight would need to be specified through further research.

The model is organized following a timeline, subdivided into four steps (T_0, T_m, T_1 and T_2 respectively; see Figure 3.8). However, it does not aim to encompass the temporal dynamics of the mediation process; rather, it highlights the constitutive factors of mediation that result relevant to each temporal phase. T_0 represents the phase antedating a proper mediation intervention (Herrman, Hollett & Gale 2006: 24); it can be said that it aims to include all those contextual factors that will interplay during the mediation process, such as the disputants (their personal characteristics, their beliefs and attitudes), the dispute and its characteristics, and the institutional context[19] in which the problem occurs (ibid., pp. 31–32).

T_m represents the very core of the mediation process, i.e. the moment in which the parties' and mediator's discussion is developed. Here, all the variables listed concern the parties' attitude that the mediator must be able to promote in order to happily fulfil his/her institutional role. The authors categorize such variables into four sub-groups: *factors that prime readiness* are bound to the participants' (both parties and mediator) personal attitudes and to making them feel comfortable in the discussion. This category includes mediator empathy, allowing the parties to feel that what they say is heard and understood, a clear discourse, and ensuring the parties feel responsible and efficient during the process.[20] *Procedural factors concerning mediation conditions* include respect for the institutional characteristics of mediation and of the mediator's mandate, such as active participation by the parties, procedural clarity, global fairness, interactional fairness, mediator neutrality and mediator process control. *Procedural factors concerning the problem-solving process* are linked to the characteristics that the communication process in mediation is expected to have: active negotiation, talked-about issues and needs, and formulated options. Finally, the *procedural factors concerning decision-making* describe the issue of the parties' control over the outcome which, as previously said (see Section 3.1.1), sharply distinguishes mediation from other ADR practices.[21]

T_1 and T_2 represent the mediation outcomes, respectively in the short and long term. Beyond considering the change in the disputants' beliefs and attitudes after the mediation process (including their satisfaction with the process itself

19. This last variable includes the degree of institutionalization of the mediation process itself: its sponsorship, governance structures, policies, goals, the possibility to access it by all segments of the concerned population, the acquired data on its efficiency, and others.

20. A negative factor, namely a hostile environment, is also considered in this category as an element that could frustrate all mediator attempts to create a positive attitude.

21. In this relation, the balance between two opposite aspects has to be considered: the clients' possibility to shape the decision and the mediator-driven closure (Herrman, Hollett & Gale 2006: 43).

and their attitude towards the future of their relationships), *short-term outcomes* encompass the description of the resolution of the conflict and of the institutional conditions of the mediation process (efficiency, effectiveness, comparable costs). Very importantly, *long-term outcomes* include post-mediation evaluations of the disputants' beliefs and attitudes and the consideration of durable changes in their relationships.[22] Moreover, in the long run, the durability of the agreement is also considered together with its effects on the wider context, like the fostering of restorative justice and the parties' reduced recidivism (ibid., p. 53).

Figure 3.8 (reproduced from Herrman, Hollett & Gale 2006: 24) represents all the mentioned variables linked to the temporal phases in which the results are particularly relevant.

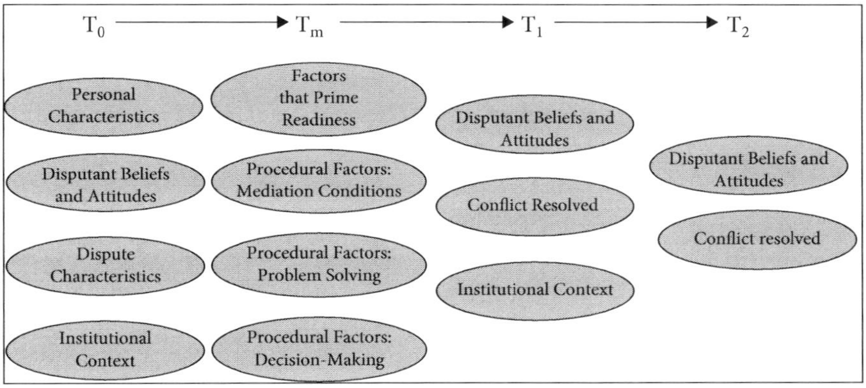

Figure 3.8. Herrman, Hollett and Gale's comprehensive model of mediation

In comparison with Wall and colleagues' framework, two aspects are shown to be of particular relevance in this scenario.

First, the phase preceding the mediation interaction proper is more precisely specified in its constituency. In particular, two factors emerge as relevant. The former consists in everything concerning the mediator's and the parties' personal and interpersonal characteristics, including the disputants' beliefs and attitudes (for instance, their willingness to participate in the process, their expectations and motivations, and so on). The latter concerns the institutional (restricted and broader) context in which the mediation process takes place, i.e. the type of

22. As said when considering Wall, Stark and Standifer's (2001) model (see Figure 3.7), evaluating the long-term durability and effectiveness of mediation can be a delicate task. However, Herrman, Hollett and Gale quote some studies that have tried to measure the improvement in the parties' interactions (ibid., see in particular p. 53).

programme in which mediation is inscribed, the geographical area, and so on. The influence of context is considered as essential in the model. As the authors put it:

> "Any form of conflict resolution occurs in a social context – within a family, a group, a community, a nation – that encompasses techniques, symbols, categories, rules, and values relating to conflict and conflict resolution." (ibid., p. 22)

The dispute characteristics, that is the nature of the conflict that has arisen (including legal constraints, and institutional/interpersonal relationships and dynamics touched by it), are also specified in the definition of the antecedent factors, which turn out to be of particular relevance to understand mediation dynamics.

Second, the model also sheds more light on the importance of considering the outcomes of mediation in the short and long term. Coherently with the consideration of the dispute context, outcomes in the institutional context (beyond the modification of the parties' attitudes) are also considered. Indeed, consideration of the possible changes at the level of the institutional context opens the way for the study of possible beneficial effects on the prevention of future conflicts in those environments in which a mediation has succeeded.

Overall, the *comprehensive model* offers some valuable aid to the identification of variables relevant to the construction of a mediation scenario, but the interplay of such variables during the phases of the mediation process is neglected. Thus, it is a rather static model, which can offer a scenario of mediation but not its process, which would be necessary for a complete ontology of mediation that could be useful for the study of communication.

3.2 The script perspective

The construction of a scenario of mediation is essential in order to understand the main factors determining this process in terms of the individuals involved, their institutional roles, their relationships, their motivations, the reasons why they get involved in mediation and, finally, the expected outcomes. These aspects are, indeed, connected and can be understood in the framework of the process that implements the *pragmatic structure* of mediation; namely the *script* dimension of this practice, which turns out to encompass some specific salient knots.

The script dimension may be added by considering the *stage models* of mediation, which give a dynamic representation of the pragmatic dimension of the mediator's mandate, i.e. they make explicit all the passages of a correct mediation process. Indeed, the elicitation of the stages of the mediation intervention is one of the issues that has been tackled extensively in the literature, because it is of immediate use for the training of mediation professionals. The enumeration of stages is elicited by taking into account the practitioners' activities and is, thus, descriptive. However, it also tends to become normative, since the description acquires the authority of a list of stages fixed during decades of practice. Although, of course, there are many individual variations, the fundamental structure of a mediation process is universally acknowledged and has given rise to the so-called *stage model* of mediation. Here, the recent version presented in Kovach (2005) is cited as a reasonably comprehensive picture of the current practices of mediation[23] (see Table 3.2).

The *preliminary arrangements* normally include all those aspects that do not directly concern the proper mediation process. Several mediators present a sort of contract before the beginning of the process, which includes fees, the selection of the mediator, and other meta-issues.

In many cases, the mediator presents, in a more or less detailed way, an *introduction* to the practice of mediation and its possible advantages.[24] Within this

23. Notice that, as Kovach observes, the succession of the phases is only ideally linear, because each phase can be repeated during the process. See Kovach (2005: 306): "I break mediation into these stages *not* to suggest linearity, but rather to highlight some of the important things that happen in most mediations". In this way, Kovach also responds to critiques on more naïve versions of stage models that are based on strict temporal linearity (see the critiques advanced in Antes, Turner Hudson, Jorgensen & Kelly Moen 1999).

24. The mediator's introduction normally makes the reasons for using mediation as an alternative to court explicit to the parties; in other words, it points to the advantages of mediation in comparison to other dispute resolution techniques. Here, I shall mention two examples of introductory discourse. The first is the beginning of a transcription of an actual family mediation session taken from a corpus of transcripts (around one hour each) from three different mediation agencies in western and southwestern American cities, which Scott Jacobs kindly allowed me to study (see Jacobs 2002: 1405 for a more detailed description of the corpus): "I'm going to begin by telling you, about this process and why you're here and what we can hope to accomplish by your being here. Um, before, you go before the court to present your case or instead of hopefully, um, you come here to the conciliation court and our job is to assist you to see if you can talk through some of your issues, and work out a plan for your children, whereby they can be with you the father and you the mother. Um, because although you're getting a divorce from each other, you're not getting a divorce from your children, and your children need both of you, and the plan, the job before both of you is to work out some plan, where they can be with you as their mother and they can be with you as their father um, so if that could be worked out here, then (you could) write up an agreement, a plan, that you two have come up with with my assistance, and then that becomes an order of the court, and enforceable, in other words you have to live up to then what you've agreed to do. But you have a right not to agree to anything in here, and if you do not then you go on before the court and (put) on your case and the judge makes an order, and then (…) a law in your family and you are required to live up to that. Um of course I encourage you as much as possible to try and

phase, the rules of the process (number of sessions, time, communication rules, etc.) can be discussed. Of course, the more the clients are accustomed to this process, the less such an introduction is necessary.

The following phases may be more or less separate, depending on the application context and on the mediator's style. The parties (or their representatives) can make *opening remarks* through "an uninterrupted presentation of their views of the case or dispute" (Kovach 2005: 307). Kovach also mentions the possibility of explicitly foreseeing a phase of *venting*, which allows parties to express their emotions; this phase is often diluted throughout the process.

In other cases, the parties' views of the case emerge, together with further information about the conflict and its context, through the mediator's questioning (*information gathering*); the mediator also tries to concentrate on the parties' interests beyond their announced positions (*issue and interests identification*). The identification of issues allows the mediator to perform an activity of *agenda setting*, where he/she may propose to tackle some issues before others. The mediator's choice is guided by his/her perception of what the best order is for achieving the resolution of the conflict. These tasks can in some cases be fulfilled through individual colloquia with the parties, called *caucus*, or *shuttle mediation*. In particular, this technique is largely used in international mediation, or in particularly difficult cases of commercial mediation or, again, in delicate processes such as victim–offender mediation (see Section 2.2.3.1). Other mediators, especially those

work things out here because then this will be an agreement that you two have devised, and you know your children and yourselves much better than any judge ever will".

The second example is taken from Friedman and Himmelstein (2007): "Lasciatemi descrivere più dettagliatamente il mio approccio alla mediazione. L'obiettivo qui, in realtà, è di vedere se posso aiutarvi a prendere delle decisioni, basate su cosa è più importante per voi, lasciandovi alla fine in una situazione più vantaggiosa per entrambi rispetto a quella che otterreste con una causa giudiziaria. Come vi ho già detto per telefono, voglio che sia chiaro per entrambi che non ho alcun potere decisionale. La porta è sempre aperta, nessuno è obbligato a rimanere qui se gli sembra che non abbia senso. Non posso farci niente e anche se potessi non lo vorrei. La mediazione funziona perché pensate di essere sulla stessa barca e che questa è la rotta giusta. Non farò il giudice, siete voi i giudici, e se giungete ad una soluzione che sembra giusta ad entrambi, allora abbiamo terminato il nostro lavoro, altrimenti non avete perso niente se non il tempo e il denaro che avete speso, anzi investito in questo processo. Esistono ovviamente delle tensioni, ci sono delle divergenze tra di voi. La mia speranza è che lavorando insieme potremo giungere ad una soluzione che tenga conto di cosa sia importante per ogni parte senza che l'altra debba sentire di aver dovuto rinunciare a qualcosa che le sembra importante. Ci sono un'infinità di modi per procedere, ma preferisco che si lavori riuniti tutti insieme per cercare di capire a fondo la dimensione del problema, e poi cercare di trovare la soluzione che risponda al meglio agli interessi di entrambi".

tackling interpersonal conflicts, refuse to meet the parties separately, in order to not risk losing their trust (Friedman 1993: 7).

Apparently, the most creative part of the process follows the first explorative phase: the mediator guides the parties through the *option generation* of possible solutions, the *reality testing* of the reasonableness of these solutions, and through *bargaining and negotiation*, which can translate the parties' desires into practice through an ideally serene interaction. In the end, when the mediation process has happily concluded, an *agreement* is reached, which normally includes a written contract (if necessary, revised by a lawyer). The mediator may also help the parties predefine the conditions of application of their agreements and, in some cases, foresee some further facilitative intervention in the implementation phase.

Table 3.2. Stages of the mediation intervention (Kovach 2005: 36)

Preliminary arrangements
Mediator's introduction
Opening remarks/Statements by parties
Venting (optional)
Information gathering
Issue and interests identification
Agenda setting (optional)
Caucus (optional)
Option generation
Reality testing (optional)
Bargaining and negotiation
Agreement
Closure

3.3 Provisional conclusions about the state of the art

The reconstructive approach I have adopted stems from a very specific perspective on the different studies on mediation: namely, the syntethical purpose of reconstructing a conceptual framework of this practice that can be the basis to understand how argumentation contributes to mediation.

Quite independently from the original goals of the different approaches considered, I have analysed those models that somehow contribute to shed light on the constitutive factors of mediation (scenario) and its dynamic relations (script). The different models considered are not incompatible: they can be integrated in order to elicit a unitary picture of mediation.

Taken as a whole, the different models dealing with the constitutive aspects of mediation show that, in order to understand this process, it is not sufficient to consider the dialogic exchange between the two parties and the mediator. On the contrary, it is important to consider the factors logically determining it and those following from it as well; that is to take into account the whole process from its presuppositions to its results. As emerged in the previous section, the scenario of mediation also involves reflection on the determinants of the choice of mediation (in terms of the individual's interests and of the institutional constraints) and of the implications of the mediation process on the social reality in which parties are living, including all types of short-term and long-term outcomes that can be envisaged. To this, as shown by considering the stage-models of mediation, the script dimension must be added. By focusing on the dynamic development of mediation, the script dimension allows us to consider its pragmatic structure, in which the various phases and aspects that emerged in the scenario are ordered towards the fulfilment of the specific goal of this practice – namely the resolution of a conflict.

As a general working hypothesis for the construction of an integrated conceptual framework of mediation we could assume the proposal by Herrman, Hollett and Gale (2006), to which we owe the identification of the main categories of *antecedents*, *process* and *outcomes*[25] (see Section 3.1.5). To this, in Figure 3.9, a specific focus on the script dimension is represented by the arrows, suggesting a sequence of steps oriented towards the mediation goal:

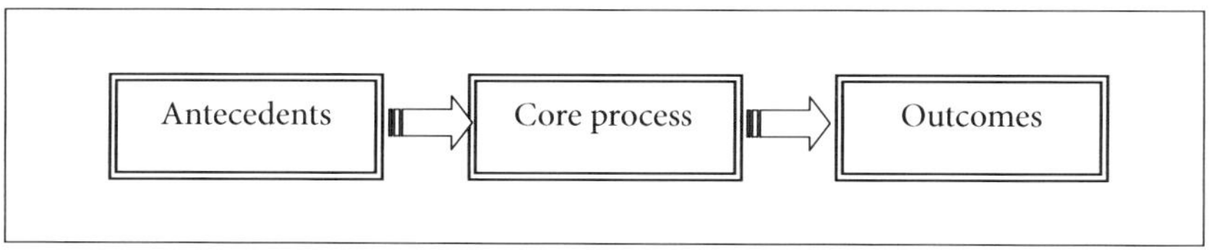

Figure 3.9. Main factors of mediation (adapted from Herrman, Hollett & Gale 2006)

The categories of antecedents, core process and outcomes are sufficiently broad to encompass all the factors emerging in the mediation models proposed until now, and can constitute a clear and solid basis – a backbone – to set up a framework of the mediation practice.

The specific content of each of these categories has been studied in the literature with different degrees of depth and specificity.

25. In Herrman, Hollett and Gale's model, outcomes are subdivided into short-term and long-term outcomes. For the purpose of identifying the general structure of this practice, however, it is possible to consider the category of outcomes as a whole.

a. Many studies, as seen, are focused on the core process of mediation. They identify its various *phases* (Kovach 2005) and elicit the main techniques and strategies that mediators employ in order to fulfil their task (Lall 1966; Maggiolo 1985; Touval & Zartman 1985a and 1985b; Wall 1981; Wall & Lynn 1993; Wall, Stark & Standifer 2001). In some cases, such techniques have been associated with precise mediator *profiles* (Herrman, Hollett, Gale & Foster 2001). It also emerges that the kernel of the mediation process is represented by the proper communicative interaction between the mediator and the parties, which includes a series of strategies and techniques that help the parties to discuss their problem. The emergence of argumentation should be identified in this very kernel, in which the mediator discreetly makes it possible for the parties to engage in an argumentative discussion oriented towards the resolution of their conflict.
b. The problem of outcomes has attracted interest for its implications at the level of evaluation of mediation in comparison with other ways of dealing with disputes (Meierding 1993; Pearson d'Estrée et al. 2001). The field of mediation studies, however, is perhaps not sufficiently mature for this kind of analysis. In fact, a thorough evaluation of mediation effects presupposes the accurate identification of the logically preceding phases and of their relations. In particular, although it is clear that antecedents have an influence on the core process, the specific nature of antecedents still deserves further investigation; moreover, their relations both to the core process and to outcomes have not been adequately brought to light.
c. Concerning the antecedents, the current picture of mediation studies uncovers some constitutive aspects of the pre-mediation phase. In particular, the main interagents – the parties (and their possible constituents, see Wall 1981) and the mediator – have been singled out. Furthermore, some factors and relations have been identified, such as the personal relationship between the parties (Wall, Stark & Standifer 2001; Herrman, Hollett & Gale 2006), as well as their beliefs and interests (Patton 2005) and the mediator's perception of such beliefs and interests (Herrman, Hollett & Gale 2006). The parties' relationship is also influenced by the institutional context (Herrman, Hollett & Gale 2006; Wall, Stark & Standifer 2001). The definition of the parties' relationship preceding the mediation intervention must also include the identification of the conflict that has endangered it. The role of conflict as a presupposition of the mediation intervention is more or less implicitly present in all models, as mentioned in Herrman, Hollett and Gale (2006). In fact, by means of an adequate analysis of the different notions of conflicts it is possible to distinguish between them many conflictual events (interpersonal or intergroup disputes, intractable conflicts, wars, and so on) and intervene properly in them.

Now we are left with the task of constructing a single and comprehensive framework for the understanding of mediation, drawing on the elements reconstructed in the overview of the literature. Such a task is a challenge to be met enthusiastically. In fact, eliciting the pragmatic structure of mediation is a necessary presupposition to start analysing how argumentation contributes to this process.

In order to fulfil this task, two further steps are necessary; these steps will be made in the conceptual block constituted by Chapters 4 and 5. Chapter 4 will lay the foundation of a framework of mediation. First, I shall elaborate on two notions – *context* and *conflict* – that have emerged as determinants for mediation but which are not adequately tackled in previous models. Second, I will present and discuss the framework per se, trying to integrate the elements that emerged in the analysis of the literature and the discussion on context and conflict.

Yet in order to complete the conceptual analysis another step is required. Chapter 5 will introduce the theoretical notions and methodologies relative to argumentation and integrate them into the framework of mediation. I shall explain how I intend to design the argumentative analysis in order to study how argumentation contributes to the pragmatic goals of mediation. The results of the empirical analysis will be discussed in Chapter 6.

CHAPTER 4

Towards an ontology-oriented conceptual framework of mediation

By introducing the categories of *scenario* and *script*, I have been reviewing the contributions to the study of mediation and orientating attention towards the characterizing features of this practice (Chapter 3). This kind of study is necessary as part of a broader attempt to understand the role of argumentation in the context of dispute mediation (Chapter 2). In fact, in order to see how it is possible for two conflicting individuals to participate together in an argumentative discussion, and how such argumentative discussion contributes to the resolution of their conflict, it is necessary to clarify how mediation is structured. It is necessary as well to have a clear conceptual model of argumentation. In more general terms, these requirements certainly hold for any research project dealing with argumentation in context.

Drawing on the resoluts of the previous chapters, it is possible to start the construction of an *ontology-oriented conceptual framework of mediation*, including the consideration of the role of argumentation in this practice. This will be accomplished in Chapters 4 and 5. In Chapter 4, I shall lay the foundation of such a framework. The illustration of a model of argumentation and its integration in the framework will be confided to Chapter 5.

Before illustrating the specific contents of the present chapter in particular, however, I need to clarify what is meant by an *ontology-oriented* framework of mediation and, in particular, by the notion of *ontology*. The traditional philosophical concept of ontology was meant to deal with questions concerning what entities exist or in what conditions they can be said to exist, and how such entities can be grouped, related within a hierarchy, and subdivided according to similarities and differences (for example, by means of a tool like Porphyry's tree; see Rigotti & Greco Morasso 2006b). For the present purposes, however, the term *ontology* builds on the following three notions: (1) "ontology of social reality" (Searle 1995), meaning a network of (institutionalized) commitments that create specific interaction fields (see below, Section 4.1); (2) ontology as it is understood within computer science and information science, i.e. a formal representation of a set of concepts within a domain and the relationships between those concepts, that may be used to define the domain and to reason about its (constitutive) properties;

(3) the notion of ontology entailed by linguistic semantics (Jackendoff 1983 and 1990). With the phrase *ontology-oriented conceptual framework*, I mean a framework of mediation that is oriented to define the main interagents required to activate this practice and identify the constitutive relations between them.

For this chapter, the mediation framework I am going to sketch will build on the results of previous studies as regards the scenario and script of mediation (Chapter 3). However, I will also clarify two crucial aspects that have been pointed to as necessary presuppositions of mediation, but whose constituency is still under-investigated.

On the one hand, the mediator works with conflicting parties who he or she will help to "transform" into co-arguers. *Conflict* thus emerges as the essential presupposition of the mediation intervention and, as such, is a concept that should be investigated in relation to the subsequent mediation discussion in order to understand the role of argumentation and how it allows movement from conflict to consent.

The parties' relationship emerges as the factor that is endangered by conflict itself. Such a relationship is thus the value that parties entering mediation want to preserve or restore, and at the same time it constitutes the close *context* of the dispute itself. It appears to be affected by various factors, from individual attitudes to external institutional variables and constraints.

In order to arrive at a convincing mediation framework, it is necessary to further investigate the two categories of antecedents represented by the parties' *relationship* and the *conflict*. First, a model for understanding the parties' relationship as the inner layer of the *context* of the mediation intervention will be proposed; within this framework, it will be possible to investigate the implications of the insurgence of a conflict. These two interrelated concepts are of particular importance for the argumentative analysis I am going to propose. In fact, I will concentrate on how argumentation changes the *status quo* of conflict within the parties' relationship and the broader context of the dispute, and on how it "transforms" the parties into co-arguers. So, in order to understand how the status quo is changed, we first have to describe it.

4.1 The parties' relationship as the context of argumentation

The mediation intervention is by nature oriented towards the reinforcement and the saving of an endangered relationship. The importance of the parties' relationship has emerged at different moments in several of the models considered in Chapter 3. Herrman, Hollett and Gale (2006) include, among the antecedents of mediation, disputants' and mediator's "personal characteristics" and "beliefs and attitudes" towards each other. Wall, Stark and Standifer (2001: 372) speak of "parties' interactions" in general, alluding to a dynamic relationship between them. The Harvard model of principled negotiation includes relationship among the seven prime factors of negotiation, warning that it can substantially determine the possible agreement.

Beside the "human face" of the parties' relationship, then, some authors (see Herrman, Hollett & Gale 2006 in particular) seem to indicate that even more formalized aspects, such as the "institutional context" in which conflicts emerge and the type of dispute that arises consequentially (e.g. a dispute over scarcity of natural resources) are important aspects that affect the parties' rapport.

In general, the parties' relationship is to be interpreted as a constitutive factor – probably the most prominent one – of the context of the discussion that occurs in mediation. Indeed, the context is constituted by a network of relationships within *social reality*,[1] which have a relevant influence on conflict history (Wehr 1979) as well as on the practice of mediation, on its methods and applications (Bercovitch 1992; Touval & Zartman 1985a and 1985b; Menkel-Meadow 1984). In the case of conflict resolution, the kernel of the context is represented by the parties' relationship, which is however embedded in and surrounded by larger portions of social, cultural, juridical, political and economic contexts, which are in turn a web of relationships. But what then is a relationship? Is there a way to define it accurately in the "context" of argumentative discussion occurring in mediation? I shall detailedly present an argumentative model at the basis of the present work in Chapter 5; here, the fact that mediation is exclusively managed by means of a communicative discussion is sufficient to say that a communication-oriented model of context will help to shed more light on the parties' relationship. For this reason, I adopt the model of *communication context* proposed in Rigotti and Rocci (2006).

Rigotti and Rocci's model provides a bridge for the antecedents and the core process of mediation. Such a model, in fact, has been conceived as a model of the context *of communication*. This means that the perspective of this model is internal to the problem of understanding and evaluating communicative events;[2] the model, in fact, aims to analyse the contextual influences on communicative events. Therefore, such an approach is particularly suited for eliciting the connection

1. The term is taken from Searle (1995).

2. More properly, the approach is explicitly situated in the tradition of research bound to the language sciences, which have shown context to be "an essential factor in the processes of the production and interpretation of speech acts, but also ... integral to the constitution of meaning itself" (Rigotti & Rocci 2006: 157).

between the parties' relationship, i.e. the most relevant antecedent contextual factors, and the proper argumentative interaction occurring in mediation.

Furthermore, this model accounts for the institutionalized and formal aspects of the parties' relationship as well as for their personal rapport. The significance of the parties' personal relationship is highlighted in particular in studies concerning family mediation (Cigoli & Scabini 2004), whereas other approaches tend to bring to light the constitutive nature of the institutional context surrounding and shaping the parties' roles (in terms of work roles, routines, hierarchy, and so on). The institutionalized context also includes the wider social and juridical context in which the conflict resolution intervention is embedded (Herrman, Hollett & Gale 2006). Both dimensions are interrelated and intertwined, though their relative weight may change depending on the type of mediation intervention. Significantly, in "hybrid" situations such as family-owned businesses, the interplay between these two aspects has to be carefully considered by the mediator (Marinoni 2001; Canyamares I Sanahuja 2002). In addition, the relationship between the parties, including its complex interplay of all the juridical, social and personal aspects, is anything but static. On the contrary, it is a growing process, which is significantly modified in the moment in which the disputants enter the mediation process. At this moment, in fact, they accept the role of parties willing to find a solution to their conflict by means of mediation and thus the role of symmetric and equally empowered co-arguers (even if their professional relationship implies a different hierarchical status). Moreover, the very presence of the mediator changes the structure of the interaction. As will become clear in the argumentative analysis of some mediation cases in Chapter 6, the presence of a third interlocutor is shown to have extreme relevance in promoting dialogue between the disputants and in helping them set up their discussion in a reasonable fashion.

It is thus worth illustrating the model of context emerging in Rigotti and Rocci's research, to try to clarify its implications for the understanding of the mediation process.

On the basis of a semantic analysis of the term *context*,[3] then specified to encompass the context of communication, context emerges as having "an 'objective' or *constitutive* dimension" (ibid., p. 166; see also Perret-Clermont 2006: 183).

3. On the basis of the analysis, context emerges as covering a relational predicate (*to be the context of*) connecting the context (x) and the contextualized (y). A first observation concerns the nature of states of affairs of both x and y, which can belong to the same world or to different worlds. In particular, the contextualized can belong to the real world or to a possible one (ibid., p. 159). About the semantic content proper of the predicate, a relationship of mutual relevance has been identified between x and y, so that "the contextualized can be properly understood only if its context is known. In fact, the context gives the contextualized

On the one hand, the performance of given communicative moves depends on the satisfaction of a series of contextual requirements. On the other hand, the context represents the target directly affected by the communicative move, as any communication is oriented towards a *habit change* (see Rigotti & Rocci 2001: 48), whose effects overflow the mere communicative dimension, permeating the social world, including the subjects involved in communication, as well as the physical reality.[4]

The authors propose a model focusing on the constitutive aspects of the context of communication, which is synthetically represented in the following figure:

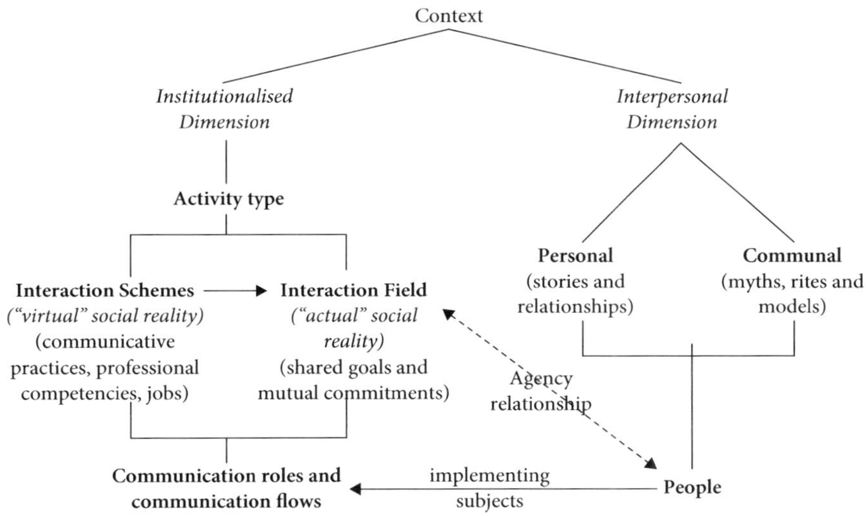

Figure 4.1. The model of context (from Rigotti & Rocci 2006)

As it appears even from a first glance at Figure 4.1, the notion of *context* includes two equally relevant dimensions: the institutional and the interpersonal dimensions. Starting with the former, it is possible to situate mediation and analogous practices. In fact, in Rigotti and Rocci's terms, practices such as mediation can be ascribed to the notion of *interaction schemes*, which are defined as:

> "...Culturally shared 'recipes' for interaction congruent with more or less broad classes of joint goals and involving scheme-roles presupposing generic

its *meaning*, in the sense that it allows us to assign the contextualized the actual function it has in relation to the immediately relevant surrounding totality" (ibid., p. 162).

4. In terms of the speech act theory (Searle 1969), this corresponds to the *perlocutionary effects* of a speech act.

> requirements. *Deliberation, negotiation, advisory, problem-solving, adjudication, mediation, teaching* are fairly broad interaction schemes; while more specific interaction schemes may correspond to proper 'jobs'". (ibid., p. 173)

In fact, if we consider the activity of mediation as the intervention of a third neutral facilitator in a conflict, this can be understood as an interaction scheme. Nowadays, as illustrated above, mediation has also become a recognized job in the field of ADR practices – which does not exclude the presence of informal practices having the same communicative structure, in other words inhering to the same interaction scheme.

An interaction scheme like mediation can be implemented in a series of *interaction fields*.[5] An interaction field is defined as "that piece of *social reality* where the communicative interaction takes place". As shown in Chapter 2, mediation has become a common interaction scheme in a number of interaction fields, from family mediation, to victim–offender mediation, and so on (see Section 2.2.3.1). The distinction interaction scheme/interaction field allows the different insights found in the examined literature to be reorganized. Mediation per se is an interaction scheme with a certain degree of institutionalization (Wall, Stark & Standifer 2001: 372). However, its actualization also depends on the specific interaction field in which the conflict is present. Following Herrman, Hollett and Gale (2006), we interpret the interaction field as a layered structure; at the core of this structure lies a specific institution (a school, hospital, business, etc.), which is surrounded by a larger context (the educational, health or economic system respectively; legislation and political norms, etc.). Albeit the fundamental features of the interaction scheme remain the same throughout its application possibilities, the interaction field contributes to the definition of the actual communication context:

> "In order to obtain an actual context I need to map an interaction scheme onto an interaction field where real commitments are present. To do so the roles of the interaction scheme need to be made to correspond to compatible roles in the interaction field. For instance, the interaction scheme of lecturing is mapped onto the interaction field of the University of Lugano to obtain the full context of my teaching". (ibid., p. 173)

In fact, while interaction schemes are virtual competences, interaction fields are pieces of social reality. Interaction schemes cannot be experienced except by seeing

5. According to Rigotti and Rocci (2006: 173): "The same interaction schemes can be found in different interaction fields: for instance we can find deliberation by a board of directors in a business and deliberation by a city council in public administration". The notion of activity type corresponds to an interaction scheme applied to a precise interaction field, for instance mediation in business, parliamentary debate, and so on (see later).

them at work in different interaction fields. Mediation, thus, does not exist per se, but it is applied to specific conflicts arising within as many interaction fields. In this relation, applying mediation to a business or to an international dispute is different because the social reality underlying the two institutions is different. This may also lead to slight changes in the actualization of the interaction scheme, as seen, for instance, when describing victim–offender mediation or organizational mediation (see Section 2.2.3.1). As a matter of fact, the connection between interaction schemes and the interaction field is so tight that together they have been considered as giving rise to the so-called *activity types*. The notion of activity type has been presented in Levinson (1979/1992) and developed within the argumentative studies by van Eemeren and Houtlosser (2005, 2007). An activity type is "a fuzzy category whose focal-members are goal-defined, socially constituted, bounded, events with constraints on participants, setting and so on, but above all on the kinds of allowable contributions" (Levinson 1979/1992: 69).[6] Some examples of activity type given by Levinson, such as *jural interrogation*, or by van Eemeren and Houtlosser (2007: 172), such as the *Dutch criminal trial*, clearly show the merger of the interaction scheme and interaction field within this notion. As the present investigation concentrates on mediation, Rigotti and Rocci's account, which allows distinguishing these two components, has been chosen in order to have a clear picture of what depends on the interaction scheme in question (i.e. on mediation), and what depends on the interaction fields upon which it is mapped.

The implementation of interaction schemes within interaction fields generates a network of *roles* that are linked to each other through corresponding *communicative flows* (Rigotti & Rocci 2006: 172). Roles depend both on the interaction field and on the interaction scheme: for instance, in the process of mediation between an organization's manager and a group of employees, the respective working roles (manager–employee) are defined by the structure of the organization (the interaction field), while the roles of parties and mediator are derived from the interaction scheme. Communicative flows are repeated and stable occurrences of communicative activities involving two or more roles that are required by the interaction scheme involving these roles. *Teaching* establishes a communicative flow binding the teacher and the pupil roles; in mediation, normally, there are communicative flows that precede the mediation intervention and that the mediator must be capable of discovering.

Distinguishing between different interaction fields is made possible because each interaction field is defined by "specific (hierarchically organized) shared

6. Van Eemeren and Houtlosser (2005, 2007) have brought to light the activity types' feature of providing constraints on the arguers' possible moves in real argumentative discussions.

goals" (ibid., p. 172), which define the interagents' mutual commitments and relations. The ultimate goal is the *raison d'être* of the interaction field itself. Roughly speaking, the goal of a business, for instance, is that of making a profit; the goal of a hospital is to provide medical assistance to patients; the goal of an educational system is to educate people, and so on. The hierarchy of goals cannot be subverted without changing the nature of the institution/organization. If the main goal of a certain hospital becomes that of making profit and that hospital, thus, decides to accept only those patients that allow the realization of this goal, its very nature becomes questionable.

Up to now, the dimension of context that has been illustrated refers to *institutionalized relations* between the interagents involved in communication, insofar as it touches on their roles within the respective interaction fields (organizations, institutions, etc.) and within various practices (as the role of mediator). However, we must not overlook that these roles may be implemented – and *are* implemented – by real human subjects, who do not constitute, as Rigotti and Rocci (2006: 174) underline, simple "fillers" of their institutional roles. Human beings precede and overcome their roles, in that their have desires, interests, and goals, which exceed what is expected by the institutionalized context in which they operate. As already stated, the parties' personal characteristics are universally considered as a determinant of the process of mediation (cf. the review in Herrman, Hollett & Gale 2006). A conceptual instrument for understanding the relation between individual goals and goals imposed by the institutionalized dimension is constituted by *agency theory*. I have introduced the concept of *agency* in Chapter 3 in order to explain some forms of conflict. In a broader perspective, agency explains how individuals assume institutional roles by taking up particular commitments. Wall (1981: 159) alludes to this dimension when he speaks of "mediator's constituents" and "negotiators' constituents": constituents are the principals, while the mediator and the negotiators are the agents.

As Rigotti and Rocci (2006: 174–175) observe in speaking of the interpersonal dimension of context, two "types of interpersonal solidarity" take place; the former concerns interpersonal relationships between the individuals (Muller & Perret-Clermont 1999), whereas the latter concerns the link between individuals and the community, i.e. their "cultural" identity. Both types of solidarity are to be taken into account in mediation. At the interpersonal level, the individuals' stories, their representations of their relationship, their "frames", are to be taken into account. When a mediator enters a conflict, he/she has to be aware and respectful of these dynamics – think, for instance, about a family conflict, or a conflict in a classroom. Moreover, the *cultural* context (ibid.), concerning the communal identities of individuals, which creates *myths*, *rites* and *models* (Cantoni 2004; Cantoni & Di Blas 2006: 234–237) also influences the possible proceeding of mediation.

As can be deduced from these examples, the *culture* of a specific interaction field is not to be exclusively conceived as the more crucial and traditional identity of the individual, namely that pertaining to the community where the individual has grown up: his/her hometown (sometimes his/her nation), his/her religion, his/her linguistic community. Indeed, there are forms of cultural identity that concern individuals on different levels, as they are involved in more than one interaction field: in a certain sense, an employee "belongs" to the "organizational culture" of the firm where he/she works, but this kind of tie does not comprehensively describe his/her culture, which will be complemented by other (normally more important) elements. One could imagine culture as a cradle that welcomes the individual into the world; various communities position themselves as many "strata" progressively enlarging the original cradle.[7] The family is normally very close to the individual, thus this identity is very significant to him or her; whereas the organization in which he/she works is normally less determinant, as shown by the fact that moving to another workplace is often experienced by individuals as a non-traumatic event.

Therefore, culture is a dimension that has always to be considered by mediators who are confronted with not only the so-called "ethnic" conflicts, where the cultural element is evident and preponderant, but also the more "ordinary" kinds of confrontation. The overlapping of different cultural identities is a complex factor, which mediators should take into account when entering a dispute (Avruch 2003; Lowry & Littlejohn 2006). For example, mediators working with conflicts

7. I do not claim to discuss the meaning of *culture* and its implications here. It is however worth recalling the conceptual approach I rely on in this work, namely the Tartu school of semiotics' definition of culture, which highlighs how this dimension is inherent in every human interaction (Lotman & Uspenskij 1987; see also Gatti 2003). Culture is defined by two fundamental aspects. On the one hand, cultural identity implies knowledge of a system of signs that become a grammar for human interaction (languages, symbolic codes, rites, metric systems for dealing with space, time, energy and economic value), and of instruments that allow developing them (technical skills). But having the same cultural identity is not only speaking the same language or sharing some code. People who have the same culture also belong to a community based on the sharing of a "hypertext", conceived of as a network of shared experiences (texts, in a broad semiotic connotation), which include the community's history and "mission", its religious faith, its scientific and non-scientific knowledge, values, institutions themselves, and foundational texts. Single individuals are not "confined" within one cultural identity, but they have different cultural identities that correspond to as many communities to which they belong. In non-pathological situations, these multiple identities do not make individuals schizophrenic, since the different communities to which the individual belongs are not indistinctly articulated; they form a sort of "multilayer cradle" for welcoming the human baby into the world (Rigotti 2005b).

in family businesses must be aware of the multidimensional relationships endangered by conflict (Marinoni 2001; Canyameres I Sanahuja 2002).

Two more specific considerations about the contribution that this model of context could bring to the study of mediation could be added. First, from a theoretical point of view, the endeavour of constructing a comprehensive framework of mediation must take into account the fact that the antecedent conditions, in relation to the establishment of an ontology of conflict, incorporate two distinct elements. On the one hand, the context is made up of the roles and flows, covered and vivified by human beings, mainly bound to the interaction field (institutions, businesses and the like) in which mediation intervenes. On the other hand, the very fact that parties agree to enter a mediation process somehow changes their "status" and creates new roles and flows with their respective commitments, which also affect the interpersonal dimension. For example, the chief manager of a business and his/her employee, by discussing their case through mediation, foreground their nature as human beings with equal argumentative dignity, while the asymmetries of power created by their unequal hierarchical status are not relevant to the mediation discussion. A good mediator will ensure that the roles created by the interaction scheme of mediation become predominant in the discussion. Consequently, the goal and characterizing features of the interaction scheme of mediation turn out to constitute an important part of the antecedent conditions that shape the communicative core of the process of mediation itself. Therefore, it should be stressed again that context is not a fixed datum which pre-exists the parties' interactions and is not modified by them (cf. Grossen 2001: 64). On the contrary, the parties' relationships giving rise to context are modified according to the development of mediation.

Moreover, in order to further specify the role of mediation, it is necessary to consider the relation between the structure of interaction fields and interaction schemes. It has been said that interaction fields are distinguished by their main shared goal, and that they present a structure of hierarchically organized goals that ultimately aims at this shared goal. Interaction schemes are activated in order to fulfil one of the hierarchically ordinate goals of the interaction field in question. In this sense, for instance, deliberation is activated in those interaction fields in which decisions have to be made by more than a single individual – from parliaments, to boards of directors, and even to enlarged families. Mediation, in this respect, has a specific nature. Unlike deliberations in parliament and many other interaction schemes, mediation is not constantly activated within an interaction field: it intervenes, as do the other conflict resolution practices, in response to the insurgence of a conflict (Greco Morasso 2007).

Such definition carries important consequences at the level of specification of this interaction scheme. On the one hand, mediation can be crucial, as its application responds to the goal of restoring the normal functioning of an interaction field, or even of improving its interactional dynamics. On the other hand, in cases of conflict mediation is applied as "firemen's work", but conflicts are not continuatively hosted by interaction fields (except for some very chronic and difficult situations). This means that such an interaction scheme is not continuatively applied to specific interaction fields, but is a possibility that can be exploited if necessary. This turns out to be a very specific feature of mediation, which distinguishes it from other interaction schemes. In fact, interaction schemes such as teaching, curing patients and promoting health, scientific debate, and so on, more specifically characterize as many interaction fields (schools, hospitals, research groups or larger scientific communities), as they correspond to their ultimate goal. Mediation, on the other hand, is applied as a means to fulfil a subordinate goal that can sometimes emerge in an interaction field, namely that of eliminating potential obstacles to its wellbeing or flourishing.

Such a nature also determines the fact that mediation can fit the goals of a variety of interaction fields and, consequently, it can be applied to conflicts of a different nature, as the proliferation of applications of the professional practice of mediation to different institutional and social contexts demonstrates (see Chapter 2).

The nature of occasional intervention that characterizes mediation is highlighted by the fact that the mediator is often an external individual who intervenes in the interaction field with the declared function of activating a specific interaction scheme. In any interaction field, resolving conflicts may be considered a subservient goal in relation to the main goal. In fact, the presence of conflicts may slow, damage, or even hinder the realization of the main goal, by disturbing or destroying the relationships between the interagents.

4.2 Conflict: The starting point of any mediation practice

From the analysis of context just presented, conflict emerges as an event that may endanger the delicate equilibrium of interpersonal and institutional relationships constituting a fragment of social reality, namely an interaction field. Conflict is thus naturally to be seen as a crucial presupposition of a conflict resolution intervention in relation to the preservation of an interaction field. However, as remarked in Section 3.1.3, the literature on conflict seems to oscillate between two different meanings of this term; namely, *incompatibility of positions* and *interpersonal struggle*. The first meaning seems a more abstract, propositional opposition; while the second meaning has to do with a conflict involving human beings in their intellectual and also psycho-social dimensions. This latter type of conflict is most likely to generate mediation interventions, whereas the incompatibility of positions recalls the notion of *difference of opinion* which is the basis of an argumentative discussion (van Eemeren & Grootendorst 1982, see Section 5.1.2).

It is not clear whether these two types of conflict are interrelated or not; and such ambiguity is not admissible in a study focused on *argumentation in mediation*. In my view, the lack of clarity about conflict determines the need for a *semantic analysis* of this term in order to grasp its proper meaning; this will allow a definition of its role in the mediation process. Semantic analysis is a possible analytical instrument to clarify concepts. The approach adopted here is based on a semantic-pragmatic account, namely Congruity theory (see Rigotti, Rocci & Greco 2006; Rigotti & Cigada 2004, pp. 77–111; Greco Morasso 2008).[8]

4.2.1 Semantic analysis of *conflict* and related terms

The method which the semantic analysis proposed here relies on stems from a theoretical and methodological approach denominated *Congruity theory* (see Section 5.1.5.1 for a more detailed account). First proposed in Rigotti (1993) as an approach to the analysis of textual sequences, Congruity theory rests on a pragmatic account considering communicative texts as actions, having thus a pragmatic goal. It interprets the whole textual structure as a hierarchy of interconnected predicate-argument structures, which are activated at different (semantic and pragmatic) levels, and which respond to the pragmatic aim of the text (Rigotti & Rocci 2001; Rigotti 2005a). The notion of *predicate* is at the core of the theory, and, from a methodological point of view, the analysis is centred on predicates present in texts at various levels: "A *predicate* is conceived as a possible "mode of being", a general notion that subsumes more specific ontological[9] distinctions such as those between properties and relations, states and events, actions and non-actions" (Rigotti 2005a: 78). Such an approach allows analysing texts at the level of simple structures manifested by lexical and syntactic structures (from predicates like "to conflict with", to simple sentences), but it also accounts for more complex structures, like higher-level pragmatic predicates which assume as arguments text sequences, and may have no linguistic manifestation at all. In Congruity theory terms, "doing a semantic analysis means to rewrite natural language utterances in terms of predicate-argument structures" (Rigotti, Rocci & Greco 2006: 259). Within this framework, the semantic analysis of lexical items also takes into account the communicative situation in which they occur. In other words, it may be said that this form of semantic analysis is not independent from the pragmatic

---

8. The semantic analysis of conflict reported here was first presented in a paper published in the journal *Pragmatics & Cognition* (Greco Morasso 2008). I am grateful to the editor, Marcelo Dascal and to John Benjamins for permission to report large portions of that text here.

9. For the meaning of the term *ontological* as it is conceived of here, see the introduction to Chapter 4.

perspective, as it considers the semantics of lexical items as it emerges from their textual uses.

In more detail, analysing a predicate-argument structure, be it at any level in the text hierarchy, means identifying the conditions that the predicate imposes onto its argument places, namely *presuppositions*, and effects produced in reality if the predicate is true (i.e. if the corresponding mode of being takes place), namely *implications* of the predicate (Rigotti & Rocci 2001). If implications allow specifying the proper meaning of the predicate, presuppositions define the conditions of *congruity* for the predicate to assume specific arguments to cover its argument places.[10] In the present case, since semantic analysis aims at conceptually clarifying conflict-related notions, it is focused on the ontological constituency of these specific modes of beings. The task is theoretically a crucial one – since, as Aristotle warned in his first book of *Topics*, if the terms we use are not clearly defined, we risk being misled in our reasoning.

Examples of the application of the method of semantic analysis based on Congruity theory to clarify lexical predicates and identify their pragmatic implications have been given in Rigotti, Rocci and Greco (2006) and in Rigotti and Rocci (2006), focused respectively on a central notion of argumentation theory, namely *reasonableness*, and on *context*. As in those cases, the semantic analysis performed here is supported by empirical evidence taken from a 100-million-word corpus of current English words, named the British National Corpus (henceforth BNC), consisting of 3,261 written texts from a variety of genres (90 million words) and 863 transcribed oral samples (10 million words). It can be accessed online through a dedicated client called SARA, which can carry out sophisticated queries, build concordances and perform standard relative frequency calculations. For the present research, the corpus has been exploited mainly in order to have a complete picture of the actual uses of the words that have been investigated; in particular, the insights gained from the literature on the relation between incompatibilities

10. Congruity theory is shown to have important similarities with other semantic and pragmatic approaches. In particular, Pieter A.M. Seuren (1998, 2000) analyses the semantics of predicates in terms of *preconditions* (presuppositions) and *satisfaction conditions* (implications). A similar approach to semantic analysis is to be found in Fillmore; see, for instance, Fillmore (1971), where the author analyses verbs of judging, like "to blame", "to criticize", and "to accuse". Moreover, see the works by Igor A. Mel'čuk on the meaning-text linguistic model (Mel'čuk 1997) and on the communicative organization of utterances (Mel'čuk 2001). About pragmatic predicates, see the approaches to text coherence introducing the notion of *relational predicates*, i.e. predicates that take text units as arguments, and impose specific conditions onto them. Different authors speak of *discourse relations*, *coherence relations*, *rhetorical relations*, *rhetorical predicates*, etc.

and interpersonal conflicts are tested against semantic evidence. The results of the semantic analysis are then interpreted in order to elicit their pragmatic implications on the subjects involved in conflict. The goal of the analysis, thus, is reconstructing the meaning of conflict and its implications for human relationships. Identifying the social relations that are endangered by conflict is in fact the first step towards its resolution.

The term *conflict* is a noun belonging to the category of abstract names that do not represent *entities* of the (possible or real) world, but are rather *names of predicates* or *modes of being*. They can be defined as *depredicative* names (Rigotti & Cigada 2004: 209). Abstract names, thus, may indicate states of affairs, events, actions, as well as properties, etc. When semantically analysing an abstract name, it is useful to recall its corresponding predicate(s). In this analysis, beyond the noun *conflict*, the verb *to conflict*, the verbal phrases "to be in conflict", "to enter (into) conflict", and "to bring someone into conflict", and the adjectives *conflictual* and *conflictory* have been analysed.

It might be the case, as it is for *conflict* and its related terms, that a single word covers different predicates, which are distinguished in the analysis by considering the relevant features of (a) the number of arguments, (b) the quality of arguments (or essential traits of the presuppositions imposed by the predicate onto its specific argument places) and (c) the order of arguments (ibid., pp. 95–106). When two uses of the same word differ under one or more of these respects, then different predicates have to be distinguished. In the case of the terms related to *conflict*, two fundamental meanings have been identified through the semantic analysis, which will be illustrated in Sections 4.2.1.1 and 4.2.1.2 respectively.

Before facing the specific traits of these two meanings, it might be useful to have a first look at this family of concepts through its etymology. "To conflict with" derives from the Latin verb *confligo* (*cum* et *fligo*), which can be rendered as "to bump into", or "to collide".

4.2.1.1 *Conflict as hostility between individuals (conflict 1)*

The first meaning identified in the semantic analysis closely recalls the etymological value of the considered forms, having to do with a struggle between two or more human subjects (persons or groups of persons), which is characterized by hostility and by the reciprocal endeavour of "eliminating" one's adversary. Emerging from the BNC corpus, a series of linguistic forms are frequently associated with this meaning. First, "to be in conflict (with)" (analysed in the forms: *to be in conflict, is in conflict, are in conflict, was in conflict, were in conflict*), which has a durative value, often manifests this first meaning, although this verbal phrase can also indicate the second meaning (see Section 4.2.1.2). The ingressive forms "to enter conflict" and "to enter into conflict" exclusively refer to this first meaning; the same is true for the expression "to bring someone into conflict with" (to cause someone to enter into conflict), in which the ingressive is submitted to a causative. The verb "to conflict", instead, is almost exclusively associated with the second meaning, which will be explored in the next section. The very rare occurrences of the verb "to conflict" related to the first meaning can be found in the form "conflicting" (see Example IV in this section), which is quite close to the durative value of "to be in conflict". The adjective *conflictual* has brought to light some occurrences of this first value. The noun *conflict*, which makes the event of conflict become a topic, is largely present with this meaning in the corpus, but it can also refer to the second meaning (see Section 4.2.1.2).

Some examples in which this first meaning emerges are the following:

I. *He* ***was*** *constantly* ***in conflict with*** *the religious and legal authorities of his day.*
II. *As far as we are concerned, if nurses* ***are in conflict with*** *their employer – and they are the least-able section of our society to fight – it is incumbent upon workers to take a stand to support nurses and other workers.*
III. *But of all Koresh's dubious activities it was gun dealing that would* ***bring him into conflict with*** *authority.*
IV. *Clulow and Vincent (1987) describe the role of the Divorce Court Welfare Service as "no-man's land between the interests of parents and children, between the* ***conflicting*** *parents themselves, and ultimately between the interests of the State and the individual; the meshing of private complaint and public response".*
V. *Before the Gulf* ***conflict****, about two million Arabs and 250,000 non-Arabs visited Jordan each year.*
VI. *While the party contains many who actively seek peace and reconciliation, it would be wrong to think of them in any sense as overcoming the basic* ***conflictual*** *components of bloc power in Ireland.*
VII. *Hitler had no wish to provoke an armed* ***conflict*** *that he was not certain of winning.*

All these forms can be considered together as reflecting a predicate C1 whose semantic analysis can be formulated as follows:

C1 (x_1, x_2, x_3): Presuppositions: x_1 and x_2 exist; x_1 and x_2 are human (single or collective) subjects; there exists some form of relationship between x_1 and x_2 which is in some degree a co-operative relationship; x_3 is an issue (understood as an object of interest) in which some form of difference between x_1 and x_2 emerges| Implications: x_1 and x_2's relationship is 'shaken'; a new state of affairs is established, in which the relationship between x_1 and x_2 becomes questionable because of the divergence on x_3; each agent (x_1 and x_2) tries to prevent the adversary party from obtaining the desired good; success in this operation is perceived as a condition to obtain his or her own good.

From the examples reported above, it clearly emerges that x_1 and x_2 can be either individuals or (more or less institutionalized) groups (nurses, like in Example II, or nations, as implicitly indicated in Example VII). The hostility between x_1 and x_2 – the "parties" in conflict – may involve different degrees of violence, including physical violence; the expression "armed conflict" in Example VII indicates an extreme form of physical contraposition which is typical of wars.

It is noteworthy that the positions of x_1 and x_2 are reciprocal; that means that, in order to have a conflict in the strict sense of the word, both parties need to recognize it. Of course, in the initial phases of a conflict, there may be a situation in which one party feels hurt and the other party does not perceive that; nonetheless, in the full conflictual phase, both parties are reciprocally hostile. To have a proper *conflict* both parties need to acknowledge their adversary.

As specified in the analysis, the proper meaning of C1 implies that a pre-existing co-operative human relationship of any sort – at least that co-operative relationship which is commonly expected from members of humanity – becomes questionable, or enters a state of crisis. One could wonder, however, if conflict is always a negative state of affairs, or if, rather, there are some cases in which the relationship that becomes questionable was negative, and, consequently, conflict turns out to be a positive event. Indeed, a human relationship can be considered negative in two (very generally defined) cases. First, if there is a substantial lack of trust (*fides*) between the involved subjects; for instance, in the case where one party betrays the other, or breaks a contract. Second, a relationship may be negative if it does not correspond to the real needs of the involved parties, i.e. it is inappropriate, or incongruous. In these cases, questioning the existing relationship may be positive. C1, however, always implies at least a negative projection of the future, since it develops under the risk of escalating into a violent conflict, thus assuming the form of physical collision.

Particular attention is to be devoted to the identification of the third argument (x_3). In fact, this argument is so frequently left implicit in the corpus that its elicitation in the semantic analysis may even seem strained. Indeed, the presence of x_3 can be indicated in a number of different ways.

First, it is sometimes explicitly specified, as in the following example, where the issue is articulately expressed: "*In March 1985, he came into conflict with the Lord Chancellor over an article he had written for* The Daily Telegraph *on Government pressure on the judiciary to shorten sentences and on the inadequacies of the prison system*". When the main issue of the conflict is expressed, the construction "conflict over" is very frequent. Another less frequent construction found in the BNC corpus to indicate x_3 is "conflict about": "*This concern has been manifest in the debate over intergenerational conflict about access to resources*".

In other cases, the main issue of the conflict (x_3) can be indirectly indicated in expressions like the "Northern Ireland conflict", or "Gulf conflict" (Example V); in these cases, the indication of the main "protagonists" of conflict (x_1 and x_2) are also indirectly indicated.[11] Here, the main issues and even the conflicting parties of the respective conflicts are assumed to be well known; thus, the identification of the geographical area is sufficient for metonymically recalling them, and expressions like "Gulf conflict" work as proper nouns.

Finally, the third argument can be left implicit if the characterization of x_1 and x_2 is specified in such a way that it allows the identification of x_3. If we consider, for instance, Example I, the characterization of the second argument ("the religious and legal authorities of his day") turns out to be a clear indication of the kind of issues involved in the conflict, which will very likely be related to religious and legal aspects. Even more clearly, a sentence such as *"He had a long-running conflict with the rabbis"*, also found in the BNC corpus, implies the presence of a conflict of a religious nature. If a person was a rabbi's neighbour, for instance, and he was in conflict with the rabbi over his garden hedge, we would expect a different characterization of x_2, such as, *"He had a long-running conflict with his neighbour"*, which would sound more fitting in terms of the categories used for describing x_2.

The presence of x_3, however, can be more or less emphasized and specified from case to case. The implications of this fact will be discussed further when tackling the results of the semantic analysis (see Section 4.2.2).

4.2.1.2 *Conflict as a propositional incompatibility (conflict 2)*

The broader meaning of *conflict* as an incompatibility of positions or goals, which is identified in some of the theoretical accounts examined above, also finds correspondence in the BNC corpus. This meaning presents a slight metaphorical connotation, as one is tempted to imagine "conflicting opinions" or "conflicting interests" as two opposite armies fighting each other. Concerning its linguistic manifestation, the verb "to conflict", which has been analysed in the forms *to conflict*, *conflict*, *conflicts*, *conflicted*, and *conflicting*, is always associated with this meaning. This is used with an atemporal value, analogous to that of "to equal" in mathematical calculations like "2 + 3 *equals* 5". Occurrences of

11. Notice, however, that though the syntactic structure of expressions like "the Northern Ireland conflict", "armed conflict", or "intercultural conflict" seems equivalent, the specification preceding the name *conflict* may assume extremely different values from the semantic point of view.

"to conflict" referring to the first meaning, noted above, can only be found in the form "conflicting", which can be interpreted, in these cases, as "being in conflict". The verbal phrase "to be in conflict (with)" (analysed in the forms indicated above) can also be related to this second meaning; in these cases, the same atemporal value identified for "to conflict" prevails. The noun *conflict* is present with this second value, as it clearly emerges from expressions such as "conflict of opinion", "conflict of evidence" or "conflict of interest". However, the prevailing function of the noun is to indicate the event of an interpersonal conflict (C1). The adjectives *conflictual* and *conflictory* are also used with this meaning.[12]

Some of the examples in which this second meaning (C2) has been identified are the following:

I. *If a State concludes a treaty that* ***conflicts with*** *its obligations under an earlier treaty, other parties to the former treaty (although third parties to the subsequent one) can regard that State as remaining bound by its commitments to them.*

II. *His point of view* ***conflicted with*** *the spirit of the age and, despite his example, the glorious art of true fresco died out, its practice being incompatible with the new social attitude to time.*

III. *Liz Sayce, MIND's policy director, said the study's general optimism* ***conflicted with*** *earlier reports.*

IV. *Egypt protested at FIFA's original date of 28 March as it* ***conflicted with*** *a religious festival.*

V. *To the extent that maximizing profits* ***conflicts with*** *the public interest, the solution from this perspective is not to modify corporate objectives, but to strengthen the limiting conditions within which companies are required to operate.*

VI. *Yet the government as promoter at times* ***conflicted with*** *the government as regulator, particularly in the area of competition policy.*

VII. *In this poem, as in 85, the Poet claims that his Muse is 'tongue-tied'; in 76, 102, 103 and 105 he gives* ***conflicting*** *reasons, all ingenious, why he writes such repetitive or uninspired poetry.*

12. For reasons of completeness, it should be added that the adjective *conflictual* covers two further predicates, namely C3 and C4. In both these cases, *conflictual* identifies a one-place predicate. C3 identifies human actions or activities that typically become sources of conflict, as in the example *He stresses the way in which the acquisition of a gendered subjectivity is necessarily* ***conflictual*** *and involves struggle,* where x_1 is a human action or activity that generates conflicts (in the sense of C1); in C4 (a value confirmed also by the only occurrence of *conflictive* found in the corpus), x_1 is some social reality that is often affected by conflicts, as in the example *If post cold-war Europe is not to be violent and* ***conflictual*** *then the sources of rivalry and mistrust need to be addressed head-on.*

VIII. *All of these decisions involve dilemmas in which equally important values* ***are in conflict*** *and however one resolves the dilemma, potential problems will arise.*

IX. *The apparent* ***conflict*** *of evidence is still not completely resolved, but there is a possible explanation.*

X. *New York publishers echo accusations of a* ***conflict*** *of interest in the choice of Knopf without prior competitive bidding.*

XI. *There is an inherent* ***conflict*** *between the demands of local autonomy and the principle of 'territorial justice', requiring that citizens in different geographical areas secure comparable treatment.*

XII. *For example, a union representative may feel a* ***conflict*** *between his need to fulfil a spokesman's role for his constituents, and his need to act responsibly as an employee of the company.*

XIII. *In this epoch the military elite was subordinate to the political elite, and the economic elite was divided, pursuing* ***conflictual*** *economic goals due to the massive expansion of the frontier.*

XIV. *Are Marx and Aristotle* ***conflictory*** *or reconcilable?* (This example was found on Google.)

In relation to the number of arguments involved, the predicate C2, which these examples make reference to, only foresees two arguments (x_1 and x_2). Its semantic analysis can be formulated as follows:

> C2 (x_1, x_2): Presuppositions: x_1 and x_2 are two possible states of affairs (propositions); | Implications: x_1 and x_2 are incompatible, i.e. mutually exclusive.

In order to clarify the nature of the states of affairs that might conflict in the sense identified here, it might be useful to recall the real arguments covering the argument places x_1 and x_2. The set of arguments found covers the following: points of view (*Example II*); theories, statements, reasons, arguments (*Examples III, VII, IX and XIV*); obligations (*Example I*), rules, duties, roles (*Examples VI and XII*), codes, laws, principles; goals (*Examples V and XIII*), interests (*Examples X and XI*), needs, values (*Examples IV and VIII*).

This meaning of *conflict* brings to light the mutual exclusiveness of x_1 and x_2, which implies the need for a solution which can be of different types. If we are in front of "conflicting evidence", we might need to investigate further in order to discover which pieces of data correspond to reality; if we face an incompatibility of goals or values, a pragmatic decision is needed, which should be made in accordance with a reasonable hierarchy of goals: in Example XI, for instance, if the demands of local autonomy are considered more important than the principle of "territorial justice", the principle could be suspended in this particular circumstance.

4.2.2 The degeneration of disagreement into a fully developed interpersonal conflict

Beyond helping to identify two distinct uses of the term *conflict*, the semantic analysis presented in the preceding sections gives some clues for interpreting the relation between propositional incompatibilities of the type C2 and interpersonal conflicts of the type C1. These latter define the full conflicts that are presupposed by mediation and other conflict resolution practices, although, as will be shown in Chapter 6, one of the tasks that a mediator must perform in order to help parties resolve their conflict (C1) is to identify the original incompatibilities (C2) that might have provoked it and that represent the *issues* originating the conflict.

When analysing C2, an initial characterization of the arguments x_1 and x_2 as "states of affairs" (propositions) has been given. There are, indeed, different levels of incompatibility or alternativity that can be touched on in C2 situations. A first level is constituted by a mere propositional incompatibility. In this case, for instance, if there is a fixed amount of financial resource to be distributed between two persons, A and B, it is unavoidable that the more A gains, the more B loses. Analogously, in a democratic system, if two candidates are running as president, the more votes one gets, the more he or she "steals" votes from the other. On a second level, incompatibility concerns *beliefs*: one cannot believe and not believe the same thing at the same time. Finally, the incompatibility can concern *commitments*: the same person cannot be committed to two contradictory positions at the same time (once he/she has resolved possible interior conflicts and has decided to support a position in public). Of course, the incompatibility of beliefs and commitments cannot be accepted at the level of the single individual, who is expected to be consistent in his or her beliefs or commitments, but there can be incompatibilities of beliefs or positions held by different human subjects. Such incompatibilities turn out to be the true origin of the conflict C1. In fact, when a propositional incompatibility involves the level of beliefs and, even more, when it touches the level of commitment, the degree of *personalization* increases. In other words, the human subjects assume social positions as "parties". At this point, a reaction can be triggered that brings C2 to degenerate into a real interpersonal conflict C1.[13] Such degeneration is based on reasoning that could be formulated

13. Felstiner, Abel and Sarat (1980–81) analyse the antecedents of disputing, starting from substantial distress and injustice and moving to the accusation of someone imagined as responsible for the injustice. In particular, they claim that, although sociological analyses have focused on official and formal institutions of conflict management (courts etc.), "the antecedents of disputing are as problematic and as interesting as the disputes that may ultimately emerge" (ibid., p. 633). Here, they introduce a well-known step-analysis of the generation of

as follows: "If you do not esteem my position (my goal, my desire, etc.) you do not esteem me as a person". This reasoning stems from an argument scheme, or *locus*, namely the *locus from the product to the producer* (Rigotti and Greco Morasso 2006b). The *maxim*, i.e. the inferential principle that the argument is based on, can be formulated as a very general law: "the quality of the product mirrors the quality of the producer". Indeed, we often apply this rule in our reasonings: a good cook, i.e. someone who deserves to be esteemed as a cook, is somebody who "produces" (prepares) good dishes. If a cook's culinary creations were all of bad quality, we would not consider him/her a valuable cook. Similarly, when a person undertakes a commitment, he/she is bound to it as the producer of this "communicative product", and the acknowledgement of his/her position can be interpreted as the acknowledgement of him/herself as a person. Thus, questioning one's view can sometimes threaten one's identity. Certainly, such reasoning is not always legitimized; on the contrary, in many cases it is not. However, it is undoubtedly the case that its application is common, and generalizing it to all cases is a subtle temptation.[14]

It is true that facing a difference of opinion sometimes turns into a positive acquisition of the involved subject and to the establishment of a much more mature identity, whereby dialogue and confrontation with others become a source of personal richness (Grossen & Perret-Clermont 1994: 256). But – at least in some cases – differences of opinion can generate overt hostility, disagreement, and personal opposition – in other words, a real conflict of the type C1. In Dascal's (1998) terms, the different communicative ways of dealing with a difference of opinion are positioned in a dichotomy having *discussion* and *debate* as poles. A discussion can be interpreted as an argumentative exchange in which all parties are committed to the search for truth and, though coming from different positions, are open to considering or even conceding to opposing views. At the opposite pole, we find disputes where the only aim of the participants is to win, irrespective of the truth of their case. In disputes, the adversaries lack respect for each other and, thus, are ready to use manipulative devices in order to win their cause. To this can be added conflicts that can escalate so much that they overcome any communicative category and become non-communicative events. The dichotomy discussion–debate can thus be viewed as a pole of a higher-level dichotomy between communicative and non-communicative ways of dealing with conflicts.

---

the dispute sub-divided into the stages of *naming*, *blaming* and *claiming*. The attention to the process of development of conflict is also present in Nader and Todd (1978: 14ff., quoted in Nothdurft 1997: 10).

14. Such a temptation is particularly poisonous in asymmetrical relations.

In general, the hypothesis can be made that the more a person feels identified with but also "dominated" by his or her positions, the more he or she will be inclined to interpret any criticism on the positions accordingly, as an attack on his or her identity. This does not mean to suggest that individuals should be indifferent to any values they hold, especially when these touch on the most important level of their identity. This would be unrealistic, because human beings normally have non-negotiable positions on certain issues.[15] What emerges from the analysis performed here is that if somebody has a "solid" identity, he/she will not feel personally questioned by objections concerning his or her positions and will more easily engage in a discussion where he/she is requested to justify them without feeling threatened.

The observations made here on the implications of C2 at the subject's identity level lead us to discuss the well-known principle of the conflict resolution practice that proclaims "separate the people from the problem" (Fisher, Ury & Patton 1991: 17). This account acknowledges that the subjective relationship between conflicting parties is crucial in the conflict resolution process: "You are dealing not with abstract representatives of the 'other side', but with human beings. They have emotions, deeply held values, and different backgrounds and viewpoints; and they are unpredictable. So are you" (ibid., pp. 18–19). However, separating the relationship from the substance of the problem is considered as an ideal move for conflict resolution. If this is interpreted as trying to solve the problem by putting aside its relational dimension ("*I am sorry but I have to fire you; but it's nothing personal!*"), it may be an unhappy effort, and a very quixotic one.

The degeneration process going from C2 to C1 is witnessed by the semantics of the predicate C1 itself. In fact, the presence of an original incompatibility C2 that has given rise to conflict can be found in the third argument (x_3) of C1, which represents the main issue of the conflict. The fact that, as said, x_3 can be more or less explicitly focused on depends on how much C1 has escalated. When, in fact, C1 is not managed for a certain amount of time, the parties' reciprocal attempts to hinder the realization of the other's goals may turn into a *global conflict*, whereby they ultimately try to eliminate each other. In such a degree of conflict escalation, the original C2 may be progressively left in the background, or even

15. Atran and Axelrod (2008) argue that, counterintuitively, people's "sacred values" (family, country, religion, honour, justice and so on) should not be set aside, nor should they be the last consideration in conflict resolution discussions. In particular, offering material benefits in exchange for giving up a sacred value actually makes settlement more difficult because people see the offering as a personal offence. The results of their research show that, despite people's unwillingness to negotiate inviolable values, showing *respect* for the other party's values may open the door to dialogue even in conflicts that are claimed to be intractable.

completely forgotten. Thus, in dealing with exacerbated and long-lasting conflicts (be they at the interpersonal level, or at the level of more or less institutionalized groups), identifying the main issue, or even a set of relevant issues, is already an important step towards the resolution of the conflict itself; indeed, this is one of the mediator's tasks in the process of mediation (see Chapter 6). Thus, the hypothesis can be made that the focus on x_3 within C1 and the escalation of the conflict are in inverse proportion: the more the issue of the conflict is specified and delimitated, the less the conflict tends to assume a global dimension, and the easier it is to manage. On the other hand, the less the presence of x_3 is clearly emerging in the linguistic formulation, the more exacerbated the conflict. In these cases, a reasonable intervention for conflict management and resolution may become very difficult.

Going back to C2, it should be noticed that a particular kind of propositional incompatibility is more inclined to turn into C1: the so-called *conflict of interest*. Since interests and goals are bound to an agent's potential intervention on reality, this fact can be better explained by introducing a *theory of action*, since interests and goals are bound to an agent's potential intervention on reality. Following Rigotti (2003), action can be defined as the intervention of a human (rational and willing) subject who, on the basis of his knowledge of the actual world and of possible worlds, activates a causal chain in order to pursue his desire to reach a new corresponding state of affairs (see Figure 4.2).

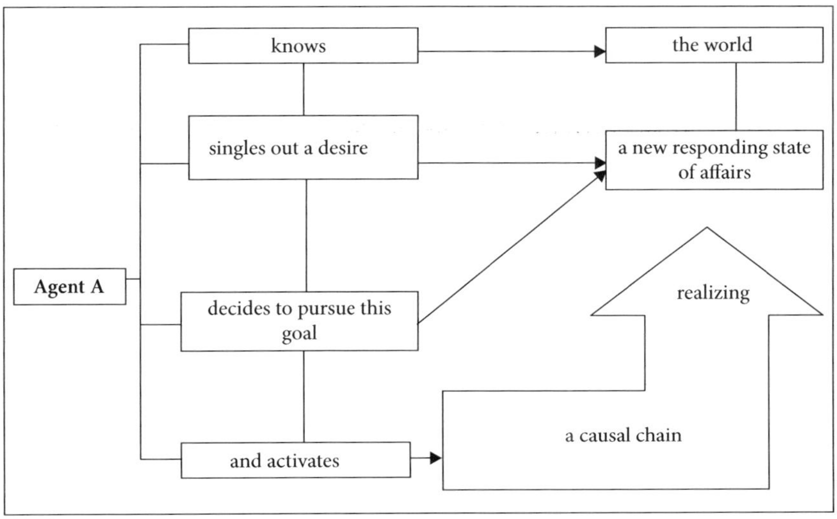

Figure 4.2. Structure of action (Rigotti 2003)

When two agents have a conflict of interest, as far as they decide to pursue their goal, their reciprocal positions tend to become *competitive*. This can happen for two main reasons. The first is that the new responding states of affairs they desire may be contradictory, i.e. they could not become at the same time part of the real world: if it is necessary that agent A's good is the possible world Q, and it is necessary that agent B's good is the possible world $\neg Q$, since Q and $\neg Q$ are contradictory, it is impossible that these two worlds are realized together in the real world. Consider, for example, a political competition where only one of two candidates will become president. Since the desired good (the election as president) is exclusive, the two candidates have contradictory interests, i.e. they imagine and wish the realization of contradictory states of affairs. In such cases, if both agents deliberately pursue their respective interests, an interpersonal competition arises where the fulfilment of A's desire automatically turns into B's ruin; the Latin saying "mors tua vita mea" represents this situation crudely but quite clearly. The second cause of degeneration of conflicts of interest into proper interpersonal conflicts takes place when the interests of the agents are per se not contradictory, but the realization of their respective desires is impossible, because it exploits an exclusive causal chain. For instance, imagine that two citizens' associations would like to propose alternative measures for promoting the cultural development of their town: one would like to improve the library service, whereas the other one wants to open a new museum. Of course, the two interests are not *conflictual*; but the city council only has a limited budget, and therefore only one of the projects will be accepted. A competitive situation is also generated in this case, which may lead to a real interpersonal conflict.[16]

As a final observation, one might wonder whether the conflict of interests that parties perceive always corresponds to a real propositional incompatibility. *Fortunately not* is the answer. In fact, when two persons appear to have incompatible interests, the search for a win-win solution seems to be in vain. However, it is important to verify whether the opposition between A's and B's goals reflects a real opposition between the fulfilment of their desires, or whether it is only a perceived opposition. In the latter case, if the conflict is based on an apparent incompatibility, the resolution will clearly be easier. Dascal (2008) discusses how sometimes the resolution of an incompatibility (or more properly, in his terms, a *dichotomy*) occurs through a de-dichotomizing strategy, i.e. through the acknowledgment that the poles of the dichotomy, if taken in a pragmatic perspective, allow for intermediate alternatives in the actual use that is made of

16. In both these cases we have the so-called *distributive* solution, which is opposed to the *integrative* solution, in which joint gains are possible (see Princen 1992: 35–36).

them within an argumentative debate. It is argued that, often, the dichotomization is an *oversimplification* of the presence of a complex difference of opinion. This observation is particularly precious for conflict studies, because the underlying and maybe complementary concerns of the parties may be incorrectly "represented" by a "clear" contradiction at the superficial level of positions. Thus, we might say that interpersonal hostilities can be hidden behind a so-claimed ontological dichotomy that, on closer inspection, could be reinterpreted and dissolved.[17] Conflict resolution studies have rightly devoted much attention to this topic, as witnessed by the well-known Harvard principle "focus on interests, not positions" (Fisher, Ury & Patton 1991: 3, see also Section 3.1.2). In this relation, it is worth reporting a famous "myth" which is transmitted to new generations of conflict resolution practitioners with the aim of warning them of this possible discrepancy between the parties' image of their advantage and their actual advantage. The story can be told in the following terms: two old sisters have a single orange to share, and both declare that they need the whole fruit. After a long conflict, they agree to a distributive compromise. They each take half the orange, and end up with a very small glass of juice for one sister and a very small cake made with the orange peel for the other. Of course, if the two sisters had focused on their real desires rather than on their positions, they would have noticed that the former were compatible: the one sister could have enjoyed more orange juice, and the other one could have had the whole peel for her cake. Both sisters would have been more satisfied. The principle that conflict resolution practitioners want to convey by this anecdote is clear: one should be aware of possible discrepancies between the parties' positions, which can be contradictory, and their real concerns, which often turn out to be complementary or, in any case, compatible.[18]

17. Here, it is first of all important to distinguish between contrary terms and contradictory terms, of which the one consists in the other one's negation. See in this relation the discussion in Petri Hispani *Summulae logicales* 3.32 (ed. Bochenski 1947: 33). Moreover, even concerning contrary terms, as Gatti (2000: 33) remarks, Aristotle, in his *Categoriae*, observed that such terms are not necessarily the opposite poles of a dichotomy, like odd and even numbers. In some cases, contraries do admit intermediate terms, as in the case of white and black, which admits an infinite set of grey tonalities in between. This was developed in the medieval doctrine of oppositions, which distinguished among contraria *mediata* (which admit some intermediate terms) and *immediata*.

18. Uspenskij proposes the challenging hypothesis that even cultural differences can often express deeper complementarities. A significant example is given in Uspenskij (2005), where it is shown that the differences about benediction with the sign of the Cross that can be found in the different Christian traditions are, in reality, expressions of different perspectives

4.2.3 Towards a new "conflict mapping guide"

When in 1979 Paul Wehr proposed his *conflict mapping guide*, he developed a valuable tool for intervening into social and international conflicts, constructed on the basis of his experience in the field (Wehr 1979: 18). This tool aimed to achieve "a clearer understanding of the origins, nature, dynamics, and possibilities for resolution of the conflict" (ibid., pp. 18–19). The conflict mapping guide approach has, indeed, numerous merits. Above all, the map is a particularly well-suited instrument for identifying a series of factors that emerge as relevant in the process of conflict conceived, in this case, as overt hostility (C1) between persons, social groups, or nations. In particular, Wehr's map is founded on the identification of the conflict *history*, *context*, *parties*, *issues*, *dynamics*, of the *alternative routes to a solution(s) of the problem(s)*, and of the *conflict regulation potential* (ibid., pp. 19–22).[19] Moreover, the mapping guide accounts for the continuous evolution of the conflictual situation, which can be constantly developed and modified by the parties' interaction, and by the intervention of third neutral parties as mediators.

on the same relationship between human beings and God (see in particular pp. 43–49, and pp. 56–57, Footnote 13). This profound complementarity, however, as it generates an actual – one could say "physical" – difference, has led to reciprocal accusations between the different Christian traditions, in particular between the Orthodox and Catholic communities (ibid., see in particular Ch. 5).

19. The main factors identified by Wehr are the following (see Wehr 1979: 18–22): *Conflict history*, concerning the evolution of some events into a conflict; *Conflict context*, which includes, "geographical boundaries; political structures, relations, and jurisdictions; communication networks and patterns; decision making methods" (ibid., p. 19); *Conflict parties*, including third parties interested in a successful resolution of the dispute; *Issues*, which can be numerous, although there is often a prevailing topic; *Dynamics*, which concerns the evolution of the conflict. Wehr underlines the following points in the conflict dynamics: precipitating events, issue emergence, transformation and proliferation, polarization, spiralling, stereotyping and mirror-imaging; *Alternative routes to a solution(s) of the problem(s)*, concerning suggestions about the conflict settlement coming either from the parties, or from uninvolved observers; *Conflict resolution potential*, concerning "resources for limiting and perhaps resolving the conflict" (ibid., p. 22), among which internal limiting factors, external limiting factors (like an external authority capable of imposing a solution), interested or neutral third parties trusted by the conflicting parties, and techniques of conflict management (managed by third parties and/or by the parties themselves). From this latter element, it emerges that the conflict map can include not only actual states of affairs, but also possible worlds. In a process of conflict resolution, the possible alternatives for the settlement are important resources to be considered in the analysis of the conflict.

However, the origin of the conflict does not come to the fore in the model, which is conceived of as an instrument for intervening in conflicts that are already overtly acknowledged by the parties. Furthermore, although the model mentions the possibility of *issue emergence, transformation and proliferation* (ibid., p. 21), the relation between issues management and conflict development is not explained. Again, with regard to the typology of conflict issues (*facts-based, values-based, interests-based* and *non realistic*, p. 20),[20] a more detailed account of the concept of "issue" that may generate a conflict would help prevent possible sources of conflict or effectively intervene in them.

In relation to all these aspects, the semantic analysis performed here can help define the basis for integrating Wehr's conflict mapping guide in a theoretically more justified and comprehensive framework. As shown in the results of the semantic analysis, the identification of two main meanings of the term *conflict* – conflict as interpersonal hostility (C1) and conflict as a propositional incompatibility (C2) – and the analysis of the degeneration of C2 into C1 help to shed more light on the origin of conflict and on its dynamics. This can help in constructing a model of conflict resolution intervention; in particular, as already mentioned, it is important to note that the intervention in a conflict of the type C1 cannot abstract from the consideration of its origin, namely C2.

In Figure 4.3, a sketched ontology of the conflictual situation is represented whereby, following the results of the semantic analysis, the essential factors of conflict and the essential relations between them have been highlighted. This ontology can work as a matrix for elaborating a new integrated conflict mapping guide. Of course, in order to develop a tool for conflict study and conflict resolution interventions, the matrix has to be further developed. However, it already helps identify some aspects that indicate many directions of research on crucial issues for the prevention and management of conflicts.

20. The typology proposed by Wehr would require further justification. According to the author (Wehr 1979: 20), *facts-based* issues concern "disagreement over *what is* because of how parties perceive *what is*". *Values-based* issues are bound to disagreement about what *should* be, as determinant of some form of decision (for example, about a policy decision). *Interests-based* issues concern disagreement bound to a conflict of interest or, more properly, over "who will get what in the distribution of scarce resources", such as power or economic benefits. In this case, the author does not justify why any opposition of interests necessarily has to do with the distribution of scarce resources (as seen previously, other cases are possible). Finally, *non-realistic* issues is a mixed category including any other aspect not falling into the first three categories, such as the parties' style of interaction or quality of communication. Concerning this last category, it is not clear why such kinds of problems are considered unrealistic.

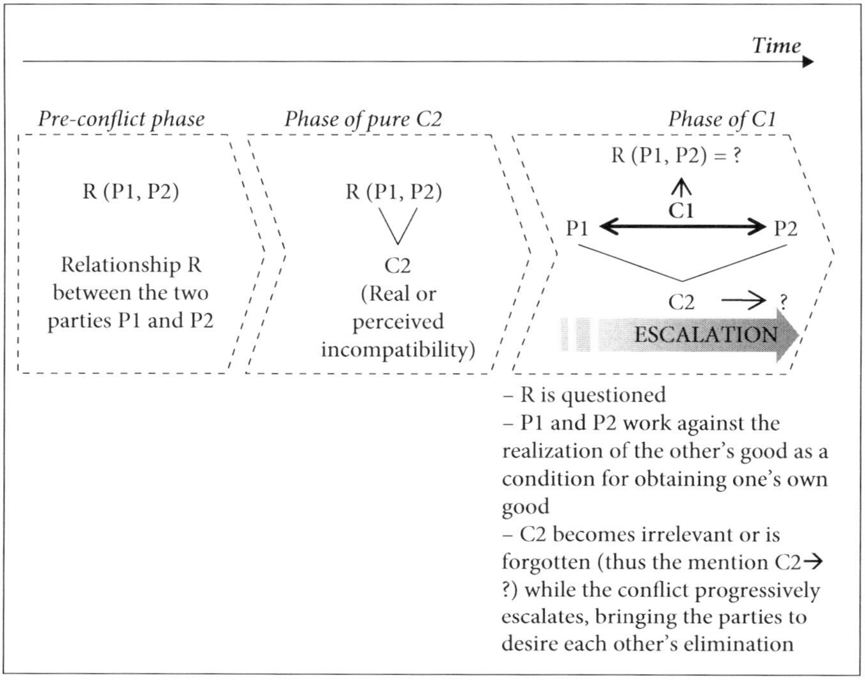

Figure 4.3. Matrix for developing a new conflict mapping guide

The temporal development of the conflict origin and escalation, which is indicated in Figure 4.3, should not be understood as an unstoppable degenerative mechanism. Indeed, many crucial aspects can be considered for the study of conflict and for planning effective conflict resolution interventions that block this development.

1. In relation to the pre-conflict phase, the first question to be answered is whether R is really a positive relation for P1 and P2 or not.
2. In relation to the phase of pure C2, it is important to verify whether C2 is a real incompatibility or if it is only perceived as such by the parties. As mentioned above, sometimes the degeneration into conflict C1 is avoided once parties perceive that their apparent contraposition manifests deeper complementarities.
3. When the proper interpersonal conflict has arisen (phase of C1), it is important to understand how the conflict could be managed without letting it further degenerate. Conflict resolution interventions, such as mediation, constitute precious instruments in this relation, as they are conceived as tools

to intervene in proper C1 conflicts. Some authors (see Glasl 2004),[21] relying on their professional experience, suggest how to use the various conflict resolution practices in relation to the different phases of escalation of C1.

4. A crucial point is the passage from C2 to C1, which opens the way to some reflection on conflict prevention. Here, the hypothesis can be suggested that the sound management of C2 situations largely depends on how much space for sound discussion and argumentation is foreseen by the context.[22] In other words, if a certain institution, or a certain interpersonal relationship (like a friendship relationship) does not envisage any space for confrontation and discussion – including not only the possibility of advancing positions and/or arguments, but also the space for expressing one's emotions and personal commitments[23] to those positions and arguments – in its written or unwritten rules, the presence of a difference of opinion or of another contraposition of the kind C2 will more likely turn into a full conflict of the kind C1; parties, in

21. Glasl (2004: 197ff.) analyses the different models of conflict escalation that have been proposed in literature and puts forward, also on the basis of his professional experience as a counsellor and mediator, a "step-model" of escalation.

22. Grossen and Perret-Clermont have approached this topic, in particular concerning its psychology, in their work *L'espace thérapeutique* (1992), in which they focus on the context of the therapeutic relationship. In particular, the contribution by Grossen focuses on the moment of first interview in psychological consultations and interprets it as the institutional moment in which the patient is legitimated to pose his/her problem, namely to ask his/her *question* to the psychotherapist. The definition and co-construction of *question*, in Grossen's analysis (Grossen 1992: 165–166), becomes the central kernel of the therapeutic consultation. In relation to the present analysis of conflict, it can be hypothesized that the moment in which the patient's problem can legitimately become a question and, thus, a communicative object that can be tackled by communicative means, is particularly important in relation to a reasonable management of the problem itself. In relation to this, on the basis of the literature on doctor–patient or patient–psychologist interactions, Grossen concludes that "La manière dont psychothérapeute et patient définissent l'objet de la demande dépend à la fois du contexte social et institutionnel dans lequel la demande est présentée, et de la dynamique propre aux interactions" (ibid., p. 169). So the space that is left for tackling certain issues, in a certain institutional context and in the interpersonal rapports realized in it, influences the development of the interaction.

23. Dumont, Perret-Clermont and Moss (1995) analyse the positive effects that a framework of friendly relationships can have on the cognitive progress made by children in co-constructing moral reasoning.

fact, having no space for expounding their reasons, will feel more threatened in their personal identity[24] and dignity.

4.3 Proposal for a comprehensive ontology

In light of the discussion of the mediation models analysed in Chapter 3, and considering the particularly important conceptual knots of context and conflict, it is now possible to sketch a blueprint for a comprehensive ontological framework of mediation, which ideally includes all relevant factors and relations constituting this practice. Of course, the final word on such a framework needs to be spoken after more empirical verification and consequent theoretical adjustments (see Chapters 6 and 7 in this relation). The endeavour of starting to construct it, however, should not be abandoned, because arriving at a framework of mediation is necessary in order to understand the argumentative dynamics in this practice and, more generally, to analyse specific constituent aspects of this practice in the context of their relations. In the following, the framework will be expounded in its main aspects, mentioning the contributions offered by the different traditions of mediation studies.

Of course, as in any graphical representation, Figure 4.4 depicts an oversimplification. It is impossible to visually express all the aspects and insights considered in Chapters 3 and 4 in a single picture. For this reason, I shall briefly discuss the framework, partly relying on the discussion presented above. In any case, the usefulness of a graphical representation is to provide an overview of the process of mediation; the argumentative dynamics will be mapped against this background.

24. In relation to this, it is interesting to quote the analysis presented in Arcidiacono (2007) and in Pontecorvo and Arcidiacono (2007), concerning the management of conflictual situations arising from differences of opinion in families. The analysis is based on empirical data deriving from video recordings of discussions during dinner of Italian families with at least two children, one of whom is a teenager. By looking at the excerpts of the conversations, it is clear that the teenagers frequently engage in argumentation with their parents – often "challenging" them with provoking standpoints (see Arcidiacono 2007: 97 and 103–104; Arcidiacono, Pontecorvo and Greco Morasso 2009). It seems that sometimes the implicit request for the reason for certain rules which is hidden in their challenges is not taken up by the parents, who seem somehow reluctant to accept their children's argumentative challenge. However, it may be that the excerpts presented only represent the most conflictual episodes found in the corpus of conversations analysed; one could hypothesize that, in those families in which argumentation is more fostered, the intergenerational confrontation is also more productive.

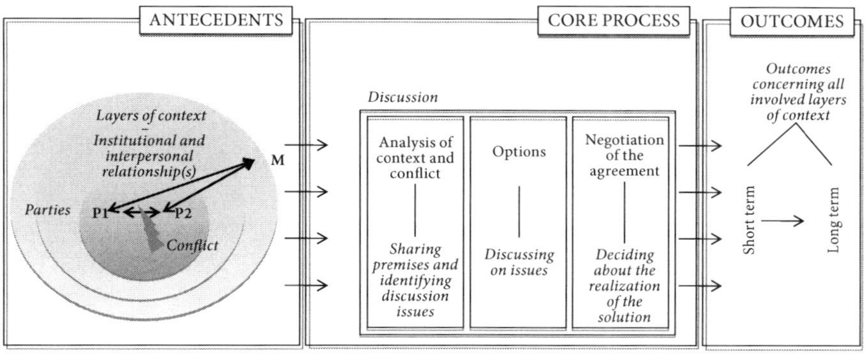

Figure 4.4. A mediation framework

The three categories of *antecedents*, *core process* and *outcomes* proposed by Herrman, Hollett and Gale (2006), including all subcategories, deserve to be maintained as broader areas indicating both the essential mediation constituents. In the antecedents, the context is considered in its stricter and wider dimensions. The core circle represents the parties' institutionalized and interpersonal relationships, while surrounding circles intend to represent other significant stakeholders and relationships, among which are the *constituents* (Wall 1981: 159). Within the parties' context, a conflict arises; focusing on the dynamics of conflict, we can go back to the conflict mapping guide (see Figure 4.3) to identify its relevant factors and understand its dynamics. The conflict mapping guide can be read in two directions, which are equally important for mediation. First, it shows how a difference of opinion may degenerate into an interpersonal conflict. Second, assuming that mediation starts from an interpersonal conflict, it shows that it is necessary to find a way to go back to the origin of a difference of opinion in order for a reasonable argumentative discussion to be started in mediation.[25]

The parties' decision to enter mediation transforms them into co-arguers and brings the mediator into the context. Such a choice, as already noted, intrinsically modifies the context itself, by adding important elements to the antecedents.

25. In a discussion during his intervention within the doctoral programme Argupolis (February 2010), Marcelo Dascal made me think that perhaps this is not always possible. There are conflicts, indeed, which seemingly are not over anything, but are pure conflicts without a contended (abstract or physical) object. I tend to think that even in cases of pure conflict, there must be some initial object of struggle, which is later forgotten, while the conflict degenerates into a form of global hostility. But I cannot exclude the possibility that human beings sometimes fight for the sake of fighting. In this latter case, clearly mediation would be inappropriate.

The influence of antecedents on the core process is not only bound to the parties' interests and personal characteristics (Patton 2005; Herrman, Hollett & Gale 2006), but also to the mediator's personal interests (see in particular Touval & Zartman 1985a and 1985b).

After this, the core communication process of mediation starts. Following Kovach (2005), I have identified the different stages that constitute this interaction. For the purpose of a communicative analysis, I propose to regroup such stages into three main phases whose communicative functions are distinct. The first phase represents the analysis of the antecedents (context and conflict) guided by the mediator. In fact, normally the antecedents are not known to the mediator at the beginning of his/her encounter with the parties. In relation to the mediation stage model presented by Kovach (2005: 36), the first six stages (*preliminary arrangements, mediator's introduction, opening remarks/statements by parties, venting, information gathering, issue and interests identification*) can be regrouped in this phase. In particular, this is the moment in which the mediator searches for the parties' common ground (Carnevale 1986), their interests and the Best Alternative to a Negotiated Agreement or BATNA (Patton 2005; Fisher, Ury & Patton 1991; Carnevale 1986). The analysis of the conflict and of the relationships it affects can be seen as a process by which the mediator and the parties walk the inverse path of the *conflict mapping guide* in that, starting from a situation of an escalated conflict, they go back to its origin and implications, as shown in Figure 4.5.

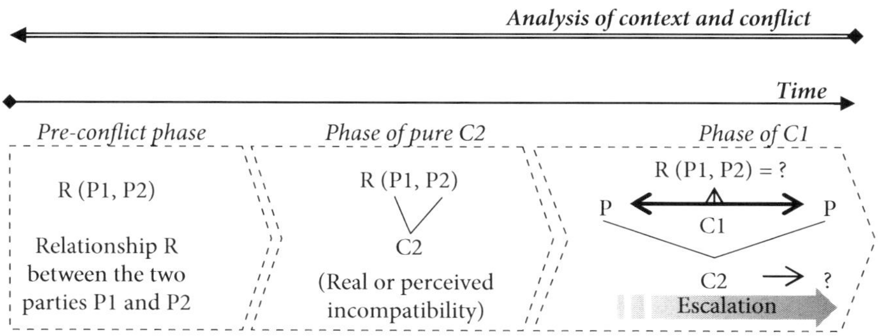

Figure 4.5. The mediator's analysis of context and conflict in relation to the conflict mapping guide proposed in Figure 4.3

The importance of this phase should not be underestimated. Indeed, proposals such as that of Wehr's conflict mapping guide originated from an awareness of the importance of studying the antecedents of mediation. In mediation of interpersonal conflict, normally this phase is accomplished simply in the discussion between the mediator and the parties (Kovach 2005).

The second phase, in which *agenda setting, caucus, option generation* and *reality testing* are included, marks a shift in the process from the establishment of a dialogical setting to the discussion of specific issues that constitute options for conflict resolution (Patton 2005).

The third phase (including *bargaining and negotiation*, *agreement* and *closure*) encompasses the negotiation on the draft of a solution set out by the parties and the final agreement. The signature of the agreement closes the core process of mediation and opens the problem of implementing the assumed decision on the short and long term (Herrman, Hollett & Gale 2006). Such a process, which can sometimes be very sensitive, represents an important starting point leading to the proper *outcome* of the mediation process (Meierding 1993; Pearson d'Estrée et al. 2001; Li 2001; Long 2003; Kelly 2004).

The outcomes involve, according to Wall, Stark and Standifer (2001), effects on the disputants, the mediator and other third parties; for Herrman, Hollett and Gale (2006), such third parties are in particular represented by the institutional context. The distinction into short-term and long-term outcomes introduced by these authors also raises the issue of the durability of the agreement.

Facing this framework, a study focusing on argumentation in mediation could certainly consider different aspects. For example, following the path opened by van Eemeren et al. (1993), Jacobs (2002) and Aakhus 2003, one could study the different mediator's communicative techniques, such as questions and reformulations, and match them onto the various phases of the core process of mediation. In this respect, even a quantitative analysis of the occurrences of certain techniques in the different phases could be an interesting starting point to describe how mediators manage the discussion practically.

Alternatively, the focus could be on the relation between the employment of given argumentative moves and the mediation outcomes. In this case, it would be possible to connect certain argumentative strategies with more or less successful outcomes of mediation.

The present study is concerned with a fundamental question about the structuring of the argumentative discussion in mediation. It can be maintained that argumentation occurs in the core process in which the communicative interaction takes place. It is still in the core process, by means of the communicative interaction, that parties involved in a "happy" mediation process experience the *change in attitude from disputants to co-arguers* that I have described in Chapter 1. To my knowledge, at present there are no analyses of how this change in attitude happens; how argumentation is structured so to help this change; how the mediator contributes to this in the different phases of the process; how the antecedents of mediation are analysed in the core process; how options are generated; and how parties agree to discuss them. The present study aims to answer this type of question.

In order to select mediations in which the disputants' change in attitude is likely to happen, I have selected successful cases of mediation. The results of the argumentative analysis will be presented in Chapter 6. Before this, the research questions and the theoretical instruments concerning argumentation will be presented in Chapter 5.

The presentation of theoretical instruments for the analysis of argumentation (Chapter 5) ideally represents a close focus on the ontology-oriented conceptual framework of mediation built up to now. It will concentrate in particular on the core process, which, as noted above, is communicative in nature. Argumentation processes certainly occur in this phase. However, the literature on mediation and conflict resolution does not consider adequate instruments to analyse a communicative interaction, let alone its argumentative ingredients. For this reason, in the next chapter, I will rely on instruments deriving from argumentative studies. In this respect, the proposed conceptual framework is interdisciplinary in nature. In fact, it is the result of four disciplinary ingredients: (1) selected studies on mediation and conflict resolution, presented in Chapters 2 and 3; (2) theoretical approaches to conflict in various disciplines (Section 3.1.3); a model of context deriving from communication analysis and introduced in order to better explain how mediation can be a context of application of argumentation (Section 4.1); and (4) theoretical instruments to study argumentation in mediation (Chapter 5).

CHAPTER 5

The argumentative perspective

An integrated ontology-oriented framework of mediation

In the preceding chapters, we have been laying the foundation for a conceptual framework of mediation (Chapter 4) based on different approaches to this conflict resolution practice (Chapters 2 and 3). This conceptual framework is the basis required for a research project that, like the present one, is focused on argumentation in the context of dispute mediation. Such a focus still requires that we integate the argumentative perspective into the conceptual framework of mediation. This integration is a further step in the conceptual analysis of this practice, and represents a first result in the perspective of the study of contextualized argumentation. In fact, it is important to analytically define the role that argumentation plays in mediation. In this sense, the present chapter completes the previous one. A first Section (5.1) will discuss a selection of argumentative theories, models and concepts that I adopt in the present work. Their integration into the ontology-oriented conceptual framework of mediation previously outlined will then be discussed (5.2).

Such a conceptual integration will show where argumentation is expected in the context of dispute mediation; it will equally explain in which senses the commitment to a standard of reasonableness undertaken by the participants in a sound argumentative discussion might favour the resolution of a conflict. Yet, we are left with some open questions about how argumentation is actually realized in a successful mediation process. Hence the need for an argumentative empirical analysis of mediation cases, whose structure and design will be discussed in Section 5.3. In the concluding section of this Chapter (5.3.1), as an integration to the design of the argumentative analysis, I shall discuss some relevant methodological issues. The results of the empirical argumentative analysis will be presented in Chapter 6.

5.1 Argumentation theories, models and concepts

The argumentative approach on which this investigation is generally founded is based on the pragma-dialectical account of argumentation, integrated by the research carried out by the Lugano research group involved in the project Argumentum.[1] From the pragma-dialectical account, the theoretical framework developed here inherits the general view of the argumentative phenomenon, its embeddedness in communication, and the crucial role of reasonableness to define the critical attitude typical of argumentation (see Section 5.1.1). Moreover, it draws on the model of a *critical discussion* (Section 5.1.2) as a fundamental grid guiding the analysis of the real argumentative practice, assuming it in its integrated version, which also accounts for the rhetorical or persuasive aims of arguers through the notion of *strategic manoeuvring* (Section 5.1.3).

According to van Eemeren and Houtlosser (2002), parties develop their strategic manoeuvring along all the stages of a critical discussion. Concerning the proper *argumentation stage* in particular, in which the co-arguers bring forward arguments in support of their standpoint or against the counterparty's standpoint, the present research integrates the model of a critical discussion with the Argumentum Model of Topics (AMT), aiming in particular at establishing tools to analyse and evaluate the inferential structure of arguments (Section 5.1.4).

Finally, following up on the pragma-dialectical principle of the embeddedness of argumentation in social life and communicative practices,[2] this research complements the argumentative analysis, which remains however its primary focus, by a semantic-pragmatic account of the communicative interaction that allows consideration of the wider communicative context in which argumentation takes place (see Section 5.1.5).

5.1.1 Preliminary remarks on the nature of argumentation

The present investigation concerns argumentation in the context of mediation. In the preceding chapters, it has been necessary to reconstruct an ontology-oriented framework of mediation, largely based on studies in conflict resolution. This framework represents the context of the argumentative discussion in

1. Argumentum (www.argumentum.ch) is an online courseware on argumentation, whose realization (2004–2008) was funded by the Swiss Virtual Campus (Greco Morasso 2009b). The project developed thanks to the collaboration of three partner institutions: the Institute of Linguistics and Semiotics at the University of Lugano, the Institute of Psychology at the University of Neuchâtel, and the Department of Sociology at the University of Geneva. The didactical aim of this project has been paired by a common research effort aimed at finding a theory of argumentation embedded in the communication sciences.

2. Van Eemeren and Grootendorst (2004: 55) remark that argumentation is always a contribution to a *communication* process and that "argumentative discourse and texts are conceived as basically social activities".

mediation. However, the argumentative discussion developing in mediation is a part of this conceptual framework, because the argumentative discussion is embedded in this context. Therefore, in what follows, some conceptual tools deriving from the tradition of argumentative studies will be integrated with the goal of ideally completing the ontology-oriented conceptual framework presented in Chapter 4. Although some annotations about argumentation have already emerged throughout the preceding chapters, the nature of argumentation will now be defined more thoroughly.

In very general terms, argumentation is a constitutive part of human communicative exchange. As such, argumentation is present in a number of communicative practices, discourse genres and social contexts (see van Eemeren 2008; Rigotti & Greco Morasso 2009b). In argumentation, an arguer personally engages in proposing a standpoint – a position he/she is convinced of – to his/her interlocutor. The latter can accept or reject the proposed standpoint, which can be a theoretical statement but also a proposal of practical action. What is distinctive of a sound argumentative practice is the fact that the acceptance of such proposals is based on the critical testing of their validity; in other words, the arguers commit themselves to prove their respective positions, analyse the reasons that support them, and decide on the most reasonable one.

This kind of critical commitment is essential for the decision-making process taking place in the parties' discussion in mediation. In fact, as stated in the opening sections of this research, mediation has already been the subject of argumentative study. As a matter of fact, the meaning of reasonable confrontation and critical testing of arguments in support of given positions is very much compatible with the aim of mediation practice. Significantly, Herrman, Hollett and Gale (2006: 22) assume as one of the essential presuppositions of their *comprehensive mediation model* that "Verbalising individual positions and stories provides the speaker and listener with an opportunity to develop a greater understanding of underlying needs and *to stimulate higher-level reasoning*" (emphasis added). This observation highlights the issue of the *quality* of the parties' decision, which in sound mediation practices should be supported by a healthy reasoning in order to be durable and to really meet the parties' interests.

The concept of *critical testing* and of *reasonableness* were identified as central to argumentation (van Eemeren & Grootendorst 1994, 2004). The dimension of criticality (defined as adherence to evidence and correct reasoning) involves in argumentation a complex interplay of relevant aspects. The reasonableness demand, in particular, should not be opposed to the notion of rationality, conceived of as logical consistency and coherence, namely as non-contradictoriness of reasoning, which guarantees the truth of conclusions derived from true premises. However, rationality is not sufficient to found all the possible cognitive and pragmatic decisions a human being is obliged to face (van Eemeren & Grootendorst 1994: 12). This turns out to be even clearer in the domain of conflict resolution, in which pure rationality is certainly insufficient for taking into account the complexity of the dimensions involved in conflict.[3] In conflict resolution, as in the other domains of human social life, a more complex attitude of reason is required, which must take into account the complexity of factors determining a situation. This kind of *esprit de finesse* is as difficult to define as essential for argumentative practices. Some of its essential traits have been discussed in Rigotti and Greco (2005) and Rigotti and Greco Morasso (2009a), and then confirmed by the results of a semantic analysis of the term *reasonable* (Rigotti, Rocci & Greco 2006; see also Greco 2005a).

Most decisively, what defines a reasonable attitude is the commitment to finding a resolution of the difference of opinion that is worthy of the *human quality* of the interlocutors. First, when trying to make a reasonable decision or verify the truth of a certain opinion, "two heads work better than one". In fact, the interlocutors can help each other take into account an important aspect that one of them might have neglected, or discover a manipulation, or keep a reasonable level of abstraction in defining a situation, etc. Second, each interlocutor in an argumentative exchange is committed to assuming a reasonable attitude. The argumentative interaction, thus, aims at promoting reasonableness by definition. Third, a direct implication of this is that the arguer does not want to obtain his/her interlocutor's assent at any cost; in fact, consent is not built through violence, but rather through using language and reason for discussing and evaluating possible arguments. In conclusion, reasonableness, as it is reached through an argumentative interaction, involves respect for the other's reason. Indeed, the practice of mediation is founded on the belief that even in cases in which dialogue is blocked, the intervention of a third person, armed with purely communicative and argumentative means, can serve the purpose of reasonably solving a conflict. This turns out to be consistent with the principle of optimism professed by Aristotle in the first book of his *Rhetoric* (see the translation by Rhys Roberts 1924): "Rhetoric is useful because things that are true and things that are just have a natural tendency to prevail over their opposites". Indeed, if human beings were not attracted by positives more than by negatives, a role like that of a mediator would make no sense.

3. According to Dascal and Marras (forthcoming), Leibniz, who devoted a lot of attention to this matter, introduced the hypothesis of a "judge of controversies" able to *weight* arguments rather than *compute* them. The judge of controversies seems to recall a more *reasonable* than only *rational* attitude.

Within the pragma-dialectical perspective (van Eemeren & Grootendorst 1984, 1994, 2004), the concept of reasonableness is closely linked to the discussion between two arguers: where the standpoint of one is subject to the critical control of the other, it is possible to solve a difference of opinion in a reasonable fashion, and to establish a reasonable foundation for one's own actions and beliefs.[4] Within this framework, ten constitutive rules for maintaining the requested standard of reasonableness within the discussion have been pointed out (van Eemeren & Grootendorst 1984, 1992). The rules owe their validity to the fact that they make the implications of a truly argumentative attitude explicit. In this sense, their nature is not normative or regulative, but it is rather *constitutive*, as it defines the traits of a truly argumentative commitment. In other words, the rules make explicit the speech acts that are functional to the goal of a critical discussion, namely the resolution of a difference of opinion. They thus constitute the ideal tracks of a reasonable discussion.

5.1.2 The model of a critical discussion as a grid for the analysis

The pragma-dialectical approach to argumentation, initiated by van Eemeren and Grootendorst in the 1980s at the University of Amsterdam, proposes a model of critical discussion as an ideal definition of an argumentative discussion developing according to the standard of reasonableness. This model is assumed, in the present research, as a general framework for the analysis of argumentative strategies in mediation. The model is intended as a grid for the analysis, having both a heuristic and a critical function (see Section 5.3.1.1). In fact, the model helps in identifying argumentative moves as well as in evaluating their contribution to the resolution of the difference of opinion. Because this model elicits the constitutive phases of a sound argumentative discussion, it can be integrated into the conceptual framework of mediation presented in Chapter 4, which presents the constitutive elements of the scenario and script of a mediation process. The integration of the model of a critical discussion into the framework outlined before permits us to ask relevant questions about how argumentation contributes to the fulfilment of the pragmatic goals of mediation: how are the phases of a critical discussion actually realized in a successful mediation process? At which point do parties become co-arguers and why is this possible? These questions are at the basis of the empirical part of my work, which will be developed in the next chapter.

4. Within the pragma-dialectical approach, reasonableness is one of the philosophical bases of argumentative analysis. In this relation, see van Eemeren and Grootendorst (1994, 2004: 18–22) and the discussion in Rigotti and Greco (2005) and Rigotti, Rocci and Greco (2006).

The model of critical discussion proposes four ideal stages, which do not mirror the actual temporal proceeding of the argumentative discussion, but are the essential constituents of the reasonable – i.e. *critical* – discussion. In the *confrontation stage* of a critical discussion, the difference of opinion emerges: "it becomes clear that there is a standpoint that is not accepted because it runs up against doubt or contradiction" (van Eemeren & Grootendorst 2004: 60). In other words, the protagonist puts forward a standpoint, and the antagonist reacts to it either by casting doubt on it (giving rise, thus, to a *non-mixed* dispute), or by presenting an alternative standpoint (which originates a *mixed* dispute). In the *opening stage*, the protagonist and the antagonist "try to find out how much relevant common ground they share (as to the discussion format, background knowledge, values, and so on) in order to be able to determine whether their procedural and substantive 'zone of agreement' is sufficiently broad to conduct a fruitful discussion" (ibid.). This stage is particularly relevant, because the whole activity of argumentation is based on the confident possibility of finding a reasonable solution through discussion with the counterpart. This attitude of confidence also involves the disposition to find common premises on which both parties agree, and on which they can evaluate their difference of opinion. In the *argumentation stage* of a critical discussion,[5] arguments in support of the standpoint(s) are advanced and critically tested (ibid., pp. 60–61). Finally, the critical discussion is concluded, with the *concluding stage*, "in agreement that the protagonist's standpoint is acceptable and the antagonist's doubt must be retracted, or that the standpoint of the protagonist must be retracted" (ibid.).

In the argumentative reality, the model of a critical discussion can be implemented according to different discussion types. The nature of the difference of opinion arising, in fact, determines different types of confrontation between the parties. This turns out to be particularly important in the case of mediation, which, as already noted, is an interaction scheme intervening in response to a difference of opinion that has already degenerated into a conflict. It is thus particularly important to specify the instruments allowing the various types of disputes to be distinguished (namely, the various discussions arising from different types of difference of opinion) which might be involved in such a conflictual situation.[6] In pragma-dialectical terms, when the protagonist of a critical discussion

5. The other three stages are not, of course, irrelevant for argumentation; not only do they represent as many essential moments of a critical discussion, but also they frequently require argumentative moves for the fulfilment of their own tasks.

6. Here, I refer to a recent version of the pragma-dialectical view of the dialectical confrontation profiles presented in van Eemeren, Houtlosser and Snoeck-Henkemans (2007).

puts forward a standpoint, and the antagonist only expresses some doubts about it, a *single non-mixed* dispute has been externalized. Alternatively, if the antagonist not only casts doubt on the protagonist's standpoint, but he/she also puts forwards a personal opposing standpoint, the dispute becomes *mixed* (van Eemeren, Houtlosser & Snoeck-Henkemans 2007: 21–22). The alternative mixed/non-mixed, thus, refers to the type of parties' involvement in the discussion; one could say that in mixed disputes both the antagonist and the protagonist have the burden of proof of their respective standpoints. What happens more frequently, and we could add particularly in intricate situations like conflicts, is that the dispute does not only present a standpoint (or two contradictory standpoints) on the same issue (a *single* dispute), but it becomes multiple. A dispute can be *multiple in a quantitative sense* if the standpoints advanced concern more than one issue; such types of dispute (which can be mixed or non-mixed) could thus be split into as many single disputes for the analysis. A dispute can be *multiple in a qualitative sense* if the antagonist presents not only a contradictory standpoint, but also a *contrary* standpoint, whose successful defence would turn into a defence of the former as well (ibid., p. 23). A dispute multiple in a qualitative sense can also arise if the antagonist does not express any contradictory standpoint but only a contrary one. Van Eemeren, Houtlosser and Snoeck-Henkemans give the following example of a dispute multiple in a qualitative sense (ibid., p. 22):

> Per: This state visit to China is no more than sheer opportunism!
> Åse: That's not true at all. I think it is a sincere attempt at ideological reconciliation.

In this example, if Åse succeeds in demonstrating that the state visit to China in question is indeed a sincere attempt at ideological reconciliation, given the logical relation subsisting between contrary and contradictory statements (cf. also Gatti 2000), she will also fulfil the task of demonstrating that this visit is not sheer opportunism. The dispute is thus multiple in a qualitative sense as it reflects the complexity of the standpoints' relations to the issue.

5.1.3 The notion of *strategic manoeuvring* as an instrument to understand the mediator's contribution to argumentation

More recently, van Eemeren and Houtlosser (2002) introduced the notion of *strategic manoeuvring*, moving to an *integrated model* of a critical discussion. This integrated model allows accounting for the arguers' personal desire to win the cause (*rhetorical aim*) and for its dialectical counterpart (*dialectical aim*), which is identified with the interlocutors' commitment to maintain a standard of reasonableness. I assume this integrated version of the pragma-dialectical model because of its more comprehensive nature, which allows it to take into account the parties' and mediator's interests and personal goals. In fact, these interests and goals are crucial to the process of mediation (see the Harvard model of principled negotiation, Section 3.1.2).

In this section, I shall first briefly expound the meaning of strategic manoeuvring in the pragma-dialectical account. Then I shall discuss this notion in connection with the conceptual framework of mediation (Chapter 4), eliciting the particular traits that strategic manoeuvring assumes in the context of this framework.

The notion of strategic manoeuvring allows reconciling "a long-standing gap between the dialectical and the rhetorical approach to argumentation" (van Eemeren & Houtlosser 2005: 27), and takes into account the arguers' personal motivations for engaging in a critical discussion. Indeed, the fact that an arguer is personally involved in his/her cause is not something to be considered bad in itself, but a natural situation that allows the sound development of argumentation. Precise choices at the level of strategic manoeuvring characterize each stage of a critical discussion. Each stage, in fact, is defined by a specific dialectical aim, and, "because the parties involved want to realize this aim to their best advantage, they can be expected to make the strategic moves that serve their interest best" (van Eemeren & Houtlosser 2002: 138). The strategic moves available concern three aspects in particular. First, they foresee the expedient choice from the possibilities constituting the *topical potential* associated with a specific discussion stage. These possibilities include potential discussion issues in the confrontation stages, premises to be selected as starting points in the opening stage, *loci* and arguments in the argumentation stage, and possible conclusions in the concluding stage (ibid., pp. 139–140). Second, the moves made in each stage of the discourse should also be made in a way that is adapted to *audience demand*, namely with the addressee's preferences (ibid.). Finally, appropriate presentational devices at the communicative and stylistic level, "exploiting the Gricean maxims of Manner in a specific and deliberate way" (ibid., p. 140).

Some specific remarks about the concept of strategic manoeuvring in relation to the ontology-oriented conceptual framework of mediation (Chapter 4) are necessary. In fact, while in other interaction schemes, such as, for example, adjudication, it is easy to imagine that both the defence and the crown will do their best to manoeuvre strategically in order to win their cause, in mediation the situation is more complex. Parties, if they are able to argue with each other – which, as will be shown in Chapter 6, is not always the case – can be assumed not to renounce their rhetorical aims, which mirror their interests. Mediators, however, whose argumentative strategies are at the core of the present investigation, have the status of third neutrals, which may induce someone to erroneously consider them as disinterested interlocutors; in other words, they might seem to lack any form of strategic manoeuvring. Indeed, as for the concept of neutrality, this must be understood as a mediator's lack of direct interest in one or another specific outcome rather than as a complete lack of interest in the dispute itself.

On the contrary, it has often been highlighted that mediators are interested in the resolution of the conflict; as Susskind (2000: 131–132) puts it, speaking as a public dispute professional mediator:

> "I'd feel surprised if most mediators didn't feel disappointed if they failed to help the parties in a dispute reach a resolution".

Analogously, Touval and Zartman (1985a and 1985b), focusing in particular on the dimension of international mediation, analyse the personal advantages motivating a third party to enter a process of mediation. Some of these reasons could also involve selfish interests (for instance, economic rewards). Princen (1992a) distinguishes, from the point of view of the *interest* of third parties in the disputants' conflict, between *neutral* third parties and *principal* third parties. In either case, however, he recognizes some level of interest on the side of the mediator in the resolution of the dispute. At a closer look, it clearly appears that a disinterested mediator would be lacking respect for the parties and their concerns. Mediators should be interested in the resolution of the conflict, at least from a pure contractual point of view, as well as for their personal motivations and professional honour. That said, mediators' interests may derive from both their genuine passion for conflict resolution and for other reasons of convenience (career or other rewards). In any case, the mediator's rhetorical goal can be considered, in general, as finding a resolution to the dispute. As pointed out first by van Eemeren and Houtlosser (2005), and elaborated on by van Eemeren (2010), while, in principle, the mediator's task is only to facilitate the resolution process, in practice mediators also aim to exploit the room for strategic manoeuvring that is left to them in order to contribute to an arrangement. This is differently performed along the stages of a critical discussion (van Eemeren 2010).

5.1.4 The Argumentum Model of Topics (AMT): Analysis of the inferential structure of arguments

In the framework of the model of a critical discussion integrated by the notion of strategic manoeuvring, a specific theoretical instrument allowing us to analyse the topical potential of the argumentation stage is represented by the Argumentum Model of Topics (henceforth AMT), which aims at eliciting the inferential configuration of the arguments that are advanced in support of given standpoints. The model was first proposed in Rigotti and Greco Morasso (2006b) and then illustrated, refined and expanded, with the help of a certain number of different applications, in Rigotti (2006, 2008, 2009) and Rigotti and Greco Morasso (2010). Some further examples of its possible applications have been provided in Bigi (2007), Christopher Guerra (2008), Filimon (2009), Palmieri (2009), Palmieri and Rigotti (2010) and Greco Morasso (2007, 2009a, 2009b).

As for the theoretical framing of the AMT model, for the present purposes it is sufficient to say that it has been elaborated by taking into account the contribution of the ancient rhetorical tradition (in particular, *Topics*, *Rhetoric* and *De Sophisticis Elenchiis* by Aristotle, and *Topics* by Cicero), and the late ancient and medieval elaborations by Boethius (*De topicis differentiis*), Peter of Spain (*Summulae Logicales*) and Buridan (*Summulae de dialectica*). But the AMT model, far from being only a revision of ancient doctrines, is also positioned in the framework of the current research and debate on argumentation, and in particular on *argumentation schemes*. Rigotti (2008, 2009) elaborates in more detail on the ancient and medieval heritage revived and reinterpreted by this model, whereas Rigotti and Greco Morasso (2010) show its added value for the analysis of the inferential configuration of arguments, in comparison with other modern approaches to the study of argument schemes. Here, such theoretical discussion is omitted in favour of an application of the AMT model that is expected to indirectly contribute to show its explicative force.

The analysis of argumentation based on this model offers, on the one hand, very precise detail of the inferential configuration of arguments. On the other hand, it highlights the relation between the arguments and their premises, i.e. to explicitly connect arguments with the opening stage and, more particularly, with the context of the argumentative interaction (Rigotti 2006). The AMT can therefore be integrated in the analytical reconstruction of argumentation based on the model of a critical discussion (Rigotti & Greco Morasso 2010). In the pragma-dialectical account, the analysis of the choice of arguments is already foreseen as a part of the reconstruction of the topical potential relative to strategic manoeuvring in the argumentation stage (Rigotti 2006). The AMT is primarily intended as a specific model for this stage of the reconstruction. In relation to the core process of mediation (see the framework proposed in Chapter 4), the analysis of the arguments advanced is particularly important. In fact, it is worth understanding what arguments make the discussion advance; on which premises they are built and how these premises connect with the antecedents of mediation, in particular with the parties' institutionalized and interpersonal relationship and with the broader institutional context of the dispute. I have chosen to integrate the AMT into the model of a critical discussion because, as will become clear in the characterization I am about to give, it is particularly suited for this type of analysis.

5.1.4.1 *The inferential configuration of arguments*

As remarked in Rigotti and Greco Morasso (2010), in general, modern authors conceive of argument schemes as the whole-bearing structures that connect the premises to the standpoint or conclusion in a piece of real argumentation. In Garssen's (2001: 81) words (but see also van Eemeren & Grootendorst 1992 and van Eemeren & Garssen 2009):

> "The link between the argument and the standpoint is appropriate if the acceptability of the premise is 'transferred' to the standpoint by means of the 'argument scheme' that is being used".

In the AMT perspective, the completeness of this "transfer" is not exclusively entrusted to the logical–inferential dimension of maxims. In relation to this, the distinction proposed by the pragma-dialectical approach between *procedural* and *material* starting points in the opening stage (Houtlosser 2002: 20) can be re-read following Rigotti and Greco Morasso (2010). These authors apply it as an instrument to specify how, in argument schemes, there is a dimension overcoming the logical principle. In particular, in Rigotti and Greco Morasso's understanding, the argument scheme combines a *procedural* starting point, coinciding with the inferential connection (maxim) that is activated, with a *material* starting point guaranteeing the applicability of the maxim to the actual situation considered in the argument. In other words, the notions of *material* and *procedural starting points* are applied to identify the different nature of premises at work in the argument scheme. The precise reconstruction of these different types of premises and the discovery of their intertwining connection is one of the main tenets of the AMT (ibid.).

In what follows, I shall first describe the type of premises constituting the procedural starting point; then I shall focus on the types of premises constituting the material starting point. As regards the procedural starting point, according to the AMT, three levels emerge in the relationship between *loci* and the entire argument schemes (see ibid.).

The ***first level*** is represented by the *locus* itself, as the source from which arguments are taken: "unde argumenta ducuntur", according to Cicero (see Reinhardt 2003) or, according to the medieval tradition, the *habitudo*, a term that can be properly interpreted as the "ontological relation" on which a certain argumentative reasoning is based. Consider the relationship between definiendum and definitum, the cause–effect relationship, the analogy (comparability) relationship, and so on. Such ontological relations are evoked by the *names* of the loci themselves: one speaks, for example, of the locus *ex* auctoritate, or of the locus *ab* oppositis, and so on, nowadays translated into English with the expression "argument from" (from authority, from opposition).

Yet, merely quoting the name of a locus does not show how the ontological relation determines the inferential configuration of arguments. In order to explain this, beyond the locus, the AMT integrates the analysis of their inferential configuration with two further levels.

Second level. Each *habitudo* gives rise to a series of *inferential connections* called *maxims*. For example, the locus from the final cause (see Rigotti 2008) presents a series of possible maxims each of which leads to a subclass of possible arguments. Consider the following examples of maxims:

1. If a certain goal is to be achieved, it is reasonable to activate a causal chain allowing it to be reached
2. If no causal chain is available, the goal cannot be achieved
3. If a certain behaviour is not oriented towards a goal (as it cannot be considered a proper human action), it cannot be endowed with any property typically congruous with human action (responsibility, merit, guilt and so on).

Third level. Each of these maxims activates a *logical form*, such as the *modus ponens* or the *modus tollens*. More specifically, provided that a certain ontological relation is the case, any inferential connection or maxim generated by it activates through its application a logical form in an argument scheme. For example, the maxim "if the cause is the case, the effect is too" activates the logical form of *modus ponens*. Different maxims may activate identical or different logical forms. Thus, when the locus from genus and species is instantiated, the maxim "what holds for the genus, holds for the species too" analogously activates a *modus ponens*. But, going back to the locus from cause and effect, the questionable maxim "if the effect is the case, the cause is too" activates the logical form of "false" *modus ponens*, which is usual in symptomatic argumentation.[7] Another maxim pertaining to the same locus, "if the effect does not take place, the cause does not either" activates the logical form of *modus tollens*. Moreover, if the locus from immediate opposites is instantiated and p and q are immediate opposites, the maxim arises "if one opposite is the case the other is not", which activates the logical form of an exclusive disjunction.

In the AMT perspective, these three levels give an accurate description of the procedural starting point of argument schemes.

As already remarked, according to the AMT, the procedural component is not sufficient for a complete reconstruction of argument schemes. Indeed, argument schemes claim to account for the relation between *real* arguments used in real-life discussions and real standpoints which they support. Therefore, beyond the procedural starting point now reconstructed, we also have to shed some light on what is considered, in the AMT perspective, a specific "material starting point" that is invoked to complete the inferential process and, at the same time, to enhance

7. In fact, the symptomatic argument, very common in all forms of explanation (for example, in the formulation of medical diagnoses), starts from the relation connecting an effect to its (possible) cause. The relation between effect and cause is normally unnecessary, since the same effect might be produced by different causes. Yet, ideally, a good symptomatic argument should identify the most probable (ideally the unique) cause for a given effect.

the persuasiveness of arguments based on these argument schemes.[8] In fact, the validity of the maxim is not the only condition for the soundness of an argumentative move: another level of premises must be taken into account (Rigotti & Greco Morasso 2006b; Rigotti 2006; Rigotti 2008; Rigotti & Greco Morasso 2009a). Beyond specifying the various levels that should be taken into account in the reconstruction of argument schemes, the AMT also accounts for the material starting point that is inherent in real arguments.

A very simple example of argument, presented in Rigotti (2009), which can be considered as part of an advertising campaign, is reproduced here in order to show the analysis of the inferential structure of arguments allowed by the AMT. Such an example can be imagined as taken from an advertising message, claiming in a very overt fashion: "This butter is natural. It is made from fresh Alpine milk". The first step of an argumentative analysis allows identifying the standpoint (this butter is natural) and the argument used to support it (it is made from fresh Alpine milk). The following representation mirrors the numerous examples proposed in van Eemeren, Grootendorst and Snoeck-Henkemans (2002):

1. This butter is natural.
1.1 It is made from fresh alpine milk.

Concerning the representation of standpoint and argument, the AMT tends to highlight the problematic nature of the standpoint, signalled by a question mark, and the supporting nature of the argument, signalled by an arrow:

(?) This butter is natural.
➔ It is made from fresh Alpine milk

The two representations, in this case, can be considered equivalent from the point of view of a first identification of standpoint and arguments. The "principle of support" (Garssen 2001) linking argument and standpoint, however, remains quite obscure at this point, and needs to be further specified in terms of topical analysis if the inferential configuration of this argumentative move has to be made explicit and evaluated. In this sense, the AMT aims to provide some instruments for fulfilling the analytical reconstruction, by presenting a synergic representation of arguments that allows eliciting various levels of their implicit

8. Persuasiveness is not exclusively based on the validity of a procedure. To put it synthetically, it is rooted in how much the actual arguments used are anchored in the "material" common ground of the participants in the critical discussion (Rigotti 2006). In this sense, a further component in the reconstruction of the inferential structure of arguments has to be included, accounting for this "aboutness" of the actual use of argument schemes.

premises and highlights their connections by reconstructing the whole inferential configuration of the argument (see Figure 5.1):

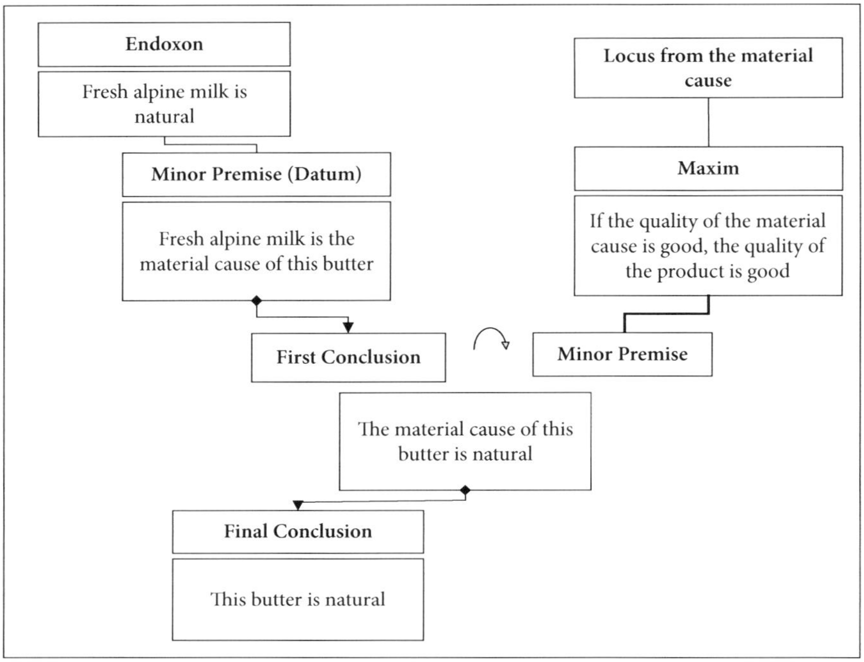

Figure 5.1. Synergic representation of the inferential structure of an argument (Rigotti & Greco Morasso 2006b)

The general principle underlying the reconstruction of the inferential configuration of this argumentative move is that of finding those explicit or implicit premises that are necessary in order for the argumentative move to be valid. Such operation is part of an *analytical reconstruction* of argumentation (van Eemeren & Grootendorst 2004).

First, the standpoint to be supported, which has already been identified, becomes the final conclusion of the reasoning, insofar as it is the statement that the whole argumentation intends to demonstrate. Then, on the basis of the argument identified, it is possible to elicit the locus on which the argumentation is based (First level).

In our case, the "naturality" of the advertised butter is connected with the main ingredient constituting it, i.e. in more general terms, with its *material cause*. The *habitudo* in question is thus the relationship between a product (in this case, an edible product) and its material cause (its ingredients). More specifically, it is now possible to identify the maxim actually working as a major premise of the syllogistic reasoning based on this argument scheme, which can be formulated as: "If the quality of the material cause is good, the quality of the product is good" (Second level).[9] Combining the maxim with the final conclusion, it clearly emerges that the minor premise, still missing in the reconstruction, should be: "The material cause of *this* butter is natural", thus applying the general principle stated by the maxim to the specific product in question. As a Third level of the procedural component, we can thus reconstruct the following logical form: "If the quality of the material cause is good, the quality of the product is good; well then, the material cause of this butter is natural; therefore, this butter is natural". The logical form so sketched is inferentially valid *if* all the premises are true. Yet the truth of the second premise is not derivable from the maxim; it should be derived from outside, namely from a *material starting point* (Rigotti & Greco Morasso 2010). In other words, the truth of this premise must be provided with some effectual backing belonging to the interlocutors' material common ground. This backing is necessary in order to exhaustively represent the inferential configuration of a real argument, as the maxim, in order to actually work, needs to be applied to an appropriate situation (Rigotti 2008). In other words, fresh Alpine milk must actually be considered a *natural* "material cause" (a natural ingredient). This statement of value represents a premise of the reasoning; such a premise, however, does not consist in an inferential connection, but rather in an assumption based on knowledge of the natural Alpine environment, of traditional methods to breed cows, and so on. Thus we could say that this is a typical instance of a *material* starting point. In this connection, Rigotti (2008, 2009) proposes to reconsider the Aristotelian notion of *endoxon* (see Tardini 1997):

> "Endoxa are opinions that are accepted by everyone or by the majority, or by the wise men (all of them or the majority, or by the most notable and illustrious of them)". (Topics 100b.21)

An endoxon is an opinion that is accepted by the relevant public or by the opinion leaders of the relevant public. In this relation, the notion of *relevant* public

9. Needless to say, other maxims can be generated by the same locus. Another group of important maxims related to the material cause, besides "If the quality of material cause is *bad*, the product is *bad*", is bound to the concept of *resource*. See, for instance, "If the needed resources are not available, a given action cannot be performed". In general, the set of maxims bound to a locus can be generated starting from an accurate semantic analysis of the maxim (see Rigotti 2008).

is very important because it turns out to coincide with the *audience demand* (van Eemeren & Houtlosser 2002): it is the protagonist and antagonist in the concerned critical discussion who must agree about the material starting points in order to resolve their difference of opinion. In the case proposed above, it is up to them to accept the naturalness of Alpine milk. More precisely, as it has been argued in Rigotti (2006), the endoxical component is rooted in the context of the argumentative discussion that is constituted by the parties' institutionalized and interpersonal relationship.

For this reason, the AMT accounts not only for the logical aspects of the development of argumentation, but also for its embeddedness in the parties' relationship, and thus in the context of argumentation. This is one of the main reasons why I have chosen to integrate the AMT into the pragma-dialectical model of a critical discussion. Via the analysis of argument schemes, the AMT allows us to verify how the antecedents of mediation – in terms of values, common knowledge about the context and factual information – play a role in the actual arguments advanced in the discussion. In other words, the AMT is a tool for the reconstruction and analysis of argumentation which connects at the conceptual level the argumentative discussion with the antecedents of a mediation process. In this way, it is well suited to study how arguments are actually context-bound (Rigotti 2006) and is therefore in line with the interests of the present investigation.

Still in connection with the material starting point, one also has to add a factual premise to the general premise represented by the endoxon (Datum), which is likely to be accepted if it corresponds to the repeated observations of the participants in the critical discussion: the fact that Alpine milk is actually the material cause of this particular butter, which is explicitly exploited by the selling company. Potential customers have no direct evidence that fresh Alpine milk is one of the ingredients of the butter (as they have not assisted in the production process) but it is an assertion whose truth the selling company must strictly conform to, and which is normally covered by legislation on commercial activities. From a logical point of view, the association of the endoxon with the datum leads to the conclusion[10] that "The material cause of this butter is natural". In the AMT, this premise represents the junction between the material and the procedural starting points (see Figure 5.1).

The "quasi Y-shaped" graphical representation presented in Figure 5.1 has been introduced in the AMT in order to highlight the *crossing of lines of reasoning stemming from premises of different nature* (procedural and material) that are present in real argumentation. It aims to provide a complete account of all the

10. In this case, a categorial syllogism is activated.

inferential nodes (based on syllogistic reasoning) that are at work in argumentation (Rigotti and Greco Morasso 2010).

It is also important to specify that such a reconstruction of the inferential configuration of actual argumentative moves is preliminary to their *evaluation* in terms of soundness. In this relation, many aspects could be elicited with regard to the considered example: for instance, the above-mentioned endoxon clearly shows its context-dependence, as the image of the Alps as a natural place where happy cows graze and produce natural milk is only valid in certain geographical and cultural areas, while it is unknown in others. Moreover, the validity of the maxim itself, although it cannot be questioned as a general logical rule, can be discussed insofar as it can be limited by other concurrent factors. For instance, milk is certainly the most important material ingredient in butter; but if other ingredients are unhealthy, the butter cannot be claimed to be natural. Furthermore, if a very natural butter is stored with no attention to its conservation, its quality decreases in a few hours. Finally, it is important to be aware that the datum concerning the actual composition of the butter, being based on an auto-certification by the selling company, can surely be subject to fraudulent claims, which should be verified.

Considerations of this kind constitute an evaluation of the logical soundness of argumentative moves and discourses, and allow the identification of potential mistakes, fallacies and other manipulative processes. The elicitation of all the components constituting the inferential configuration of arguments allows us to specify the appropriate critical questions with which to evaluate argumentation. As Christopher Guerra (2008) has remarked, specific critical questions could be associated with each node of the quasi-Y structure of the AMT, particularly in relation to the endoxon, datum and maxim.

5.1.4.2 *Taxonomy of loci*

On the basis of the First level of the procedural component, namely the different loci on which argument schemes are founded, a taxonomy has been constructed (Rigotti 2009). Such a taxonomy, drawing on the medieval distinction between *intrinsic*, *extrinsic* and *middle* loci, proposes a reinterpretation of it based on the categories of modern linguistics, which more clearly account for the different relations (loci). The opposition intrinsic–extrinsic was chosen in the Middle Ages in order to characterize the degree of proximity of the locus to the standpoint; in other words, intrinsic loci tended to be bound to *habitudines* which refer to a single state of affairs in reality (cause–effect, *definitio–definitum*), while extrinsic loci tended to be bound to *habitudines* which refer to alternative states of affairs in reality, their most general and representative category being that of *opposition*.

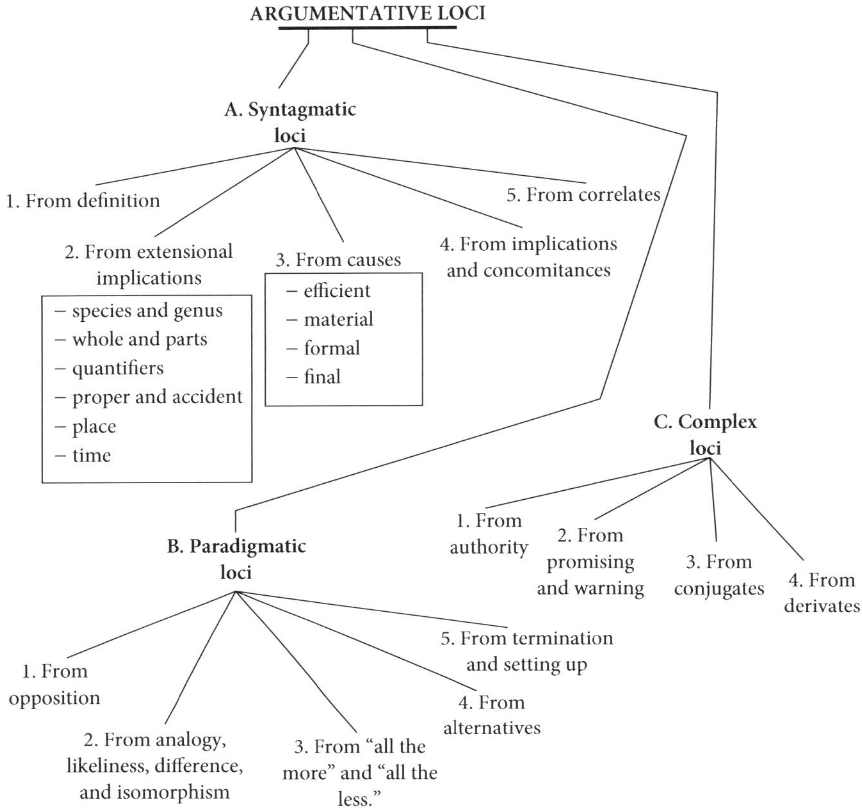

Figure 5.2. Taxonomy of loci in the AMT

As it is shown in Figure 5.2, three main categories of loci are included in this taxonomy. The first one is represented by *syntagmatic* loci, whose distinctive feature is to be connected with aspects that either have been established in the standpoint or that coexist with it. The notion of syntagm, introduced in modern linguistics, accounts for these kind of *in praesentia* relations. In medieval works, in particular the commentary to Peter of Spain's *Summulae Logicales* written by Buridan, the logical relation on which this kind of loci is based is said to refer to a single state of affairs in reality. Such a state of affairs is normally complex, such as the one encompassing cause and effect, or an action and its implications. Among the syntagmatic loci, the following ones can be enumerated: *locus from definition*, *loci from extensional implications* (species and genus, whole and parts, quantifiers, proper and accident, place, time), *loci from causes* (in particular, locus from the efficient cause, from the material cause, from the formal cause, from final cause, and from instrumental cause), *locus from implications and concomitances* (of the standpoint), and *locus from correlates.*

The category of *paradigmatic loci* draws on the linguistic category of relations in absentia (or paradigmatic), and regroups all those loci that are bound to the standpoint through a relation of alternativity. Included in this category are the *loci from opposition* based on different types of opposition (systematized in the *square of oppositions*, see Rigotti & Greco Morasso 2006b) the *locus from metaphor*, the *locus from analogy* (with the subcategories, of likeliness, difference, and isomorphism), the *locus from "all the more..." and "all the less..."*, the *locus from alternatives*, and the *locus from termination and setting up*. In terms of modern semantics, these loci refer to the comparison of one or more possible worlds.

Finally, the third category has been named *complex loci* both in order to account for the contaminations between the two preceding categories – indeed, frequently actual arguments present aspects that can be ascribed to both syntagmatic and paradigmatic loci – and in order to consider the extra-discursive elements that can be included in these loci. For instance, the *locus from authority* is surely part of the complex loci because, although its structure is mainly based on the efficient cause, it refers to an extra-discursive aspect, as the efficient cause of the standpoint, from which the authority is taken, is the speaker uttering it (see Rigotti 2006).

5.1.5 Argumentation as a communicative interaction

It is necessary now to point to some more general assumptions about the process of communication, of which argumentation is considered a relevant component. The reasons justifying such framing are twofold, and refer to two different levels of focus in the analysis.

On the one hand, argumentation should be considered in its proper context of the communicative interaction, as it is in general widely acknowledged in argumentation studies.[11] This is particularly relevant in the case of mediation,

11. See van Eemeren, Houtlosser and Snoeck-Henkemans (2007: 3): "Pragma-dialectics on the other hand acknowledges explicitly that argumentative discourse is part of a communicative activity. That is why the argumentation that is advanced is always analyzed in relation to the way in which the verbal interaction between the participants in the communication process proceeds. Bringing forwards standpoints and argumentation and responding to the (real or assumed) standpoints and argumentation of others are viewed as socially motivated moves in a collective process of conflict management".

because the core process (see the mediation framework in Chapter 4) does not automatically start as a well-defined argumentative discussion. The mediation interaction begins with the mediator's effort to open communication between the parties. Consequently, an argumentative discussion in mediation is not to be taken for granted; it is already the result of good communication. It is thus particularly important to consider argumentation in its broader context of a communicative interaction. Therefore, although the argumentative analysis of texts requires a necessary abstraction process that focuses on the argumentative aspects, this analysis needs to be integrated in a perspective that considers the whole development of the communicative interaction. Indeed, even the selection of argumentatively relevant traits of the discussion can only be adequately fulfilled if the goals of the communicative interaction are considered. Relational aspects, repetitions, phatic communication and other features may be judged relevant or irrelevant from the argumentative point of view also in relation to the contextual factors.

On the other hand, a second reason for introducing some notions of communicative analysis concerns a micro-level. As argumentation also includes the exploitation of semantic nuances, ambiguities, as well as rhetorical aspects at the level of speech acts, use of metaphors and other elocutive aspects, the analysis should not neglect specific linguistic aspects, which may have more or less direct argumentative functions.

5.1.5.1 *Accounting for the communicative dimension: The perspective of Congruity theory*

Congruity theory (Rigotti 1993; Rigotti & Rocci 2001), already introduced in Chapter 4 for the semantic analysis of *conflict*, starts from the interpretation of texts as communicative actions, and interprets the meaning of such a communicative action as a hierarchy of semantic-pragmatic predicates. This hierarchy goes from lexicalized units, such as the ones bound to conflict, to higher-level pragmatic predicates, which are analysed in the same terms of presuppositions and implications.[12] Connective predicates are to be interpreted as relational predicates (see Gobber, Gatti & Cigada 2006) assuming among their arguments text sequences, speaker, hearer and context. The structure of a connective predicate can thus be represented as follows:

12. See Rigotti (2005a: 81): "Moreover, in Rigotti and Rocci (2001), it is argued that not only we can explain the different lexical or grammatical presupposition triggers in terms of predicates that impose presuppositions on their arguments, but it is also possible to treat in similar fashion the *coherence* and *illocutionary felicity* of entire texts".

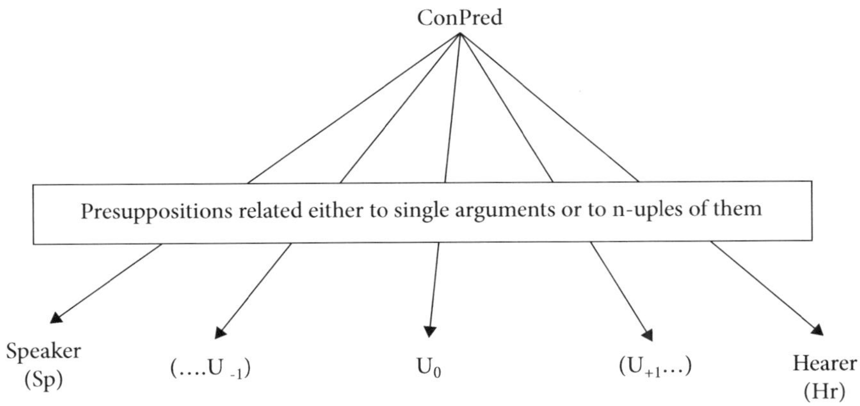

Figure 5.3. The structure of a connective predicate (Rigotti 2005a: 83)

The connective predicate relates all these arguments to each other, insofar as it "characterises the utterance by specifying what the speaker does to the addressee with her utterance" (Rigotti 2005a: 82). The pragmatic nature of the interpretation of texts proposed by Congruity theory clearly appears from this definition. This account is pragmatic both because, as said, it rests on the interpretation of texts as communicative actions, and because it involves the context of communication as an argument of the connective. The hierarchical network of predicates, thus, is ultimately dominated by the predicate that more directly evokes the communicative meaning of the text.

Congruity theory can be virtually applied to any communicative text, including argumentative texts (Rigotti 2005a). The instruments to analyse argumentative sequences more specifically have already been introduced; as for Congruity theory, it is assumed in the present research because it allows a broader perspective on the analysed data and therefore can serve as a basis for considering relevant communicative aspects that integrate the argumentative account of mediation on which this research is focused. In fact, the mediation interaction is clearly a text where more than a single sequence is present, and though the argumentative nature of the mediation interaction has been proven, not only argumentative passages are present.

In particular, mediation corresponds to a dialogue, i.e. to "a communicative interaction where the participants can (and are expected to) alternate, more or less regularly or frequently, the roles of speaker and hearer" (Rigotti 2005a: 91). Now, as has been shown in Rocci (2005), Congruity theory can be applied to monological as well as to dialogical texts. In the latter case, it is possible to interpret and analyse in great detail by means of the notion of connective predicates co-operative local moves which have been called *dialogue games*, and which involve a common goal between the interlocutors beyond their individual goals. As Rocci (2005: 105) shows, connective predicates are less abstract than dialogue games, as they allow us to analyse the functioning of the single communicative move. However, the hypothesis can be made that dialogue games, which are "considerably more abstract" (ibid.), regroup classes of connective predicates.

Significantly, Congruity theory, interpreting texts as hierarchies of predicates, allows us to focus on the fact that the ultimate action performed through the text itself – coinciding with the connective predicate of the highest level – involves the participants in the communicative interaction (see the roles of speaker and hearer in Figure 5.3). Not coincidentally, Rigotti (1993: 48–49) pointed out that the most important change in social reality produced by communication operates on the subjectivity of the interlocutors. Elaborating on the implications of this at the relationship level, Cigada (2006: 140) speaks of *emotive congruity* (*congruité emotive*), namely the possibility and capability to emotionally participate in the communicative exchange, as a constitutive dimension of communication. Thus, the evaluation of the congruity of the arguments of the connective predicate dominating a given communicative text must also take into account the complexity of the human subjects involved in communication.

It is clear that such a delicate balance becomes even more complex in the case of communication in mediation, which follows an antecedent conflictual phase, in which the conflicting parties are certainly lacking congruity at the relational level. In fact, the escalation of a conflict is a process by which the parties' relationship gradually deteriorates, up to the moment in which each party only wants to vanquish his/her adversary and considers him/her to be the real problem (the real origin and source of the conflict). In such a situation, we are certainly far from the ideal of co-operative communication, and from a well-balanced dialogue from the emotive point of view.[13] Thus, the importance for the mediator to be able to cope with emotive aspects and to be empathetic with both parties has often been highlighted.[14] Such capability should be understood as aimed at enabling both parties to "find their own place" as human beings within the communicative process.

13. The fact that even less-than-conflictual polemical exchanges can be very challenging from the point of view of the involved subjects has been pointed out by Dascal (2003 [1989]). See also Greco Morasso (2008) for this aspect.

14. Dealing with interpersonal aspects and emotions is considered very important in the training of mediators. More specifically, it has been argued that mediators' training should devote more attention to the management of emotions and the development of emotional intelligence, conceived of as "the capacity for recognizing our own feelings and those of others, for motivating ourselves, and for managing emotions well in ourselves and in our

5.2 Argumentation in the core process of mediation

Along with the presentation of the argumentation theories, models and concepts developed in Section 5.1, I have been discussing how they fit the core process of mediation as it is described in the ontology-oriented conceptual framework (Chapter 4). Generally speaking, what is expected to happen in a successful core process, namely the identification of the problematic issues in the parties' conflict, as well as the shift to their resolution, is best achieved by means of an argumentative discussion. In fact, the arguers' commitment to critically found their decision and renounce to violence for a reasonable decision-making process is a good framework for a conflict resolution process in which disputants remain responsible for the outcome. In this sense, there can be no mediation without trust in human beings' capability to tackle their conflict by means of a reasonable argumentative discussion. For these reasons, the argumentative dimension introduced in this chapter integrates and completes the framework presented in Chapter 4 at the conceptual level.

Yet this conceptual integration leaves some important questions unanswered about how an argumentation space can be opened between two parties in conflict, and what the mediator's role is in this respect. In order to answer these questions (raised in Chapter 1), it is necessary to look at the argumentative reality of successful mediation processes. We are going to reconstruct the phases of a critical discussion in mediation and verify how they are structured and how mediators contribute to the parties' discussion without taking a particular side or advancing standpoints about the conflict outcomes. We shall also reconstruct the prominent features of the mediator's strategic manoeuvring, considering the recurrent arguments and argument schemes that contribute to the resolution of the conflict. Finally, I shall integrate the argumentative analysis in a broader consideration of the mediation process as a communicative interaction, by considering the perspective of Congruity theory. As this research is focused on contextualized argumentation, I shall devote particular attention to the relation between the development of argumentation and the context (interaction scheme of mediation and various interaction fields) in which the argumentative discussion is embedded. More specifically, the design of the empirical argumentative analysis will be illustrated in the following Section (5.3).

relationships" (Goleman 1998: 317, quoted by Schreirer 2002: 100). Emotions are identified as an essential component in conflict resolution (Jones & Bodtker 2001; Shapiro 2002).

5.3 Designing an empirical argumentative analysis of mediation

The ontological framework of mediation presented in Chapter 4 and enriched with the argumentative perspective in Chapter 5 constitutes a first set of results of the present research with regard to the conceptualization of the mediation practice. It presents a "blueprint" of a process of mediation, in which some moments appear to be particularly crucial. This blueprint also shows that, during the mediation process, there is effectively a mutation of the disputing parties into real co-arguers able to discuss specific options for the resolution of their conflict and to negotiate on the details.

The research questions from which this investigation originated are oriented towards an understanding of the correspondence of the structure of the argumentative discussion in mediation with the fulfilment of the pragmatic goals encompassed by this practice. As mentioned in the previous section, though argumentation is clearly required for the achievement of these goals, we still need to analyse the argumentative reality in order to understand how such achievement is actually made possible. The design of the empirical research has been constructed to clarifiy this point. The analysis has been organized according to a complex design, constituted by *two analytical steps*. The task of identifying the main features of argumentation in the context of mediation is largely accomplished by the first step, while the second step has the function of verification and confirmation.

First step. One of the cases of the corpus, which is particularly representative of a successful mediation process because parties completely solve their problem and restore a new ground for their relationship by arriving at a formalized agreement, is selected as the source of the empirical data. The aim of this step of the analysis is twofold:

1. I shall do a *phenomenological analysis* of the whole core process of mediation constituted by the communicative interaction in this case, from its beginning to the resolution of the conflict. This phenomenological analysis is preliminary to the argumentative analysis; it is necessary to understand how the core process of mediation is actualized in the mediator's and parties' discussion. I shall go through the discussion and identify the different phases of the core process of mediation identified in the core process of the mediation framework. I shall also represent the main communicative moves that make the transition possible from one phase to the other. Finally, I shall pay attention to the type of chronological development of the discussion, considering if the phases are linearly subsequent, if there are repetitions, and so on. In this way, we shall arrive at a picture of how the communicative discussion in the selected mediation case has developed and how it corresponds to the

"ideal" conceptual model of a mediation process. The phenomenological analysis is expected to identify the major changes in the parties' interaction; possibly, it will show the increasing confidence between the parties, their possible increase in "emotive congruity", their change in discussion style and the phases that bring a resolution of the conflict. However, the *reasons* for these changes cannot be explained by this type of approach.

2. It is the task of the argumentative analysis to investigate such reasons. The argumentative analysis will be based on the concepts and models introduced in this chapter. I shall undertake an analytical reconstruction of the critical discussion occurring in the mediation process, trying to verify to what extent and how the argumentative practice corresponds to the ideal model. In particular, I shall define how the stages of a critical discussion are realized in such a complex interaction, in which arriving at an agreement requires a long and complex communication process. Moreover, I shall analyse in detail the contributions of the three participants to the discussion: the protagonist, the antagonist and the "third" participant, the neutral but active mediator. While doing the analytical reconstruction of argumentation in this case, I shall pay particular attention to the *mediator's strategic manoeuvring*. I shall try to elicit the *characterizing aspects* of his strategic manoeuvring; I shall monitor those aspects that help the parties be "transformed" into co-arguers; and I shall verify whether this passage corresponds to a true progress of the conflict resolution process in mediation, namely if it brings parties closer to a reasonable resolution of their conflict.

Second step. The results of the first step will allow restricting the focus of the analysis by focusing on the crucial aspects of the mediator's strategic manoeuvring which emerged in the first step. Such aspects will be verified on a larger evidence basis, constituted by all the other five cases of the corpus (see Chapter 6). This second step will allow specifying: (a) whether the prominent aspects of the mediator's strategic manoeuvring that emerged in the first step are confirmed considering a larger evidence basis; (b) whether other prominent aspects emerge.

Moreover, the possibility of comparing different applications of mediation will offer the possibility to investigate how the institutionalized and interpersonal dimensions of *context*, conceived of in terms of *interaction scheme* and *interaction field* (see the definition discussed in Chapter 4) influence the development of the argumentative discussion and, thus, the process of conflict resolution.

The double-step research design delineated here is seen to have different advantages. First, it allows for the management of the empirical data that, on the one hand, consents a progressive zooming in on those aspects that are relevant to the research questions of the present investigation. In this sense, such a research design provides a progressive refinement of the research questions, which are re-oriented by the results of the first step. At the same time, however, the second step also allows us to account for unexpected results that can emerge from the analysis of the other cases.

5.3.1 Methodological considerations

Having briefly outlined the design of the empirical component of the research, it is still necessary to illustrate some methodological considerations about the advantages and limitations of an argumentative analysis (5.3.1.1) in the specific context of a mediation interaction (5.3.1.2).

5.3.1.1 *The analysis of argumentative interactions: Features, advantages and limitations*

Some remarks on the methodological rationale underlying studies in argumentation have been proposed by Jackson (1986), Jacobs (1986), van Eemeren et al. (1993) and van Eemeren and Grootendorst (2004). In particular, Jackson (1986) has examined the methodology of argumentation studies and, more generally, of discourse analytic approaches based on *analytic induction* (ibid., p. 129).[15] In more

15. In relation to the social sciences, in particular, Jackson argues against the common view that discourse analysis and other accounts founded on analytic induction would lack methodological validity. In particular, Jackson maintains that methodology should not be confused with specific and routinized procedures considered as rules to be followed in doing research. Methodology is "a way for generating arguments for empirical claims"; in this perspective, "specific design and analysis procedures are seen not as guarantors of correct conclusions, but as routinized solutions to argumentative problems" (ibid., p. 131). In this sense, the specific routinized principles of empirical enquiries used in the social sciences turns out to be a standard means to reach the goal of empirically founded claims. As a means, they can be seen to have an instrumental rather than absolute validity. Therefore, "analytic induction offers no pre-existing argumentative structure into which empirical claims can be slipped. But this does not mean that it has no method, nor does it mean that the claims are non-empirical" (ibid., p. 133). More specifically, Jackson observes that, with regard to the relation between claims and empirical evidence, "the most salient characteristic of discourse analytic research is the use of examples drawn from conversation or other discourse as data" (ibid., p. 138). In relation to this, Jacobs (1986) further examines and discusses the validity of this method, based on the argument from example: "There is a genuine sense in which examples have a demonstrative power within the framework of discourse analytic argumentation. That demonstrative power is grounded in the idea of an institutional fact and in the claim that intuitions are social facts to be accounted for. [...] In comparing and contrasting examples of language structure and language use, the discourse analyst is involved in finding out how our social knowledge makes language appear. By selecting for analysis examples of a variety of types, the analyst can (1) bring those intuitions into bold relief, showing that we in fact have them, and (2) argue for the correctness of technical descriptions based on those intuitions, justifying the description

detail, van Eemeren et al. (1993) and van Eemeren and Grootendorst (2004) specifically situate the pragma-dialectical approach to argumentation within this kind of approach and provide some methodological principles.[16]

The fundamental concept at the basis of the methodology also employed in the present work is that of *reconstruction*:

> "The aim of a pragma-dialectical analysis is to reconstruct the process of resolving a difference of opinion occurring in an argumentative discourse or text".
> (van Eemeren & Grootendorst 2004: 95)

Indeed, the reality of human interaction made possible through communication is far more complex than any disciplinary approach may suggest. Thus, making an argumentative analysis of a text means reconstructing those aspects of it that are relevant to the argumentative purpose of resolving a difference of opinion, and neglecting other aspects. Of course, this does not mean that the other aspects pertaining to the complexity of human communication are not relevant, but only that there is a necessary abstraction from the real object to the *formal object* that is relevant to argumentation studies (Rigotti & Cigada 2004: 59–61). The concept of reconstruction is in no case to be conceived of as a process of text manipulation that neglects or revisits the empirical data, but only as a focus on the argumentative traits of a more complex communicative interaction.

In particular, the process of reconstruction implies four kinds of *transformation* (van Eemeren & Grootendorst 2004: 100–110), which might be said to help focus on these traits: *deletion*, *addition*, *permutation* and *substitution*. Deletion consists in leaving out parts of the data that are irrelevant; addition consists in including the implicit argumentative material that can be inferred from what is uttered explicitly; permutation concerns the disposition of the data, which can be rearranged in order to interpret it in light of the model;

---

by the way in which the described features are required for having the intuitions we do" (ibid., p. 166). This is how the examples drawn from the corpus selected for the present work are used. A rationale for the selection of the corpus is explained below.

16. As a whole, the methodological approach to the argumentative analysis derived from pragma-dialectics tends to be defined as an *analytic, a priori, rational* approach (van Eemeren et al. 1993). Each of these attributions corresponds to the extreme of a dichotomy in which approaches to analysis and reconstruction can be viewed. It tends to be analytic because the empirical data (oral or written texts) are analysed from an external perspective. It is a priori because it starts "from a theoretical stance taken toward the phenomena" (ibid., p. 53). It is rational because it assumes that the organization of verbal interaction is to be found neither in sequencing (at the level of behaviour regularities) nor in conventions, but in deeper rationality (ibid., p. 55).

and, finally, substitution may interpret vague or imprecise formulations of communicative moves and provide clearer formulations that help to highlight the argumentative nature of such moves.

It is thus clear that the argumentative reconstruction of a text is not a trivial task, since on the one hand, the data that the analyst considers are often mixed with non-argumentative passages, while on the other hand they may leave part of the argumentation implicit. Indeed, the fact that argumentation in real human interaction is not completely explicit is a distinctive feature of human communication, already pointed out by the Aristotelian notion of *enthymeme* (Tardini 1997); thus the relevance of the process of reconstruction.

Van Eemeren et al. (1993) have analysed the basis for the justification of the analyst's reconstruction of the process of argumentation. Part of the grounding is of an *empirical nature*, insofar as it is bound to ethnographic evidence or to the natural speaker's awareness of the use of language, which gives information about the use of communication in general, as well as cues deriving from how the participants themselves understand what is going on in their communicative exchange. To this, van Eemeren and Grootendorst (2004: 112) add the specific knowledge of the context in which the argumentative interaction takes place, which often sets up expectations and conventions that may justify a specific reconstruction. This is in line with the approach adopted in the present investigation, in which a large section has been devoted to the reconstruction of the context of the argumentative discussion in mediation. In general, as van Eemeren et al. (ibid., p. 44) put it, "This evidence can be assembled both to justify the analyst's intuitions empirically about what is being argued and to augment those intuitions so as to go beyond a naïve reading of the discourse".

A second major source of justification of the reconstruction is *normative*. In fact, the analyst of argumentation assumes the participants to be co-operative and to act in a reasonable way, and holds them accountable for meeting such expectations (ibid., p. 45). For this, the model of a critical discussion – which is assumed, in our case, in its integrated version, including the strategic manoeuvring and integrated by the AMT in its specific component of topical potential in the argumentation stage – plays a fundamental role, insofar as it plays a heuristic and critical function. As van Eemeren and Grootendorst (2004: 58–59) put it:

> "The model of a critical discussion performs both a heuristic and a critical function in the analysis and evaluation of argumentative discourse and text. The heuristic function is that of being a guideline for the analysis: the model serves as a guide in the detection and theoretical interpretation of every element in, and aspect of, the discourse or text that is relevant to a critical evaluation. The critical function is that of serving as a standard in the evaluation: the model provides a series of norms by which it can be determined in what respects an argumentative

exchange of ideas diverges from the procedure that is the most conducive to the resolution of a difference of opinion".[17]

It is clear that what is relevant to the normative account guiding the analysis depends on the research purpose. In general, however, the analysis is guided by some strategies directly deriving form the normative account. The most general strategy is called the strategy of *maximally reasonable reconstruction*, which gives maximal credit to the speakers, considering them as contributing to the resolution of a difference of opinion.[18] Such a strategy works as a guiding principle under uncertain conditions but the justification of the analysis must always be in accordance with the empirical grounding, including knowledge of the specific context of argumentation.[19]

Methodologically, the pragma-dialectical approach to argumentation also includes the presentation of the analytical reconstruction by means of an *analytic overview* of the critical discussion, which helps bring to light "which points are at dispute, which parties are involved in the difference of opinion, what their procedural and material premises are, which argumentation is put forward by each of the parties, how their discourses are organised, and how each individual

17. About the heuristic and critical functions of the model, van Eemeren, Houtlosser and Snoeck-Henkemans (2007: 17) explain: "Assuming that argumentative discussions and texts and the argumentative moves made in such argumentative discourse have – at least potentially – the objective of resolving a difference of opinion in a critical way, we believe this model can be considered a template for the crucial tasks that parties involved in the difference of opinion have to perform. If it turns out that language users do not fulfil all these tasks in everyday argumentative discourse or do not fulfil all of them completely, it still holds true that all the tasks specified in the model are functional for scrupulously resolving a difference of opinion, and so, technically, they should be performed one way or the other. Consequently, one of the uses of the model is to identify moves which in real world cases are not explicitly or completely expressed. Even in the case of moves that are apparently (or even actually) fallacious, we are of the opinion that it is methodologically acceptable to use the ideal model for conducting a critical discussion to identify these moves as argumentative moves".

18. Such a principle is then instantiated into two more specific strategies. On the one hand, the strategy of *maximally argumentative interpretation* requires that the argumentative force (or status) is attributed to those speech acts that may have it. On the other hand, the strategy of *maximally argumentative analysis* means that each single argumentation is accorded a maximum of argumentative force (p. 114ff.)

19. In this sense, as van Eemeren and Grootendorst (2004: 117) observe, there is an open character to the argumentative analysis based on pragma-dialectics: "In principle, there is always the possibility that in the course of the reconstruction process, other, and better, options, come into view that are more plausible, and have to be taken into account". Such a status of interpretive work-in-progress may perhaps be attributed to all qualitative analyses of human interaction.

argument is connected with the standpoint that it is supposed to justify or refute" (van Eemeren & Grootendorst 2004: 118). In the present research, the analytic overview is adopted. Some elements typical of the mediation interaction are included, together with the representation offered by the AMT.

5.3.1.2 *On the confidential nature of the mediation intervention: Some methodological cautions*

Human interactions, in general, can be classified in accordance with the dichotomy of having as opposite poles their openness versus their confidentiality. For instance, a corpus made of newspaper articles is, by its very nature, in the public domain; a more restricted segment of the public attends university lectures, which are less open to the general public but also not private meetings; but certain mediation interactions – together with many other kinds of activity types, such as doctor–patient consultation, financial consultation, and so on – are confidential[20] by nature, so that their development is never made public and it is difficult to access them even for reasons of scientific research.[21] In some cases, the final mediation agreements acquire a public status, but generally, the process of

20. Mediation, indeed, can be considered one of the contexts in which one can find instances of confidential interactions. See in this relation Kerbrat-Orecchioni and Traverso (2007: 1–2): "Les confidences sont attendues dans les conversations familières (où elles servent précisément à construire la 'familiarité'); elles sont fréquentes dans certains sites comme les petits commerces ou les salons de coiffure, et plus encore dans certains contextes institutionnels comme les consultations médicales ou les entretiens thérapeutiques". Mediation is certainly a context in which parties are required to disclose part of themselves in front of the mediator and – which sometimes can be more difficult – in front of each other. It can be imagined that, in such situation, the presence of some external observer such as the researcher could be disturbing; in all cases, then, the collection of data must be conducted carefully, taking into account the problem of confidentiality.

21. In an already mentioned project on conflict settlement conducted at the Institut für Deutsche Sprache in Mannheim, Germany (see Footnote 17 in Chapter 2), the collection of data constituted a very sensitive issue. As the researchers report (see in particular Nothdurft 1995b: 8–13), at the beginning, collecting data on real interactions of conflict settlement was so hard that it seemed impossible. Such difficulty was not coincidental, but rather it was due to the fact that the confidentiality of this type of interaction is an essential component of it. As Nothdurft (ibid., p. 10) puts it: "In Interviews, die wir mit Teilnehmern der Tarifschlichtung nach dem Metallarbeiter-Streik 1983 (Eisenmann, IG Metall, für die Arbeitnehmer- und Dr. Grenz, Daimler-Benz, für die Arbeitgeberseite) führen konnten, wurde von den Beteiligten deutlich gemacht, wie wichtig es für den Erfolg solcher Schlichtungen ist, daß sie unter Ausschluß der Öffentlichkeit stattfinden. Erst die 'Hermetik' der Situation und das Vertrauen der Beteiligten darauf, daß bestimmte Dinge nicht an der Öffentlichkeit kommen, ermögliche Verhandlungsprozesse und Verhandlungszüge, die für die Herstellung einer Übereinkunft von großer Wirklichkeit seien".

mediation, including the discussion and the arguments put forward, is not filed in the records (Herberger 1986: 231, quoted in Nothdurft 1995b: 11). As Princen (1992a: 4) has observed, this determines, first of all, a real problem for scientific research, because the confidential nature of mediation can hinder the analysis of this process. The problem, however, is not only a practical one. It also has theoretical implications, because including an external observer into a process that is confidential by nature may modify the very nature of the interaction. For this reason, the presence of researchers during the mediation interaction is limited; in some cases it is possible, in particular when parties agree to have someone to supervise the mediator; in other cases, observers are introduced to the parties but then watch the interaction from a separate room.[22] At other times, the interaction is video-recorded, so that no external observer is present. In general, it can be said that external intervention does not necessarily change the nature of the interaction, but it must be planned cautiously.

Indeed, the problem of confidentiality of data is reflected in the methodologies for collecting data employed in mediation studies; in fact, many of the analyses only rely on *indirect* sources for investigating conflict and mediation. In this regard, considering the transcriptions of entire mediation interactions turns out to constitute a delicate as well as valuable empirical basis, necessary for an argumentative view on mediation.

In general, two widely accepted methods can be identified in the literature on mediation: the *case-study approach* and the *media-based content analysis* approach.

In the case-study approach, evidence is taken from the analysis of a single mediatory event in which the author has participated. The empirical data are therefore constituted by the writer's direct observation, often corroborated by recording or notes and completed by subsequent interviews. The most famous case analysed in this way is former American President Carter's mediation between Israel and Palestine at Camp David (Princen 1992a; Matz 2006). But numerous other experiences of intervention are quoted; in particular, this method is very often employed for the study of ethnic conflicts (see for example Povey, Cattell & Michell 2005; Davidheiser 2006; Levine 2005). Particularly in the case of ethnic conflict, the kind of experience from which data are drawn in this approach is not necessarily a complete mediation process; often, these studies refer to a minor event within a complex and protracted conflict, such as a *peace workshop*, where

22. Isabella Buzzi, head of a mediation centre in Milan, confirms that she sometimes allows observers to be present during the interaction; in other cases, observers can watch the interaction through an internal audio-video system (I. Buzzi, interview with the author, June 10, 2008).

some representatives of the parties are invited to talk together and present their reasons to each other.

The case-study approach clearly presents some advantages, among which is the fact that it provides direct and fresh experience on real practices of conflict resolution through the evaluation of best practices. Sometimes, a methodology used in a particular case may have proven successful and thus can claim to be extendable to similar interventions. This is the case, for instance, of Levine's (2005) process phases or of Broome and Murray's (2002) account of the mediator's job in a peace workshop. However, this method clearly contains some weaknesses: for example, Malhotra and Liyanage (2005: 911) remark that the evaluation of the results of such cases is normally drawn too quickly and without a solid basis of evidence. More generally, the fact that the author is directly involved in the interaction and relies on the participants' memories of the discussions rather than on more objective recordings obviously creates problems over the reliability of the materials.

A well-established alternative to the case-study approach is the content analysis of media reports. Such a methodology clearly allows overcoming the problem of confidentiality by relying on public data published in the media. Of course, this is particularly suited for international conflicts and other public events that are of interest to the media, and cannot be applied to the study of interpersonal conflicts. In this relation, different corpora of data on conflictual events have been constructed, and, most interestingly, codebooks have been organized for the study of salient features of conflict and conflict resolution initiatives. The most-often employed software applications for the creation of data sets on international political behaviour are the Kansas Event Data System (KEDS, see http://web.ku.edu/keds/index.html) and the more recent Textual Analysis by Augmented Replacement Instructions (TABARI, see http://web.ku.edu/keds/software.dir/tabari.html), both developed by Philip Schrodt and his collaborators (Schrodt 2006). Such applications need to rely on previously elaborated conceptual frameworks in order to code data and identify relevant categories; in this relation, some well-known frameworks are WEIS (created in 1976), COPDAB (created in 1982), PANDA, then extended into the Integrated Data for Event Analysis (IDEA) in 1997 (see http://www.vranet.com/idea/), and CAMEO, created in the early 2000s (see Schrodt et al. 2005). The presence of different coding frameworks is a consequence of the fact that identifying semantically relevant categories is a process presupposing a specific framework of conflict and mediation,[23] which is

23. See the detailed illustration that the research group led by Jacob Bercovitch provides for the rationale of the codebook he proposed in 1999 as a result of the Mediation Project (Houston 1999).

not necessarily shared by all researchers, and which also depends on the reality of the conflict to be analysed.[24]

Very few studies rely on a type of data and methodological approach which is similar to the present one (see Glenn & Susskind 2010). However, it is noteworthy that the (actually not very numerous) studies that concentrate on the argumentative nature of mediation have managed to present results emerging from the analysis of empirical data consisting in transcriptions of mediation interactions (Section 2.2.1).

Moreover, as this manuscript was in the final stage of preparation for publication, a special issue of the *Negotiation Journal* came to my attention, devoted to the study of the negotiation communicative interaction through a close analysis of discourse and conversation (see in particular Glenn & Susskind 2010). This new stream of research is encouraging, as it witnesses the increasing awareness in conflict resolution research and practice of the importance of a close and focused approach to the study of the real communicative interaction in dispute resolution. In the authors' words: "We believe in the value of looking closely at actual talk, studying how the participants in a negotiation session come together and do what they do. Doing so helps us understand how negotiation works, how to listen better, how to take action more effectively, and how to teach and train about the art and practice of negotiation" (ibid., p. 118).

24. Schrodt et al. (2005: 2–3) justify their choice of creating a new coding framework (namely, CAMEO) on the basis of the fact that the preceding ones were either aimed at studying a too large body of politically different events (such as PANDA/IDEA) or, as in the case of WEIS and COPDAB, they were based on "implicit assumptions" (ibid.), which were inappropriate for the study of the kind of conflicts they were dealing with. For example, they claim that WEIS and COPDAB (both created during the Cold War period) are too state-centred and neglect all non-state actors who may play an important role in conflict and mediation (ibid., p. 2).

CHAPTER 6

Results of the argumentative analysis

Responses to the research questions and exceeding evidence

This chapter completes the present research on argumentation in the context of dispute mediation by illustrating the results of the argumenative analysis of some successful cases of mediation. These results will clarify how the argumentative discussion is realized in mediation and how mediators contribute to this important achievement, which in turn is a determinant condition for the resolution of the parties' conflict. As previously argued, the empirical analysis of a corpus of mediation cases represents a necessary complement to the previous conceptual blocks: namely the identification of the main mediation features (Chapters 2 and 3) and the outline of an ontology-oriented conceptual framework of mediation, including the argumentative dimension (Chapters 4 and 5). In fact, without an empirical observation, it would have been impossible to detect how the integration of argumentation in the context of dispute mediation happens in practice.

The structure of this chapter reflects the research design presented in Chapter 5 (Section 5.3). After describing the rationale for the selection of cases that will be analysed (6.1), I shall present the two steps of the empirical argumentative analysis respectively in Sections 6.2 and 6.3. The results of the first step, constituted by a detailed analysis of a particularly representative case, will orientate the second step, in which these results are tested against a larger evidence basis.

The results of the argumentative analysis are discussed in this chapter, while some general conclusions about this research and about argumentation in context will be drawn in Chapter 7.

6.1 Rationale for the selection of an empirical corpus

The objectives of this research, which is oriented towards understanding the role of argumentation in the mediation process, need to identify a corpus of mediation cases that can be considered successful, insofar as they represent the restoration of relationships endangered by conflict.

In order to fulfil this requirement and to answer the problem of confidentiality in a theoretically and practically satisfying manner by providing a reliable set of data for the argumentative analysis, the present research is based on a corpus of pre-recorded mediations whose distinctive feature is that of constituting an acknowledged basis for the training of mediators. In this sense, the empirical corpus, which will be described in detail below, is constituted by *exemplary interactions, from which mediators learn to mediate.*

The cases that constitute this corpus are mediated by two renowned mediators, namely Dr John Haynes and Dr Larry Fong, who are considered authorities in the field of mediation. John Haynes, in particular, "was a pioneer in the field of family mediation,[1] a respected author and practitioner, an international trainer, and the founding president of the Academy of Family Mediators", as presented by the Association for Conflict Resolution (www.acrnet.org). As a mediator in private practice, he mediated more than 5,000 interpersonal disputes. He is the author of various volumes on divorce and family mediation, among which is *The fundamentals of family mediation* (1994), as well as a number of publications on conflict resolution.

Since 2001 an award dedicated to his memory – the John Haynes Distinguished Mediator Award – has been given once a year to a distinguished practitioner in the field of mediation. But in order to understand Haynes's contribution not only to the practical development of the practice of mediation, but also to the constitution of the "spirit" of the practice itself, it must be considered that John Haynes's example has been and is much more than that of a successful and capable practitioner. He is considered a pioneer in the field of mediation also in the sense that he somehow interprets the "human attitude" that is considered the ideal of any mediator.[2] Some of his discourses, like the so-called "Vienna Speech" (Haynes 2004), are considered a moral will for mediators. In particular, Haynes

1. There is a particular episode in his biography that shows his role as a pioneer of the mediation movement. In 1978, Haynes was awarded a Ph.D from the State University of New York at Stony Brook, where he discussed the possibility of applying mediation to the field of family relationships and divorce. It is reported that, at his defence of thesis conference, one mentor commented "It's very impressive, but will anyone else ever be able to duplicate it?" (Haynes, Haynes & Fong 2004: 275). The flourishing of mediation activities in the subsequent period witnesses that Haynes was "prophetic".

2. See the description of possible candidates for the John Haynes Distinguished Mediator Award on www.acrnet.org: "In keeping with his legacy, the candidate should demonstrate innovation, creativity, and outstanding competence in published writings, training, and practice, maintain personal and professional integrity and respect for others, and embrace a sense of humour and humility about our standing as fallible beings".

always declared that the reason for his engagement in mediation and the basic principles guiding his practice stemmed from his personal experience as a Quaker (Haynes, Haynes & Fong 2004: xvi)[3] and, in particular, from a positive view of human beings' capability of recognizing what is good.[4]

Significantly, the first winner of such an award has been Larry Fong, Haynes's former colleague and friend, with whom he had reinterpreted and developed his practice in light of the so-called "Milan Mediation Model", a methodology derived from the systemic therapy method.[5] Nowadays, Larry Fong, who holds a Ph.D. in psychology (1987), works as a private mediator and arbitrator in Calgary, Alberta (see his personal homepage at http://www.fongmediate.com); moreover, as an international mediator and trainer, he has consulted in 13 different countries. He sat on the board of the Alberta Family Mediation Society (Past President), Family Mediation Canada (Past President) and the Academy of Family Mediators (Past President).

A second more important reason, yet connected with the first one, concerns the exemplarity of the corpus; in fact, the selected cases can be said to have a paradigmatic function in the training of new mediators. Indeed, these cases have been video-recorded and the mediator-training videos have been distributed worldwide. This means that these mediations are used as an example from which new mediators can learn. Significantly, Carl D. Schneider, head of a mediation service in Bethesda, Maryland,[6] which also serves as a training agency, uses the following words in describing the training tapes: "No one else has put together anything like these tapes. [...] *They have trained a generation of mediators*" (emphasis added). Indeed, John Haynes himself has trained over 20,000 professionals in more than twenty countries[7] and implemented mediation training programmes within

3. Quakers have a long experience in non-official and official mediation and peacemaking (Princen 1992a: 186–213; Bailey 1985).

4. In his own words: "There is 'that of God' in everyone. While it is difficult, when caught in the middle of the parties' maelstrom, to believe that either one has virtue, each person does carry an inner wisdom. The mediator seeks 'that of God' in each person, to be able to reconnect him or her to that inner wisdom" (Haynes & Haynes 1989: 3).

5. Larry Fong has been working with John Haynes for a long time, but his professional practice as a mediator also stems from his intercultural background as a second-generation-born Chinese Canadian (Haynes, Haynes & Fong 2004: xvii).

6. Schneider leads *Mediation Matters*, see http://www.mediationmatters.com.

7. The list of countries in which Haynes worked as a mediator trainer is impressive and covers large areas of the world: Argentina, Austria, Australia, Canada, Germany, Great Britain, Ireland, Italy, The Netherlands, New Zealand, Northern Ireland, Norway, Poland, Russia, Scotland, Singapore, South Africa, Spain, Switzerland, United States of America and Uruguay.

international court systems throughout the world. The training tapes are part of Haynes's and Fong's engagement in teaching.

Moreover, given the reasons expounded above, the sample of mediation sessions that constitute the corpus may be claimed to be representative of the practice as they are widely recognized as paradigmatic examples by professionals themselves. Indeed, these cases show how mediators *should behave*, and, in this sense, studying argumentation in these cases equals studying argumentation in a canonical case.[8] In this relation, all the cases can be considered as successful, because they somehow show the restoration and improvement of the parties' relationship.[9]

The selection criteria for the compilation of this corpus is in accordance with the purpose of mediations which are as canonical and "basic" as possible in the realm of ADR practices. First of all, only *interpersonal* conflicts have been selected (see Chapter 2 for the discussion on this topic), involving two or three parties as well as the mediator. Moreover, in the selected cases, all the parties had equal negotiating power, namely they were free to maintain their relationship or to break it. Therefore, mediations that involved children or teenagers in conflict with their parents have been excluded. As the success of a mediation case is defined in this investigation as the possible restoration of the parties' relationship in pre-conflictual terms, cases of divorce mediation have also been excluded.[10]

---

8. Of course, this does not deny or neglect the importance of personal and cultural factors in interpreting mediator work. It is clear that any cultural community where mediators are involved and, even more, any single mediator, are significantly free as to how to live the practice. However, the fact that the training tapes are used worldwide for the training of new mediators shows that these two mediators are assumed to be "models" for learning the fundamentals of the practice.

9. Although not in every case do parties arrive at a formal agreement, yet in all cases a single mediation session was sufficient to reach a solid basis of understanding between the parties that allowed future personal negotiations on their problem. In an interview with the author (September 7, 2005), one of the two mediators involved in these cases, Larry Fong, declared that in no case were they asked by the parties to meet again, which they consider a sign of the parties' improvement in their relationship. Further analysis about the long-term outcomes of the parties' agreement (for example, interviews after some years) is lacking from these cases, which is a limit of the present work. However, the fact that these cases have been selected as a basis for training and as paradigmatic of how to conduct mediation guarantees that, from the point of view of the pragmatic goals of mediation, they are considered successful.

10. In fact, divorce mediation, as highlighted in Chapter 2, presents a slight difference in relation to other applications, which however should not be underestimated. In fact, the

Considering the very specific and fine focus of the argumentative analysis, a selection of six cases (as a whole, about six hours of interaction) has been considered adequate, since it allows for the management of a reasonable amount of materials and, at the same time, for the selection of sufficiently diversified cases.

In fact, first of all, within the sphere of interpersonal conflicts, the choice has tended to include a quite significant variety of application domains (interaction fields) of mediation. In accordance with the goals of the present research, in fact, the analysis is oriented towards the investigation of the argumentative dynamics in relation to the pragmatic goals of mediation as an interaction scheme that can be applied to a variety of interaction fields (see Chapter 4). In this sense, selecting different interaction fields on the one hand eliminates the risk of generalizing field-bound argumentative dynamics. On the other hand, it offers the equally important possibility of verifying whether there is any contextual influence, due to the interaction scheme to which mediation is applied, on the development of the argumentative discussion, the choice of arguments, and so on.

The involved interaction fields, which turn out to be equally various and representative of major applications of mediation, are shown in Table 6.1:

Table 6.1. Domains of application of mediation emerging in the corpus

	Case 1	Case 2	Case 3	Case 4	Case 5	Case 6
Family m.						■
Business m.		■			■	■
Community m.	■			■	■	
– School m.			■			
– Organizational m.	■					

conflict between the parties is not resolved with the restoration of the preceding relationship, but with the instauration of a new different relationship. Since one of the main issues in mediation has been shown to be the relation between conflict, parties' relationship, and the very process of mediation, having equivalent cases from the point of view of the possibility of restoring the initial relationship seemed to me very important for the uniformity of the corpus. This does not mean that divorce mediation necessarily presents different argumentative dynamics. The selection has been made to concentrate on a corpus as uniform as possible from the point of view of the goal of the mediation in terms of restoring the parties' relationship. Other studies of mediation (see in particular van Eemeren et. al. 1993) have tackled cases of divorce mediation; the analysed excerpts refer more properly to child custody mediations. Child custody consultations are similar to the cases selected here, because they respond to the same requisite of aiming at restoring a relationship which is already present.

The most frequent interaction fields – family mediation, business mediation, and some very common forms of community mediation – are thus included in the sample. The combination of family mediation and business mediation presented in Case 6 is also very frequent (see Chapter 2). The variety of application domains is also essential for understanding the relation between the process of argumentation and all the dimensions of *context* that emerged in Chapter 4.

Beyond the interaction fields considered, the corpus is however quite diversified also for the geographical, temporal and cultural origin of the cases. Cases from 1 to 3 have been mediated by John Haynes, while cases from 4 to 6 have been mediated by Larry Fong. Cases 1 to 4 were recorded in the 1980s in Canada (Alberta),[11] while Cases 5 and 6 were recorded in the years just after 2000 in the Netherlands. These characteristics have been purposefully weighed up in order to avoid as much as possible too much dependence on the personal characteristics of a single mediator[12] or on cultural factors related to temporal and geographical variables.

6.1.1 Narratives of the cases making up the corpus

For illustrative purposes, the six cases constituting the corpus will be presented by means of a short narrative of the conflict as it emerges during the mediation discussion. Such description is only meant to introduce the cases, and does not have any analytical claim. The description is focused on the emerging traits of the conflict, while the moves towards its resolution will be explored below via the argumentative analysis. Names and identifying information on the disputants have been modified for reasons of privacy.

Case 1: Harassment complaint
Mediator: John Haynes

This case concerns a conflict between a university Professor, Philip F., and one of his students, Ann. Ann is a mature student and Professor F. is responsible for

11. The former set of tapes has been produced by Kent Taylor (Haynes & Haynes 1989: xv), while the latter has been produced by Sjoerd Homminga from Edumonde Mediation, the Netherlands.

12. Ideally, it would have been useful to include a higher number of mediators involved in the selected cases in order to avoid the risk of personalization. However, as proven above, no equivalent to these video-recorded interactions currently exists at the level of professional acknowledgement and recognized authority in the field of professional mediation. Moreover, the fact that Haynes and Fong are indicated as *models* to be followed by other mediators has allowed me to overcome the doubt that their practice is considered too individually bound. In a way, it can be said that even their personal characteristics and style are considered a best practice, not to be assumed necessarily, but certainly taken into account.

a special programme for students with particular commitments (especially family commitments) who cannot attend the university programme on a regular basis. F. is in charge of helping these students keep on track, by suggesting specific assignments to them, answering their questions, etc. Part of this special programme includes private meetings beyond the regular course timetable, where students can discuss their academic issues with him. Ann has filed a sexual harassment complaint against Philip concerning his behaviour during some one-to-one consultations. The mediator has been asked to intervene by the academic vice-president who is in charge of regulating these kind of issues in the university. Both parties have met separately with the vice-president who has advised them to try to mediate their issue before going through the normal academic procedure for handling such problems. Both of them have agreed to this suggestion. It clearly emerges from the parties' discussion that the case can be tackled through mediation because the complaint concerns events that do not constitute per se a clear case of sexual harassment, though it may be a case of ambiguous or unsuitable behaviour. More precisely, the problem concerns some invitations to lunch and dinner and the accusation by Ann that Philip once placed his hand on her knee, while Philip's position on this second aspect varies throughout the discussion. The lack of clarity between Philip and Ann is, indeed, the problem that has given rise to the conflict.

Case 2: Business conflict
Mediator: John Haynes

Two friends, who have been working together for a long time as collaborators and co-owners of a business making and selling bagels, find themselves involved in a conflict that encompasses both their working relationship, thereby endangering the very survival of their very successful business, and their interpersonal relationship, which is spiralling down together with their families' friendship. In particular, the workload is subdivided between David, who bakes bagels, and Robert, who is in charge of maintaining customer relationships and of distribution. Such a division of labour leads to a different organization of working time. David must wake up very early in the morning and work "in front of the oven", as he puts it; Robert, after making bagels' deliveries, usually contacts clients and talks to them, sometimes while playing rounds of golf. Both David and Robert are very happy with the other's working skills, and they are satisfied with the business, which has a very sound basis. David, however, is resentful of Robert's lifestyle, which he regards as much more comfortable than his own. He wants to mechanize the business, but Robert is afraid that the debt that would be involved in this operation would be too heavy a burden on their families. During the discussion, it emerges that this problem is also affecting the relationships between their respective wives and children, who have grown up together as friends; they too now find themselves entrenched in a spiral of complaints. As for the "style" of the conflict, while David puts forward a number of complaints and threatens to leave the business, Robert tends to deny the existence of the problem at all, while claiming that his work too is hard.

Case 3: Conflict at school
Mediator: John Haynes

The principal of a school invites the mediator to meet a third-grade teacher, Claire, and the mother (Lisa) of one of her pupils (Kevin), who is not present during the mediation. The conflict concerns the behaviour of Kevin, which Claire finds unacceptable, immature and unsuitable for a third grader. She has suggested putting Kevin down to the second grade at the beginning of the year. But Kevin, who is the son of an American diplomat, and has therefore travelled abroard quite a lot of his life, has already attended the second grade during the previous year in the United States. Therefore, his parents do not want to make him repeat the same academic year. Lisa claims that Claire is not engaging enough in helping Kevin, and, more, that she is against her son. For this reason, she directly addressed the principal of the school, who then suggested mediating the case. Claire, on the other hand, says that she has done everything possible to help Kevin, but that he is not mature enough for the third grade. One of the major problems seems to be that he never completes his work in class, nor is he willing to complete it at home. She says that Kevin leaves his work at school and that at home he is often left alone and that his parents do not check on what he should be doing. Lisa answers that she is not aware of the homework that Kevin has because she does not get it… and so the discussion goes on as a cumulus of reciprocal accusations from Lisa and Claire, who question each other's roles and skills.

Case 4: Adoption
Mediator: Larry Fong

The mediator is confronted with a problem about the adoption of a very young child (Rudolph is only five days old) by a couple who are unable to conceive a child of their own. The mediation session involves, as well as the mediator, the potential adopting parents (Harrison and Jenny) and the natural mother (Vivian). From a legal point of view, Vivian still has the possibility, some days from the moment she gave birth, either to definitively sign the papers concerning the adoption or to decide to keep the baby. During these days, however, it has emerged that the adopting couple and Vivian had a confused idea of the relationship that should be maintained between the baby and his natural mother. Vivian wishes to keep some contact with the baby; but what she means by "contact" (namely, some visitation rights) is far from what the new parents had understood by "contact". The new couple is afraid of somehow confusing Rudolph and would prefer Vivian not to see him at all. The agreement that the parties had signed before Rudolph was born was ambiguous on this aspect. The discussion is held in an emotionally surcharged environment. Vivian has given birth five days before the mediation session and is about to give her son to another family, while Harrison and Jenny have been waiting for a baby of their own for a long time and now risk losing Rudolph.

Case 5: Banker versus caterer
Mediator: Larry Fong

In this case, Tim, a banker, had entrusted Polly, the chef of a specialty items catering service, with the task of preparing a magnificent reception for the celebration of his bank's 100th anniversary. The conflict arises because, on the very day of the reception, a significant amount of the food appeared to be rotten. After this regrettable event, which has seriously damaged the bank's image, Tim refuses to refund Polly's small business, which has a huge debt with its suppliers. Polly claims that the food had been correctly delivered by her collaborators a couple of days before the reception, and that the damage was caused by the incorrect storage methods used by the bank's staff. The commitments between Polly and Tim had not been explicitly written in the usual form of a contract, but remained on an informal level, which makes the solution less evident. Besides, the parties' conflict is made more complex by the presence of some interpersonal ties between them: Polly and Tim had met in primary school and, since then, had remained friends, seeing one another from time to time. The present problem risks therefore not only any possible business deals in the future (and, may cause the failure of Polly's business), but also the parties' future friendship.

Case 6: Father and daughter in business
Mediator: Larry Fong

Therese has been hired as a director of one of the divisions of her father's (Paul) real estate business. While she was on holiday, Paul fired one of her employees, whom she claims to be one of the best workers in their business, without consulting her. Therese is very upset and does not accept the firing and, above all, the fact that her father makes important decisions without consulting her; Paul is determined to affirm his working position as founder and "boss" of the business, and the subordinate role of Therese as one of the directors. The situation is complicated by the fact that, as it emerges after about 20 minutes of discussion, the fired employee, James, was held by Paul to be Therese's boyfriend (although she never confirms this interpretation). The problem gradually turns out to involve a more general lack of communication (and listening) between father and daughter, which risks endangering their personal relationship and Therese's future within her father's business.

6.1.2 Conventional procedures for the transcription of oral data

The texts to be analysed, being mediation sessions, are typically *oral* texts. This kind of data needs some preparatory work in order to make it suitable for analysis; in particular, the texts have to be transcribed in such a way that allows maintaining the oral traits as much as possible.[13] For this task, the present research has relied on a well-developed methodological framework of conversation analysis (Hopper, Koch & Mandelbaum 1986; van Rees 1992; Traverso 1999; see also Glenn & Susskind 2010).[14] Within this framework, the studies in argumentation that have analysed mediation sessions (see Section 2.2.1) can be seen to have set up a standard of transcription (as concerns the relevant aspects to be indicated in the notation), which has been taken into account and mirrored in this research.[15]

As for the notation system, the transcription is based on Traverso (1999). The conventions are reported in the following table:

13. In this relation, see Traverso (1999: 23): "La transcription est une preparation indispensable du corpus, à travers laquelle on cherche à conserver à l'écrit le maximum des traits de l'oral".

14. Concerning the value of conversational analysis as a basis for the description of argumentation in conversations see van Rees (1992), in particular pp. 155–156.

15. The most salient aspect is that turns are numbered rather than lines. Such a notation happens to be much more efficient for the purposes of an argumentative analysis. In this sense, it is clear that "Conversational analysts use a variety of transcription systems for such purposes, the choice of system depending on the purpose which the transcription is intended to serve: there is no such thing as a single 'right' transcription system. Different systems focus on different aspects of an utterance, and which aspects are relevant depend on where the investigator's interests lie" (van Rees 1992: 157).

Sign	*Explanation*
[	Interruption and overlapping: (indicates the point at which overlap by another speaker starts)
=	Turns following one another with no interruption
wh-	Interruption of a word
Eh:	Lengthening of preceding vowel is indicated by colons
A::nd	Longer lengthening of preceding vowel
Hhhh	Aspiration
(.)	Pause of one second or less
(3)	Pause of more than one second (the duration in seconds is indicated)
↑	Rising intonation (questions)
/	Slightly rising intonation (suspension)
↓	Falling intonation (exclamations)
YOU SHOULD	Majuscules indicate emphasis
^{0}I agree^{0}	Text comprised between the signs ^{00} is pronounced with a very low volume
(SHOUTING)… +	Particular vocal characteristics are indicated in small caps inter brackets at the beginning of the excerpt. Their end is indicated by the sign +
(*looking at T*)	Essential non-verbal elements and actions are indicated in italic inter brackets
[…]	Omitted from transcription
( )	Inaudible/incomprehensible passage

Each talking turn is numbered.[16] Numeration is relative to each case (each case starts from turn n. 1); the excerpts reported in this research keep the original numeration of the whole transcriptions.

The parties' names have been changed for reasons of privacy. In the transcription, they have been indicated with their full names; while the speaker of each turn is indicated by a letter. M always indicates the mediator; the parties are indicated with the initial of their first name.[17] In the analysis, the mediator is always indicated using the masculine markers he/his. This choice is simply due to the fact that both mediators are male.

16. The concept of *turn*, as controversial as it may be from a theoretical point of view (see van Rees 1992: 22), is however the basis of the transcription system, and there is some consensus about the identification of turns (ibid., p. 28).

17. Here, the use of M for indicating the mediator seemed to be the most pertinent category. In fact, characterizing the mediator from the point of view of his socio-professional role is adequate in terms of the focus of the present work on the interaction scheme of mediation. On the other hand, the parties' professional roles, as they enter mediation, become less determinant than their equal status as human beings and potential co-arguers. Therefore, the initials of their (changed) proper names have been selected. For a discussion of the theoretical implications of the identification of the speakers in transcriptions practices see Mondada (2002).

The interaction language is English in all the cases. In principle, nonverbal aspects have not been reported in the transcription, since the focus of the present research mainly concerns the verbal development of the argumentative discourse in mediation. However, the availability of video-recordings has been exploited for a careful interpretation of verbal aspects (as suggested by Traverso 1999: 22–23).[18] Moreover, when some specific aspect of nonverbal communication (a gesture, a facial expression, and so on) is fundamental for the understanding of the verbal text, it is noted conforming to the transcription system; when a gesture (like nodding one's head) counts as a communicative move (the answer to a question, for instance) that is essential to the development of the discussion, it is considered an autonomous turn.

6.2 First step: A way out of conflict: The value of argumentation in mediation

Following the double-step research design illustrated in Chapter 5 (Section 5.3), I shall now present and discuss the results of the empirical analysis of mediation cases. The results of the first step of the analysis are presented in this Section (6.2). The second step (6.3) will build on the first; in fact, the emerged specific features of argumentation in dispute mediation will be confirmed on a larger evidence basis.

6.2.1 Phenomenological analysis of communicative moves in the core process of mediation

First, in order to understand the correspondences and synergies between the mediation structure and the argumentative salient phases, it is necessary to have a clear phenomenological representation of the phases of the mediation process, in accordance with the framework outlined in Chapters 4 and 5. I shall consider this correspondence in Case 1, which has been selected as an empirical basis for the first step of the analysis. I shall match the specific communicative moves performed by the mediator and the parties with the stages of the core process of mediation. For this purpose, it is therefore necessary to represent the *plot* of the case, in the sense proposed by Caffi (2007): namely, as a type of summary presenting the

18. The selection of only verbal aspects in the transcription has been decided in conformity with the goals of the present work. Indeed, the various possible notations of nonverbal communication on the basis of video-recorded materials are a current issue in linguistic research (see in particular De Stefani 2007: 4; Mondada 2006).

actual content of the case in the same order as it appears in the real interaction. In other words, possible repetitions of moves, shifts from one to the next phase of mediation (see Chapter 4), and returns back to the preceding phase, are all faithfully reported.[19] Such a representation makes it possible to grasp the actual development of the discussion between the mediator and the parties throughout time and to systematically elicit to which phase of the mediation process each set of communicative moves corresponds.

The representation proposed here is inspired, though largely adapted in accordance with the purposes of the present research, by the *multidimensional representation* presented in Caffi (2007: 177–185) and by the representation of *salient phases* of the interaction elaborated in Giugliano (2007).[20] The use of a synoptic table helps in visualizing the chronological development of the communicative interaction in relation to the essential aspects considered, and allows for various dimensions to be taken into consideration simultaneously.

The first column shows the phases of the core mediation process corresponding to the framework outlined in Chapter 4; in column 2, each communicative move is associated to the mediation phase to which it pertains. As previously said, the phases of the mediation process are not fulfilled in a strictly chronological order (Kovach 2005); also in the case considered here (see Table 6.2), the first phases are interrupted and restarted various times.

The second column reports the talking turns, regrouped in significant communicative moves.[21] Columns 3, 4 and 5 are respectively devoted to the first party

---

19. Caffi (2007: 163) refers to the distinction proposed by Russian formalists between *fabula* and *plot*. Fabula is defined as "the set of narrative motifs as rearranged in their logical, causal and chronological order", while plot "is the set of motifs as the appear in the story, i.e. the actual content".

20. Caffi (2007) applies her multidimensional representation to the analysis of doctor–patient interactions, while Giugliano (2007) has elaborated a form of representation allowing her to indicate the salient phases of school-teaching classes. In her work, Giuliano has tackled a type of communicative interaction (namely, a school class) to which more than two participants collaborate. For analysing this type of interaction, she proposes to specifically mention in the representation of the interaction which interlocutors are directly involved in each communicative move. I have followed this proposal, since it allows identifying more or less direct levels of relevance of each communicative move to the corresponding levels of addressees.

21. The representation proposed here, being specifically oriented towards the understanding of the communicative process that leads to the resolution of the conflict is relatively flexible. For example, it does not necessarily cover any single communicative move, but it focuses on those passages that are seen to be more relevant in relation to the goal of the interaction scheme of mediation, namely in relation to the resolution of the conflict.

(Ann), the mediator and the second party (Philip). In terms of the ontology-oriented framework presented in Chapter 4, these three interagents represent the main roles in the mediation process in Case 1. The mediator's and parties' salient communicative interventions are represented in the respective columns[22] in terms of a first approximation of the communicative actions that they are performing.[23]

The table proposed here also allows consideration of some other aspects relevant from the argumentative analysis that will follow. The initiator of each communicative move – in rough terms, this is the interlocutor who takes the responsibility for raising a new issue in the discussion – is indicated in bold. Interestingly, a prominent role of the mediator in leading the discussion in terms of the issues considered emerges in a quite clear fashion, especially at the beginning of the interaction.

Moreover, for each of the communicative actions considered, the participants to the communicative interaction are specified. In fact, it is evident that some communicative moves are purposefully directed only towards one of the two potential interlocutors who participate in the mediation session: for example, the mediator may address a question to one of the two parties; or a party may refuse to directly address the counterpart and decide to speak to the mediator only; and so on. Nonetheless, at some level the mediation discussion always involves all the interlocutors, as everyone is present and potentially listening to what is said. Some implications of what is said by one party to the mediator must surely be relevant to the other party too. In this sense, different levels of speakers and addressees can be envisaged, corresponding to the degree of immediacy of the interlocutors' involvement. For example, whoever makes a concession when speaking to the mediator, indirectly presents a proposal (an offer) to the counterpart, and even more indirectly asks for a counter-offer. In Table 6.2, the immediately involved interlocutors are indicated by the shaded boxes. Considering who is involved at each stage turns out to be quite significant. As it visually emerges from the representation, in fact, the beginning the mediation discussion is realized as a sequence of one-to-one dialogues between the mediator and one of the parties. As the discussion proceeds, the parties are able both to be involved in the trilogue together and even

22. With the exception of the discussion on options boundaries, to which all parties are equally participating.

23. In relation to the theoretical instruments for textual analysis proposed in Congruity theory (see Chapter 5), it could be said that columns 3–5 report a first and necessarily quite approximate analysis of the connective predicates dominating the parties' communicative actions.

to speak to each other without the mediator's help. This indicates the unblocking of the communicative situation occurring with the development of the case. Indirectly, this could be interpreted as a signal of the fact that a change in the parties' attitude (from disputants to co-arguers) has occurred, which raises the original questions of the present investigation. However, we still need to verify how this change is concretely made possible.

Table 6.2. Representation of the plot of Case 1

Phase	Turn	A	M	P
Phase 1	1–3		**Summarizes A's position (harassment complaint against P) and introduces mediation**	
	4	Confirms		
	5		**Asks for P's analysis**	
	6–13			Refuses to consider A's accusation
	14		**Asks for A's story**	
	15–67	Tells her story		
	68–72		**Insists on knowing P's story**	(Initially: accusations against A)
	73–86			Tells his story
	87–89		**Asks A about P's behaviour with other students**	
	90	Other students are treated differently; they have confirmed this		
	95–123		**States the issue: to identify boundaries that allow maintaining A's and P's academic relationship and persuades the parties to remain on this issue**	
Phase 2	192–253	Discussion on boundaries: – No physical contact – Type of relationship (only academic, no friendship) – Timing of A's and P's meetings – Confidentiality of the agreement		

(*Continued*)

Table 6.2. Representation of the plot of Case 1 (Continued)

Phase	Turn	A	M	P
Phase 1	254–256		**Asks P to recognize the possibility for A to draw her boundaries**	
	257			Recognizes
	258		**Asks P to recognize that A may have been disturbed by him having inadvertently crossed her boundaries**	
	259–263			Recognizes
	264–268		**(to P): Asks P to apologize for having crossed A's boundaries**	
	269			Apologizes
	270		**Asks P to directly address himself to A**	
	271			Apologizes
	272		**Asks for A's reaction after P's apologies**	
	273–277	Says that what P said has an enormous importance to her.		
Phase 2	278–280		**Goes back to discussing the agreement**	
Phase 1	281–287			**Raises doubts on A's good faith and trustworthiness and thus jeopardizes the agreement**
	288		**Asks A to repeat what she has stated at 22–226**	
	292	Confirms her willingness to continue the academic relationship with P. Expresses her disappointment because of P's lack of trust ("wild allegations")		

(*Continued*)

Table 6.2. (Continued)

Phase	Turn	A	M	P
	293–295			Expresses the main reason of his worries: some of the things that A said are not true because he does not remember them
	296	Counter-argues ("that doesn't make me a liar that you don't remember")		
	297–300		**Helps P recognize that A has admitted he crossed her boundaries *inadvertently***	
	301–305			**Restates his good faith**
	306		**Asks him to apologize to A**	
	307			Apologizes
Phase 2	308		**Turns back to the boundaries discussion and summarizes it**	
	309–331	Discussion on boundaries: – Timing of A's and P's meetings – Presence of some other person		
	332–337			**Raises a further sub-issue about A's complaints about how P looked at her**
	338–340	Commits herself not to re-open the conflict; affirms her willingness to close the problem		
	341			Expresses doubts on the basis of what A said at the beginning
	342		Asks P to revise his judgement now	

(*Continued*)

Table 6.2. Representation of the plot of Case 1 (Continued)

Phase	Turn	A	M	P
	343–351			Admits that his judgement is different now and expresses trust in A and esteem as a student; accepts the issue of boundaries.
Phase 3	352–366		**Leads a brief discussion on the implementation of the agreement reached.**	

The interaction clearly starts with what corresponds to the first phase of the mediation core process, namely with the *mediator's introduction* (turns 1–3) and by subsequent *opening remarks by the parties*, *information gathering* and *issues and interests identification* (see Chapter 4); the first phase is concluded at turn 123.

It is quite clear that the passage to the second phase (*option generation*, *reality testing* and *bargaining and negotiation*) can be performed once the issue that the parties have to discuss has been identified; in this specific case, the discussion can move to the problem of the *boundaries* of Ann and Philip's future relationship (see turn 124 and ff.). More specifically, the discussion on boundaries proceeds between the generation of sub-options, corresponding to the specific elements defining the boundaries, and the testing of their appropriateness.

However, this phase is interrupted, and phase 1 restarts, as it emerges that the identification of issues and interests is not completed. Indeed, from turn 254 to turn 277 and, again, from turn 280 to turn 307, the mediator has to lead parties back to discuss the origin of the conflict, until they commonly agree that it has been originated by a misunderstanding rather than by an evil intention.

Then phase 2 begins again at 308, adding new elements to the definition of boundaries. Eventually, the interaction is concluded with some space devoted to phase 3 (*agreement and closure*). As clearly emerges from Table 6.2, this final phase does not take too much time, probably because the implementation of the agreement is relatively simple. In fact, it only involves the two parties' interactions without directly including other persons. Moreover, nobody must be made aware of the terms of the agreement except for the academic vice-president, whom the mediator offers to inform himself.

This overview of the plot of Case 1 constitutes a necessary and valid basis for the argumentative analysis, which will be performed in the sections that follow. In fact, it offers an overview of how the pragmatic structure of mediation detailed in the framework presented in Chapter 4 is actually implemented in the case in question. However, the analysis, until this moment, remains at a phenomenological level: we see that some changes happen in the parties' style and contents of the discussion, but we do not understand why and how. The argumentative analysis that I shall henceforth follow aims at eliciting the reasons for these changes.

6.2.2 Analytical reconstruction of argumentation: A macro-text of argumentative discussions

The first significant aspects that come to light through the analytical reconstruction concern the interpretation of the mediation interaction in light of the model of a critical discussion. What first emerges is the fact that the development of the discussion does not imply a linear succession of the stages of a critical discussion nor a single dispute, but rather it involves different argumentative discussions. The kind of dispute involved, thus, is certainly *multiple* in a quantitative sense, but it is also multiple in a qualitative sense, as will be shown.

In this relation, the image of a *macro-text* can be of help for understanding the kind of complex situation that the analyst is faced with when approaching the resolution of a dispute through mediation.

Different critical discussions appear to be interrelated. They can be distinguished as for (a) the individuals playing the roles of protagonist and antagonist (and of third neutral) and (b) the issues and relative standpoints involved. Given the relations occurring between the different issues involved, such a macro-text can, however, also be interpreted not as a series of disputes, but as a single dispute, *multiple in a qualitative sense* (see the definition proposed by van Eemeren, Houtlosser and Snoeck-Henkemans 2007, reported in Chapter 5). In fact, the various critical discussions that, taken as a whole, give rise to the multiple dispute do not concern different and extraneous issues that are, so to say, "listed" one after the other (which would be a very extreme case of a dispute multiple in a *quantitative* sense). Rather, they show to be interrelated. Just to mention the most salient aspects of this qualitatively multiple dispute, let us consider that parties discuss how to resolve their dispute and, by so doing, they indirectly resolve the issue of whether finding a mediated solution to their conflict is worthwhile. Or, again, parties may discuss the appropriateness of a certain communication style, or the appropriateness of a certain issue for their mediation discussion; these disputes would constitute digressions on meta-issues that favour the development of the main discussion over the resolution of the conflict. But the dynamics through which the macro-text of discussions giving rise to a qualitatively multiple dispute is constructed will appear more clearly in an analytical reconstruction of the interaction, which will be presented in the sections that follow.

6.2.2.1 *Setting up an argumentative space*

As van Eemeren et al. (1993: 180) have pointed out, there is a critical standard in the mediation practice that, though often unsaid, represents a presupposed objective. As conflicting parties are far removed from this reasonable standard when they enter the process – otherwise they could have engaged in a discussion autonomously – it is the mediator's task to set up the premises for a sound critical discussion, which at the same time can possibly be resolutive (van Eemeren 2010). In Case 1, the mediator starts by asking parties to formulate their disagreement. Not surprisingly, their conflict emerges not as a clear difference of opinion, but as a contraposition of reciprocally hostile positions; and this happens despite the fact that a standpoint on Ann's side had previously been made explicit, at least in part, by her filing a sexual harassment complaint against Philip. But it is apparent that Philip's answer to the mediator's question is transformed into a further occasion for quarrelling:

	P	Well I really don't know what the basis of the whole thing is a:: (.) bunch of UNFOUNDED nonsense ah:: (.) I really (.) [don't know why we are here
7	A	[Well that's a bit strange =
8	P	= putting me in just an AWFUL situation some WILD allegations being made =
9	A	= Ya
10	P	A:nd (.) [and so ( ) past coming and:: (.) I really don't know what
11	A	[So I'm just (.) one of those CRAZY women/(.) you're a victim of (.) some loony single mom
12	M	Ann (.) tell me (.) what's the basis for the allegation =
13	P	= Well paranoia ( ) a lot of [paranoia

So a standpoint had been advanced by Ann's harassment complaint. Although Philip reacts to this standpoint, his reaction cannot be identified as participation in an argumentative discussion. Indeed, the standpoints advanced do not to refer to a single issue: while one party (Ann) presents a standpoint, the other one (Philip) challenges the very legitimacy of that standpoint. Philip's strategy consists in presenting his adversary as a paranoid individual; such a strategy does not merely aim at casting doubt on her standpoint but at excluding her from a reasonable discussion. This move could be considered as a fallacious attempt to violate the *freedom rule* of a critical discussion, by preventing one of the participants from expressing her standpoint, and is therefore substantially inadmissible. From a juridical point of view, even if Philip managed to demonstrate that Ann is paranoid, this would not automatically invalidate her accusation – in fact, she could be both paranoid and the victim of some form of harassment.[24]

Ann, in turn, answers by ironically designating Philip as a *victim*. This move could be read as implying that he is, indeed, a torturer. From the analytical point of view, Ann's intervention at turn 11 is a repetition and accentuation of her standpoint. However, this does not add any relevant element to the argumentative discussion.

The emotionally surcharged tone of the discussion is mirrored in the frequent interruptions, in the quick concatenation and overlapping of talking turns as well as in the emphasis given to various emotionally marked words (turns 6, 8 and 11 in particular).

As clearly emerges from this passage, the mere contraposition of different (or even opposed) standpoints is not sufficient to make an argumentative discussion. A similarity may come to mind with certain political (ideological) discourses, whereby politicians limit themselves to accusing their adversaries without assuming the burden of proving their positions and without listening to the other party's reasons. Sometimes, the exact logical relation between the standpoints – which is not necessarily that of contraposition – is not even investigated. It is clear that this sort of political discourse does not constitute a good service to the community of electors. In a similar vein, parties in conflict who simply ignore accusations do not serve their own interests well, because they lose the opportunity to verify the existence of any agreement. In mediation, it is up to the mediator to take care of the critical standards of reasonableness.[25] It might be said that the mediator has to create an "argumentative space" for the parties' discussion. In Case 1, it is clear

---

24. This would be accepted in most Western juridical systems. I am indebted to C. Fiorini and F. Centonze for their expert consultation on this issue.

25. See van Eemeren et al. (1993: 180): "The mediator's role, as portrayed in the literature, is to create conditions for rational discussion between the disputants, and it is the set of conditions that are desired that compose the underlying normative theory. Among those most frequently discussed in the literature are bilateral commitment to resolution of dispute through discussion, voluntary participation by both parties, unrestricted opportunity to raise concerns and make suggestions, approximate power equality between disputants, and consensus decision. *It is not assumed that these conditions hold prior to mediation; as mentioned before, it is the mediator's job to try to create these conditions*" (emphasis added). This operation is performed by the mediator through all the stages of the critical discussion. The initial settings of the confrontation and opening stages, however, emerge as particularly important

from the mediator's questions and remarks that he is trying to guide the parties away from a verbal war to a situation that could be interpreted as the confrontation stage of a critical discussion. By means of this guidance, he lays the basis for an argumentative discussion between the parties; in other words, he opens an otherwise blocked argumentative space.

Interestingly, Philip's attempt to depict Ann as a paranoid individual is not even considered by the mediator. Probably, this could be interpreted as a contextual constraint to argumentation: if for the academic vice-president of the university the problem was sufficiently important to send them to mediation, the mediator's strategic manoeuvring can reasonably exclude Philip's standpoint about Ann's claimed insanity from the discussion. Instead, the mediator pushes the parties' to restate their respective positions *on the issue that has given rise to conflict*. The importance of such precision should not be underestimated: the mediator does not want to hear any reciprocal accusations between Philip and Ann, but he wants them to formulate clear positions on the problem that has led them to mediation. Here, the constitution of the confrontation stage proceeds at the same time as the narration of the story of the conflict, which could certainly be interpreted as part of the *opening stage* of a critical discussion. In fact, if, on the one hand, it is necessary to retell the narrative of the dispute in order to identify the issue to which the standpoints refer, on the other hand, such a problematic issue can only emerge against the backdrop of the common ground of the parties' previous institutional and interpersonal relationship, the events and experiences they have shared, and so on.

But let us look at how the mediator actually conducts the discussion. First, he establishes the talking turns and does not allow interruptions by the other party. Between turns 12 and 14, for instance, the mediator, seeing that Philip does not answer his question about the substance of the problem (see turns 6–13 above), changes the talking order by addressing himself to Ann first:

12 M Ann (.) tell me (.) what's the basis for the allegation =
13 P = Well paranoia ( ) a lot of [paranoia
14 M [Well (.) Philip (.) hold it just one second (.) let's not describe what each other does (.) let's try to get eh into the facts Ann tell me what's what's happening↓

At turns 30–33, the parties seem to go back to reciprocal accusations; the mediator interrupts them and invites Ann to stick to the issue:

since they constitute the necessary premises for the exchange of arguments that occurs in the argumentation stage.

30	P	[III designed this program for [these people
31	A	[Oh (.) so that should give you all kinds of liberties
32	M	Okay (.) And then you (.) noticed (.) when you first joined the program (.) that (.) Philip was very helpful to [you as (.) as an academic/

Finally, only at turn 68, does he decide to move back to Philip:

68	M	O:kay (.) all right (.) I think I have a good understanding of that (.) °then Ann° (.) thank you (.) Philip/(.) what is your sense of all this =

Second, he insists on the question he has asked and does not allow parties to answer differently. The clearest example of this is the excerpt following turn (68), where the mediator insists until Philip starts answering his question at (73):

68	M	O:kay (.) all right (.) I think I have a good understanding of that (.) °then Ann° (.) thank you (.) Philip/(.) what is your sense of all this =
69	P	= Well (.) my sense is is she is ABSOLUTELY paranoid I mean we have to understand [that this ( )
70	M	[Hold (.) excuse me but don't describe what you think she thinks (.) because that is not helpful to me (.) what WOULD be helpful to me to understand would be (.) ho:w you've seen the relationship develop over the six months =
71	P	= Well she's just misinterpreting everything that takes place (.) that's that's =
72	M	= Okay (.) that's something that [Ann did (.) but how do you see (.) this relationship
73	P	[I:: (.) I helped to establish this particular program (.) in the:: Department of the Environment for (.) for the students like Ann who (.) are somewhat disadvantaged they have got children [a:nd

6.2.2.2 *"Focus on interests, not positions": The identification of a problematic issue*

It emerges clearly that the confrontation stage prepared by the mediator is precisely and firmly guided towards a specific issue, namely the origin of the conflict. Such a procedure may well be explained as a contextual constraint: mediation is aimed at resolving a conflict by definition; as a consequence, identifying which conflict is to be solved turns out to be necessary. Not coincidentally, as already pointed out in Chapter 4, the analysis of the conflict is an essential tool in mediation and a constitutive part of the first phase of this process.

In this relation, the principle "Focus on interests not positions" (Fisher, Ury & Patton 1991: 3ff.) is to be interpreted, from the argumentative point of view, as an invitation not to accept any contraposition or accusation, but to root out the parties' real concerns. These concerns are bound to the problem that began the conflict, which it is thus important to recall. In light of the analysis of conflict proposed in Chapter 4 (see in particular Figure 4.3), it emerges that what the mediator is doing is to search for the initial difference of opinion that has led the parties to disagree and which is the origin of the conflict (C2). He repeatedly refuses to be entrenched in the current status of the conflict escalation – in terms of a conflict analysis, he does not want to be influenced by the current dynamics of the interpersonal escalated conflict (C1). Reconsidering the conflict mapping guide proposed in Figure 4.3, it can be said that the mediator encourages the parties to walk the inverse path of the dynamics of conflict escalation, as outlined in the mediation process in phase 1 of the framework (see Chapter 4).

Moreover, identifying C2, which emerges as an incompatibility in the background of the parties' relationship, necessarily implies the investigation of the parties' relationship itself, i.e. of the *context* of the dispute (see Chapter 4). The mediator's guidance towards C2 has therefore the double function of confrontation and an opening stage, as has been highlighted in the previous section.

Concerning Case 1, some remarks about the nature of C2 are now useful in order to understand the process of mediation more specifically. The diagram for the analysis of the issue proposed in Rigotti and Greco Morasso (2006b)[26] can be of use in this sense (see Figure 6.1). This diagram highlights the boundary between what is already ascertained in a discussion (and could therefore be relevant for the opening stage) and what properly constitutes the problematic aspect about which parties have to argue. In Philip and Ann's case, as results from Figure 6.1 show, the parties have quite different representations of what should be proven by means of argumentation:

26. The diagram has to be read consecutively from left to right. In fact, the order of the different levels of the semantic-pragmatic structure of the issue is not accidental: it represents the implications existing between the various levels. For example, it does not make any sense to discuss the reasonableness of a necessary or impossible state of affairs, but it is possible to question its damage potential or its utility (pleasantness, risks, etc.), or, with regard to an action in the past, it is possible to discuss whether it has actually happened (true, false, probable, improbable). On the other hand, if a future action is questioned, it does not make sense to discuss its truth or falsity. These implications refer to different kinds of modality (see Rocci 2005). See also Greco Morasso (2006b) for an example of the use of this grid to analyse a dispute.

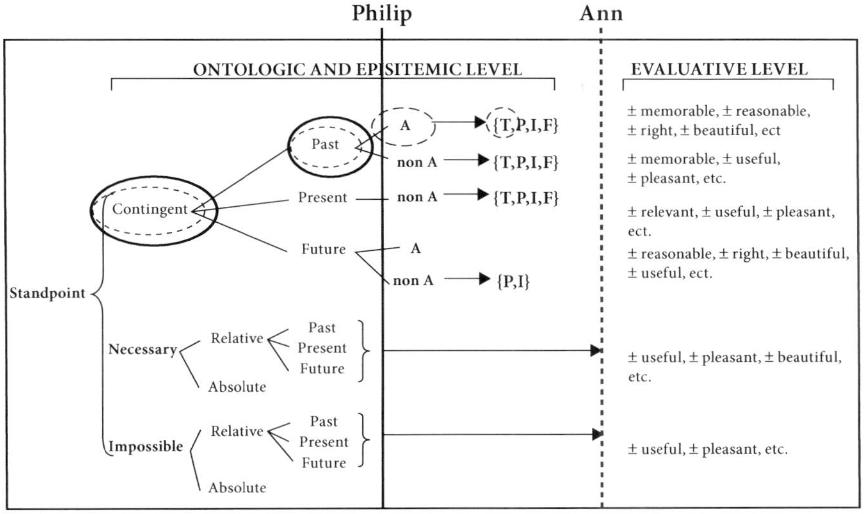

Figure 6.1. Analysis of the issue (adapted from Rigotti and Greco Morasso 2006b)

Here, C2 emerges as a fact or, better, as a series of facts (some invitations to lunch and dinner and touching Ann's knee, actually first denied but then implicitly admitted by Philip) that happened in the past. The parties, however, interpret the issue differently: for Ann, the truth of the fact in the past is not questionable; the nature of what happened and, therefore, of Philip's intentionality, is also taken for granted. The point at issue for her is at the evaluative level, and it concerns the moral quality of Philip's actions. For Philip, however, the issue is rather on an ontological level: he says he does not remember whether the events mentioned by Ann took place but, if they did, they are not to be considered as actions but rather as consequences of unintentional behaviour. Then Philip reaffirms his standpoint that his behaviour is the one he usually adopts with students, and that it is morally acceptable. Concerning the specific episode of touching Ann's knee, at first he denies having done it, but then says he does not remember doing it, and then that he comes from a more expressive cultural background where touching is allowed (thus he moves to an evaluative level, admitting that the controversial episode could have taken place).

If we consider both parties to be sincere, which the mediator appears to do as a working hypothesis, the situation can be described as follows:

a. Ann was offended by the set of actions φ performed by Philip
b. This presupposes that Ann, being in good faith, interprets φ as an action and a morally bad one
c. Philip was offended by the fact that Ann has interpreted φ as morally bad

d. This presupposes that Philip has performed the set of actions φ in good faith without thinking that Ann would have been offended
e. φ has different meanings for Philip and Ann[27]

6.2.2.3 *Selecting issues as a form of strategic manoeuvring with topical potential*

One might expect that, once the source of the conflict (the original difference of opinion C2) has been identified, the argumentative discussion will follow this path and focus on the evaluation of the parties' standpoints on this issue. On the contrary, here, an unexpected as well as crucial passage is made by the mediator, which constitutes one of the aspects that more essentially characterize the paradoxical work of a discreet arguer who, working "behind the scenes", allows the argumentative discussion to take place. The discussion on C2 has already proven not to be very productive, since it has degenerated into a conflict; therefore, it is not restarted and developed but frozen, and the mediator leads the parties away from a discussion of the original disagreement C2, but on to other issues.

Unlike therapy and adjudication, mediation is generally acknowledged to be focused on the *future* rather than on the past (see the elaboration by Bannink 2008). Mediators who practise this mean that the parties should not dwell on the conscious or unconscious deep reasons for the actions that have brought them into conflict (as parties may be invited to do in some forms of therapy); and that they need to avoid insisting on the parties' respective responsibilities (as would happen in a court). Let us take the example of a civil adjudication: a judge is expected to decide on issues such as whether a certain fact has taken place, whether this fact is a criminal offence, whether the defendant is responsible for it, and the kind of punishment a guilty defendant deserves. Mediation is a different interaction scheme that, by definition, is oriented towards a resolution of the conflict. In fact, as van Eemeren and Houtlosser (2005: 78) put it, "although theoretically the parties may be just as free to draw their own conclusions as in ordinary argumentative discourse, *in mediation they are expected to come to an arrangement*" (emphasis added). In mediation, it is expected that a solution will emerge, and that this solution, being found by the parties themselves, can *preserve or restore their relationship* as much as possible. Therefore, the kind of issues that parties can discuss in mediation is of the following nature: what can we do in order to maintain our relationship? Are solutions p, q, z… viable ones? And so on.

27. In this situation, (e) must be assumed because, otherwise, Ann's and Philip's reactions would be incomprehensible.

As said, issues like p, q, z… are commonly defined *options* for conflict resolution (Kovach 2005; see Chapter 4). *Option generation* is one of the stages of a canonical mediation script (see the framework outlined in Chapter 4). Options are in a relation of implication with the original issue C2, insofar as they constitute (parts of) possible solutions to it.[28] Therefore, it is essential for the mediator to investigate C2 first, otherwise he could not identify, together with the parties, appropriate issues to discuss. Without reaching C2, in fact, the real interests of the parties cannot emerge.

Later on, it is also meaningful for the mediator to move the discussion on to options. Let us consider the very moment in which such a movement from the past to the future – or, in argumentative terms, from issue C2 to the corresponding option (issue$_{opt}$) – happens by means of the dialogue between the mediator and Ann in particular:

45 A [Ya (.) I mean asking me things you know how was it going and are you able to manage (.) and you know it must be so burdensome having (.) children to look afte:r and (.) it's just I thought (.) why is he (.) you know (.) that was too personal for me↓
46 M Mmh
47 A That's you know I (.) I don't wanna talk about those things with you↓
48 M ^{0}Okay^0 (.) ^{0}All right^0 (.) so you need (.) more clear boundaries about the kinds of things (.) [to be talked about.
49 A [ABSOLUTELY (.) I just =
50 M = Okay =
51 A = want to go to school I wanna get my degree↓

The passage from the past to the future, i.e. to the investigation of possible worlds, happens by means of a mediator's *formulation* (or *reformulation*)[29] of a statement

28. The options can have different types of part/whole relationships with the whole of the solution: they can be complementary parts that, taken together, constitute a solution, or they can represent alternative solutions.

29. On the manifold possible uses of such a presentational device, see van Eemeren et al. (1993, in particular p. 120): "Officially, such formulations have straightforward informative and procedural functions. Clarifying positions, summarizing the status of an issue, identifying points of agreement and disagreement, closing up a stage of the discussion and moving to the next, and so on. In performing these functions, however, formulations can also give substantive shape and direction to an argument, and in that respect formulations can serve as a technique for mediators to manage the substantive character and argumentative force of a discussion without entering into the discussion as an advocate".

made by Ann.[30] At turn 47, she formulated a standpoint about the problem that originated the conflict; the anaphoric use of "those" indicates the list of things that she has just mentioned at turn 45 and that constituted a problem for her. The mediator does not investigate how legitimate it was to ask such questions in an academic relationship, or about the reasons for Ann's discomfort with such questions; rather he elicits an implication for the future of Philip and Ann's relationship. Notice that the fact that some form of relationship between the two disputants will be present in any outcome is presupposed. This is certainly to be interpreted as a *presupposition accommodation* (Greco 2003): namely, as the introduction of new "materials" (premises) in the parties' common ground by presupposing rather than asserting them. This move represents a non-canonical way of constructing the opening stage, which can often – though not always – be used in a manipulative way (ibid.), because it adds implicit material into the common ground that may escape the parties' control. In this case, the mediator's presupposition accommodation can be interpreted as legitimate due to the contextual constraints: the more reasonable solution would be to continue Ann and Philip's academic relationship without forcing one of them to move to another university. At the same time, presupposing that the relationship will survive the current problem probably corresponds to Ann's and Philip's deepest and untold interests, as will be more specifically proposed in the next section.

An analytical reconstruction of the standpoints makes this passage clearer. In order to analytically reconstruct this discussion, I have adopted the representation of the analytical reconstruction proposed by van Eemeren, Grootendorst and Snoeck-Henkemans (2002), because it facilitates a synoptic representation of the standpoints and of their respective arguments. To the standard notation, however, some further aspects have been added in accordance with the specific purposes of the present investigation. First of all, after the numbering of the arguments, the person to which the argument is directed (the *audience* or *krités*)[31] is specified. For example, "1.1.(A)" means that the argument 1.1. is addressed to Ann and not to

30. In Aakhus's terms (2003: 273–275), this can be interpreted as part of a strategy of *redirection*, by which the mediator manages to move the discussion from one issue to another. In this case, we might add, the strategy of redirection is supportive of a very specific and typical moment of the confrontation stage in mediation: the passage from the analysis of the conflict to the attempt to resolve it by assuming its possible solutions as issues for the discussion.

31. The pragma-dialectical approach uses the term *audience* to refer to the addressee of an argumentative discourse, of which the discourse should be oriented (van Eemeren & Houtlosser 2002). The ancient Greek term *krités* (from the verb *krino*, which means "to sift"), was also used in the ancient rhetorical tradition to indicate the addressee of an argumentative discussion that was in charge of making a decision about the acceptability of the proposed standpoints (see Rigotti & Greco 2005).

Philip. This is an important feature because it takes into account the fact that, during the mediation process, parties can be more or less immediately involved as interlocutors (see Section 6.2.1). Moreover, parties may accept a mediator's proposal on the management of the mediation process for very different personal reasons.

Second, the mediator's standpoint is indicated as 1_{opt}. The use of number 1 indicates that he is reformulating Ann's standpoint, namely standpoint 1; but the subscripted notation 1_{opt} indicates that the new standpoint is different insofar as it represents the shift from past to future, i.e. from phase 1 (*analysis of context and conflict*) to phase 2 (*options*) of the core process of mediation (see Section 4.3). "Opt", indeed, is a label indicating that the standpoint moves to touch the level of options.

The reconstruction of standpoints and arguments is as follows:

Table 6.3. Analytical reconstruction of turns 45–51, Case 1

Turns	*Analytical reconstruction (standpoints and arguments)*	
	Ann	
45–47	1. I did not want to talk about these things with Philip 1.1.(A) That was too personal for me	
		Mediator
48		1_{opt}. Ann needs more clear boundaries about the kinds of things to be talked about in the future.
	Ann	
49–51	1_{opt}'. Absolutely (I accept 1_{opt} as my standpoint). 1.2.$_{opt}$(A) I wanna go to school I wanna get my degree.	

Different observations can be drawn from this representation. First, it emerges at turn 48 that the mediator himself adopts a standpoint, even though, as requested by his neutral role, such a standpoint does not concern a specific solution to the conflict; rather the standpoint concerns the issue to be discussed, thus emerging as a meta-issue.[32] So, it could be hypothesized that *the mediator can in*

32. The professional position according to which the mediator is "responsible for the process" (Haynes & Haynes 1989: 3) and not for its content, which is widely accepted by mediators, can be interpreted, from the argumentative point of view, as a part of the mediator's role of agent in his/her agency relationship with the parties. From the argumentative point of view, this role primarily consists in establishing a sound discussion. Being responsible for the process, however, also means providing for an adequate physical space for the parties' discussion *in praesentia*, considering the juridical aspects and implications of the parties' case and of the parties' agreement, and also invoking the intervention of experts of specific domains if needed (lawyers or other experts).

general profess some standpoints if they refer to the meta-level of management of the discussion rather than to specific solutions.

Second, concerning the development of the interaction, it can be observed that Ann first proposes a standpoint in reference to the origin of the conflict, and says that she could not tolerate discussing personal matters with Philip. However, after the mediator reformulates her standpoint at turn 48, she accepts his standpoint (49); and the kind of backing she gives indicates that this standpoint corresponds with her real interest. The passage to options, thus, seems to be natural for Ann. The argument she proposes, $1.1._{opt}$(A), is in tune with a perspective in which the conflict will be solved in the future.

The situation is quite different for Philip, who at first does not express his opinion on the mediator's standpoint 1_{opt}. His silence, however, turns out to be a sign that he does not accept the mediator's management of the process. In fact, Philip repeatedly reacts by trying to avoid the discussion about boundaries. From turn 113 to turn 190, a long meta-discussion on the appropriateness of the discussion on boundaries involves the mediator and the two parties. The mediator emerges here as the protagonist of a meta-argumentative discussion. This is not part of the main discussion between the parties about the resolution of their conflict. However, it turns out to constitute part of a *multiple dispute in a qualitative sense* (see Section 5.1.2). This meta-discussion is connected to the parties' main discussion over the resolution of their conflict; in fact, if the mediator fails to bring Philip and Ann to talk about boundaries, they will probably be unable to discuss a solution to their problem.[33] Let us consider the entire passage:

113 M So one of the issues that we really need to sort out (.) i::s (.) ho::w to be able to maintain the academic relationship (.)
114 A Mmh
115 M Between you but to [have some clear boundaries
116 P [I don't know whether we CAN ( ) (.) because I mean I I'm really =
117 M = I'm not sure you have a choice
118 P Well I don't know that I can continue with somebody who makes these wild allegations there would have to be an independent third party there all the time to monitor it
119 A Fine (.) it may be a lot safer
120 M You may well set it up in that way (.) you may well set it up and decide that's the best way to have it so that there's no misunderstanding on anybody's part (.) Ann I think you'd feel safer and more comfortable in that situation (.) and you'd feel safer and more comfortable =

33. The mediator's direct argumentation can be interpreted, in this case, as an attempt to set the parties' agenda in order to bring them to the resolution of their conflict as soon as possible.

121	A	= I'm not leaving this program↓
122	M	So (.) the the the question is (.) you're not leaving this program (.) you're not leaving this program and I assume therefore (.) that the (.) task today is to find a way that you can both stay in the program (.) a:nd maintain a good academic relationship↓
123	A	Mmh
124	M	And to clarify (.) what the boundaries are (.) so that you're not uncomfortable (.)
125	A	Mmh
126	M	And you're not subject to charges
127	A	I just want to be able to continue and to graduate (.) and I don't want to feel I've been compromised now (.) in the faculty (.) I don't want him to take it out on me (.) I mean that's another GENUINE concern (.) that he's not going to give me the help I need (.) or he is going to penalize me in my grades↓ (.)
128	M	Okay
129	A	And especially with these sarcastic remarks or talk about me with [other professors
130	P	[Would you like to have someone around like this with these kinds of allegations [against him/
131	A	[You couldn't you know what you couldn't have me around enough before and [you are at fault
132	P	[Are you going to try to work with somebody like this/=
133	A	= Now he doesn't want me around↓
134	P	It makes it extremely difficult to [continue↓
135	A	[No you don't want me around on MY terms (.) you want me around on YOUR terms↓ (.) as long as you're pulling the strings (.) as long as you can say [we're going to lunch
136	P	[This is the ( )
137	M	My assumption is is that you should both be around on normal terms↓
138	A	Mmh
139	P	I have nothing against that I thought that's what we were doing all along you know so
140	A	He doesn't even know he is (.) [so inappropriate
141	P	[she's (.) dreaming into this all kinds of wonderful things that she thinks that don't exist at all↓ =
142	A	= Well they weren't wonderful (.) just for your information (.) that's not my idea of a wonderful thing (.) having you put your big fat hand on my knee↓
143	P	I've never put [my hand↓
144	M	[Okay now let's let's look at some of the things (.) that (.) that clearly should not happen we really should draw some clear (.) boundary lines (.) no physical contact↓
145	A	Mmh
146	M	Right↑

147 A Absolutely
148 M Does this seem right Philip↑
149 P ^{0}Absolutely^{0} that's right John that's fine by me
150 M No physical contact (.) number one (.) no lunches↓ (.) no dinners
151 P No friendship↓
152 A I never asked for your friendship↓
153 M No↓ other than academic friendship no friendship
154 A Cooperation is different
155 M But let's clearly distinguish between having an ACADEMIC relationship and a social relationship↓
156 (4)
157 A I don't think you know the difference
158 M Let Philip speak for himself↓
159 P I've always had friendly relationships with all my students I've always expressed an interest in their general well-being (.) and made them feel comfortable and welcome to the university and (.) I've NEVER in ALL the years the twenty years that I've been (.) at the university had ANYTHING like this ever =
160 A = Nobody ever complained/
161 P (2) They didn't have any NEED to complain↓
162 M In life (.) each of us ha:s (.) different boundaries about (.) what's comfortable and what's uncomfortable right↑ (2.5) a:nd (.) some people have a boundary here/(1.5) some people have a boundary here (.) and one of the tasks that always seems necessary for the person in the power position (.) is to understand that the boundaries are set by the others (2) it's sometimes hard for us and as you know I taught for (.) many years at a university (.) sometimes it's hard for us in a power position on faculty (.) to: (.) recognize tha:t (.) the boundaries eh: should be set always by the most conservative person (3) hh and I'm sensing here that one of the things that's gone wrong (.) is that (.) hh Ann you have one set of boundaries and Philip you have another set (.) and they've been crossed (.) and in crossing those those two boundaries Ann you've become very uncomfortable (.) and that discomfort is interfering with your (.) academic goals (.)
163 A Absolutely
164 M and your ability to pursue the academic goals↓
165 A Mmh
166 P What troubles me is she's suggesting far more into it than [what warranted
167 M [Okay (.) but Philip having that now happened (.) YOU're uncomfortable (2.5) the vice president for Academic Affairs knows about this (.) right↑ (.) at this moment now it's not a PUBLIC matter (.)
168 P But ( ) =

169	M	= Precisely it could become a public matter (.) and so that (.) if you (.) hold onto a position (.) that only you decide (.) then (.) it may well go to the next level (.) and my sense is (.) is that you would both like to come out of this (.) with a CLEAR set of boundaries (.) and an UNDERSTANDING of how to respect those boundaries (.) on the one hand (.) and maintaining (.) a good academic relationship (.) in the future (.) so you can be the best professor you want to be (.) [and you can be the best (.) graduate student you want to be
170	P	[Well the best I can be is if she just goes into another program if she went into another program [we wouldn't have any more problems↓
171	A	[So it's my fault↓ =
172	M	= And it would be equally true that it could be solved if you left↓ ( )
173	A	Exactly (.) and I'm prepared to go to the limit with it because I have more RIDING on this↓
174	M	Neither of you is going to the [limit
175	P	[But there are other students who want to stay in the program with me so (.) I look at this [they would all suffer
176	M	[You can have (.) You can have a relationship with them (.) based on their boundaries (.) it may be DIFFERENT from the relationship you have with Ann (.) based on her boundaries↓ (.) that's perfectly okay (.) that's perfectly okay (.) to have different boundaries in different relationships with different people (1.5) but (.) to be able to respect and understand (.) that once we cross somebody else's boundaries (.) particularly in a power position
177	P	Mmh
178	M	that unfortunately it makes them (.) it discombobulates them (.) in many many ways (.) and my sense here (.) is that it is a boundary issue↓ (2) I (.) I might let me be very very clear (.) beyond (.) the touching or putting the arm
179	A	Mmh
180	M	There's there's has there been any other activity↑
181	A	Eh: no no [I just
182	P	[There you go you see there isn't =
183	A	= Well I think because I put a STOP to it↓
184	P	No because well [because if it were more to it
185	A	[Well I made a complaint
186	M	If there were more to it that would be a very different ball game we wouldn't be discussing the boundary issue↓ =
187	P	= She thinks there might have been more that's what she's saying but there's never been anything ^{0}to suggest^0 (.) that I don't think there's any more to [this
188	M	[The question for you Philip is (.) the question for you is (.) can you reconstruct your relationship with Ann/(.) around boundaries that are different/

189	P	That depends on what those boundaries are (.) I suppose
190	M	Okay

First, the mediator reformulates his standpoint "Ann needs more clear boundaries" and disambiguates it. Then (turns 113ff.), he proposes the standpoint "You need more clear boundaries for your relationship", by highlighting how this would also meet Philip's interests. Later on, at turn 162, he refines his standpoint, which becomes: "*Ann* should set more clear boundaries for your relationship".[34] Then, it is the mediator who provides Philip with some arguments for accepting his standpoint, as shown in Table 6.4. Consider that, as it emerges in the following reconstruction, although the reformulation of the standpoint already occurs at turn 162, the first argument (namely 1.3.$_{opt}$., turns 167–169) still refers to the first version of the standpoint. The second version is supported rather by argument 1.4.$_{opt}$., presented at turns 176–178. In the whole passage, Philip is the direct addressee of the mediator's argumentation; he therefore is to be considered as the main antagonist of the critical discussion, while the mediator is the protagonist. In the following table, therefore, the notation "?" suggests that Philip has doubts on the mediator's standpoints (as in van Eemeren, Grootendorst and Snoeck-Henkemans 2002):

Table 6.4. Analytical reconstruction of turns 167–169

Turns	*Analytical reconstruction (standpoints and arguments)*	
	Philip	**Mediator**
167–169	?	1'$_{opt}$. You need more clear boundaries about your relationship.
		1.3.$_{opt}$.(P) Otherwise the thing could become public.
		1.3.1.$_{opt}$.(P). And the thing becoming public could interfere with your academic status.
162 and 176–178	?	1"$_{opt}$. Ann should set more clear boundaries about your relationship.
		1.4.$_{opt}$.(P).Because she has been discombobulated
		1.4.1. $_{opt}$. and people in a power position on faculty need to avoid that power "discombobulates" less powerful people
		1.4.1.1 $_{opt}$. And I know this because as you know I taught for many years at university.

34. Some remarks are necessary about the adopted notation. First of all, the standpoints are signalled with the same numeration as in Table 6.3._By this choice, I would like to highlight that the mediator does not formulate three different and extraneous standpoints; rather he reformulates his original standpoint in three progressively more precise versions (1$_{opt}$, 1'$_{opt}$, and 1"$_{opt}$ respectively). Moreover, the numeration of arguments starts with 1.3. because the arguments presented in this table support the same standpoint (as said, in its different versions) as in the preceding discussion (see Table 6.3). In this later phase, the expected addressee of the mediator's argumentation is clearly Philip.

In order to evaluate the strength of the mediator's arguments and their contribution to the discussion, it is useful to reconstruct in greater detail, by means of the Argumentum Model of Topics (AMT) (see Chapter 5), the inferential configuration of the two main arguments that the mediator presents to Philip (respectively, 1.3_{opt} and 1.4_{opt}).

First, it is necessary to say that both arguments are based on complex inferential structures that involve a concatenation of premises and a conclusion, which could be named an *argumentative chain* of subordinate arguments.

Argument 1.3_{opt} is based on a two-step chain, which first of all concludes that making the problem public should be avoided, and, as a second step, recognizes that the condition for this is that Ann should be left free to set her own boundaries. These two moves are based on the *locus from termination and setting up* and on the *locus from the final cause* (based in particular on the relations between means and ends) respectively. In what follows, these steps will be analysed one by one and their sequential connection will be made explicit.

The locus from termination and setting up, which is at work in the first step, connects the acceptability of a state of affairs to the acceptability of one or more of its implications. For example, if a certain state of affairs is expected to bring positive consequences, one is led to conclude, on the basis of this locus, that it has to be accepted or even welcomed: for example, one might reason the positive value of going on a diet from the expected outcome to get fit, healthier, and so on. Contrariwise, a state of affairs is to be avoided if its consequences are negative: for example, in Philip's case, the public suspicion of an affair between him and Ann should be avoided, because it would have the negative consequence of damaging Philip's professional honour.[35] This reasoning is suggested by the mediator through a communicative move that can be interpreted as a warning to Philip: "Precisely it could become a public matter" (turn 169). This warning leverages in particular on the emotion of *fear*. Fear is a future-oriented disphoric emotion (Cigada 2007: 244), which represents the desire to hinder the realization of a possible negative world: in

35. The basic version of a locus from termination and setting up would foresee, in its "negative" formulation, that if a certain state of affairs *is* negative (in the real world) it should be avoided (for instance, if the presence of high rates of infant mortality in many countries is negative – and we do know that this state of affairs is indeed part of the real world – it should be avoided, or removed). In this case, the negative nature of the concerned state of affairs is evaluated on the basis of its possible *negative consequences* in possible worlds (in the future). In this sense, and more precisely, the locus from termination and setting up is intertwined here with a *locus from the implications* which is subordinated to it. Therefore, according to the AMT (see Chapter 5), this reasoning constitutes a particular and frequently occurring type of the category of *complex loci*.

this case, *fear* refers to the possibility of losing face and maybe also one's professional and economic status. The emotion of fear is indirectly correlated to Philip's *interest*[36] in maintaining his position and reputation. In fact, the mediator points to the negative consequences on Philip's side if the "affair", even though not confirmed, is made public, i.e. if Ann goes further with the complaint (see turn 189).

From the rhetorical point of view, the mediator's formulation of this argument is quite direct[37] and does not leave much to be implied. The mediator's wording could also be interpreted as an abuse of power, even a threat (an *ad baculum* fallacy)[38] to Philip. However, the realization of negative consequences evoked by the mediator does not constitute a threat by him personally; in other words, the mediator is not the cause of the realization of his warning; rather, the realization of negative consequences mentioned is linked to the contextual surroundings in which Philip lives and operates. In this sense, the mediator's move may be considered legitimate, as the negative consequences he evokes would be realized even if he did not mention them.

The proper analysis of the inferential structure of this first step of argument 1.3 is presented in Figure 6.2. The endoxon, which is implicit in the mediator's

36. Cigada (2007: 241) argues that, in general, appeals to emotions focus "on the interest of the addressee, in the sense that the author suggests that it would make no sense to decide without considering some particular implications of his decisions". It can be said that the emotion of fear indirectly (by opposition) points to the positive interest of not losing something that one really cares for.

37. The only aspect that could be reconstructed as a *mitigating device* (Caffi 2007) is represented by the adverb *precisely* at the beginning of turn 169, which follows (and almost interrupts) Philip's objection "but" (turn 168), in turn interrupting the mediator while saying: "At this moment now it's not a PUBLIC matter" (turn 167). The mediator, in fact, seems to interpret Philip's "but" as "but it COULD become a public matter"; in this way, by means of the adverb *precisely*, he signals agreement with something said by Philip. Clearly, it is a delicate move, since Philip has been interrupted and therefore he has actually said nothing. In this sense, the adverb *precisely* is to be interpreted as a presupposition accommodation operated by the mediator (Greco 2003).

38. The fallacy *ad baculum* (literally, "from the stick") is a way of putting pressure on an opponent, thus violating the freedom rule of a critical discussion, according to which parties should not prevent each other from advancing standpoints or casting doubt on standpoints (see van Eemeren & Grootendorst 1992: 107–109). This fallacy refers to a *threat* of some kind of violence. Normally, despite the name of this fallacy, the threat remains, indeed, only a threat. In fact, as van Eemeren and Grootendorst (1992: 109) remark, "If things do not stop at threats, the name gives a literal description. But if a stick is brought into play there is, of course, really no question any more of a discussion, let alone a critical discussion". The fallacy *ad baculum* is always a manipulative move. Some warnings, however, may be reasonable moves and distinguish themselves from proper threats, as happens for the mediator's intervention in this case.

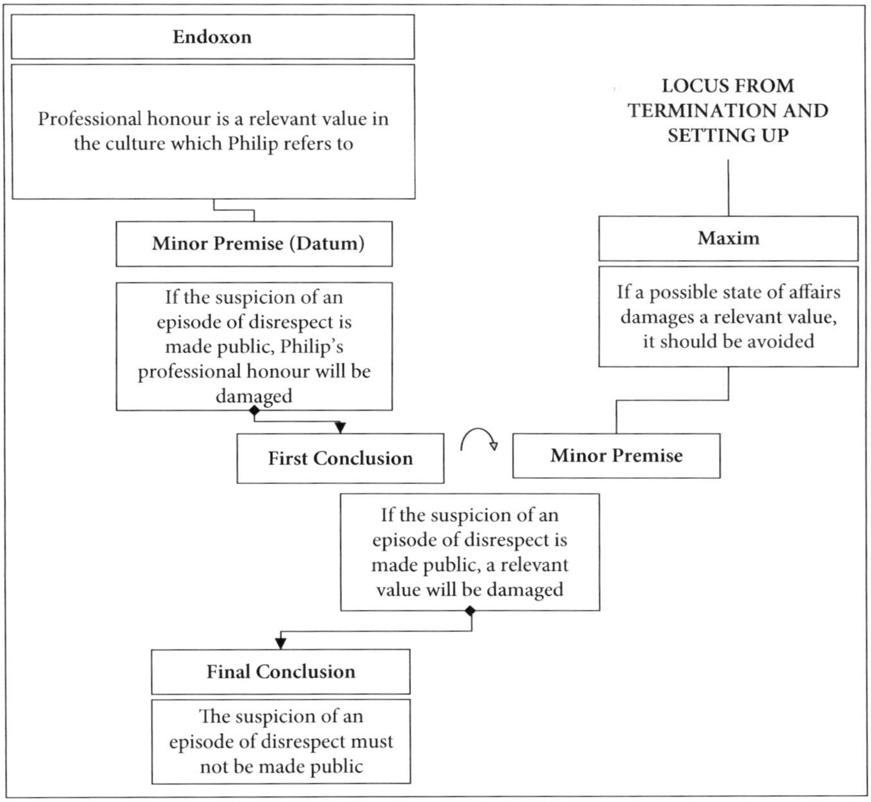

Figure 6.2. Synergic representation of the first step of argument 1.3

discourse, has been reconstructed as the statement of the importance of *professional honour*, conceived of as respect for Philip's professional mandate which is a cultural value that Philip recognizes. The minor premise (datum), which is also only implicitly present in the mediator's warning, states the possible negative consequences[39] that would follow if even a mere suspicion of an episode of disrespect involving Philip and Ann is made public. In particular, Philip's professional honour would be damaged. The mediator does not specify it more than this: certainly, Philip would at least gain a bad reputation; we do not know whether the university would move against him in a more formal way. But it is exactly the fact that the

39. Not coincidentally, this minor premise is constituted by an "if… then" clause. In fact, in this case, the minor premise represents a *possible world* rather than a real one. This is requested by the very nature of the reasoning, which, as said, combines the locus from termination and setting up with a subordinate locus from the implications (see Footnote 35 in this Chapter).

evoked future is uncertain and vague that renders it more menacing. The warning implied in this argument is well understood by Ann, who reinforces it at turn 173 by saying explicitly that she is "prepared to go to the limit", even if this would imply Philip leaving the university. Philip's counterarguments (at 175 he says that other students are interested in his programme and would therefore not want him to leave the university) appear quite weak, because this would probably not have great hold on the academic authorities who make this sort of decision.

Elaborating on the final conclusion of step 1.3, the reasoning goes on by specifying the conditions that are necessary in order not to make the accusation about Philip's behaviour with Ann public. In particular, in this second phase, the mediator's argumentation leads to the conclusion that the parties need to negotiate a clear set of boundaries. The specific maxim activated within the locus from the final cause, which is at work in this passage, concerns the relation between *ends* and *means* and, in particular, can be formulated as: "The intention of realizing a goal entails the intention of pursuing its necessary means". Now, once it is established that setting up boundaries for Philip and Ann's relationship is a necessary condition (and, actually, the only necessary condition) to avoid making their problem public (see the minor premise associated with the maxim, Figure 6.3), the conclusion follows that Ann and Philip have to set boundaries. The fact that their problem becoming public would be a negative situation has already been established in the first step of this reasoning (see Figure 6.2). The fact that the setting of boundaries actually constitutes the only necessary condition for not making their problem public is derived from another reasoning, stemming from an endoxon generally concerning the functioning of joint human actions and activities: "The co-operation[40] of a free agent must be negotiated taking into account his/her requests" and a minor premise derived (datum) from knowledge of the contextual surrounding (the academic environment) and of the previous interaction, which could be formulated as: "The fact that the suspicion of an episode of disrespect is not made public presupposes Ann as a free cause; and Ann asks to set boundaries". The datum, in this case, clarifies the only condition that Ann is asking (see turn 49, where she first states this) in order to solve the conflict without going to the next level in the academic procedure against Philip. Such a condition becomes justifiable because Ann is the "free cause", i.e. the agent necessarily involved in the co-operation to reach the desired end not to make the conflict public. Her power in negotiation is determined by the fact that Philip cannot decide not to make the problem public by himself. He must, thus, necessarily be involved in co-operating

40. Following Rigotti (2003), I define co-operation as a type of joint action involving two or more agents who pursue the same goal and try to reach it together.

if he wants to reach his goal. And, since this goal is particularly relevant for Philip, he is expected to negotiate with her on how to reach it on the basis of her conditions and requests. Notice that the endoxon evoked, in this relation, brings Ann and Philip on to the same level, despite their power differences in the academic context, and it tends to bring them to an equal status, as co-operators or co-agents, by presupposing that they can share a goal and pursue it. The equal status of the parties is requested by the interaction scheme of mediation itself; this endoxon is, thus, justified by the fact that Ann and Philip's discussion is situated in the context of a mediation process.

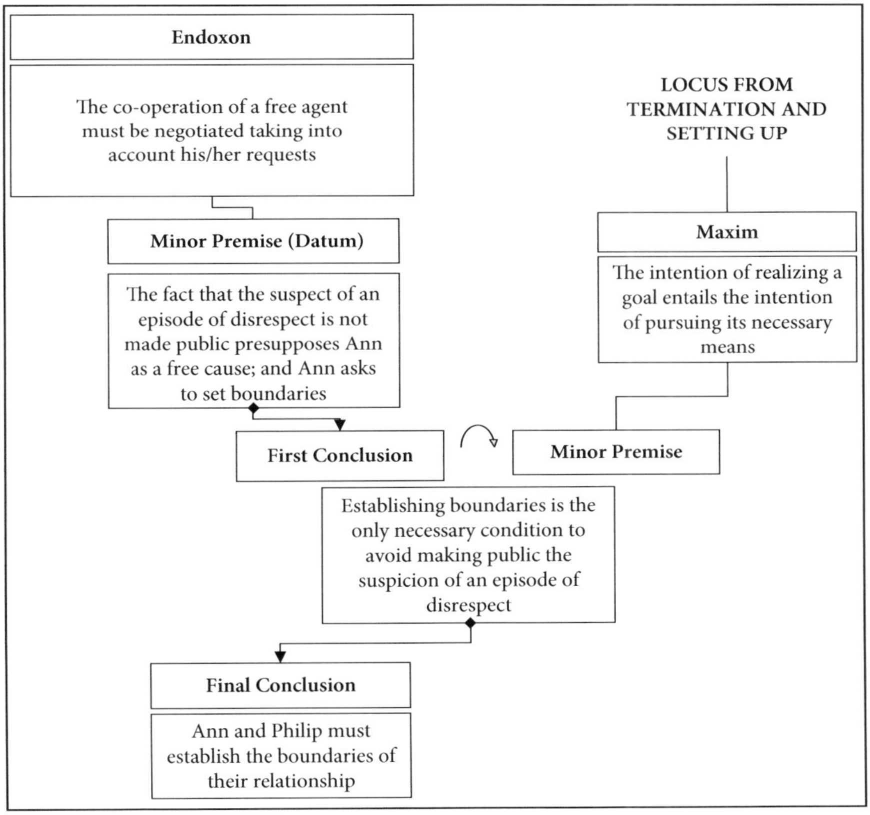

Figure 6.3. Synergic representation of the second step of argument 1.3

But the mediator does not only propose this argument to Philip. In fact, he also raises (turns 162 and 176–178) another line of reasoning, which seems to be aimed at supporting the standpoint $1''_{opt}$; namely, "Ann should set more clear boundaries about your relationship". The interpretation of this argument, however, is difficult, because the text is in itself quite opaque. Therefore, the interpretation suggested in what follows is a hypothesis on what the mediator proposes to Philip as an argument in this further line of reasoning.

Clearly, the argument is centred on the problem of a power imbalance derived from Philip's and Ann's different roles in the academic context. Philip has declared that he wants to maintain good relationships with his students (turns 159 and 175) and that he has "always expressed an interest in their general well being (.) and made them feel comfortable and welcome to the university" (turn 159). By saying this, Philip suggests a goal that he always pursues in his relationships with students, namely to care for their well-being and to make them feel comfortable and welcome to the university.[41] This seems to be part of his concept of an academic's professional ethos.

To this, the mediator's intervention at 176ff. adds that, when there is a power imbalance, as is the case in the student–professor relationship, the student, being the individual in the less powerful position, may be made uncomfortable by the professor's crossing what he/she feels to be the natural boundaries of their relationship. And this may happen even if the professor, as we assume in Philip's case, has crossed the boundaries inadvertently. The mediator, in this sense, seems to point to a contradiction between Philip's normal "decorum", i.e. the normal honourable way in which he interprets his role as a university professor, and his specific behaviour with Ann. In fact, he has inadvertently crossed her boundaries, and she has been made uncomfortable by this. Therefore, if Philip does not find some corrective measure for the problem, his goal of making students feel comfortable is not fulfilled, and this has consequences for his professional ethos. For this reason, the mediator seems to suggest that Philip should let Ann decide on the boundaries of their relationship. This would be a corrective measure against her feeling very uncomfortable (turn 162) or "discombobulated" (178). In the interpretation proposed here, the mediator's discourse can be reconstructed as a two-steps argumentative chain; the former step is founded on the locus from termination and setting up, while the latter step rests on the *locus from the instrumental cause.*

In the first step, the maxim at work can be formulated as "If an important goal is put at risk, the risk should be removed". The line of reasoning stemming from the maxim is combined with another line of reasoning stemming from the endoxon "It is part of a university professor's ethos to maintain friendly

41. The mediator seems to remind him of the importance of his goal at 169, where he presupposes that one of the most important objectives that mediation will allow Philip to reach is that he can be "the best professor he wants to be".

relationships with his/her students and to make them feel comfortable". This endoxon, as remarked above, has been declared by Philip to be part of his values. The datum associated with this endoxon is made clear by the mediator, who highlights that Ann is not comfortable at the moment, mainly because Philip has inadvertently crossed her boundaries (see Figure 6.4):

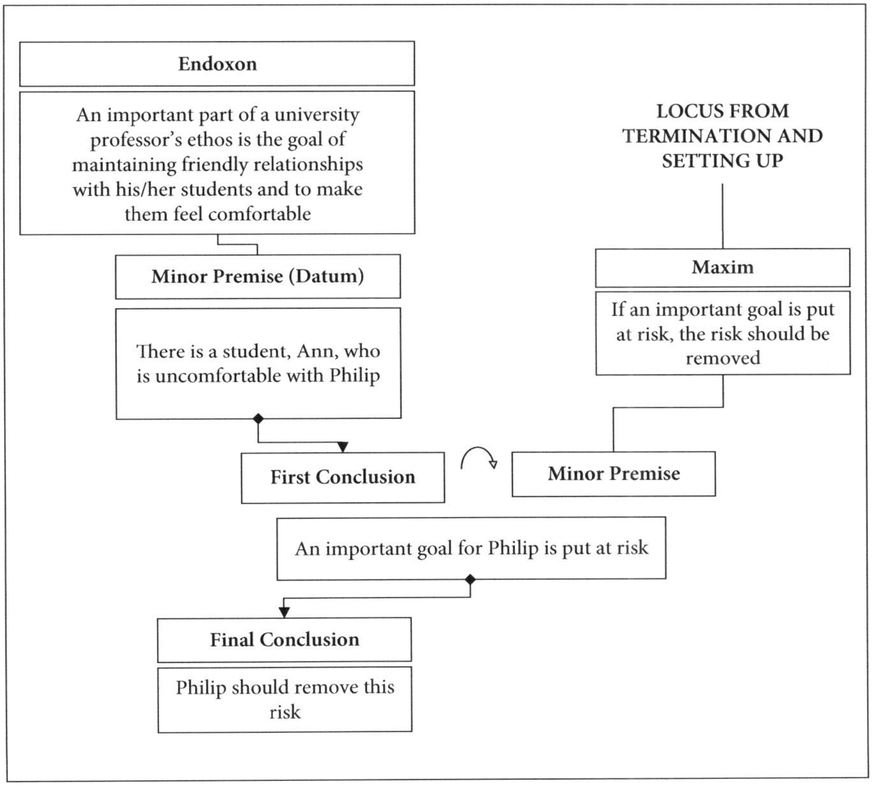

Figure 6.4. Synergic representation of the first step of argument 1.4

The latter part of the argumentation draws on the results of the former. In particular, the *locus from the instrumental cause* (see Chapter 5) is applied here (see Figure 6.5) with the following maxim: "It is reasonable to pursue adequate means for reaching an important goal". This argument shows that letting Ann decide the boundaries of her relationship with Philip is an adequate measure to stop her feeling uncomfortable; this, as shown in the former step of the argumentative chain, endangers Philip's goal of making his students feel comfortable.

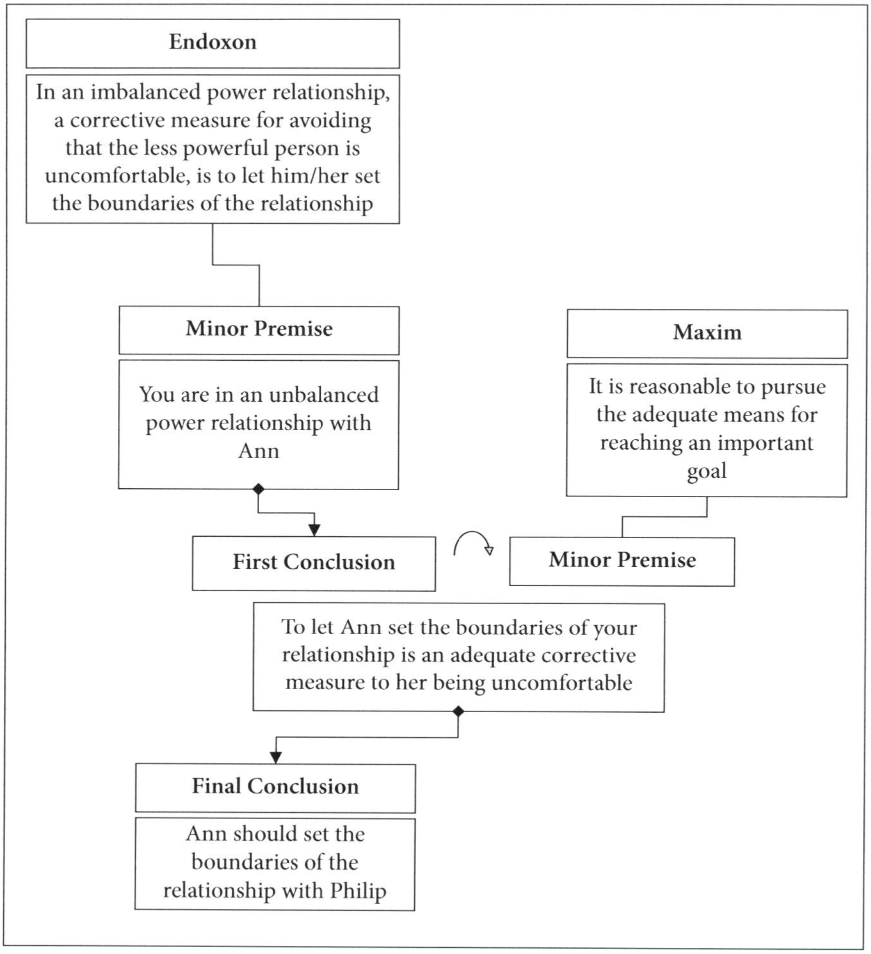

Figure 6.5. Synergic representation of the second step of argument 1.4

As said above, this interpretation is not to be accepted uncritically, because the mediator's discourse leaves much implicit and unclear. The interpretation proposed here, however, seems to me the more reasonable in the context of the argumentation that the mediator directs towards Philip. In fact, by means of this argument, the mediator manages to show Philip why letting Ann decide on the boundaries of their relationship is an advantage *to him*. The persuasiveness of this argumentation is bound at a deep level to Philip's interests evoked by the endoxon represented in Figure 6.4. This endoxon concerns, as observed, a university professor's ethos, namely, his dignity and self-esteem. Rather than being concerned with the academic duties of a university professor, this has to do with the relationships between human beings and exceeds the institutionalized dimension of Ann and Philip's relationship. The persuasive effectiveness of this move exactly consists in presupposing that this form of dignity or self-esteem exists, and that the concerned person (Philip) recognizes and desires it, i.e. that he wants to behave decorously, "the best professor he wants to be", as the mediator himself formulates it at turn 169. The mediator, here, is more than a third neutral; he dares to propose "wise advice", by means of which he probably hopes to evoke a positive response from Philip, who is expected to recognize his own deepest interest.[42]

At the evaluative level, the evoking of this endoxon is appropriate, because it is drawn from Philip's own statements. A possible weak point concerns the fact that only Ann appears to be uncomfortable with Philip; therefore, a simpler way to eliminate this risk would be, rather than reconstructing the relationship on the basis of her boundaries, to "eliminate" her by asking her to move to another programme. Indeed, Philip suggests this at turn 106. This possibility, however, is excluded by the institutional context, as the mediator promptly declares at 117: "I'm not sure you have a choice", he says to Philip, about whether to continue his relationship with Ann. Therefore, letting Ann decide about boundaries turns out to be a reasonable decision within the paradigm of possible alternatives at Philip's disposal.[43]

The fact that a university professor should try not to make his/her students uncomfortable because of the power imbalance is then supported by the mediator through an argument based on the *locus from authority* ($1.4.1.1_{opt}$ in the reconstruction proposed in Table 6.4), where the mediator confirms that the professor's honour entails this aspect on the basis of his own experience. Such an audacious observation by the mediator is probably bound to the particular contextual situation of this case; the mediator, having been an academic, can easily integrate pieces of contextual knowledge (about goals, practices, rites, and so on) that the parties have not mentioned. Notably, in this case the endoxon is further supported by means of an argument from authority based on the mediator's own experience: "you know I taught for (.) many years at a university (.) sometimes it's hard for us in a power position on faculty (.) to: (.) recognize tha:t (.) the boundaries

42. One cannot help thinking to John Haynes's principle for which mediators have to find "that of God/that of good" in each person, presupposing that each human being is able to recognize what is good.

43. The importance of the weighting of each parties' alternatives has been highlighted in the literature on conflict resolution, as shown in Chapter3. See in particular the Harvard model of negotiation (Fisher, Ury & Patton 1991; Patton 2005).

eh: should be set always by the most conservative person" (turn 162). Such an argument works as a subtle form of threat, meaning that if, one the one hand, Philip is in a power position in relation to Ann, he is not in such a position in relation to the mediator. The mediator himself, in fact, has done the same job as Philip for a while and has been in a power position in an academic faculty. By means of this move, he thus advocates the right to a peer-to-peer dialogue, and he also shows that he knows the academic context as an insider.

In a way, however, a justification for Philip can also be found in the mediator's argument, as at 176 he says that Philip can have different boundaries in different relationships, and that this is perfectly legitimate. Thereby, the mediator limits the problem to one single episode, thus implying that the possible accusation that Philip systematically embarrasses female students does not hold. The episode with Ann is indirectly interpreted as a misunderstanding in the context of a generally cordial but respectful relationships with students.[44]

As it appears from this reconstruction, it is important for the parties to accept the mediator's intervention at the meta-level in order to set up an argumentative discussion about their problem. In fact, the mediator makes sure that both of them are ready to talk about an option for the resolution of the conflict. He also provides Philip with specific reasons for agreeing to enter this discussion. As emerged from the argumentative analysis, the force of the mediator's arguments addressed to Philip largely depends on them being anchored in the institutionalized or interpersonal dimensions of context (see Chapter 4). This is a form of contextual influence on the arguers' strategic manoeuvring; the appropriateness of the arguments (topical choice) is linked to the context.

6.2.2.4 *Some remarks on the notion of* interest

What has been shown in the previous sections, in particular concerning the double line of arguments proposed by the mediator to persuade Philip about the appropriateness of starting a discussion on the boundaries of the relationship between Ann and himself (Section 6.2.2.3), has brought to light that *argumentation persuades when it touches the addressee's (or, more properly, the decision maker's) interests*. More specifically, if we consider the endoxa backing the different steps that are present in arguments 1.3 and 1.4, it is clear that some level of Philip's interests are always present: his professional honour, a positive disposition towards normal interactions with other human beings, and his unwillingness to abuse his power.

44. A similar interpretation, by the way, had already been given by Ann at 90, when she affirms that Philip is "much more detached" with other women who participate in the programme.

In relation to this, it seems opportune to investigate the very notion of *interest*, which emerges as the key to an understanding of mediation, as it is also ascertained in the literature (see Chapter 3, in particular in relation to Fisher, Ury & Patton 2001 and Patton 2005). For this purpose, first of all the notion of *interest* will be analysed in its constituency, in order to elicit its proper meaning. In this endeavour, the thorough and informative work by Cigada (2008, see pp. 61–81 in particular) opens the way to an understanding of this term. Second, the values of interest will be elicited as they explain the dynamics of persuasion in the passages examined in the previous section. This will constitute a basis on which the remaining part of the corpus will be investigated.

Moving from a careful etymological reconstruction of the ancient Latin word *interest*,[45] Cigada (ibid., p. 63) proposes a definition of "interest" as a *function with variable intensity*, which connects an advantageous state of affairs or event to an individual or a group. From this definition, the *positive* value of any interest immediately emerges. In this relation, Cigada (2006: 135) introduces the term of *proximité positive* (positive proximity) to indicate a positive experience of reality that involves, at some level, the well-being of the subjects involved.

Interest is also a polysemic word, as Cigada remarks when discussing the interpretations proposed by the *Trésor de la Langue Française Informatisé* (Cigada 2008: 66–67); and the polysemy of interest will prove to be particularly relevant for conflict resolution studies. The *Trésor* distinguishes between an *objective* interest, coinciding with a real advantage that *concerns* an individual, and a *subjective* interest, reflecting the individuals' conscious attention. The latter concept of interest implies a human subject actively claiming his interest or even "working" to realize it. But this does not necessarily coincide with the real interest of individuals nor, vice versa, is the real interest always at a conscious level. This emerges as particularly important in the resolution of a conflict, which should be guided by

45. According to Cigada's reconstruction, the Latin form *meā interest* imitates the construction of *refert*. Indeed, the impersonal verb *rēfert* would be the result of a composition between the ablative *rē* and the verb *fert*. As Meillet (1985: 567, qt. in Cigada 2008: 62) argues, *refert* is often confused with *interest*, as the value of "to make a difference" equally suits both expressions. In this way, the syntactical construction of *meā, tuā, illius rēfert* is transferred to interest, thus giving origin to the peculiar forms a*licuius interest* and *meā, tuā interest*. On the basis of the Lexicon Totius Latinitatis, Cigada (ibid.) reconstructs four main values attributed to the Latin verb *intersum*. The first one is the proper value of *to be between* two places or two temporal moments. The second indicates the presence of a *difference* between two objects (as in the example "Inter hominem et belluam hoc maxime interest", Cic. Off. 4. 11). The third value concerns the action *to intervene, to be present.* Finally, *intersum* can mean that something *belongs to* or more or less tightly *is relevant to* or *concerns* somebody or something. For a more complete analysis see Cigada (ibid., pp. 61–63 in particular) and Cigada (2006: 133–135).

the principle "Focus on interests, not positions", formulated by the Harvard School on negotiation and conflict resolution, to which we have already devoted a careful analysis (Chapter 3). The hereby presupposed opposition between *positions* and *interests* opens the way to consider interests as something that parties do not expressly declare, perhaps because they are unconscious of them. In this sense, *parties are not automatically interested in their interests*. Therefore, the task of a conflict resolution professional is, in this relation, to help parties discover their real interests. The selection of appropriate interests is clearly a part of the mediator's strategic manoeuvring with the topical potential.

In relation to this, the mediator's argumentation to persuade Philip to speak of boundaries as an issue in the discussion is really to be interpreted as the mediator looking for Philip's real interests. Philip has clearly declared his annoyance with Ann and her complaint, thus implying that he does want to engage in solving the problem. But his real interests, namely those that will move him to accept the need to discuss boundaries, are recalled by the mediator[46] rather than by Philip himself. In fact, it is the mediator who presupposes Philip's interest in his reputation and, more specifically, his professional honour as an academic. Again, it is the mediator who, by evoking an endoxon about the "normal terms" for co-operating with a free interagent, presupposes Philip's desire to be involved in normal interpersonal relationships and respect the human beings with whom he has contact. Eventually, when Philip declares his interest in his students being comfortable and welcome to the university, it is the mediator who welcomes this value as relevant and important and elaborates on it to persuade Philip that finding a way to continue his relationship with Ann is in his own interests.

As Philip's interests are mostly invoked as unsaid, *presupposed* endoxa, it clearly emerges that the mediator's operation is risky: he tries to propose arguments whose endoxical premises are intended to touch the deepest levels of the addressee's interests, but which have remained unexpressed. In this way, the mediator launches possible lines of reasoning to Philip, who has to accept the *accommodation of these presuppositions* in order to accept the arguments themselves.

Even more risky is the mediator's management of the confrontation stage, where the mediator, as seen in the previous section, moves the discussion from the issue of conflict to its possible solutions (options). Here the mediator is presupposing something that has not been explicitly accepted by the parties, namely that

46. It is true that, in Philip's case, the evoked interests are bound to the fear of losing something. But fear is not used as a threatening means; rather it is evoked to remind him of his own interests and concerns. Fear, in any case, is involved in mediation, as parties have to deal with a conflict that, as remarked, endangers the status quo of the parties' relationships.

finding a solution is possible and that their relationship can continue and flourish. *By means of a presupposition accommodation, thus, the mediator challenges the parties to recognize what their real interest is.*[47] Moreover, by considering the very nature of this kind of interest concerning the re-establishment of an untroubled relationship in the future, it turns out that, differently from what one might anticipate, the parties' deepest interests are not necessarily opposed to each other. One is inclined to think that parties in conflict have opposite or even mutually exclusive interests. Indeed, as already seen in the analysis of the notion of conflict in Chapter 4, this is not necessarily the case; in many occasions, in fact, apparently contradictory interests turn out to be complementary. But there may be something more than just the discovery of complementary interests. In fact, each party may discover that their interest *involves the counter party*, so that the interest in one's own well-being somehow turns out to include the other's well-being. It should not be neglected that parties who decide to go to mediation normally do value their relationship at some level – for this reason, they might have decided to avoid other, more violent or less friendly forms of conflict resolution. Often, parties have known each other for a long time, or they have some reason for desiring to continue their relationship on some level (in the case of Ann and Philip, they only want to maintain an academic relationship). In this relation, the concept of *relational happiness*[48] could be introduced to refer to all win-win situations in which favouring the other party also results in a deeper personal advantage.

47. A possible relation between the evoking of interests and presupposition accommodation has been proposed by Cigada (2008: 71), who more precisely hypothesizes that the interlocutors' interests "justify" the speakers' accommodation: "La notion d'intérêt, un peu plus ouverte, permet d'expliquer le développement de la relation par le phénomène de l'accommodation, que les interlocuteurs pratiquent chaque fois qui'ils offrent verbalement à l'autre la possibilité d'assumer une position de proximité majeure par rapport au centre de leurs intérêts". The mediator may be said to bring this possibility to the extreme, almost to force it, in order to challenge parties to recognize their interests and the common ground between them. Needless to say, launching such a challenge is risky, because it is somehow an intrusion into the speakers' common ground that, if accepted, radically enlarges it.

48. As Menkel-Meadow (1984: 754) remarks, considering personal gain as obviously entailing the other party's loss is a form of reductionism: "It is assumed that the parties must be in conflict and since they are presumed to be bargaining for the same 'scarce' items, negotiators assume that any solution is predicated upon division of the goods. In the language of game theorists, economists, and psychologists, such negotiations become 'zero-sum' or 'constant-sum' games and the bargaining engaged in is 'distributive' bargaining. Simply put, in the pure adversarial case, each party wants as much as he can get of the thing bargained for, and the more one party receives, the less the other party receives. There is a 'winner' in the negotiation, determined by which party got more". According to Martini, Rigotti and Palmieri (2008),

6.2.2.5 *A deep habit change allowed by the consideration of interests*

The consideration of the parties' most crucial interests shows to be directly bound with the degree and quality of the *habit change* in which parties are involved during the mediation process. Different levels of interest are associated with the different levels of change that may occur. In this sense, interest appears to have a *multilayer structure* (Cigada 2008), going from more external to more internal interests, and arriving at the ultimate habit change to do with the subjectivity of the persons involved in communication.

A paradigmatic example of the deepest habit change that can be experienced if the parties' interests are taken into account is present in the case we are considering. At a certain point in time, the mediator perceives the need to interrupt the discussion on options in order to go back and tackle "a fundamental issue" related to the disputants' interpersonal trust; indeed, before this point was clarified, the parties' negotiation was continuously undermined by a fundamental lack of trust between them; and the core process of mediation could not proceed. Having listened to each other's reasons, the parties are able to re-establish trust in each other, and can then move on to discuss the individual options. Let us consider the passage where both disputants show an understanding that the conflict originated through a misunderstanding rather than by an evil intention:

271	P	(4) I suppose so Ann if (.) if you've got boundaries that I don't know about and I've crossed them I I I guess I have a sense of regret that (.) hhhh that you feel that way but ah =
272	M	= No buts no no conditions hold it Philip right there (.) Ann (3) if (.) in the future (.) there is no physical contact no (.) lunches (.) or dinners et cetera (.) and that if there's a need for academic consultations (.) that (.) ano:ther (.) student would be participating in those consultations (.) you could benefit academically from that (.) that third mind in the room hhh (3) and given Philip's regret for having what has happened (.) how comfortable are you now about being able to move on (.) with your (.) academic career↑

this form of reductionism is bound to a certain restricted interpretation of economic theory, which, during the past century, has contributed to the spread of an anthropological conception according to which human actions are not motivated by the reasoned desires of human agents, but rather by their resentment towards others who might "steal" something from them. This conception is clearly incompatible with the effort of resolving a conflict by a peaceful means such as mediation.

273 A Eh: that's (.) much more comfortable and (.) (*crying*) that means a lot to ME (.) to have him say (.) that (.) he WAS responsible to take some responsibility in some way (.) and so that (.) I don't feel like (.) I'm just the nut (.) and (.) know that (.) eh: (.) at some level he respects ME as a PERSON and my RIGHT (.) to move you know to move just in the world (.) my world (.) as best I can↓

274 M Mmh =

275 A = And that I do respect him as an academic a great deal and ah (2) and I don't want to lose what I have (.) but eh (.) it means A LOT to hear that

276 M ^{0}Okay^{0}

277 A He I guess in his way is sorry I don't know (.) that's what I choose to hear↓

Something really interesting happens in this passage: the fact that Ann at 273 is in tears and says that Philip's words mean a lot *to her*, showing that he acknowledges her *as a person*, touches her on the deepest level, and she now feels not only safe (because the mediator will help them set clear boundaries), but also understood and *respected* as a person. Ann immediately returns the same trust in Philip: "And that I do respect him as an academic a great deal and ah (2) and I don't want to lose what I have (.)" (turn 275). Here it is likely that the parties' interpersonal conflict (C1, in terms of Chapter 4) is on its way to being extinguished.

The consequences of such a mutual recognition on the development of the argumentative interaction should not be underestimated. Indeed, the re-establishment of trust that one can perceive here constitutes a sort of "seal" on the parties' habit change, which has consequences for the discussion that follows. One episode in particular shows the occurred change. At turn 332, Philip raises an issue that Ann had previously mentioned but then abandoned: the fact that she felt he looked at her in a "strange" way. A discussion on this issue may well be opened up as part of the options for the resolution of the conflict. However, while the mediator is trying to set up such discussion at turn 333, Ann interrupts him by expressing her intention to change her future behaviour (turns 338–340), thus interpreting the issue as irrelevant, because she is not "going around looking for things".

Such a personal initiative by Ann really shows the change of perspective she has assumed: it signals that she feels comfortable about speaking directly to Philip, whom she addresses directly at 338, and that she feels that their future interaction can proceed almost on the terms of a normal interpersonal interaction. Philip, although he still needs the mediator's help at 342, finally confirms to be confident that Ann will not malevolently interpret his behaviour in the future.

332 P How do we get over this looking business that she was talking about that I look at her in some (.) strange way

333 M Oh I think you have to be aware of it (.) number one (.) you have to be aware of it (.) number one (.) and you have to be aware Ann that it is not an attempt to cross the boundary number two (.)

334 A Mmh
335 M You both have to work at it (.)
336 A Mmh
337 M You've both got to have some shift in your perceptions about it (.) and if you're aware of it (.) and (.) therefore (.) play it out differently in doing the lecture (.) and if you're aware about it (.) a:nd re (.) define it (.) it (.) from (.) leering (.) to some other form (.) then it doesn't exist (.) I mean/=
338 A = I mean I want to forget it Professor Ford I I
339 P [( )
340 A [I'm not going to go around looking for things↓
341 P Okay well that's what it seemed to me that you were sort of out to get me I must say that's how I perceived it at the (.) start of
342 I M Does it seem that now↑
343 P Well I (.) no I've got a bit more understanding (.) no
344 M All right

From the excerpts presented above, it can be deduced that the deepest effect of the movement from conflict to consent allowed by the mediator's intervention is the habit change of the human beings involved in mediation. This aspect highlights an important facet of the reasonableness involved in real argumentation, which does not only include the logical development of the reasoning, but also its anchoring in the parties' common ground which enables the parties to change. Thus, in mediation the relational and emotional aspect (the second order conditions, see Chapter 1) is really part of the argumentative dimension, since it has to be taken into account in order to construct a confrontation stage on issues that can truly meet the parties' interests and constitute viable solutions to the conflict, which fulfil the parties' expectations. What is shown in this case is that, if the deepest level of the parties' interest is overlooked, involving their mutual respect as individuals, any further discussion may be blocked.

6.2.2.6 *Going back to a "fundamental issue"*

In the case of Philip and Ann, before the explicit mutual recognition described above happened, the proceeding of the pragmatic structure of mediation and, in particular, the ongoing argumentative discussion, was blocked. As already noted, at a certain point the mediator understands that there is a need to go back to phase 1 of the core process of mediation (*analysis of context and conflict*) after having spent some time discussing the options constituting boundaries (phase 2). In fact, the discussion on boundaries turns out to presuppose premises that were not in the parties' common ground initially: as a consequence of their conflict, the parties do not trust each other, and therefore do not concede to each other the credit of co-operating in good faith. The mediator understands that the parties' mutual recognition and trust were endangered in the conflict; being recognized and trusted constitute interests deeply rooted in both parties. These interests need to be acknowledged before moving to the phase of options. In other words, the mediator realizes that the original difference of opinion C2 has not been thoroughly identified until this point; in fact, the issue of mutual respect and trust is at stake in conflict.

Consequently, the question of boundaries cannot not be thoroughly discussed because, since the parties do not trust each other in the present, they do not think that their relationship can work in the future, and believe that, even if they define boundaries, the same problem will re-emerge. The presence of the unsolved part of C2 within the discussion emerges from the fact that, although the discussion on specific sub-options has already started, and the parties have agreed on some points (no physical contact, no invitations), they go on quarrelling on what has happened and accusing each other of fallaciously reconstructing the events.

Therefore, at 254, the mediator moves to this aspect of the parties' interests and does not go back to the discussion on the options issues until the parties have reached an agreement on this "fundamental issue":

254	M	Let me come back to a fundamental issue here↓ (.) it's a FUNDAMENTAL issue↓ (4) I think we all recognize that (.) part of the problem that existed here (.) is tha::t (.) you don't like (.) to (.) have (.) a relationship that you perceive to be a professional one (.) to: (.) include (.) touching (.) or to inclu::de (.) out-of (.) normal hou:rs (.) relationship interaction (.) dinners lunches et cetera (3) you Philip (.) feel (.) that's okay (.) and that with some other students you have lunch with them/
255	P	I'm friendly with all my students↓ =
256	M	= Okay (.) now (.) the fundamental issue is this (.) can you accept (.) Ann's right (3) to draw those boundaries for herself (.) about what's comfortable for her (.) does she have that right↑
257	P	Oh she certainly does if she wants to↓
258	M	Do you accept then (.) that if you inadvertently cross those boundaries (3) that that would (.) upset her/
259	P	(2) Well I suppose it would upset her but then she should have established those boundaries which she hasn't done up to now and (.) she's just gone straight off on a tangent without establishing them [that's that's my experience
260	A	[I never had a chance to establish them
261	P	My concern is that if we continue this relationship
262	A	There's no relationship to continue↓ =
263	P	= She's going to go (.) off again on another tangent somewhere (.) and so that that really concerns me [I want this thing at rest once and for all

264 M [Okay let's then go to my next point (.) okay let's then go to my next point (.) okay let's then go to my next point (.) which is (.) if (.) you inadvertently (.) crossed those boundaries (.) partly because you didn't know that they existed (.) and that's always a problem where there is a relationship of a more powerful person and [a less powerful person

265 P [This is a [fabrication↓ ( )

266 M [Let me (.) let me just generate this other part (.) can you see that it would be appropriate (.) to: (.) express your concern of having done that (3) inadvertently/

267 P In in what way how do you mean↑

268 M (3) Do you think given those facts if that if those arguments are correct about the boundaries et cetera (.) tha:t (.) it would be appropriate to apologize for inadvertently crossing those boundaries/

269 P (4) Well (.) apologies I should eh (.) hh I could ( ) I guess if she's got boundaries that (.) are valid (.) and she feels they've been crossed I: (.) can accept that that I not only regret it but (.) I've offended her unintentionally (.) I (.) probably can deal with something of that nature

270 M Hh would it be possible for you to say that directly to Ann rather than to me↑

271 P (4) I suppose so Ann if (.) if you've got boundaries that I don't know about and I've crossed them I I I guess I have a sense of regret that (.) hhhh that you feel that way but ah =

272 M = No buts no no conditions hold it Philip right there (.) Ann (3) if (.) in the future (.) there is no physical contact no (.) lunches (.) or dinners et cetera (.) and that if there's a need for academic consultations (.) that (.) ano:ther (.) student would be participating in those consultations (.) you could benefit academically from that (.) that third mind in the room hhh (3) and given Philip's regret for having what has happened (.) how comfortable are you now about being able to move on (.) with your (.) academic career↑

273 A Eh: that's (.) much more comfortable and (.) (*crying*) that means a lot to ME (.) to have him say (.) that (.) he WAS responsible to take some responsibility in some way (.) and so that (.) I don't feel like (.) I'm just the nut (.) and (.) know that (.) eh: (.) at some level he respects ME as a PERSON and my RIGHT (.) to move you know to move just in the world (.) my world (.) as best I can↓

Then the discussion goes back to boundaries, thus enabling the parties to come to an agreement that will be directly reported to the concerned academic authorities by the mediator; thereby, they successfully accomplished the mediation process.

From the point of view of the dynamics of conflict resolution in a happily concluded mediation session, the sequence of issues should be:

$$C2 \rightarrow \text{issue}_{opt} \rightarrow \text{sub-issues}_{opt}$$

From the chronological point of view, what actually happens in the Philip-Ann session is the following:

$$C2 \rightarrow issue_{opt} \rightarrow sub\text{-}issues_{opt} \rightarrow C2 \rightarrow issue_{opt} \rightarrow sub\text{-}issues$$

These dynamics make us reflect on the fact that the movement from conflict to consent is not completed if the parties do not raise all the fundamental issues that are bound up with their conflict, because the options resulting from the discussion must truly reflect their real interests; in particular, at least in this case, mutual respect as human beings is at issue. If the conflict has not been thoroughly analysed, those interests that are endangered by it cannot wholly emerge. The options, in this case, would necessarily turn out to be partial solutions that only cover a part of the disputants' concerns. In this case, although there may be agreement on certain options, the discussion could always go back to previous points. However, the mediator has no way of verifying that all the components of C2 have come to light other than the parties' confirmation. Thus, when he thinks he has reached agreement, he tends to proceed with the options while being aware that other issues may still emerge.

6.2.2.7 *Negotiating on specific options*

The sub-issues that, taken together, constitute the definition of the new boundaries of Ann and Philip's relationship, are the following:[49]

a. Physical contact
b. Invitations
c. Having discussions in "normal times"
d. Presence of a third person during the parties' discussions
e. Use of "normal" hours for the parties' discussions
f. Philip's way of looking at Ann
g. Management of possible future misunderstandings

In this case, the "macro-text" of argumentation in mediation turns out to be completed by a series of sub-discussions on specific options. Each sub-issue$_{opt}$, in fact, gives rise to an argumentative discussion whereby all the dialectical stages can be identified. The fact that the parties have eventually accepted the mediator's standpoint "Ann must set clear boundaries" puts Ann in the position of protagonist and Philip in that of antagonist in a critical discussion.

49. In this list, all the sub-issues are considered, including those that are discussed before the shift back to phase 1, and those discussed later.

The management of the discussions on specific sub-options is quite similar in all cases (a–g); as an example, here, the treatment of issue (d) is presented. It is noteworthy that in general, as these sub-discussions are activated, some change from the initial situation of conflict emerges relative to the parties' ability to assume an argumentative attitude. Let us analyse how the argumentative discussion on (d) can be reconstructed, in order to see how the nature of the discussion is changing at this point. At turn 233, Ann proposes a standpoint: as an alternative option to the idea of meeting during regular working hours, which Philip has declared impossible, she agrees to meet with him out of regular working hours but only in the presence of a third person. Philip immediately agrees, though for a reason that is criticized by the mediator, who perceives that there is still a deep disagreement between the parties. Notice, by the way, that this sub-discussion starts before the mediator has brought attention back to C2 (see the previous section). It will be completed later, after the parties have agreed on mutual respect.

233	A	(2) Or I'll meet with another mature student we can meet together (.) if (.) if it's absolutely impossible (.) to meet during the day (.)
234	M	Okay
235	A	I'll meet with one of the other mature students and he can entertain our questions
236	M	Is that good with you ( )
237	P	Oh that's fine I I don't want to ever see her one on one again (.) because it's just impossible for me to keep up with these kind of WILD allegations that come out of her↓
238	M	It IS possible Philip if (.) we (.) recognize that (.) different people need different (.) relationships
239	P	(.) Ah if somebody else is there then that's fine↓ =

In this case, it is Ann who, unsolicited by the mediator, puts forward a standpoint (turn 233) and assumes the clear role of protagonist. In this passage, the argumentative discussion on option (d) seems to be almost useless, because the parties appear to maintain the same standpoint, i.e. that there should be a third person present during their meetings. However, after the interruption due to the discussion on C2, the mediator restates this seemingly achieved agreement at 278, and some further disagreement emerges. In particular, Philip casts some doubts on Ann's standpoint, reformulated by the mediator at 280:

279	P	= That there is going to be a third person present is that what you mean/(.) by agreement↑

280	M	Well (.) the agreement would be (.) no no physical contact (.) no luncheon invitations or dinner invitations (.) and that when (.) an academic consultation is required (.) outside of the (.) normal (.) hours that (.) another student would participate and we would arrange that NOT specifically there has to be a monitor (.) but in fact it would be (.) a three-person consultation (.) and the idea is (.) to bounce ideas around
281	P	Well that that might be (.) problematical because sometimes we have to address a particular (.) assignment that one student is doing here
282	M	Ya
283	P	But I I need an independent objective (.) an independent witness present to make sure that there is no (.) suggestions such as has been made here of improper things taking place↓
284	M	My sense is [that
285	P	[I want to protect myself↓
286	M	My sense is that you don't need an independent person (.) to know how to behave appropriately
287	P	No I don't need that (.) but I do need to to make sure that if there are any (.) more wild allegations made that that it can readily be seen that they are unfounded

Philip's reasoning is reconstructed in the following table:

Table 6.5. Reconstruction of the argumentation

Turns	*Analytical reconstruction (standpoints and arguments)*	
		Mediator (on behalf of Ann)
280		(d).1.[50] When there is a need for academic consultation, another student participates
	Philip (d).1 ? (d). 1.1. Each student has his/her own assignment (d).1.1.1. And that conflicts with my need to have someone to protect me	

This critical discussion is retrieved by the mediator at 308 and eventually concluded. Notice that the mediator reformulates Ann's standpoint twice, at 280 and 308 respectively. In contrast to what we have seen previously, however, the mediator here does not makes use of a reformulation to personally assume Ann's standpoint. In this case, Ann's standpoint directly concerns a possible solution to the conflict (or part of a solution) and, therefore, the mediator remains neutral.

50. *(d).1.* is the notation selected for indicating the mediator's standpoint (which is, indeed, a reformulation of Ann's at turn 233, on issue (d).

In this case, the reformulation can be interpreted as a mere repetition, useful for reminding parties of the status of their confrontation stage. The discussion from 308 on develops thus:

308	M	Okay (.) but then what it what it means for you I think is two things Philip (.) is one is (.) that you delineated some very clear things and those are rather simple (.) no physical contact no invitations tho- those I think are relatively simple we suggested (.) a: (.) a third (.) ah:: course of action (.) that I think would make both of you more comfortable and enable both of you (.) to move forward academically and put all of this stuff behind both of you (.) it would be that if you have a consultation outside of the normal hours hh (.) that (.) you do it on a group basis↓ =
309	P	= Which is outside of just the normal hours↑ =
310	M	= Outside ten to five
311	P	In the absence of anybody else this is going to be ( )
312	M	Or you may feel that you would not for a while until you can get greater clarity (.) about these things (.) you may not want to meet with Ann one-on-one behind a closed door (.) that's OKAY (.) there are [lots of other
313	P	[Is that okay with you↑
314	A	Absolutely
315	M	There are lots of places you can meet publicly in an academic setting (.) in a sense and still discuss academic things (.) or alternatively (.) you can begin TO to arrange the situation where more than one student (.) student (*cough*) excuse me (.) is present during an academic discussion↓ (.) eh I did that all the time because I always felt (.) that one could generate more ideas with (.) with (.) with more exploration =
316	P	= Can it be a male student or a female student↑
317	M	Does it matter↑
318	P	I don't know does it matter
319	M	Does it matter to you Ann↑
320	A	Well I don't know I don't think it matters
321	P	Obviously somebody fairly independent
322	M	Why (.) that person doesn't know they're not there (.) eh eh for any other reason than to participate in the academic (.) discussion↓
323	A	I don't want them to know about this (.)
324	M	They are not monitors
325	A	They're not there to be a watchdog↓
326	M	They're not watching you and they're not watching Ann they're PARTICIPATING in an ACADEMIC discussion↓
327	P	But if she (.) later on I cross these boundaries and then she makes an allegation later on I cross her boundaries and she makes another allegation later on I want somebody to be able to say (.) whether these things happened or didn't happen

328	M	You don't need to alert people to say (.) I want you to join in this academic discussion (.) so that if I am accused of some sort of harassment you can then (.) prove that I didn't [I don't think that
329	P	[No we don't need to say that
330	M	No we don't need to say (.) that do we what we need to say (.) is that we need to have for your comfort and (.) for your comfort we need to have a third person (.) there you may review it jointly three or six months from now you may want to come back and talk to me about three or six months down the pike (.) in the sense of knowing that you DON'T NEED that (.) in which case you can (.) can move to the (.) one on one (.) but in the next period it would seem to me to be very useful just to ENLA::RGE the numbers in the academic discussion (.) from two (.) to three (.) or even four (.) for no other purpose than to give you both a sense of comfort so that you're not WORRYING about (.) the discussions we've had today (.) when you discussing some major environmental issue (.) tomorrow

A remarkable feature of this sub-discussion (d), which can be found analogously in the other sub-discussions, is the fact that Philip and Ann have acquired a much more mature attitude from a dialectical point of view. It can be said that the passage to co-arguers has now been established, although the parties move to their new role as participants in a critical discussion in a somewhat fragile fashion, so that some mediator's interventions are still necessary. In other words, once the mediator has achieved the objective of identifying C2 and, then, of bringing the parties to discuss the options, he seems to have accomplished a large part of his work. As it appears from the excerpts above, the parties tend to stay on the issue rather than continue to accuse each other; and they tend not to mention the origin of their conflict any more. From the point of view of the management of their interaction, there are fewer interruptions and overlapping turns, so the discussion appears much more serene. Most significantly, at 313 Philip directly asks Ann's opinion on a mediator's proposal, which has never happened before.

The interaction scheme of mediation almost seems to turn into a *negotiation* (with some of the traits of a *problem-solving* discussion), where the parties aim at finding a solution that can satisfy their respective interests. The mediator encourages the parties' new attitude, by engaging himself in the discussion as a neutral advisor who only helps them define a good common agreement, as at 312, 315[51]

51. Very interestingly, at 315 the mediator, calling on his personal experience as a former academic, gives the parties a further reason why, according to him, a discussion on a group basis would be useful: "Alternatively you can begin to arrange the situation where more than one student is present during an academic discussion. I did that all the time *because I always felt that one could generate more ideas with more exploration*". Such a reason does, indeed, exceed his mediator's role, and puts him on the level of a friendly collaborator in Ann and

and 330, and by using the personal pronoun "we" when speaking of the parties' interests at 330.

Once the passage to co-arguers has happened, the conflict is some way to being resolved. Here, the parties seem to become able to negotiate their problem, since the harshest aspects of the conflict have dissolved. In this sense, one can interpret negotiation not only as a specific ADR practice, but also as the genus of which mediation is a species, which in this sense becomes a negotiation *facilitated* by an initial intervention by a mediator. This observation is in line with many interpretations of the relations between mediation and other ADR practices (such as the Harvard model of negotiation), which have been discussed in Chapter 3, as they constitute an important contribution to the theoretical elaboration on mediation.

6.2.3 Some responses and some refinements of the research questions

As has been argued in Chapter 5, the double-step structure on which the argumentative analysis is based has the advantage of allowing us to progressively refine and specify the research questions and arrive at an accurate and punctual analysis of a relatively large corpus of empirical data.

In relation to the objectives of the argumentative analysis outlined in Chapter 5, the analysis performed up to now has shown that argumentation in mediation can be reconstructed as a complex critical discussion, multiple in a qualitative sense. In it, different standpoints are put forward, giving rise to a macro-text of argumentative discussions corresponding to the pragmatic structure of this practice. In part, these outcomes emerged unexpectedly. In fact, in the attempt to analytically reconstruct argumentation in mediation, the reality of this practice emerged as more complex than expected. In this relation, the model of a critical discussion served as an analytical grid that allowed discovering the delicate interplay of discussions constituting a real mediation interaction.

In particular, phase 1 of the core process of mediation tends to host the confrontation and opening stages of the parties' main discussion, i.e. respectively the moment in which a difference of opinion emerges and is clarified between the parties who act as protagonist and antagonist, and the moment in which their

Philip's negotiation. It is, moreover, a suggestion that the mediator feels he can give to Philip on an interpersonal basis about how to improve his professional practice (beyond the resolution of this problem). This unexpected and apparently contextually incongruous move can be interpreted as a "gratuitous" move, exceeding the boundaries of the interaction scheme of mediation. More generally, it is a sign of the progressive establishment of interpersonal trust in this dialogue.

common starting points are identified. In this process, the mediator performs the non-canonical role of a third neutral, which corresponds neither to protagonist nor to antagonist. The confrontation and opening stages do not emerge spontaneously, but need to be helped by the mediator's intervention. In particular, the construction of a confrontation stage is seen to require a very complex process guided by the mediator. By this process, parties are helped to identify the issue on which they originally had a difference of opinion (C2). From that moment on, however, the discussion is shifted by the mediator from C2 to one or more issues in relation to which standpoints can be put forward, which may represent viable solutions to C2, the so-called issue(s)$_{opt}$.

Later on, in discussions on specific options, the argumentation stages can be envisaged, in which parties bring forward arguments, negotiate solutions and exchange the roles of protagonist and antagonist. It could be said that the parties' general discussion on the resolution of their conflict has a very particular argumentation stage, which is constituted by the different argumentation stages of the discussions on options. This constitutes a first reason why the dispute in mediation is to be considered multiple in a qualitative sense: if parties solve these discussions on options, they hereby find a solution to their general conflict, thus also concluding their general discussion. The concluding stage is ideally hosted by phase 3.

It can thus be said that the crucial dynamics of mediation, namely the disputants' "transformation" into co-arguers, mainly pertains to phase 1. As the passage from disputants to co-arguers happens during the first phase and, in the second phase, parties prove to be able to discuss between each other, the analysis of the remaining part of the empirical corpus considered in the present research can be concerned mainly with the first phase. A particularly critical point emerged in the passage from C2 to the various options, based on the options' correspondence with the parties' real interests which have emerged through the analysis of the conflict. This aspect will therefore be taken into account in detail.

It is interesting to note how this transformation happens through the mediator's *direct argumentation*, which is far from being absent from the discussion. Although the mediator cannot argue about one or the other solution, he is responsible for the quality of the parties' argumentative discussion: this apparent contradiction expresses the mediator's paradox (Chapter 1). Mediators seem to cope with this paradox by arguing in a very specific way, which is aligned with their professional role. In fact, in analysing Case 1, besides the mediator's intervention in the construction of the confrontation stage of the discussion about the resolution of the conflict, the mediator has also emerged as a protagonist of some of the discussion, which corresponds to *meta-discussions* on crucial passages. In particular, I have shown how the mediator personally assumes the standpoint of the parties' need to discuss the *boundaries* of their relationship. The mediator's direct argumentation emerges as functional to the constitution of the parties' confrontation stage – in fact, he argues for the issue that they should debate. This is a second reason for considering the mediation discussion as a particular type of a multiple dispute in a *qualitative* sense. In fact, if the mediator had failed to win his case, the discussion between the parties would be blocked.[52]

We can now match the results of the first step of our empirical analysis with the mediation phases that have emerged from the ontology-oriented conceptual framework of mediation presented in Chapter 4. The representation in Figure 6.6 represents a first answer to the question raised in Chapter 1 about how argumentation helps fulfil the pragmatic goals of mediation. In fact, in order for the script of mediation to proceed, following the phases of the core process, a complex macro-text of argumentative discussions – a dispute multiple in the qualitative sense – needs to be activated. In this multiple dispute, the mediator is seen to play a particularly active role in the setting up of the confrontation and opening stages. Distinctive of the multiple dispute of mediation is the argumentation stage, composed by the sum (indicated with Σ in Figure 6.6) of the argumentation stages of the sub-discussions opened up by the different options which the parties are considering.

It is evident that such a multiple dispute, which can also be considered a macro-text of argumentative discussions, is peculiar to mediation as an interaction scheme imposing a specific institutional mandate. Such a macro-text of discussions does not generally arise spontaneously, as is the case in ordinary discussion; indeed, it is tightly connected to the nature of the interaction scheme of mediation and it is wisely and intentionally managed by the mediator. In this sense, the *context* of mediation, in terms of the characteristics of its interaction scheme, seems to influence the nature and development of the various discussions involved, in particular for the selection of viable issues. This observation partially anticipates the answer to a question that can only be thoroughly answered by comparing the influence of context in the various cases of the corpus, which represent many applications of mediation to different interaction fields.

52. Given the institutional embeddedness of the interaction scheme of mediation in a precise interaction field, namely the university in which the problem has arisen, an unsuccessful outcome of mediation would have very negative consequences on the parties. Here, the mediator's proposal of a specific issue for the discussion is to be interpreted as his attempt to fulfil his institutional mandate; in fact, he chooses an issue that is relevant to the resolution of the conflict. If he failed to win his cause, negative consequences would follow also for the parties; Philip, in particular, could be prevented from maintaining his academic position in the faculty.

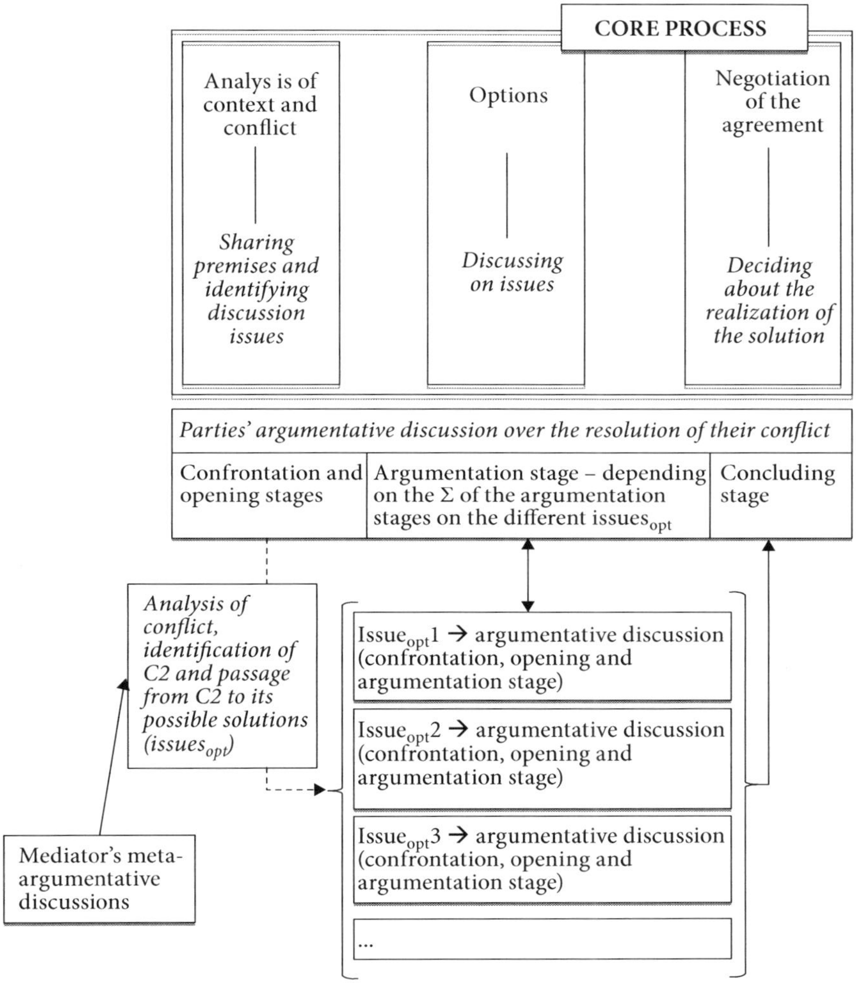

Figure 6.6. Representation of the macro-text of argumentative discussions in mediation

The mediator's special role of third neutral does not keep him from being a participant in the critical discussion and having a personal strategic manoeuvring. As seen in Chapter 2, studies in the argumentative strategies of mediation have rightfully brought to light the relevance of some *presentational devices* of the mediator's argumentation and have expounded their dynamics and weight at the level of strategic manoeuvring. From the analysis of this first step, it emerges that an equally crucial role needs to be attributed to the mediator's strategic manoeuvring with the *topical potential*, in particular in relation to the delicate raising of the parties' interests in different stages of the critical discussion and in the appropriateness of the mediator's arguments to the institutionalized and interpersonal context of the dispute. As van Eemeren and Garssen (2009: 6) remark, although in strategic manoeuvring the three aspects of topical potential, audience demand and presentational devices are inextricably connected, "in argumentative practice the one aspect is often more prominently manifested than the other". In our case, the mediator's strategic manoeuvring with the topical potential certainly emerges as a key instrument in the setting up of the parties' argumentative discussion.

From this latter observation, some considerations can be drawn, which will be taken into account in the following step of the analysis.

First, two moments have emerged as essential concerning the mediator's management of the topical potential in the confrontation and opening stages of the parties' main discussion: the identification of C2 through the analysis of the parties' conflict and the movement from C2 to the options for conflict resolution that respond to the parties' interests. The analysis of the broader corpus (Cases 2–6) will thus be based on the identification of these two passages.

Second, a keystone of the movement towards the resolution of the conflict seems to be the consideration of *interests*. Interest has emerged in several passages as the resolutive factor, both in the confrontation stage, for the identification of the relevant issues, and in the argumentation stage, as the real "engine" of the resolution of the conflict. Particular attention will thus be devoted to the elicitation of interests.

6.3 Second step: The features of the mediator's argumentative contribution

On the basis of these considerations, it is now possible to design a more precise analysis of the remaining part of the corpus.

The analysis will focus on the first phase of the mediation process in particular, by verifying how the passage from disputants to co-arguers actually occurs and how it helps disentangle the parties' conflict and brings them to discuss possible solutions to their problem. The cases from 2 to 6 have therefore been analysed in their pragmatic structure and the relevant communicative moves pertaining to the first phase of the mediation process have been selected. The analysis that will be presented in the following sections is relative to this phase only.

The particular significance of the mediator's strategic manoeuvring with the topical potential in relation to the construction of the parties' confrontation and opening stages, which has been described in the previous section, will be tested against the whole corpus of empirical data (Section 6.3.1). The presence of the mediator's meta-argumentative moves will also be verified (Section 6.3.2.). Furthermore, the possible function of the elicitation of parties' interests as crucial knots allowing the resolution of the conflict will be considered as well.

Certainly, the results of the first step of the analysis constitute guiding principles to orientate the research on the other cases. However, they equally constitute hypotheses to be verified on a larger evidence basis, from which unexpected results are expected, which somehow surprise and exceed the research questions. For this reason, the analysis will also be open to possible refinements or corrections of the conclusions drawn after the first step on the basis of other possible specificities of the mediator's argumentation.

A further component of the analysis concerns more specifically how the *context* contributes to the shaping of the argumentative process that is present in mediation (see Section 6.3.3). Context can be expected to influence the development of the argumentative discussion (van Eemeren & Houtlosser 2005; Rigotti 2006; van Eemeren 2010). In part, we have already seen how the mediator's arguments are anchored in the context. The comparison of different domains of applications will allow a discussion of the role of the specific interaction field to which mediation is applied.

6.3.1 Manoeuvring strategically with the topical potential in the confrontation and opening stages

From the point of view of argumentation theory, the two most significant tenets emerging in the present investigation are (a) the presence of a multiple dispute generated in the mediation process and, thus, bound to this interaction scheme and (b) the mediator's crucial role in constructing the topical potential in the various stages of the discussions.

In analysing Case 1, the first phase of the mediation script was identified with the crucial moment of argumentation in mediation in which the parties, as a result of the mediator's guidance, began to abandon their conflictual attitude and learn to become co-arguers. The analysis will be based on the other cases (Cases 2–6) in order to verify the presence and constituency of the most significant strategies that emerged in Case 1. The mediator's strategic manoeuvring with the topical potential in the confrontation stage of the discussion on the resolution of the conflict is represented in particular by two moments: first, the mediator's analysis of the conflict through his search for the identification of C2, which is the issue originating it; second, the shift from C2 to the options constituting possible solutions to this issue, which is typical of the confrontation stage in the mediation practice. In the rest of this chapter, the presence, relevance and contextual conditions of both these moments will be discussed on the basis of how they emerge from the other cases of the corpus.

6.3.1.1 *The analysis of the conflict: Towards the identification of C2*

The mediator's guidance of the parties towards the exploration of the origin of their conflict (through the identification of the major issue C2) is seen to be relevant in all cases of the corpus. In no cases are parties able to analyse their conflict by themselves.

Although the two mediators considered in the present research always start with the same question, i.e. they begin by asking the parties what their problem is, the parties' answers are diverse and give rise to different kinds of deviation from the dialectical profile of a confrontation stage (van Eemeren, Houtlosser and Snoeck-Henkemans 2007: 26–27).[53]

In some cases, the parties' accusations and reciprocal reproaches are far from constituting a confrontation stage. In such cases, the mediator starts by insisting on hearing the narrative of their conflict (their reciprocal roles, the chronological development of their conflict), thus helping them to find C2 and to specify their positions on this issue. A prototypical example representing this kind of situation is the business and interpersonal conflict involving two friends and co-owners of a business, David and Robert (Case 2). In particular, David's complaints about Robert tend to address his personality and his role within the business; in this case, the conflict has clearly escalated to a situation of interpersonal hostility (C1). Robert, in turn, insists on denying the very existence of any conflict.[54] Overall, the constituency of C2 is, in this case, completely unclear. The mediator fights on two fronts: he has to repeatedly ask David to identify a clear issue that makes him resentful – see in particular turns 22 and 66 – and, at the same time, he has to

53. As a matter of fact, the parties' presentation of their problems frequently turns out to be a fundamental deviation from the dialectical profile of a confrontation stage. Very often there is no real *confrontation* of the parties' standpoints, which tend to refer to different issues, whose relations are not investigated by the parties. The mediator's intervention is thus necessary from the very initial phase of the parties' discussion in order to set up a sound confrontation stage.

54. The strategy of denying the conflict, often called *avoidance*, has been identified as one of the possible attitudes that parties entrenched in a conflict of the type C1 can assume more or less consciously (see Glasl 2004).

overcome Robert's attempts at arguing that, since his work is necessary, the problem raised by David is meaningless:[55]

22 M The (.) the bottom line is okay (.) you feel tha::t the labour costs are too high and (.) could be brought down in some way (.) you feel that (.) the: selling costs are too high and could be brought down/
23 D Well not even (.) I don't even feel that the selling costs (.) are that high everything is in line (.) I just want =
24 R = Well (.) you're here to complain about my expense account↓

[…]

66 M So what is it (.) David (.) that (.) golfing makes you resentful↑
67 D Well (.) basically that he's out there in the open (.) in the sun (.) having fun (.) and I'm in front of the oven and can't (2) well hell (.) you know (.) I guess if being in front of the oven is what I did for leisure (.) maybe I'd enjoy it
68 M Mmh
69 D But I really feel that (.) yes (.) either I've got in have a whole lot more time off (.) and be up (.) in the mountains with my family doing whatever I want to do (.) just to even up the situation and have that time to spend with my family
70 M Would would would you be more comfortable if Robert didn't (.) play golf↑
71 D [Well (.) depending what he was doing↓
72 R [I'm maintaining our [customers
73 D [Well depending what he's doing with his time (.) I guess/
74 R We've got to maintain our customer relationships↓ =
75 D = No fair enough (.) you know Robert is good at (.) is good at (.) good at what he does↓ =
76 R = Well (.) we have increased sales every year
77 D Yes =

55. Part of Robert's argumentation is developed in these passages: see turn 24, where he tries to present David as advancing useless complaints; see also turns 72, 74, 76 and 78, where he quite clearly supports the standpoint that he cannot do otherwise but continue in his way of handling the relationships with the customers, since this way has proven successful. This kind of argumentation shows to have a certain weight – as David seems to acknowledge at 75; nonetheless, the fact that Robert uses it to exclude any possible problem that David may have, and refuses to engage in the construction of a confrontation stage, makes it a fallacious move in this stage of the discussion. In fact, Robert exploits this reasoning to hinder David in opening an argumentative discussion, thus violating the *freedom rule* of a critical discussion, which states that every arguer has the right to advance a standpoint (or to cast doubt on a standpoint). Notice that the mediator does not follow Robert's line of reasoning for the moment, perhaps as he understands that this would block the discussion.

78	R	= I mean (.) it hasn't been as if we've gone backwards/
79	D	That's true but (1.5) I just feel that for the compensation and for the fifty-fifty split (.) I do more than fifty percent (.) and I want to change that (.) either I want to change that [or I'm going to have to get out of the situation
80	R	[( )
81	M	So your feeling is that you're doing more than (.) your half/
82	D	Oh (.) I know it↓
83	M	Okay (.) Robert (.) what's your perception↑

At the beginning, as David's answer is evasive, the mediator's question at 70 seems to be purposefully provoking, because it is clear that the problem cannot be actually centred on the fact that Robert plays golf. At 75, David accomplishes the retraction of the standpoint that the mediator has provokingly suggested to him, and he confirms this at 77. This exchange helps David to specify his existing concern – as it emerges at 79, "that's true, *but* I just feel that for the compensation and for the fifty-fifty split I do more than fifty percent and I want to change that". David's standpoint is reformulated by the mediator at 81. David proves to accept it (by reformulating it, in turn) at 82.

Analogously, a circuitous route to the construction of a confrontation stage on C2 is to be found in Case 5 (*Banker versus caterer*), in which the description of the conflict development precedes the clear formulation of the parties' standpoints on C2. Also in this case, the mediator gives the parties some time to express their discomfort and resentment by narrating how the conflict arose. First, he repeatedly asks what the problem is, i.e. he pushes the parties to identify a clear issue (C2) bound to the conflictual events they have experienced. Only in a second phase, once C2 has been identified, does he ask the parties to formulate precise standpoints on this issue. It must be remarked that, in this case, C2 emerges as a very specific problem, which can easily be transposed at the level of options for conflict resolution. The point mainly concerns how much of Polly's expenses is to be paid by each of the parties. In this case, helping the parties to precisely formulate their standpoints quickly facilitates the resolution of the problem: Tim, for instance, admits he does not want to pay *everything* but he is prepared to pay *something*. Polly, in turn, confesses she does not expect the whole amount to be paid but only *some* of it.

Even in those cases in which the parties' standpoints emerge in an apparently clear fashion, it should be noticed that their reciprocal positions do not normally appear in a sound argumentative discussion. This happens, for example, in Case 6 (*Father and daughter in business*) in which, as early as turn 10, just after the mediator has asked about the parties' problem, the daughter and director of the business (Therese) succinctly presents the nature of the dispute with her father, while clarifying her position on the issue at turn 12:

10 T [Eh:: (.) Dad has a real estate agency eh:: eh:: (.) I WORK (.) there (.) I'm I'm one of the directors and ah:: I was on vacation and (.) eh:: while I was on vacation with a good friend (.) my father fired (.) one of our (.) the BEST people we have and:: (.) well th- the guy's name is James he called me while I was (.) skiing in Austria (.) and I came home and (.) my father just doesn't want to talk about it ( )
11 M Mmh =
12 T = And he just says well you've to accept it and that's it that's why not and:: wh- I know I don't agree with that

Immediately after this, the mediator asks Therese's father to complete this presentation of the problem. The father (Paul) replies by describing his view of how the problem developed, i.e. with a move that pertains more to the opening stage. Quite soon, however, he returns to the presentation of the respective standpoints in a fashion that, not surprisingly given the conflictual background, is very much centred on himself even when describing Therese's point of view:[56]

20 P And Therese is very angry about that because she says she thinks he is (.) her employee which is not the case
21 M Mmh
22 P Because I'm the boss
23 M Mmh
24 P And Therese is director (.) and I've (.) of course (.) there are some plans for the future (.) but she has to learn a lot
25 M Yes =
26 P = I'm responsible I'm taking the decisions (.) and now I think she's angry that I didn't (.) [contact her
27 M [Mmh
28 P [and ask her opinion about that
29 M Mmh
30 P I didn't think it was necessary she had to go on holidays

56. When two people have difficulties in talking to each other, they also have problems in *listening* to each other. Listening, indeed, is by nature an essential component of dialogue. As Cantoni et al. (2008: 214) remark, in Latin the action of being silent is indicated by means of two verbs: *sileo* and *taceo*. The former refers to the silence of entities that in any case cannot intervene – in this sense, a wood could "silere" – while the latter is a communicative concept, referring to the intentional silence of a human being who is listening and, thus, intentionally leaving room for the interlocutor. The importance of listening in communication is acknowledged by conflict resolution professionals, who include in mediation training courses *active listening* (see for instance Philips 1999), which can be realized by numerous techniques, such as *looping* (repetition and summary of the parties' statements).

In fact at turn 20, although correctly recalling Therese's standpoint, Paul provides an argument that rests on his personal interpretation: "because she thinks he is (.) her employee", while Therese has never (and will never) claim unique responsibility for the firing of employees. Paul's move in this case could thus be considered a *strawman fallacy* (see van Eemeren & Grootendorst 1992). Paul, then, slightly corrects himself at turns 26 and 28: "And now I think she's angry that I didn't (.) contact her [...] and ask her opinion about that". Paul's reaction to his daughter's remarks creates a mixed dispute. His standpoint can be inferred from what he says at turn 26: "I'm responsible I'm making the decision", so Therese does not have the right to be angry because, indeed, the decision did not concern her directly. At this moment, Paul seems to have raised a multiple dispute in a qualitative sense: while for Therese, the issue is whether or not her father had the right to fire the employee, for Paul the problem is whether or not Therese has the right to comment on these kinds of decisions.[57] Of course, if Paul succeeds in demonstrating that Therese has no right to comment on his decision, her standpoint will automatically be defeated.

In sum, despite the apparently definite setting up of an argumentative discussion proposed at 10–12, the parties' confrontation stage appears not to be clear: Therese does not accept Paul's characterization of her point of view, nor does she provide an alternative formulation.

It is interesting to observe the moves by which the mediator brings the parties to a true confrontation stage. In a first move, the mediator decides to summarize the difference of opinion in a fairly generic way, by referring to the disagreement on what happened:

41	M	You both disagree
42	T	^{0}Ya^{0}
43	P	Well Therese is very upset about that
44	M	Is it fair to say that both disagree about what- what happened/
45	P	Yes

Then he quickly turns back to further investigate the very nature of the difference of opinion itself. He seems not to be persuaded that the episode first announced by the parties, i.e. the firing of an employee (James), can really be understood as the issue originating their conflict. Following the case shows that

57. The fact that Paul somehow modifies his position at 29, saying that he did not ask Therese's opinion because she was absent and, thus, implicitly recognizing that the decision could also concern her directly, magnifies the confused presentation of the problem.

the mediator's intuition is right, since more general issues concerning the relationship between father and daughter emerge as problematic, while the firing of James appears to have worked as a *casus belli*. Thus, although a first form of confrontation stage is sketched at the beginning of this case (turn 44), the real constellation of problematic issues will emerge only later and through the mediator's guidance.

An apparent counter example can be found in Case 4 (*Adoption*), which presents one of the clearest instances of the confrontation stage: it is one of the parties who, asked by the mediator about the problem, reconstructs the respective standpoints synthetically and precisely. Such a reconstruction will never be questioned later in the transcription of the case:

7	V	= Sure (.) well (3) as you know I gave birth five days ago (.) and: I would like to have some (.) visiting rights with my (.) child they're waiting to adopt the (.) child and (.) they don't want me to have any visiting rights (.) =
8	M	= Mmh
9	V	^{0}that's (.) why we're here^0

Even in this case, however, such a description fails to fully identify the origin of the problem, which arises from a misunderstanding of the terms *adoption* and *visiting (rights)* due to the fuzzy semantics of natural language. At this point in the discussion, however, neither Vivian nor the adopting parents seem to be aware of the fact that their diverging positions derive from a previous misunderstanding of the implications of their decision respectively to give the child in adoption and to adopt him.

6.3.1.2 *From C2 to options*

Let us now consider another salient moment which emerges from the analysis of Case 1. I shall discuss how the mediator moves to *options* in the other cases of the corpus. The relevant passages concerning the movement from the origin of the parties' conflict, namely C2, to the options for its resolution are reported in what follows:

Case 2: Business conflict

81	M	So your feeling is that you're doing more than (.) your half/
82	D	Oh (.) I know it↓
83	M	Okay (.) Robert (.) what's your perception↑

84 R I don't see it as that↓ (.) I mean (.) I'm putting in as many hours as he's putting in and I'm there early in the morning and (.) and I'm doing the sales work I'm making sure that the (.) deliveries are ready for the drivers when they come in in the morning to take the product out (.) eh you know I go on from there I make sure everything is done before I go and meet with the customers (.) it's not always on the golf course obviously you've got to have meetings with them in their offices and so on
85 M Mmh =
86 R = But certainly the other side of it is something that has to be done (.) I mean you've got to keep that up/
87 M So (.) how do we understand that in terms of what we're talking about↑ (.) your your sense is you'd like to increase the mechanization↑

In this case, the shift to options is very subtle. It concerns the abandonment of the previous, actually quite long and difficult, discussion on the origin of David's and Robert's conflict, in favour of a focus on ways to solve the problem. The shift emerges at turn 87; the use of the linguistic expression "you'd like to" signals an orientation towards the future, in contrast with the previous questions asked by the mediator (see for instance 81: "So your feeling is that you're doing more than (.) your half").

Case 3: Conflict at school

46 M Mmh (.) so here's another thing (.) we are getting some clarity and I have a SENSE that what we're going to do this afternoon (.) is get more and MORE CLARITY (.) ah:: so that (.) you can each do what's (.) best for (.) Kevin 'cause I think it's clear (.) that you both want what's the best for him (.) in the context of what's: needed for all of the other kids in the class as: [as well

In Case 3, after a highly charged discussion between the parties (a schoolteacher and a pupil's mother), the mediator can only hypothesize a vague issue-option, which he expresses in the notion of *clarity*: "what we are going to do this afternoon is get more and MORE CLARITY" (here, the issue-option is also emphasized). The shift from the conflict to its resolution is explicitly motivated by being oriented to the parties' shared *goal*: doing what is best for Kevin, the boy in question, in the context of his involvement in a class. From the preceding discussion, the conflict appears to have degenerated into an interpersonal struggle of the type "mors tua vita mea". Probably for this reason, the mediator finds it opportune to remind the parties of what their goal *should be*, in conformity with their interest in Kevin's well-being.

Case 4: Adoption

75 M Okay (.) okay (.) so one of the issues that (.) may arise is not (.) IF you tell him (.) you're his birth Mom but for most couples (.) it is not only an if it's WHEN (.) so we have a number of things to (.) agree to here before you walk out today (.) so one is you want to make sure that Rudolph doesn't forget (.) that (.) you're (.) his Mom (.) you want to ensure that (.) Rudolph (.) always feels as though (.) you never abandoned him (.) and you want to ensure that you have a: (.) GOOD relationship with Rudolph (.) and we still have to discuss the parameters of what this is going to look like (.) just in principle on those (.) three issues alone (.) without looking at what it's going to look like↑ (.) or HOW often or whatever (.) what are your impressions about what (.) Vivian is saying (.) today (.) about WHAT (.) is going to be good for (.) Rudolph

Analogously to Case 3, the shift to the proper discussion on options, i.e. to phase 2, happens through the mediator's selection of the issues on which they are going to talk, also signalled by the introduction "we have a number of things to agree to here before you walk out today", and by the fact that the mediator makes the parties' goals explicit. Also in this case, the general issue is identified as what is better for the baby, Rudolph.

Case 5: Banker versus caterer

187 M Mmh I'm sure we'd talk about the money (cough) (.) the exact amount in a minute (.) (cough) (5) You must have something in your mind about (.) what you'd be willing to pay (1.5) But I'm thinking more (.) of what was like when the two of you were young (.)

188 T Mmh

189 M And you're growing up (1.5) and what would happen if (.) Polly became the banker ↑ (2) a::nd you became (.) the eh:: (.) eh:: (.) person who (.) was very good at (.) eh:: (.) buying (.) exotic fruits and (.) give the items across the world (.) if this problem occurred (.) and (.) you (.) were eh:: (.) the (.) person who (.) helped (.) the catering↑

190 T Mh

191 M And (.) she was the banker↑ (1) You know just by:: (1.5) fate (1) The ( ) passed and you were upset ways [right↑

192 T [Mmh

193 M (2) And you did this favour for your good friend (2) what would you want from (.) Polly↑

194 T What do you mean by (.) You did this favour for your good friend↑

Case 5 is distinguishable for the rhetorical strategy the mediator chooses to add to the options. By using the parties' former good relationship, the mediator dares to suggest an inversion of the roles as he asks Tim what he would want if he were in Polly's position. This *role change* can be interpreted as the assumption of the other's point of view, namely, in this specific case, Tim's understanding of Polly's *perspective*.

More generally, the notion of *perspective* provides interesting insights into the understanding of the dynamics of change in communication. As Graumann and Kallmeyer (2002: 1) remark, the objects of reality are always necessarily viewed by some point of view, bound to the individual's position in space. Such points of view necessarily change when the individual changes his/her position or viewpoint in space. But, the authors argue, moving is not the only way in which human beings can be faced with different perspectives on the same objects: through *communication*, in fact, human beings "learn what other see from their vantage-points and they learn to take the others' perspectives". This acquisition, however, may not be as easy as it could seem from this statement. In fact, as the authors remark, different perspectives can be associated to opposing roles in antagonistic dyads. This kind of situation has been studied mainly by social psychologists (ibid., p. 2). In this sense, in a situation in which opposing parties have different perspectives on their problem, *assuming* (or trying to assume, even as a working hypothesis) *the other's perspective* can become a way to reasonably handle a difference of opinion without letting it degenerate into a full conflict.

This kind of observation seems to be supported by the results of a recent analysis proposed by Schwarz, Perret-Clermont, Trognon and Marro (2008) concerning learning processes intended to foster conceptual change about proportional reasoning. During an experiment that the authors analyse, one of the two young students involved in the learning process, called Itay – after some discussion in which he and his companion, Shay, bring forward different perspectives – admits that his own conclusion "does not prevent him from considering Shay's different conclusion as not being completely at odds with his conclusion" (ibid., p. 69). Following this move, the authors notice that the interaction changes and becomes "unblocked": Shay feels free to appropriate Itay's objection and to elaborate on Itay's argument; he even explains to the adult experimenter, who is present during the interaction, why Itay's doubt on his previous standpoint is justified. The authors argue that "Itay seems to open the way for Shay to appropriate his doubt through a concession" (ibid., p. 70) which also gives Shay the opportunity to save face (ibid., p. 69). This move can be read as Itay's acknowledgement of Shay's *perspective* as legitimate.[58]

58. The authors do not use the term *perspective*, but I believe that Itay's move can be interpreted as the legitimation of his interlocutor's point of view, which in turn, as the authors observe, engenders the latter's assumption of Itay's doubts (see ibid., p. 70).

This example of the friendly management of a disagreement is taken from a co-operative non-conflictual interaction. A similar situation would be unlikely if we replaced Itay and Shay with two disputants at the beginning of a mediation session. In the latter case, as seen, the disputants are normally entrenched and somehow blocked in their respective positions. Given these reflections, what the mediator does with Tim and Polly in the case analysed here emerges as particularly relevant in relation to the resolution of their conflict. In fact, it can be observed that the mediator asks Tim to change his perspective in a situation in which, without the mediator's intervention, it would be really difficult for the parties to arrive at a mutual understanding. By following Case 5, it can be noticed that this mediator's move is decisive: in what follows, Tim stops complaining about what happened and starts proposing to negotiate some form of solution to their problem. By doing this, he presupposes that it will be possible to continue his relationship with Polly in some way and that the practical arrangement is "a matter of negotiation" (see turn 225). The inversion of perspective, thus, in this case appears to have a positive influence on the discussion.

Case 6: Father and daughter in business

In Case 6, the passage to options takes longer and is complicated by continuous returns to the conflict. The salient moves are all centred on Therese's *wishe*s for her father's behaviour in the future. The mediator tries to shift the discussion to consider this issue, which allows taking the parties' future co-operation for granted and elaborates on the possible facets of such co-operation. The subsequent mediator's attempts to consider this issue are reported here:

134	T	Well:: (.) We didn't really have a discussion about that he said (.) do you wanna be the director of one of the:: (.) the offices and I (.) worked with other firms so he knows that I can do that and:: (1) well (.) I'm not just another employee and being ( ) of the family well (.) we didn't have much discussion about that no
135	M	Mmh (.) In a way do you wish there were more discussion/(.) or less discussion/
136	T	I:: (.) I wish that (.) dad would listen to people a bit more
137	M	That dad would (.) listen to (.) people a bit more
138	T	Ya
139	P	Oh well if they say (.) things that make sense (.) that make sense it's all right

[...]

154	M	Mmh (.) when Therese said eh (.) she:: (.) wished (.) that you would listen (.) to people more
155	P	Mmh
156	M	What people (.) were you talking (.) about↑
[…]		
174	M	Mmh (.) When you were saying (.) Therese that you wish that your father would listen to people more (.) were you one of those people also↑
175	T	(2) I wasn't talking about myself
176	M	Mmh (1.5) [you were
177	T	[but it would be nice
178	M	What would be nice ↑
179	T	If I could have (.) ad- ad- adult conversations with my father without him (.) saying every three seconds well (.) I'm the boss
180	P	But dear we already have adult conversations about the business (.) and about your life (.) so what's wrong
181	M	So what would these conversations (.) look like Therese did you have to (.) describe to your father (.) what (.) a conversation (.) would look like that would make (.) YOU feel (.) listened to (.) what would it look like (.) could you explain that to dad ↑
182	P	Tell me (.) what's wrong ↑
183	T	(2) Ah:: (2) Well if- you don't really listen do you ↑ I mean (.) [( )
184	P	[I listen
185	M	So:: (.) Therese (.) you have to tell your dad (.) what you would like (.) so:: (.) why don't you tell him what you do want (.) what you (.) would like him to do for you

The mediator's strategy seems to be progressively consolidated because, albeit with frequent interruptions, he insists on asking Therese to describe a possible world that would correspond to her interest.

6.3.1.3 *Strategic manoeuvring with interests*

As has already emerged from the analysis of Case 1 (see Section 6.2.2.4 in particular), the category of *interest* seems to be a keystone for understanding the passage from identifying the origin of the conflict (C2) to imagining new possible solutions. Some remarks are necessary here, in light of the results of the analysis of the whole corpus, and in particular in relation to the mediator's *strategic manoeuvring with the topical potential* in the confrontation stage. In fact, this aspect of strategic manoeuvring prominently emerges in the whole corpus.

First, in all cases, focusing on the *future* of the parties' relationship, and thus presupposing that such a relationship will exist, meets the parties' deepest interest, i.e. that of saving their relationship or – better – of restoring it on a more solid and mature basis. This interest, though normally not made explicit by the parties, is however the motivation for their choice of an alternative dispute resolution practice like mediation.

Moreover, in all cases, evoking interests is performed by means of a *presupposition accommodation* (Greco 2003; see also Section 6.2.2.3 and 6.2.2.4). In fact, by asking how the parties' relationship will work in the future, the mediator presupposes that it will work; and this is probably the parties' deepest concern. As seen in the previous section, such a strategy is even clearer in Case 5, where the mediator "forces" one of the parties not only to imagine their relationship in the future, but also to imagine it through the other party's eyes by assuming her perspective.

In some cases, the retrieval of interests is solicited by the mediator's reminder of a *goal* shared by the parties, as in Cases 3 and 4. Interestingly, in both these cases, what is at issue is not only the parties' rapport, but also another person (a young boy or a baby, whom both parties love and feel responsible for), who risks being damaged by their conflict. An interesting example of what has been called *relational happiness* (Section 6.2.2.4) emerges here. The parties' true interests are compatible as, at one level, they involve some common good, namely the happiness of a child, who would benefit from the fact that parties will have a peaceful relationship in the future. In the case of the conflict at school (Case 3), this is fairly clear. For the child's mother, in fact, it is better that her son have a good relationship with his teacher; at the same time, it is in the teacher's interest that her pupil has a calm home environment. Unfortunately, in this case, the mediation process seems to be insufficient to unblock the conflict; and the parties do not seem to be disposed to renounce their interests in damaging each other. At a certain point, the mediator specifically questions their role as a mother and as a teacher respectively, and finds it opportune to remind the parties of their mutual interest in the young boy's well-being.

6.3.2 Mediators' meta-argumentation

It has already been observed in Case 1 that mediators explicitly argue on meta-issues. In fact, beyond assuming the task of controlling the parties' topical potential in the confrontation stage, the mediator also argues directly in specific discussions on meta-issues. Here, again, the extremely crucial role of the *topical potential* has emerged in relation to the choice of adequate premises.

6.3.2.1 *Uncharted waters*

A first example of the mediators' argumentation on a meta-issue is taken from Case 6, in particular from the passage between phases 1 and 2, in which the mediator tries to make the parties shift to options. At 188, following repeated interruptions by Therese's father while she is trying to explain what she would regard as a good relationship in the future, the mediator asks Paul to reflect on the fact that, if he does not know what Therese is going to say, he must wait and listen in order to understand before making any judgement. The relevant excerpt of the dialogue is the following:

188	M	Okay but let (.) let me just make sure I (.) I know that Therese has finished (.) because (.) and I want you to speak just about yourself Therese not about other employees not about other people (.) but I want you to describe your father (1.5) what (.) you (.) need (.) from (.) him
189	T	(3) ah::
190	M	Is it something new for you to (.) listen to this something different/(.) or you've heard this before
191	P	Mmh well no there were no problems and then no now I think (.) you are occurring also those [problems
192	M	[No (.) Is it [something new
193	P	[the the firing of this James (.) [is
194	M	[is her describing to you your daughter describing to dad (2) something that she needs between father and daughter (.) is it something new to you/(.) to hear this/or have you heard this (.) before/
195	P	Eh well eh:: we had the normal quarrels between father and daughter and and there's nothing wrong with that and (.) of course I listen to her (.) I love her so I do I listen to [her
196	M	[Yes (.) as a father
197	P	Yes
198	M	As she describes what she needs from you as your daughter (.) would you have heard this before (.) or is it something new to you↑
199	P	(2) Well ye- yes so far it's new that eh:: (.) I don't know that anything was wrong to that point
200	M	Yes
201	P	(*to Therese*) is it something wrong↑
202	M	Ya (.) So let me make sure I understand this (.) it's something new for the both of you/(.) would that be fair enough to say this↑ (.) or would it not↑
203	T	(3) eh:: (.) well (.) this is the first time I told you (.) I think
204	M	Mmh
205	P	Ya =
206	M	= So this is a new experience for the both of you (3) would that be::/(4)

207 P But that's becoming ( ) problem
208 M Hold on I need to know (.) how you've done this before (.) it sounds to me (.) like this is a new (.) experience (.) for both of you (.) am I on the right track↑
209 T Ya
210 M Dad↑
211 P I guess so yes
212 M Ya (.) and if it is a new experience for the both of you (.) then (.) we're in UNCHARTED waters (.) we don't really know where we go
213 P I don't understand this because (.) we are talking about the firing (.) of James
214 M And if we are in uncharted waters (.) then (.) maybe we should (.) try to make sure we understand (.) where we're going
215 P Mmh
216 M Yes↑
217 P Yes↓ I wonder
218 M So why don't we find out where your daughter is going with this ↑ (.) and just listen to what she has to say
219 P (1.5) Okay speak up
220 M Because it is something new
221 P We are here now (.) it's paid for so (.) speak up

The mediator's reasoning suggests the metaphor of navigating in uncharted waters, where one cannot know the direction in advance. If one finds him/herself navigating in uncharted waters, he/she has to first understand the direction in which he/she is going. Now, such imagery applied in this case suggests that Paul's "navigation" is not under control and he needs to stop his customary way of proceeding until he understands his new situation. Clearly, in order to understand the direction in which he is heading, Paul needs to listen to what Therese is saying, as the mediator suggests at 218.

This reasoning is founded on a locus from the instrumental cause, already described in Section 6.2.2.3. As in that case, the reasoning exploits in particular a maxim based on the relation between means and ends, assuming that, if something is needed, it is reasonable to do whatever ensures it. In other words, if a certain goal is to be pursued, it is reasonable to pursue its means. The complex inferential structure emerging from the analysis of this argument, presented in the synergic representation in Figure 6.7, encompasses two lines of reasoning stemming from as many endoxa. The former (endoxon A) states that people need to know what is unknown and relevant to them. The mediator asks Paul to confirm that what Therese is saying is a new experience for him; although its relevance is unquestioned, because we know that Paul loves Therese. The latter endoxon (endoxon B) is an equally general principle stating that, if someone asks to be listened to, he/she is willing to say something. Therese, indeed, *is* willing to say something, but she could not say it because of Paul's repeated interruptions. As she wants to talk, listening to her becomes, for Paul, the means for knowing what she wants to say. The two lines of reasoning starting with endoxa A and B respectively, taken together, lead to the conclusion: "Paul needs to know what Therese feels, and it is possible for him to know it by listening to her". This conclusion, in turn, is associated with the maxim, leading to the conclusion that, for Paul, listening to Therese is reasonable.

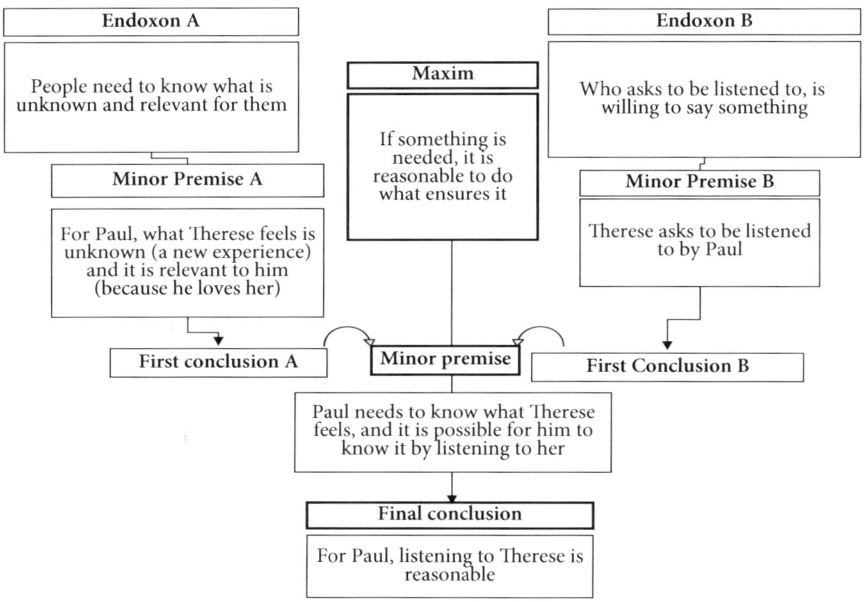

Figure 6.7. Synergic representation of the "uncharted waters" argument

Some considerations can be made on this reasoning. First, it has to be noticed that, from turn 188 to 211, the mediator verifies the hold of the premises of his reasoning – in particular, of the Minor Premise A, i.e. the *datum* (see Figure 6.7) together with the parties. By this procedure, he is preparing the way for its argumentation to be accepted by the parties. From a rhetorical point of view, this way of constructing arguments is didactical – maieutic, one could say – insofar as it brings parties to recognize the premises from which a conclusion will inescapably and quickly be drawn.

Furthermore, the mediator makes use of an effective metaphor, through which he not only forces Paul to recognize that he needs to stop and listen to his daughter, but he also suggests an image of his work as a mediator. In fact, by using the pronoun "we" at turns 212ff., he presents himself as *navigating together with the parties*.[59] It is literally true that the mediator does not know what Therese is going to say, and by this, he also conveys the idea that he is participating with the parties (father and daughter) in the process of exploring their conflict, thus empathically assuming the burden of their difficulties and the hope of finding a solution.

6.3.2.2 *The golden goose*

Another significant example of the mediator's argumentation, founded also in this case on an effective metaphor, this time drawn from a popular fairy tale, can be found in Case 2. At the end of the session, the mediator summarizes the status of the discussion (namely, the consolidated *commitment stores* of the parties, to use Hamblin's terms)[60] and prepares the parties for their future work. At this point, the

---

59. As a matter of fact, the quality of the parties' relationships that are built up in mediation also depends on the mediator's attitude and involvement in the process. Many studies focus in particular on the personal qualities and skills that a mediator must be seen to have in order to intervene effectively in a conflict. Some of the mediators' characteristics are defined by their very role within the practice: mediators must be able to help parties discuss their problem without directing them towards a specific solution (thus the mention of mediators as *facilitators* or, chemically speaking, as *catalysts* of the resolution process). However, mediators are responsible for the process (Haynes & Haynes 1989: 3), i.e. they must guarantee that the parties are truly involved in a mediation intervention, by avoiding the parties' shifting to other kinds of practices and dialogues. In order to fulfil their task, they must be *neutral* and *reliable*. Some insights into the issue of the mediators' reliability, interestingly, derive from the literature drawing on intercultural conflicts, where the problem of mutual trust is felt to be particularly urgent (see Greco 2005b). For example, moving from their experiences in mediating intercultural conflicts (in particular in Australia and Malaysia), Honeyman, Goh and Kelly (2004) identify two essential qualities that any mediator must possess in order to be trusted by the parties: *connectedness* and *authority*. In their own definition, "By *connectedness*, we mean a sense on the parties' part that the mediator is, in some way, 'one of us'. By *authority*, we mean a sense on the parties' part that, even while being 'one of us', the mediator is a person of more than average seriousness of purpose, experience, and gravitas" (ibid., p. 501). These two factors concern not only ethnic conflicts, but are indeed necessary for mutual understanding and trust between all mediators and disputing parties.

60. Hamblin introduced the expression *commitment store* in order to indicate the speaker's "repository" of previous statements that imply as many commitments on his/her side: "A speaker who is obliged to maintain consistency needs to keep a store of statements

parties have already learned to trust the mediator for the work he has been performing during the session. It could be hypothesized that, for this reason, he dares to directly present a meta-standpoint which is crucial as it is directly connected with the very goal of the mediation practice. At turn 406 he declares "There's got to be a solution", which can be more explicitly reconstructed as "it is possible to find a solution to your conflict through mediation". Mediation, in fact, would guarantee a solution compatible with a common future as business partners and friends, while an adjudicative solution would certainly risk a deterioration in their relationship. In this sense, such a standpoint clearly recalls the aim and value of mediation. Even more interestingly, the argumentation supporting this standpoint is based on a metaphor that points to the value constituted by the very successful business that the parties own and in which they work together:

401 M [...] eh: and all the time I think (.) keeping in mind (.) that (.) one of the things you really want to do is (.) you've got a golden goose here right↑ (.) and it would be crazy to kill the golden goose↓
402 R That's what I've tried to tell him
403 M It's laying the golden eggs you've got a [golden goose
404 D [I'm the GOOSE↓ =
405 R = Ah: (.) [you're not
406 M [You've got a good bottom line (.) you'd be CRAZY to kill it↓ (.) there's got to be a solution↓ (.) there's got to be a solution↓ (.) [...]

The mediator not only highlights the value of their business through the image of the golden goose, but he states explicitly that it would be a pity (literally: "it would be *crazy*") to lose such a value due to the parties' conflict (see turns 401 and 406). Such reasoning clearly rests on a *locus from termination and setting up*, whose inferential dynamics have already been discussed in Section 6.2.2.3. The representation in Figure 6.8 shows that, in this case, the mediator evokes an endoxon that reminds the parties of the importance of profit in a business context. More, as pointed out explicitly by means of the metaphor, their business is not just reaching its goal, but it is even *exceeding* their expectations. This confirms and increases the persuasive force of the whole argumentation.

---

representing his previous commitments, and require of each new statement he makes that it may be added without inconsistency to this store. The store represents a kind of *persona* of beliefs: it need not correspond with his real beliefs, but it will operate, in general, approximately as if it did. We shall find that we need to make frequent reference to the existence, or possibility, of stores of this kind. We shall call them commitment-stores: they keep a running tally of a person's commitments" (Hamblin 1970: 257).

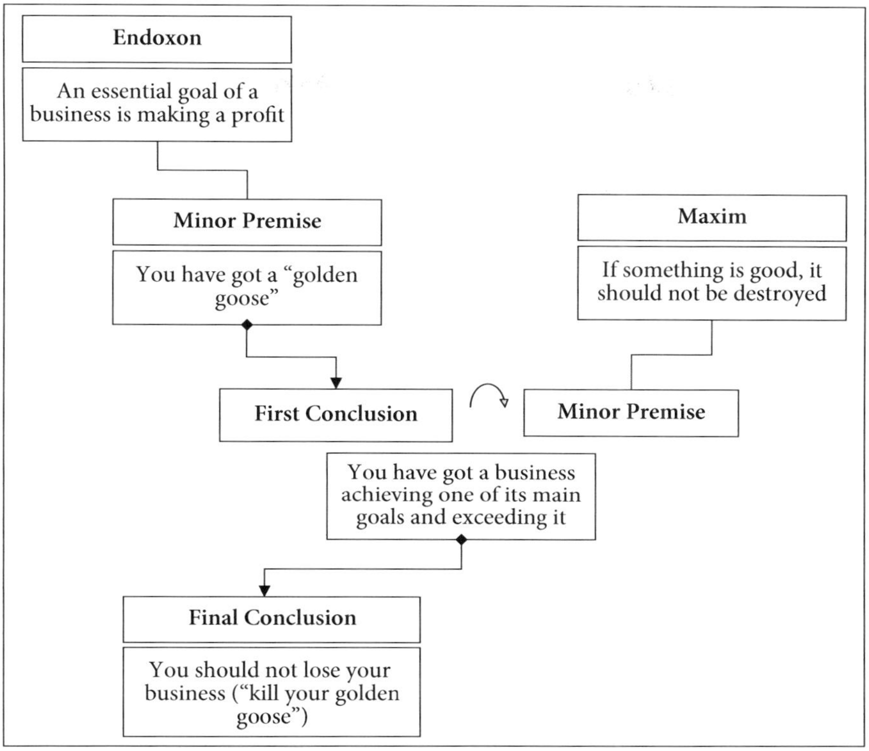

Figure 6.8. Synergic representation of the "golden goose" argument

6.3.2.3 *A particular function of questions: The mediator as a heuristic advisor*

In the cases analysed up to now, the mediator has always assumed a standpoint in the assertive form, either by reformulating the parties' positions, or by means of a personal initiative (as in the "golden goose" example). There is, however, another and more discreet way in which the mediator can suggest possible arguments to the parties, i.e. by means of *questions*. The role of questions as a specific aspect of the presentational devices of the mediator's strategic manoeuvring has been pointed out in several studies (see in particular van Eemeren et al. 1993 and Jacobs 2002). In some specific cases, the mediator uses questions in order to suggest possible lines of arguments for the parties to verify and accept (Greco Morasso 2007). The mediator, in other words, can be said to work as a *heuristic advisor*, providing the parties with suggestions of arguments that ultimately support what has already been identified as the most crucial meta-standpoint of the whole mediation practice, namely "It is possible to find a mediated solution to your conflict". These suggestions are based on hypotheses that the mediator makes on the solution of the conflict. As Haynes and Haynes (1989) observe, a good mediator makes hypotheses on the possible solutions of the conflict, but has to verify them with the parties, who have to make the decision on their conflict.[61] Asking questions is thus a discreet but effective way to verify the hypotheses[62] and make the parties reflect on possible arguments that could lead to the resolution of their conflict.

Several instances of argumentation through questions have been found in the corpus. Here, in a very interesting example taken from Case 5, the mediator appeals to the parties' interpersonal relationship, which is troubled by the conflict, in order to consolidate their commitment towards a positive settlement of the conflict itself:

302	M	[But let me (.) ask a question here (3) you know I don't know what the value of your friendship is (.) between each other (.) but (.) ah:: (.) if (.) things didn't work out (.) today (.) will that friendship be lost↑

The argumentation behind the mediator's intervention in this case is indirect and quite complex. It originates from two questions he asks, one indirectly and the other explicitly, both based on the problem of *friendship*:

1. "I don't know what the value of your friendship is": this indirectly questions the importance (value) that parties attribute to their friendship;
2. "If things didn't work out today, will that friendship be lost?": the second question concerns the relevance of the present conflict to their friendship, i.e. how deeply their friendship would be affected if the conflict were not resolved.

Two main hypotheses of arguments for strengthening the parties' commitment to conflict resolution underlie the mediator's questions, giving rise to an argument chain. Through asking questions, he subjects these hypotheses to the parties' verification, and asks for their acceptance. Both hypotheses are founded on the

61. See Haynes and Haynes (1989: 28): "Good mediation also requires that we test our hypotheses through questioning and revise, modify or discard them according to the information we receive from clients".

62. Haynes and Haynes (1989: 26) theorize the use of questions in order to verify the hypotheses: "The mediator begins by collecting basic data. While collecting these data, she develops a hypothesis and then tests that hypothesis. When it appears to be correct, she confirms the hypothesis by asking the couple about it directly. When they indicate that the hypothesis is correct, it guides the mediator's behavior and line of questioning".

locus from termination and setting up in its complex version that encompasses a reasoning on the *implications* of the present states of affairs, as in the case examined in Section 6.2.2.3.

The former part is considered first. In this case, the maxim can be formulated as follows: "If a certain state of affairs is important (very positive), it should not be interrupted". This maxim is activated, in this case, as it is applied to an endoxon about the positive value of friendship:

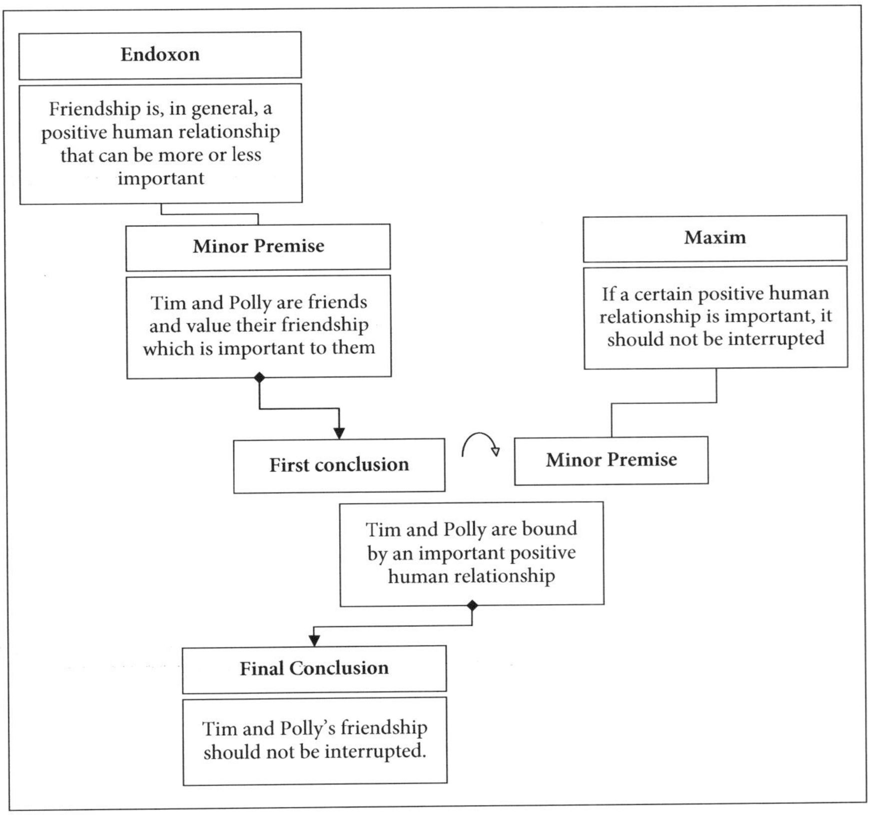

Figure 6.9. Synergic representation of the first step of the "friendship" argument

Although the mediator had previous evidence that the parties considered themselves to be friends, the minor premise pertaining to the syllogistic chain which assumes the endoxon as a major premise is still the most problematic point, because it sets this issue in the foreground, and requires that the parties now expressly confirm the importance of their relationship.

Before considering how parties respond to this suggestion, let us turn to the analysis of the mediator's intervention in its second part. The hypothesis concerning the relevance of the conflict for the parties' relationship is built on a second maxim of the same locus, which can be expressed as: "If a *possible* state of affairs endangers some value that should be kept, this state of affairs must be removed". In this case, the state of affairs concerned is not evaluated for its present negative traits, but for the negative implications that it may bring about. Here, as in the argument presented by the mediator to Philip in Case 1, concerning the problems that would follow if the conflict with Ann should become public (see Section 6.2.2.3.), the emotion of *fear* of losing something that one values as important plays a crucial role.

In the present case, the endoxon on which the mediator builds his argument concerns the very nature of conflicts, which are assumed as states of affairs that normally endanger the conflicting parties' friendship and make them hostile to each other (Chapter 4). This argument is seen to have an analogous structure to the first part analysed above. The minor premise associated with the endoxon can be formulated as "Polly and Tim are friends and have a conflict between each other *of such a nature that it can endanger a relationship of friendship*";[63] from this syllogistic chain, it follows the first conclusion that "Polly and Tim's friendship is endangered by the conflict".[64] The first premise is thus exploited as a minor premise by the above-mentioned maxim, and generates, through a syllogistic process, the eventual conclusion: "The conflict should be removed". The following synergic representation shows the inferential structure of the argument:

63. The mediator's question ("if (...) things didn't work out (...) today↓ (.) will that friendship be lost↑") aims directly at ascertaining and establishing "in public" this minor premise, which constitutes the "datum" driven from the parties' experience. In particular, such a minor premise is constituted by two pieces of data: first, the acknowledgement of the fact that Polly and Tim are friends, which is assumed from previous declarations made by the parties themselves. Second, the ascertainment of the nature of their conflict, which turns out to be a real interpersonal conflict that, as such, can endanger a relationship of friendship. This second part of the premise should be "filled in" by the parties who are solicited by the mediator's question.

64. The fact that Polly and Tim's relationship of friendship is important to them is not discussed in this part of the reasoning, as it has been established in the preceding part.

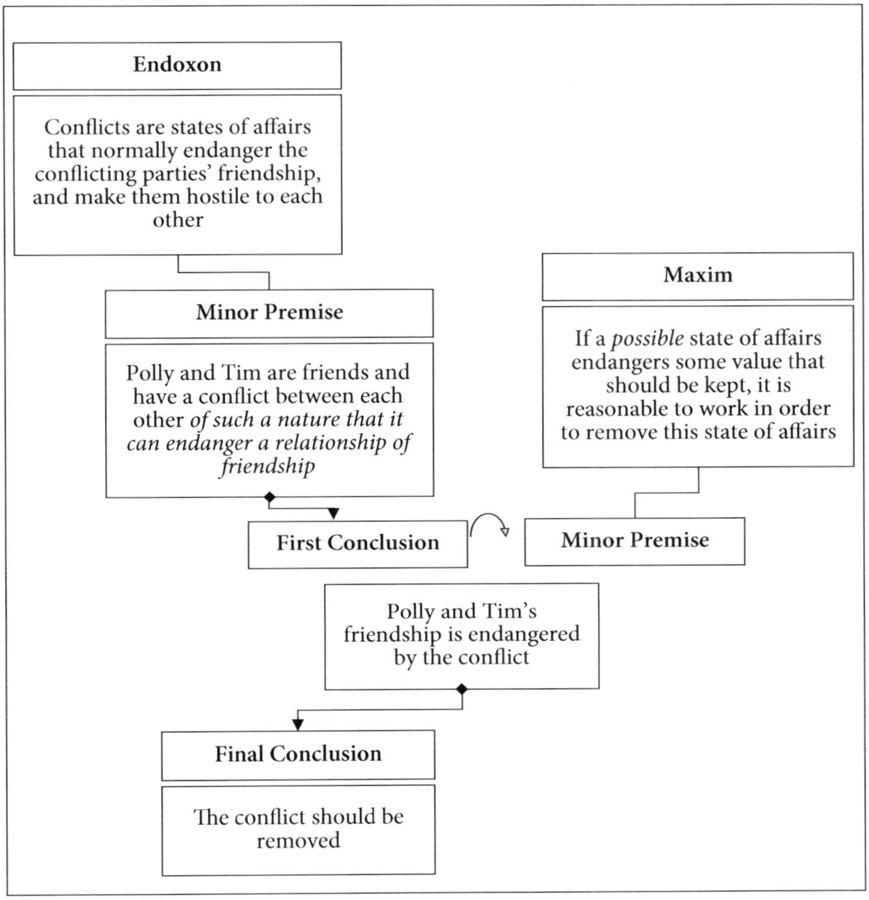

Figure 6.10. Synergic representation of the second step of the "friendship" argument

In this second example, it is even clearer that the mediator offers the parties the materials to construct an argument that is developed by the parties themselves. In particular, it is Tim who develops the steps of this argument in answering the mediator's questions:

303 T (4) Well eh:: (.) there is only one reason why I'm sitting here (.) eh yes I think that if we don't solve this eh:: (.) we we probably eh:: (.) at least we won't have business together =
304 P = No =
305 T = and (.) probably that we won't won't see one another (.) again eh
306 M Mmh
307 T And (.) well (1) that's not a disaster (.) but it's a pity

308 M Mmh (.) Mmh (.) (*Polly nods*) (2) So I don't kno:w (1) what the value of your friendship would be (.) but (.) there would be a loss
309 T Yes↓
310 M Yes↑

It is interesting to see how Tim confirms the mediator's hypotheses step by step. First, he "confesses" that keeping his friendship with Polly is the only reason why he has decided to try to solve the conflict through mediation ("There is only one reason why I'm sitting here"), and that this relationship is of importance to him, at least to a certain extent ("Well. That's not a disaster, but it's a pity"). Second, he confirms that, if the conflict is not resolved, the friendship will probably be lost ("At least we won't have business together, and probably we won't see one another again"). Polly confirms Tim's development of the mediator's suggestion, by saying "No" at 304, and nodding in agreement almost all the time he is speaking. The parties, having accepted the mediator's hypotheses, which he restates at turn 308, commit themselves to the conclusion: "The conflict should be removed", thus implicitly recognizing the reasonableness of the conflict resolution efforts and of the sacrifices needed for keeping their friendship.

Moreover, it is interesting that an analogous argument is also present in Case 2, in which, besides the conflict on the management of the workload in the parties' business, an interpersonal dimension also emerges:

47 R You know (.) my wife his wife our kids his kids we all get along but that's starting to affect things too =
48 M = Uh: hum
49 R I mean (.) I'm getting static from my wife and I'm sure you are from Jane too (.) you know what I mean↓ =
50 D = Absolutely↓ (.) I mean (.) she feels very much the way I feel except that she (.) expresses it a lot louder
51 R Well =
52 D = She doesn't [she she's
53 R [I hear that every time I come home =
54 M = So you've got a double issue here/
55 R Oh: yeah↓
56 M You want to keep the good social relationship as well as keep a good business [relationship/
57 D [Yes↓
58 R [Well certainly (.) yes (.) we recognize that (.) that's why (.) we've come to see somebody like yourself =
59 D = We were friends before we were partners↓
60 M Mmh (.) all right

The mediator reformulates the parties' concerns at turn 56, by pointing out the value of the relationship that their conflict is making impossible to preserve, which not only involves the two of them, but also their families.[65] Such reformulation can be interpreted as an argument supporting the reasonableness of the efforts to find a mediated solution. Otherwise, the relationship could be irremediably broken. This argumentation can thus be reconstructed as a variant of the previous example, equally resting on the locus from termination and setting up, and evoking the value of friendship as an endoxon.

The mediator's reformulation brings to light the deep interest of both parties, which they immediately confirm at turns 54–56: it is, again, the desire of not damaging their friendship and that of their families. Interestingly, in this case, the parties' interest is far from corresponding to the other party's ruin. In fact, being friends, the parties include in their deepest level of interest the satisfaction of both of them as well as of their families. This is a case in which the desire of *relational happiness* (see Section 6.2.2.4) emerges, being "discovered" thanks to the mediator's intervention.

6.3.2.4 The locus from termination and setting up *as a distinguishing feature of mediation*

The fact that in several cases the locus from termination and setting up has emerged as the determinant in the mediator's argumentation is not coincidental. On closer inspection, it appears that such a reasoning scheme is determinant in a process such as mediation because it is strictly bound to the pragmatic statute of mediation. In fact, as seen in Chapter 4, the conflict that parties are experiencing, by its very nature, endangers their relationship – be it interpersonal as a friendship, or more institutionalized, as in collaboration in a business – and makes them fear that something they care for can be compromised or lost forever. In this sense, accepting to go to mediation is explained by the hope of winning one's cause in the profound sense of maintaining a positive relationship which often, as pointed out (Section 6.2.2.4 and *passim*), implies some form of relational happiness. It is thus very important that the mediator, when arguing for the possibility of finding a mediated solution, indicates the possibility for the parties to keep their relationship and to maintain it in the future.

---

65. The pressure the parties feel from their wives, and the fact that they are actively contributing to the conflict behind the scenes, also emerges later (see turns 243–263 in particular). Interestingly David says that decreasing his own workload "would also decrease the pressure I'm getting *from the home front*" (turn 252). The war metaphor *home front* is indicative of the kind of global conflict in which the parties feel entangled.

Therefore, the frequent use of the locus from termination and setting up, whose *habitudo* exactly touches the relations between a present state of affairs and the possible worlds that can originate from its modification, is evoked to sustain the reasoning about the value of the parties' rapport and the opportunity to mediate the conflict in order to preserve it. Normally, the maxim evoked is, "If something has a value, it should not be interrupted/given up/terminated/lost".

As remarked in the analysis of Case 1, the application of the locus from termination and setting up to appropriate endoxa may evoke specific *emotional dynamics*, which should not be overlooked in the context of the resolution of a conflict. In particular, the locus from termination and setting up may move parties from the dysphoric emotions bound to conflict to euphoric emotions (Cigada 2007) related to its possible positive solution, such as, in particular, *hope*. This passage is bound to the parties' consideration of the value that risks being lost in their struggle. The reasoning relying on the locus from termination and setting up also invites the parties' involvement in the resolution of the dispute: in fact, saving the endangered value becomes a common enterprise in which parties find themselves co-operating.

The specific values at stake are, of course, bound to the endoxa evoked by the concrete arguments put forward or suggested by the mediator, which foreground the importance of the parties' relationship – their "golden-goose" business, or their interpersonal rapport. This is not surprising, as endoxa constitute shared premises pertaining to the parties' common ground, i.e. to what they share and accept.

What is rather surprising is that the emotional dynamics activated seem to be strictly correlated with the choice of the locus from termination and setting up. Thus, the abstract logical structure of a locus, which is seemingly inert from the point of view of the hold on the arguers' emotional involvement, turns out to predispose precise emotional dynamics. In the case of the locus from termination and setting up, in particular, parties are solicited to think of the valuable relationship that they risk losing, to *fear* that they may actually lose it, and to *hope* that they can save it through mediation. So, the emotional dynamics moving from fear to hope seem to be strictly connected to the logical dimension of the locus, in particular with the formulation of the maxim. If adequate endoxa are provided, i.e. if parties acknowledge that they actually have some relationship to preserve, the emotional dynamics are properly activated.

More generally, it could be imagined that specific dynamics from the emotional point of view could be associated with the topical choice in the argumentation stage, not only in relation to the locus from termination and setting up, which is considered here as a distinguishing feature of mediation, but also in relation to other *loci*. The hypothesis advanced here, however, would certainly require further investigation on a larger corpus of interactions taken from different activity types.

6.3.2.5 *Arguing discreetly is still… arguing*

Although the mediator cannot assume the role of a protagonist in the critical discussion on the resolution of the conflict, his role is nonetheless extremely important and more leading than it might seem at a first glance. By means of strategic manoeuvring within the topical potential, the mediator takes the helm of the discussion, and the parties have to trust him enough to feel calm while navigating with him. In fact, asking questions and raising particular issues he assumes an active role, as questions always pre-define the "horizon" of the expected answers (Rigotti 1991).

The emergence of the parties' trust in the mediator's guidance is however not easy; parties may feel uncomfortable about being asked questions they are not prepared to answer, or having discussions on issues they would prefer to avoid. A particularly significant example of this can be found in Case 6, where the mediator's way of leading the case is repeatedly questioned by one of the parties. This indirectly shows that parties clearly perceive the mediator's decisive leading role in selecting issues, controlling their commitment store (Hamblin (1970: 257), and so on, as well as the "educational work" he does.

Let us consider the various episodes in which Paul, the father and boss of the real estate agency, stops the mediator and questions his ways of proceeding.

88 P [Do you- excuse me (.) do you think that it is at all relevant↑ (.) of course you are leading but (.) is this a relevant question↑

89 M Well (.) maybe I'll ask your daughter first and (.) if it's not relevant she will tell me

90 T I have no idea which direction you're going but if you think it's a relevant question okay well (.) Evelyn ↑ (.) I don't think she would care (.) one way or the other

By means of this first interruption, Paul contests the mediator's questioning of the attitude of his younger daughter, who is not involved in the conflict. From Therese's answer at 90, it clearly emerges that she is more confident in working with the mediator, and perceives the discussion to be completely guided by him.

In what follows, several other interventions by Paul signal either surprise for having to deal with certain issues (turn 106) or disappointment (213, 226, 228 and 382):

106 P Eh ↓ I didn't expect that question (*P and T laugh*) eh:: (.) well we have a good relationship (.) I mean I have a good relationship and Evelyn and I have a good relationship and Therese and Evelyn have a good relationship so I'm doing (.) it's all right

[…]

213 P I don't understand this because (.) we are talking about the firing (.) of James

[…]

225 M So (.) If I might help you let's talk about James in a minute (.) I need to know what YOU want (.) from your father (.) when you talk to your father because (.) he's here trying to understand what you need (.) yes↑

226 P Yes but there's no relation here I (.) [^{0}suppose^0

227 M [ABSOLUTELY (.) but I need to know what's in her mind because (.) I don't know (.) and I think you're waiting to hear this

228 P (2.5) Well if (.) if you think it's necessary let's do so but (.) I can't:: (.) get it at the moment

[…]

382 P (3.5) But (.) where are you getting to↑ (.) because we are here for the problem (.) with James (.) and the way (.) she reacted on that

383 M Absolutely↓ (*cough*) (.) and I am prepared to talk about that just a second and one more question (2) Therese if things don't get better here/(.) because I don't know enough about the two of you if things cannot be resolved today/(4.5) what would (.) what does Therese do (.) next/(.) you've talked about that:: you've discussed about it with your father/

Finally, when the mediator has helped to make C2 emerge, Paul accuses the mediator of having made "a major problem out of nothing" (391–399) and challenges him to argue about his choice.

391 P [Excuse me but I think you make make a major problem out of nothing

392 M Mmh (.) [So

393 P [And you're ( ) (.) away (.) and you're creating (.) actually (.) a problem between (.) Therese and me (.) which is was not there (.) till this time

394 M Ya

395 P And now she's angry (.) and she thinks of resigning (.) and she's disappointed

396 M Mmh =

397 P = That she did not know my plans (.) for the cases of emergency (.) so what are you doing actually (.) we (.) [we are here to discuss

398 M [You're worried (.) you're worried about the questions I asked (.) or the answers you got↑

399 P Aha↓ Well I think your questions (.) brought up an answer (.) and ( ) a totally new problem which was not there till this moment (.) so what is all about here↑ =

400 M = Well I- you might well be right (.) may I ask Therese than↑ (.) just to make sure (.) Therese (.) have you been thinking about leaving the company (.) before you came in today↑

401 T (2) Not really (.)

402 M Mmh

403 P [You see↑

404 T [Ah:: (.) because I never really knew (.) what your ideas were for the company I HOPED (.) that somehow you trusted me more [and:: and::

At 398, the mediator provokingly asks Paul whether he is worried about the questions or the answers Therese gives to those questions. Indirectly, this is a way of asking whether Paul wants to avoid the truth about the origin of his daughter's resentment towards him. In this sense, of course, Paul's difficulty in accepting the mediator's management of the confrontation stage is also explained by the fact that Paul does not want to acknowledge the origin of the conflict. He does not hide the fact that he would prefer not to solve it by argumentative means but wants Therese to obey him. Although he has agreed to enter a mediation process, he remains fearful of losing his hierarchically predominant role until nearly the end of the session.

6.3.3 The role of *context* in the argumentative discussion

In the second step of the empirical analysis, the consideration of all the cases of the corpus also allows a comparison of the different *interaction fields* (see Section 4.1) to which the *interaction scheme* of mediation is applied, giving rise to business mediation, family mediation, school mediation and so on. This permits some conclusions to be drawn on the specific weight of the interaction field and the interaction scheme in relation to the definition of the argumentative strategies.

As pointed out by van Eemeren and Houtlosser (2005), the reality of the argumentative practice influences the parties' strategic manoeuvring by imposing specific constraints onto it. In terms of the ontology-oriented conceptual framework of mediation built in Chapter 4, focusing on the context of argumentation in mediation means understanding how the antecedents of mediation influence the core communication process. In this case in particular, the constraints posed by the context on the mediator's strategic manoeuvring also turn out to be opportunities for the mediator to accomplish his task. If we reconsider the data analysed until now from the perspective of how the context is present in these argumentative discussions, two aspects emerge prominently, both concerning the topical potential: first, the selection of issues led by the mediator in the parties' confrontation stage and, second, the topical choice in the mediator's construction of arguments, involving both the argumentation stage and the opening stage (as concerns the choice of relevant premises). The second dimension seems particularly relevant. Some significant aspects are discussed in Sections 6.3.3.1, 6.3.3.2 and 6.3.3.3.

Concerning the topical potential in the confrontation stage, it should be noted that, within a certain context, both the interaction scheme (in our case, the practice of mediation) and the interaction field impose constraints on the disputants' possible choices. It may be argued that each interaction scheme more or less strictly predefines the paradigm of possible issues to be tackled in the communicative interaction, as already remarked. In mediation, once the facts that have originated the conflict are established, attention is concentrated on considering the future of the parties' relationship.

However, the parties' *conflict* in itself provides more specific but equally important constraints on the selection of the issues (options) to be discussed. Indeed, the options that may possibly lead to the resolution of the process are to be defined in relation to the conflict that has emerged within the interaction field, insofar as they must be possible solutions to that specific conflict and take into account the interests it endangers. Otherwise, the options may not correspond with the parties' true interests, and risk not being considered as proper solutions.[66]

Yet the weight of the context can also be felt in the very constituency of the arguments used by mediators for orientating the disputants towards the resolution of their conflict, as it emerges from the analysis of their inferential structure (see Section 6.2.2). As Rigotti (2006) has shown, there is a clear connection in particular between the endoxon evoked and the constituency of the context in which a given argument is presented. Not coincidentally, in all the cases analysed here, the mediator makes sure he is relying on premises that are accepted by the parties. When arguing about uncharted waters (Section 6.3.2.1), and about the parties' friendship (Section 6.3.2.3), as it has been pointed out above, the mediator explicitly asks parties to confirm their commitment to such premises. In the case of the golden goose (Section 6.3.2.2), such confirmation is not necessary because the financial solidity and the good perspectives of the parties' business has already emerged repeatedly during the discussion.

It is also noteworthy that the different dimensions constituting context may more or less be put to the fore by the topical choice performed by the mediator. The metaphor of the golden goose, for example, works because of the value of the parties' business, i.e. on the need to preserve their institutional relationship. On the other hand, a different focus is present in the arguments that recall the

66. Some of the studies concerning the argumentative nature of mediation, such as Jacobs and Aakhus (2002a), have tackled the problem of the quality of the mediator's management of critical discussions between the parties, pointing out that sometimes mediators seem to push the parties towards a type of rationality that is defined as "bargaining", which avoids them engaging in real critical discussions during the mediation process. Now, it is undoubtedly true that, in some very extreme cases, bargaining on concessions without analysing the real issues of the conflict is the only reasonable way to proceed (think, for instance, about negotiations with terrorists holding hostages), but in normal cases of mediation of interpersonal conflicts this may be identified as a sign that the mediators' intervention is of low quality. In fact, if mediators do not help the parties develop a well-founded opening stage, their discussion on options will suffer. A conflict of interest or, more specifically, an *agency problem* (see Chapter3) may even arise: once the mediator is paid for his work in the process, he may not be interested in whether the parties reach a well-founded agreement. Many mediators, however, speak of a feeling a deep level of personal satisfaction bound to having helped parties truly understand each other.

extreme importance of the parties' friendship as leverage for settling their conflict. In these cases, it is the interpersonal relationship binding the parties that is called into question more frequently.

6.3.3.1 *Context and the crucial role of the opening stage*

Our analysis shows that a well-constructed opening stage brings to light the essential aspects of the context that will then serve the resolution of the conflict: in particular, the parties' relationship – how much they care for it, and how much and under which respects the conflict endangers it, as well as what they still agree upon, what they want to preserve, and so on. Therefore, a well-constructed opening stage turns out to be crucial in mediation,[67] as witnessed by a series of tools developed by mediators for reconstructing it. For instance, when a family is involved, a visualization system has been developed that is known as *family genogram* (Parkinson 1997; Marzotto & Tamanza 2004), whereby a visual representation of the institutional and interpersonal roles within the family is designed together with the parties, and serves as an acknowledgement of the contextual (institutionalized and interpersonal) relationships (see Figure 6.11). In light of the interpretation of context proposed in Chapter 4, which takes into account the weave of institutional and interpersonal relationships generating it, the family genogram could be read as a possible realization of a "map of context":

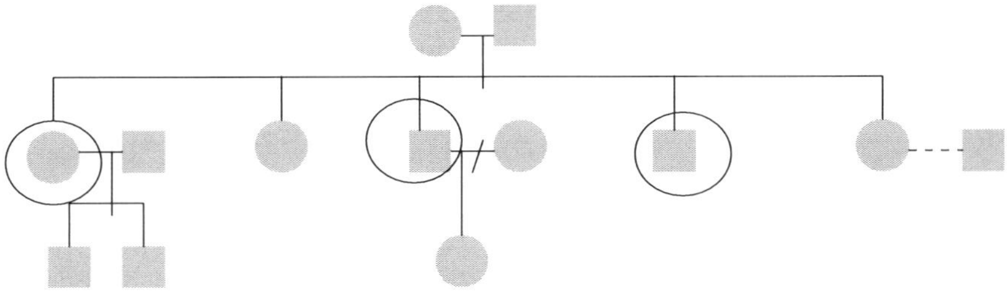

Figure 6.11. An interpretation of a family genogram in a family owning a business. Here, the usual form of the family tree is complemented with further information representing the institutional and interpersonal relationships between the members. Circles represent women, squares represent men; horizontal lines linking two members indicate that they are married, (dashed lines represent engagement relationships); circled members are actively working in the business.

67. The opening stage, as such, is a concept defined in relation to a single critical discussion. It is clear, however, that in a complex situation identified in mediation, once some elements have been put to the fore and have become part of the parties' common ground, they may be exploited in different discussions by activating different opening stages. This is, in general, quite a natural situation: the same pieces of common ground may constitute different opening stages in as many discussions.

Often mediators also employ a flipchart or analogous visualization tools in order to represent the progressive reconstruction of the parties' interaction field (Haynes & Haynes 1989: 23).

Many aspects are included within the opening stage in mediation: the description of the *context* (Rigotti & Rocci 2006) in which the interaction takes place, the nature of the conflict and the issue around which it has originally developed, including the parties' reasons, and so on.[68] The search for this agreement is normally reconstructed by the interlocutors themselves during everyday conversations. In mediation, however, the interlocutors' initial status as conflicting parties tends to hinder co-operative management of the argumentative discussion.

Such a process of exploration pertains to the opening stage of critical discussion, insofar as it constitutes a sort of commitment store (in the sense proposed by Hamblin 1970: 257ff.) of the parties' assumptions, values, etc. in relation to which their difference of opinion, which has degenerated into a conflict, first emerged. Indeed, while for the mediator the information he gets on the context is new,[69] for the parties it is, in general, more like "visualizing" and re-establishing their mutual commitments.

Mediators construct the opening stage by asking questions about the parties' institutionalized and interpersonal relationship. This helps to define the relationships that have been affected by the conflict; sometimes a clearer definition of the conflict itself needs to be restated. Let us consider Case 5, which is paradigmatic in this respect, since it involves both a relationship of friendship and of business. As early as turn 19, the mediator asks the parties about their relationship:

19 M [Ya 'kay (.) and (.) (*cough*) you said you've know each other since primary school (.) do you mean you actually have been friends for that long/(.) or you just met in primary school

Then, the mediator asks about the institutionalized aspect of the parties' relationship by asking information about how their contract had been formalized. Quite early on, at turn 88, he asks whether the parties have signed a contract, since this is the most common way to formalize a business relationship. After having heard that no formal contract was set up in this case, however, at turn 96 he asks for information

68. Not surprisingly, within the initial phase of a canonical mediation process, much time is devoted to the investigation of these aspects by means of the mediator's questions (Kovach 2005; see Chapter1).

69. Indeed, in all the cases analysed within this work, the mediator knows almost nothing about the parties before the beginning of the mediation process. This is a quite normal situation in many mediation experiences (some exceptions, like mediation of international conflicts, are mentioned in Chapter2).

about the informal way in which they have been handling their business. At 99–108, the reciprocal trust characterizing the parties' professional relationship is affirmed.

88	M	[Okay (.) There's a lot of information I need to know so I hope you don't mind we're jumping around but- (.) did the two of you (.) ehm:: (3.5) have a contract with each other/ something written on paper:: that (1) set out your expectations of each other and (.) how much to spend or:: (.) what hap- (.) what happened
89	P	^{0}No^{0}
90	T	In fact I gave her (.) blank cheque (.) Ehm (.) maybe that was not (.) exactly the ideal of which you SHOULD do business but eh (.) well since we that we have known one another known one another for such a long time (.) I KNOW that (.) she has an excellent job er: shop er:: (.) and I just thought that to be a GREAT party so she had to do (.) that much of what she could do (.) I was not really VERY much interested in the cost
91	M	Mmh (.) Mmh (.) 'Cause it supposed to be a special event
92	T	Exactly
93	M	Once in the lifetime. (.) ya↑
94	T	Ya
95	P	Mmh
96	M	(*cough*) But ↑ (.) when the two of you met (.) and you talked (.) did you give her an idea (*cough*) excuse me (.) an idea (1) of what she was 'posed to do↑ (3) How did she know what to order how did she know (.) how much↑ (2)
97	T	Ehm:: (.) I I I think it (1) my- my secretary was to give you the- the list of the attendants [wasn't she↑
98	P	[Ya she gave me
99	T	And if then Polly knows (.) VERY WELL (.) how much we have to order eh:: per person etcetera so (.) we didn't (.) actually discuss the details of the:: ( )
100	M	Mmh
101	P	And during the period afterwards I sometimes called and he said Okay if it's good for you (.) you know your business
102	T	Ya
103	P	He trusted me and (.)
104	T	Ya
105	P	[I trusted him
106	T	[If it helped (.) or to define quality (.) it would have been exactly as I wanted it to so that is not the point
107	M	Mmh (.) Mmh
108	P	^{0}Exactly^{0}

Analogously, in Case 6 the mediator, having been informed about the fact that Therese is Paul's daughter, asks about their business and interpersonal relationship at different points during the interaction. In particular, he asks: (a) if Paul has other children and, learning that Therese has a younger sister, Eveline, he asks about the plans for her career, and about the relationships between the father and the two sisters; (b) how long Paul's business has been in existence; (c) how Therese became a member of Paul's business – whether she was invited, whether her role had been discussed, and so on; (d) how Paul founded the business (his career); and (e) Paul's intentions for the future. Defining the institutionalized and interpersonal context of the parties' relationship helps to establish the value that the relationship endangered by the conflict has for the parties.

6.3.3.2 See, I wasn't around when you had your conversations: *A note about how mediators justify their requests for information*

One of the functions that questions can have in mediation is to let the common premises constituting the parties' opening stage emerge. In relation to this, it is remarkable that mediators' often seem to feel a need to explicity justify requests for information about the parties' relationship and about their conflict.[70] The kind of reasons they provide for these requests refer to their own lack of information, since they are external to the parties' relationship and conflict. In the following table, various rhetorical choices for formulating such justification are reported:

Table 6.6. Mediators' justifications of his requests for information

Case N.	*Turn N.*	*Speaker*	*Formulation of the communicative move: justification of the request for information*
Case 2	290	M	= What I want to know is: is if you mechanize (.) in this (.) you see (.) I know nothing about your business I can only ask questions
Case 2	312	M	= Okay↓ (.) help me because I'm just an eater of bagels and I don't know anything about producing them at all (.) ah: I just assumed that everything was mechanized these days but (.) what are your competitors doing↑ (.) what's what's what's what's going on [in the field↑

(*Continued*)

70. In fact, since deciding on the outcome of the conflict is the sole responsibility of the parties involved, some might consider it sufficient that they know all the relevant information without the mediator being made aware of it. Thus, if it is evident that both parties have all the information that the mediator is asking for, they might consider it meaningless to relate it to the mediator – if not invasive. For example, in Case 6 the mediator has to manage the fact that one of the parties (Paul, the father) explicitly questions the relevance of his request for information (see Section 6.3.2.5).

Table 6.6. (Continued)

Case N.	*Turn N.*	*Speaker*	*Formulation of the communicative move: justification of the request for information*
Case 4		M	Good afternoon: (.) you know I (.) I have the sketchiest of information as to (.) who you are (.) and: perhaps you could just take the time for me right now to kind of let me know (.) ah: (.) what your names are and who you are with I don't know if (.) you two are together or you two are together (.) can we start with you (.) you know if you
Case 5	88	M	[Okay (.) There's a lot of information I need to know so I hope you don't mind we're jumping around but- (.) did the two of you (.) ehm:: (3.5) have a contract with each other/ something written on paper:: that (1) set out your expectations of each other and (.) how much to spend or:: (.) what hap- (.) what happened
Case 5	172	M	So (.) the problem is (.) she paid seventy-five thousand (.) and: you don't want to pay anything↑ (1) or:: she paid seventy-five thousand (.) and you're willing to pay something↑ (.) I I don't quite understand (.) see I wasn't around when you had your conversations so: (.)
Case 6	125	M	Ya (.) You know (.) knowing that (.) she came into the business remember that there's MUCH information I don't know (.) but when she came into the business (.) did you have dreams of what she would be doing inside this successful business of yours↑ Did you have pla::ns dreams/
Case 6	227	M	[ABSOLUTELY (.) but I need to know what's in her mind because (.) I don't know (.) and I think you're waiting to hear this

The mediators' questions are thus justified as a sincere request for information, which can be considered a question's canonical pragmatic function (Gobber 1999: 72). However, further superior pragmatic functions are implicitly associated with this, and somehow hidden behind it. Gobber (1999: 73), citing Wegener (1991[1885]: 67–68) remarks that there is a hierarchy of pragmatic functions in the communicative act of asking for information, and that possessing that piece of information only very rarely constitutes the final goal. Indeed, it is often subordinated to other goals: the final goal of a question may be for someon's benefit – either the one asking the question, or the one being asked.

First, in asking for information, the mediator highlights precise portions of the parties' common ground, bringing them to the fore and thus evidencing some of the common features that are relevant to resolving the conflict. In particular, the fact that parties are "forced" by the mediator's asking to re-state some of their existing commitments, even though they are aware of these to some extent, focuses attention on these commitments. Moreover, those commitments that are re-stated by the parties receive a sort of "refreshing" and re-commitment from the parties. In this sense, the updating of the commitment store allowed by the mediator's questioning is essential for the parties to understand the terms of their existing relationship that is under threat in the conflict. Consider, for instance, that, through mediation lines of questioning, in Case 2 both parties re-state in front of their adversary that the bottom line of their business is more than satisfactory; or that, in Case 5 the parties admit that their friendship is important to them. The mediator's questioning more or less directly helps construct a portion of relevant common ground about the importance of the parties' institutionalized or interpersonal relationship that can then be exploited in order to resolve the conflict, insofar as it clearly emerges that losing such a relationship equals wasting a value of some sort.

Second, making explicit the terms of the relationship endangered by the conflict also brings to light the meaning of the conflict itself, by specifying its relevant context.

Furthermore, a "side effect" of the mediator's asking about something that the parties are convinced they know may be that unknown aspects of the parties' relationship emerge about which the parties themselves were unaware. In Case 6, for instance, the explicit commitment of Therese's father to his daughter's future in the business is, indeed, an important step towards the parties' orientation towards a positive solution, even though initially Therese seems to be far from being positively affected by it:

408	P	Therese I told you when you started working for the firm (.) eh:: (.) I expect you:: to (.) eh (.) get (.) experience (.) in (.) five years time (.) you have experience (.) to (.) manage the whole business and I it was not specific (.) in my plans (.) eh:: that you (.) are (.) definitely becoming (.) the CEO (.) after five years when I'm leaving (.) the company (.) but of course that is my plan and you FELT (.) I MUST (.) assume that you felt (.) eh:: that that was my plan (.) and what you did not know was that (.) OF COURSE in case of emergency (.) I have a plan for this [kind of ( )
409	T	[At least you could have talked to me about it instead of surprising me here with this
410	P	But it was not of your business it was not (.) [it was not relevant
411	T	[it was not of my business↓
412	M	So let me::
413	T	[Right what what what

414	P	[When you ask me what would you do how would you deal with it when you died [( )
415	M	[Let me make sure (.) eh (.) I can keep things on track because we're running out of time
416	P	Mmh
417	M	And unfortunately we did not book enough time for the session (.) I did not know (.) that these problems between the two of you:: were much bigger than I think the two of you (.) know (.) but (.) I need to know (.) ehm (.) Therese is there anything that your father can say or do for you today/(.) that would make you feel comfortable about growing (.) inside this successful company/
418	T	(4) It would help if you ah:: (.) include me in your plans

In particular, at 408, Paul admits for the first time that he had planned to be succeeded by Therese in leading his business in the future. Moreover, he says he imagined Therese had understood that this future was foreseen for her in the business, and that all the alternative provisions he has made (like finding an *ad interim* director if he had some problems while Therese was growing up in the business) would only be activated in cases of emergency. It is true that Therese seems not to take up her father's admission (see turns 409 and 411); however, when the mediator goes back to leading the discussion (turns 415 and 417), he moves from the issue that has preceded this exchange, i.e. Therese's threat of resigning, to an option-issue bound to the resolution of the conflict, which he formulates as "Therese is there anything that your father can say or do for you today *that would make you feel comfortable about growing inside this successful company*?". Here, Paul's "confession" about Therese's professional future – which has not been clearly stated until after a long discussion – is highlighted by the mediator, who asks Therese for the *conditions* that would make her comfortable with such a professional perspective. The alternative of resigning then seems to become irrelevant. An analogous question is then addressed to Paul. Eventually, the parties decide to go out to have dinner together in order to discuss the future of "their" business. Thus, after this first session of mediation, the parties' communicative interaction is transformed into a problem-solving discussion to be continued without the help of a mediator.

6.3.3.3 *The clarification of misunderstandings as a specific feature of the opening stage in mediation*

The mediation context also influences the construction of the opening stage at the level of the *clarification of misunderstandings* based on semantic ambiguities. Such misunderstandings, in fact, could lead to an unclear presentation of the parties' relationships that are at stake in the mediation process.

On the one hand, as van Eemeren and Grootendorst (2004: 60) notice, "there is no point in venturing to resolve a difference of opinion through an argumentative exchange of views if there is no mutual commitment to a common starting point".[71] On the other hand, major problems may arise if parties think that such a common starting point exists when it actually does not, because they have based their agreement on ambiguous terms or expressions; in other words, they have been misled by words. In his first book of *Topics*[72] Aristotle wrote of how the development of the argumentative discussion might be blocked by ambiguity in the words that are chosen:

> "It is useful to have examined the number of meanings of a term both for clearness' sake (for a man is more likely to know what it is he asserts, if it has been made clear to him how many meanings it may have), and also with a view to ensuring that our reasonings shall be in accordance with the actual facts and not addressed merely to the term used. For as long as it is not clear in how many senses a term is used, it is possible that the answerer and the questioner are not directing their minds upon the same thing".

The negative effects that ambiguity may have on the management of conflict have also been noticed in the literature on conflict resolution. In their groundbreaking work on conflict resolution *Getting to Yes*, Fisher, Ury and Patton (1991: 5) examine a case of diplomatic breakdown between the U.S. and the Soviet Union during the time when President Kennedy was in office, which shows how the ambiguities of a single term can bring failure to a conflict resolution initiative. Concerning this episode, the authors observe:

> "A critical question arose: How many on-site inspections per year should the Soviet Union and the United States be permitted to make within the other's territory to investigate suspicious seismic events? The Soviet Union finally agreed to three inspections. The United States insisted on no less than ten. And there the talks broke down – over positions – despite the fact that no one understood whether an 'inspection' would involve one person looking around for one day, or a hundred people prying indiscriminately for a month".

71. Though it might be said that ultimately human beings always share some material starting point – at least those traits defined by their common nature – it might be the case that, in some discussions, parties do not recognize any common starting point.

72. The proposed translation is taken from Pickard-Cambridge 2004. For the original text, see Aristotelis *Topica et Sophistici Elenchi* in Ross (1958 ed.).

In this case, the ambiguity of the word *inspection* made the parties' negotiation for managing their conflict – a broad conflict, in this case, if we consider the whole context of the Cold War – useless: the parties did not even find a solution. The clarification of the term *inspection* might have helped to specify the terms of their reciprocal positions. But it might also be said that, had they found a solution on a number under those conditions – let us say six inspections – the agreement would still not have been solid, since, as the authors point out, nobody understood what was meant by an inspection.

Therefore, the solution of ambiguities that may arise in the parties' discussion is one of the tasks that should be performed in a dialectically sound opening stage. In those cases where a specific activity type requires the presence of some "leading figure", as is the case of the mediator who accompanies and leads the conflicting parties' discussion, it is then the task of such a leading figure to make sure that this kind of ambiguity does not arise.[73] In this sense, various instances of requests of *usage declaratives* performed by the mediator may be found in the process of mediation. The purpose of usage declaratives, among which *definition*, *precization*, *amplification*, *explication* and *explicitization* are included, is "to ensure mutual *comprehension* of the interlocutors' speech acts (van Eemeren & Grootendorst 1984: 109). In terms of Congruity theory (see Chapter 5), this kind of communicative move corresponds to a class of connective predicates that regulate the interruption of an ongoing discussion to make the interlocutors discuss their presuppositions.[74]

---

73. Compare the analysis of a doctor–patient consultation in Bigi, Cigada, Gobber and Greco Morasso (2007), where the opening stage is led by the doctor, who makes sure that the patient understands the premises necessary for making a decision on his diagnosis and therapy.

74. In Walton's (2007) terms, this kind of discursive move can be interpreted as a *clarification dialogue*. The aim of a clarification dialogue is "to help one party in a dialogue to understand an obscure or otherwise problematic utterance of the other party" (ibid., p. 174). In this sense, clarification dialogues are to be distinguished from explanation, because they concern a sort of "semantic negotiation" at the level of terms or expressions (i.e. at the linguistic level) rather than the expounding of the causal relations between facts or events in the real world. Notice that, from a theoretical point of view, dialogues should not be confused with activity types or interaction schemes: the term dialogue is used here in relation to the more "local" notion of *dialogue games* (Mann 2002), which indicates the sets of joint goals that define the co-operative dimension of a dialogue, and allows for the distinguishing of the different dialogues, such as deliberation, negotiation, information seeking, and so on. Some of these dialogue games, like information-seeking dialogue, or clarification dialogue itself, are not to be seen as argumentative in nature. However, they can be understood as local dialogic connective predicates that serve specific functions in the context of an argumentative exchange;

These requests open a space for meta-reflection that is semantic in nature, because it aims at the definition of terms or expressions and at the same time performs the pragmatic function of adjusting the parties' common ground. This does not equal to directly putting forward argumentation, but it clearly has argumentative implications, as it allows defining a clear opening stage.[75] Indeed, establishing a sound opening stage is of particular relevance in mediation, where parties need to find an agreement starting from a situation of conflict in which finding common premises for the discussion can be particularly difficult, and misunderstandings can occur frequently. The analysis of the corpus has brought to light some instances of requests for definition, precision or explicitation operated by the mediator for the sake of the parties' mutual understanding. In this relation, Case 4 is exemplary,[76] because the parties' misunderstanding is directly bound to the core of their conflict (C2). In fact, when the child's natural mother presents the problem to the mediator at turn 7, she says that the adopting parents do not want to give her visiting rights; just after this presentation, she affirms – and then repeats afterwards – that her having contact with the baby was part of the agreement signed with the adopting parents and prepared by the legal advisors (turn 15):

6	M	Okay (.) eh can (.) can you give me an idea in a nutshell ah (.) my secretary said that I was gonna have (.) three people coming today (.) can you give me an idea in a nutshell (.) why you are here today eh: (3) Vivian would you like to give me an idea please↑ =

---

and it is reasonable to interpret their goal as subordinate to the goal of the stage of critical discussion that is concerned.

75. See the interesting remark proposed in Berthoud (2004: 3): "Parler des mots est notamment lié à la non-transparence de la signification, et particulièrement dans ces moments du discours où des objets ou des événements ne se laissent pas aisément mettre en mots, où les mots cessent d'aller de soi […]. La difficulté de s'entendre sur les mots, les précautions à prendre pour nommer une réalité résistant à une catégorisation trop stricte, la recherche des mots mieux ajustés, le jeu sur les extensions lexicales, font émerger dans le discours des séquences où sont négociés et thématisés des choix de dire, la responsabilité de la formulation, la justification du choix de telle ou telle formulation". Such an observation about the moments in which words *stop going automatically*, i.e. stop being a goal-directed instrument and become a problem in themselves, highlights that, from the argumentative point of view, the negotiation and clarification of meaning is a move typically pertaining to the opening stage, as it allows precisely defining the premises on which parties agree as a point of departure for their discussion.

76. A revised and simplified version of this communicative exchange has been discussed in Walton (2007) as an example of clarification dialogue.

7	V	= Sure (.) well (3) as you know I gave birth five days ago (.) and: I would like to have some (.) visiting rights with my (.) child they're waiting to adopt the (.) child and (.) they don't want me to have any visiting rights (.) =
8	M	= Mmh
9	V	^{0}that's (.) why we're here^{0}.
10	M	Okay I understand so we have a: (.) a: (.) is it a boy or a girl↑
11	V	Little boy (.) Rudolph
12	M	Rudolph↓ (.) okay (.) and: five days ago Rudolph was (.) born and (.) we have (.) did you have other arrangements with (.) Mom and Dad (.) previously to this/I'm not sure
13	V	Well (.) I've signed the papers (.) ehm (.) but I'm still in my (.) my waiting period (.) I still have (.) you know (.) time to (.) decide what I really want to do
14	M	Mmh
15	V	And the arrangements were that (.) I would be able to have some ^{0}contact with him^{0}
16	M	Mmh mmh (.) okay (.) so (.) all three of you have worked together before (.) we have Rudolph who is born now (.) we have a situation where (.) e::hm it might be unclear as to what kind of arrangements there were about (.) visitation or something like that is that↑ (.)
17	V	[Yeah
18	M	[Does that put it in a nutshell for you↑
19	V	Yeah Rudolph is at their house now↓
20	M	Okay ^{0}okay^{0} (3) what has she left out↑ what would you like to include can you give me a little bit more framework of what you think the: (.) problem is today that brings you here↑
21	J	(*looking at H*) Well (.) when we (.) when we adopted Rudolph I mean we ADOPTED him we expected that he was going to come into our FAMILY (.) and be our CHILD (.) and (.) you know we've met with Vivian and we talked TALKED before the baby was born and (.) my our OUR understanding was that (.) the BABY now we know the baby is Rudolph was going to come and live with us and be OUR CHILD =
22	H	= For 100 percent (.) that was our understanding↓

At turn 16 the mediator identifies that the origin of the conflict may include a lack of clarity on the problem of visitation rights. Janice's presentation of the case, at 21, followed by her husband's intervention at 22, confirms that there has been a problem in understanding the terms of the agreement. The problem emerges progressively, helped by the mediator's questioning; in particular, at 30, Janice, questioned by the mediator,[77] points to the ambiguity of the word *contact*, which has been at the origin of the misunderstanding:

27	M	So (.) then you felt (.) happy and satisfied that that was going to be a good home (.) are you saying that's the way it is now or not saying↑
28	V	Yeah↓ but (.) I had agreed that (.) I had talked to them about it about having agreements of (.) me being able to (.) to see him (.) have contact with my child
29	M	With Rudolph↑ mmh I see you nodding your head (.) does that mean (.) yes or (.) or no↑
30	J	Yes (.) (*nodding*) my understanding (.) was that (.) by CONTACT (.) you know Vivian was free to write letters and:
31	M	Mmh
32	J	Send pictures on holidays
33	M	Mmh
34	J	Christmas (.) birthdays (.) that kind of thing (.) and (3) but I had never I don't think we ever (.) CONSIDERED (.) Vivian (.) seeing (.) Rudolph and spending TIME with him (.) I just think it's it's a very very confusing situation for everyone including Rudolph (.) when he gets older
35	M	Harrison check this out (.) Is this the same kind of/
36	H	Yes my understanding was (.) that (.) the contact (.) would be: (.) up until the point where she (.) surrendered the baby to us after signing the papers

Then it is the mediator who offers the parties the opportunity to clarify their misunderstanding at 41, where he asks about a segment of the opening stage concerning factual knowledge of the parties' preceding negotiations. In other words, he asks them to *define* what they meant by "visitation":

41	M	Mmh (1) okay (.) help me out with something (.) Vivian I need need to understand a little bit more (.) is it your impression that (.) ehm (.) during the negotiation phase with (.) Mom and Dad here (.) that (.) it wasn't clear to you (.) about what (.) visitation meant/was it not discussed/and then if I might then I'll ask both of you what your general impressions are
42	V	No↓ I pretty well got the impression I said I wanted to have contact with my (.) my boy and: (.) that's why I signed the papers they had agreed that I would have contact
43	M	Mmh (.) mmh (.) did they say anything about what (.) kind of (.) contact↑
44	V	No (.) no we didn't really talk about it

77. Notice that the mediator not only makes the discussion proceed in terms of new information that emerges, but also encourages specific interlocutors to commit themselves by taking positions. The analysis of connective predicates allows taking this fact into account, since connective predicates assume speaker and hearer among their arguments.

45 H That was the problem the AMBIGUITY (.) of the way things were presented to us (.) by our legal counsel and: it's becoming quite a quite a (.) big issue for us right now because we have an inability to (.) conceive children on our own (.) and: (.) and (.) the adoption process is an almost impossible (.) mass of paperwork and (.) red tape so (.) when the opportunity came to adopt Rudolph (.) we jumped (.) we just jumped at it we very much (.) truly want the baby↓

46 M That's generally my experience what happens is that (2) couples who want to adopt (.) are excited (.) and (.) moms who (.) are: (.) going to (.) consider (.) eh (.) giving up (.) their child (.) to a family have a lot going on in their MIND at once (.) so (.) it might appear that it would be easy for eh something like this to slip by (.) I need to know (.) from you Vivian what is it that you do want↓ because I still don't know yet I know you want (.) access (.) I hear (.) eh Harrison and Jenny saying what (.) they think (.) you want (.) but I personally don't know what you want yet (1) for you and Rudolph/

Here, a constellation of related ambiguities emerges; and these very ambiguities have originated the conflict. Two particular concepts are related and entrenched in the misunderstanding: *contact* (*to have contact with someone*) and *adoption* (*to adopt*). A very concise semantic analysis[78] of these two terms can help an understanding of where the problem lies:

> To have contact with (x1, x2). x1 and x2 are human beings | x1 and x2 have some not too tight but regular form of relationship.

Indeed, *contact* is used for covering different (more or less regular) frequencies of encounters: regular contact (once per week) as well as very occasional meetings. For Vivian, in this case, contact meant seeing her baby regularly; while for Jenny and Harrison it meant being allowed to send some postcards on special occasions. Clearly, such interpretations are bound to equally diverging interpretations of Harrison and Jenny's role as adopting parents:

> To adopt (x1, x2, x3). x1 and x2 are a couple of potential parents, x3 is a child who for some reason cannot be grown by his natural family | x1 and x2 commit themselves to raise x3 *as if* he/she were their natural child.

Here again the problem has not been defined in clear terms. In fact, one might argue, even though adopting parents want to raise the child as if they were its natural parents (with the same love, care, and so on), this does not however

78. See Chapter4 for a detailed expounding and application of the method of semantic analysis adopted in the present work.

necessarily exclude the possibility that the child can have some form of contact with its natural parents.[79]

Now, while the need for clarification emerges from the parties' statements, the possibility of clarifying them is clearly offered by the mediator's interventions. By analysing them at the level of *connective predicates* (see Chapter 5), in fact, it is clear that he is leading the parties to clarify their ambiguities:

Turn	*Text*		*Connective predicate*
20	M	Okay °okay° (3) what has she left out↑ what would you like to include↑ can you give me a little bit more framework of what you think the: (.) problem is today that brings you here↑	C (S, U_{-1}, U, A):[80] With U[81] the mediator asks J's opinion about V's preceding statement
35	M	Harrison check this out (.) Is this the same kind of/	C (S, U_{-1}, U, A): With U the mediator asks H to assume a personal commitment on the other interlocutors' difference of opinion
41	M	Mmh (1) okay (.) help me out with something (.) Vivian I need need to understand a little bit more (.) is it your impression that (.) ehm (.) during the negotiation phase with (.) Mom and Dad here (.) that (.) it wasn't clear to you (.) about what (.) visitation meant/ was it not discussed/and then if I might then I'll ask both of you what your general impressions are	With U the mediator asks V to recognize the misunderstanding in the preceding discussion

79. The issue is, of course, very complicated and sensitive. Here, I simply suggest that using a term like "adoption" without defining it can lead to misunderstandings.

80. Here, the elements enclosed in brackets are the arguments of the connective predicate in question. S refers to the speaker, A to the addressees. U indicates the utterance, while U_{-1} and U_{+1} refer to the co-text, namely to the preceding and to the following co-textual material respectively. Notice that many of the mediator's interventions are at a meta-communicative level, as he asks parties to take a position on the preceding discussion (thus, the argument U_{-1} is always present). This is required by the clarification dialogue, as the mediator must bring the parties to acknowledge their misunderstanding.

81. Here, "U" is used for "utterance", while the participants to the interaction are indicated with the initials of their proper names except for the mediator.

46	M	That's generally my experience what happens is that (2) couples who want to adopt (.) are excited (.) and (.) moms who (.) are: (.) going to (.) consider (.) eh (.) giving up (.) their child (.) to a family have a lot going on in their MIND at once (.) so (.) it might appear that it would be easy for eh something like this to slip by (.) I need to know (.) from you Vivian what is it that you do want↓ because I still don't know yet I know you want (.) access (.) I hear (.) eh Harrison and Jenny saying what (.) they think (.) you want (.) but I personally don't know what you want yet (1) for you and Rudolph/	C (S, U_{-1}, U, U_{+1}, A): With U H confirms the presence of a misunderstanding in the preceding discussion and interprets it as a normally occurring phenomenon in similar situations

The definition of what was meant in the past by "visitation" and "contact" is clearly part of the opening stage, because it aims to clarify the premises from which the further discussion for conflict resolution can be developed. This segment of discussion, opened by a direct mediator's request for a usage declarative (definition of "visitation", see turn 41) provides the opportunity for the parties to acknowledge each other's reasons for their standpoints, and to realize that a misunderstanding arose about their interpretation of the visiting rights. Once this clarification takes place, they can avoid accusing each other of having changed their mind after the first agreement, and move on to discuss the real issue of the best solution for the baby. In this case, the mediator's function as a support to the parties' critical discussion is quite evident, because he tries to help them avoid unclear formulations, as requested in rule 10 of a critical discussion.[82] This requirement was clearly not fulfilled in the preceding discussion, and now the mediator has to put it forward in the present situation.

Case 4 probably presents the clearest instance in the corpus of the role of a request for a usage declarative operated by the mediator. However, different evidence comes from the other cases, in which the mediator either resolves a misunderstanding, or asks for definition, precisation or explicitation in order to avoid

82. This is the formulation of the rule according to van Eemeren & Grootendorst 1992: "*The usage rule*: Parties must not use any formulations that are insufficiently clear or confusingly ambiguous, and they must interpret the formulations of the other party as carefully and accurately as possible".

any possible misunderstanding deriving from words or expressions used in an unclear fashion.

In Case 1, some precisations are needed in order to set the new boundaries of Ann and Philip's relationship as unambiguously as possible. See the mediator's attempt to distinguish[83] between a friendly institutionalized relationship and a friendly interpersonal relationship at 153 and 155:

150	M	No physical contact (.) number one (.) no lunches↓ (.) no dinners
151	P	No friendship↓
152	A	I never asked for your friendship↓
153	M	No↓ other than academic friendship no friendship
154	A	Cooperation is different
155	M	But let's clearly distinguish between having an ACADEMIC relationship and a social relationship↓

The situation is slightly different in Case 5, in which the mediator accidentally discovers a difference of opinion by using a word to define Polly's work for Tim – the word *favour* – which he does not accept:

193	M	(2) And you did this favour for your good friend (2) what would you want from (.) Polly↑
194	T	What do you mean by (.) You did this favour for your good friend↑
195	P	[It was a FAVOR
196	M	[You helped there your good friend (.) You are the:: ah (.) ah (.) caterer (2) if you were caterer instead of (.) Polly (.) and she was the banker↑ ()
197	P	You don't think that was A FAVOR (.) from me↑
198	T	(3) I think ah:: (1) I GAVE you the POSSIBILITY (.) to eh:: (.) to do a good job (.) that you you would get eh:: (.) a good payment for it that's not exactly what I call a favour [no
199	M	[Ya (.) so (.) then (.) I may have misused (.) the word↑

In this case, it is Tim who, at turn 194, advances a request for clarification, at the same time implicitly conveying a doubt on the presupposed statement "what Polly did for you is a favour". Thus, in this case the request for definition gives rise to a subordinate critical discussion that is bound to the interpretation of the events of the conflict. Indeed, the word *favour* semantically indicates some (single and limited in time) action gratuitously performed by a subject (x) for the good of

83. In this case, a dissociation (see van Rees 2005) is operated on the notion of *friendship*, which for the purposes of the interaction is subdivided between "academic friendship" (which can be interpreted as a friendly working collaboration in the institutionalized roles of professor and student) and "friendship", meaning a more intimate interpersonal relationship.

another subject (y). It is implied that (x) was not expected to perform the action in question, but that this is made from the "goodness of her heart".

Therefore, accepting this characterization of Polly's work for him would mean for Tim putting their business relationship in the background, which he does not want to accept, and above all putting himself in the position of someone who is expected to do something in exchange for Polly's favour. Polly's interpretation of her work, however, fits very well with the mediator's characterization. Therefore, she immediately contrasts Tim's doubt both at 195 and at 197. The mediator, at 199, seems to ignore the implications of Tim's question; he appears more concerned with resolving his "gaffe" than with understanding why Tim has reacted so immediately. Polly, however, has grasped the deeper meaning of this reaction, as she shows at 195. It must be said that, in this case, the mediator quite surprisingly tries to close this subordinate discussion without concluding it, which seems to put the quality of his intervention in question. Interestingly, however, after some discussion, Polly goes back to the point:

268	P	[Ya (2) But (.) I- I want to make one thing clear. It was a favour from me (.) that I::
269	M	Mmh
270	P	NOT (.) that I had the opportunity but (.) I I called (.) to (.) places all over the world I have: (.) worked late to get everything right eh: (.) there were some problems abroad I (.) I managed to control them (.) so there were some favours for you
271	T	[Eh
272	M	[Eh
273	P	It's good to realize that
274	T	Did you realize as well that your (.) name was on the ( ) that (.) all the guests (.) have had this:: (.) oh (.) ( ) party with your name?
275	P	Yes of course =
276	M	= Mmh =
277	T	= It's a:: =
278	P	= Of course and that's a shame what's you said it's a shame but it's not (.) basically it's not my problem
279	M	So it sounds like (.) the two of you (.) for the two of you (.) this was an embarrassment for both of your (.) businesses.
280	T	^{0}Certainly^0 =
281	M	= Your name on the card:: (.) your party:: (.)
282	T	Mmh
283	M	Yes↑
284	P	(2) Mmh
285	M	Ya
286	P	Ya you're right

Polly does not want to leave the discussion unresolved, and without providing her reasons for interpreting what she did as a favour; such reasons are expounded at 270. After Tim's reply, the mediator eventually manages to make the discussion move on to the consequences of what happened, which has provoked an embarrassment for both businesses (turn 279). In the passages reported here, clarification occurs almost without the help of the mediator, as the parties attempt to explain their interpretation of the facts. In this case, it could be said that the mediator is only the "trigger" that activates the development of the discussion. Here, it is the interaction scheme itself that provides the parties with some room for presenting to each other the reasons for their concerns. However, the mediator's reaction, especially at the beginning, risked the failure of the task of the opening stage, because he missed an opportunity for clarification in this case. The fact that in spite of this, the parties do not leave the issue unresolved shows the importance of clarification in mediation.

CHAPTER 7

Conclusive remarks

The main reason that brought me to investigate argumentation in the particular context of dispute mediation is the importance of what is at stake in mediation. Mediation, in fact, is an important and widespread *conflict resolution* practice, in which one can see the enormous benefits of a well-conducted argumentative discussion as a means to deal reasonably with and possibly solve conflicts. Mediation, thus, seemed a good benchmark to understand how argumentation can contribute to the establishment of communicative practices in society based on human beings' ability to engage in reasoned dialogues rather than exert violence or other coercive, non-rational means to achieve goals and, particularly, to solve conflicts. Conflict is a ubiquitous phenomenon in our everyday life, both at the level of our interpersonal and group relationships and within the broader international scenario. It is thus particularly urgent to find paths and ways to deal with conflictual situations and relationships in a reasonable fashion, so that it is possible to preserve existing relationships and build new and better ones.

Looking back to the results of my research project as well as to the path that has made it possible to achieve them, I can conclude that my expectations have been exceeded. Not only is argumentation a part of dispute mediation, but it has emerged as constituting a fundamental key to the achievement of the goals of this practice. The establishment of a well-founded argumentative discussion appears to affect the quality of the conflict resolution process. Conversely, the principles that constitute the "spirit" of a good mediator attitude according to the professionals in this practice – such as "Focus on interests, not positions" (see Chapters 2 and 6) – are *de facto* almost exclusively realized by argumentative means.

Also exceeding the original expectations was the clear-cut emergence of prominent features of the mediators' argumentative strategies in relation to the construction of an argumentative discussion (see Section 7.2). Such features characterize dispute mediation from the point of view of the structuring of the communication process and could thus be adopted as a "model" to test the quality of the argumentative discussion in mediation in future research projects.

In this final chapter, I shall first give a retrospective evaluative overview of the previous Chapters (7.1). This overview is not intended as a simple summary of the research project; it is called *evaluative* because I highlight the main results that have been achieved. I shall then devote specific attention to one particular set of results, which I believe more directly concerns the community of argumentation scholars dealing with or interested in dispute mediation; namely prominent features of the mediators' argumentation (7.2). Finally, moving on from the results of the analysis of dispute mediation, I shall abstract some general considerations about the study of argumentation in context (7.3). In this final section, I shall also mention some of the professional fall-outs that this type of study can produce.

7.1 A retrospective evaluative overview

The study of argumentation in context developed in this volume originates from a puzzling consideration about the insurgence of argumentation in dispute mediation (Chapter 1). Conflicting parties enter mediation in anything but a reasonable mood; they are often overcome with emotion caused by their conflict and unable to communicate with each other. However, in successful cases, after one or more mediation sessions an argumentative discussion between the parties is established and parties become able to conduct a dialogue with each other. In this volume, I have characterized this change as the parties' *change in attitude* from disputants to co-arguers. The main goal of this research project has been to understand how this change in attitude is possible, how an argumentative discussion is established and what the mediators' role is in encouraging it. This study has been possible by integrating an analytical conceptual analysis and an empirical effort.

The analytical component is constituted by the progressive construction of an ontology-oriented mediation framework able to map the context of dispute mediation and its intersections with argumentation. First, I have mapped the context of dispute mediation in Chapters 2 and 3 via a progressive refinement of its main characteristics. The reconstruction of mediation as a context of argumentative interaction has been based on an interdisciplinary synthetic approach. In other words, I have based the analysis on insights derived from studies in conflict resolution that have singled out the defining traits of this conflict resolution practice. However, this stream of studies lacked a unitary perspective able to give a comprehensive picture of mediation. For this reason, the approach adopted in Chapter 3, which tries to integrate the best from each existing approach, has given as a result a synthesis that is per se an advance in the study of mediation. During the last years, the need for a comprehensive framework of mediation has been increasingly felt to be urgent in professional elaborations and in scientific studies. Some very recent attempts clearly signal the need for such a model, as is manifestly suggested in Herrman, Hollett and Gale (2006). In general, although there is a variety of approaches that propose interesting insights into various aspects of a mediation *scenario* (the network of essential factors and relations constituting a mediation interaction) and *script* (the expected process of a successfully managed mediation interaction), no comprehensive conceptual framework has been elaborated, which is able to combine the scenario and the script perspectives and founded on a conceptual analysis based on an interdisciplinary overview of the literature. The integration of the scenario and script dimensions makes the framework particularly suited for the study of the communication and argumentation dynamics that are concretely at work in a mediation process. The script dimension, in fact, highlights the pragmatic structure of mediation, namely its general goal and the specific subservient goals, distributed in specific phases.[1] In this way, it is possible to analyse how argumentation contributes to the achievement of each specific goal of mediation.

However, in order to be suitable for the study of the role that a well-founded argumentative discussion plays in mediation, the picture emerging from the above described reasoned synthesis of current approaches to mediation still needed some conceptual integrations, which are provided in Chapters 4 and 5.

In Chapter 4, I elaborated on two very important concepts that were in need of clarification, namely the parties' relationship as a *context* for their communicative-argumentative interaction and the parties' *conflict*. In fact, although primary importance is attributed to these notions in the literature, their proper meaning remained quite unclear. Concerning context, a model drawn from communicative research (Rigotti & Rocci 2006) has been integrated in order to complete the study of mediation as a context of argumentative interaction. This model, originally conceived as a tool for analysing the context of communicative interactions, facilitates the assumption of an argumentative perspective on mediation. The model permits an understanding of what is meant by *relationship* between the parties, which aspects of their institutionalized and interpersonal commitments are concerned, and so on.

Conflict is a crucial notion for mediation, being a necessary presupposition of any conflict resolution intervention. Despite its importance, however, there are relatively few studies devoted to the understanding of its proper constituency. Conflict is seen to be polysemic, if not an ambiguous word; and conflict resolution studies suffer from a situation of such uncertain semantics. The semantic analysis

1. Understanding the script dimension has been helped, in the present research, by my involvement in a professional mediation training course, which facilitated me in eliciting what is expected by mediators in each phase of a successful conflict resolution process. I attended the course organized by the Scuola Universitaria Professionale della Svizzera italiana (SUPSI) from March 2007 to January 2008. I obtained the Certificate of Advanced Studies in Mediation and the Use of Mediation Techniques on the Workplace.

proposed in Chapter 4 (see also Greco Morasso 2008) has led to clarification of the dynamics of escalation from some form of disagreement (a difference of opinion on an issue or some incompatibility of interests)[2] to situations of interpersonal hostility; these dynamics are represented in a *conflict mapping guide*.[3] Such an analysis of the concept of *conflict* suggested some cues that have successively allowed enriching the analytical instrumentation applied to the empirical data. As confirmed by the outcomes of Chapter 6, understanding how conflict develops is something that any mediator needs. Normally, in fact, when parties ask for external help to solve their problem, a conflict has already arisen and, very often, the original difference(s) of opinion that have provoked it are not clearly identified by the parties, who seem to be more interested in damaging each other rather than in limiting their disagreement. In this connection, the outcomes of the argumentative analysis in Chapter 6 have also shown that the mediator has to walk the inverse path of the escalation of the conflict and arrive at the identification of the original controversial issue in order to help the parties solve their interpersonal conflict. The analysis of the notion of conflict is another specific result deriving from the present analysis of argumentation in dispute mediation. As well as this, the dynamics of conflict escalation described in Chapter 4 could even open a parallel vein of research into how conflicts can be *prevented* by establishing adequate spaces of mutual understanding, allowed by argumentative discussions.

These two integrations of context and conflict allowed the construction of an ontology-oriented framework of mediation, presented and discussed in Chapter 4. As this framework is intended as a basis for the study of argumentation in the context of mediation, it was still necessary to integrate the argumentative perspective at the conceptual level. This task was undertaken in Chapter 5, in which the argumentative theories which are adopted in the present research are presented and their integration into the framework is discussed. What primarily

2. Some full interpersonal conflicts originate from differences in the parties' perspectives or "ideological" contrapositions; others originate from competitive situations deriving from conflicts of interests. Both cases can be viewed as generating differences of opinion that, if not managed, degenerate into full interpersonal hostility. What normally happens in a conflict of interests is that the parties not only know that the realization of their interest is incompatible with the realization of the counterparty's interest; but they also claim that their position (their willingness to achieve their own interest) is *right* and that the counterparty is wrong in opposing it. Full interpersonal struggles usually arise from this situation.

3. The task pursued by the conflict mapping guide presented in Chapter 4 offers an instrument to understand conflict. In this relation, this instrument, apart from its value as a theoretical investigation of the constituency of conflict, can also serve the more practical purpose of being a possible matrix for designing tools for conflict resolution interventions.

emerges from such an integration is that the core process of mediation, in which the parties' change in attitude is likely to happen during their communicative interaction, is made possible by the presence of an argumentative discussion. In other words, argumentation strongly contributes to the fulfilment of the pragmatic goals of the interaction scheme of mediation: *the successful change in attitude of the parties who learn to be co-arguers becomes the condition of a happy outcome of the mediation process.* This latter may be defined as the re-establishment of a "revised version" of the parties' previous relationship.

At the end of Chapter 5, the need for the empirical component in the research project is discussed. In fact, although the ontology-oriented conceptual framework built in Chapters 4 and 5 already represents a theoretical advance in the study of argumentation in the context of dispute mediation, still the questions that originated the present research could not be answered by means of this conceptual analysis alone. It is necessary to focus on exactly how the argumentative discussion is realized in mediation, and how the mediator contributes to the parties' change in attitude and helps them become co-arguers. The design of the empirical analysis is expounded in Chapter 5, while its results are presented and discussed in detail in Chapter 6. The argumentative results are particularly important in the present research effort. For this reason, I shall devote particular attention to a review of the main results that have emerged from the argumentative analysis in a specific Section (7.2).

Before addressing these results, however, I would like to advance some cautions about the choices and the necessarily following limitations that characterize this research project. From the methodological point of view, in order to define the role that argumentation plays in a happily concluded mediation process, a corpus of transcriptions of successful mediation cases has been compiled. This corpus, whose selection criteria have been discussed in detail in Chapter 6, is constituted by exemplary mediation cases ("best practices"), also used as an example-basis to train mediators in a number of countries worldwide.

The selection of these cases has necessarily implied some limits, which signal the need for further research. The two mediators considered, John Haynes and Larry Fong, are acknowledged as professional models by other mediators and currently no equivalent collection of cases exists which can be used by practitioners as a training tool. However, the fact that this set of mediations is limited to only two mediators raises a problem about the extent to which the strategies and techniques identified are based on the two mediators' individual characteristics rather than a standard interpretation of what mediators should do. As a matter of fact, however, the use of these cases in training shows that Haynes's and Fong's way to handle a mediation process is considered canonical and exemplary, and their individual characteristics are acknowledged as a term of comparison for other mediators.

A further limit of the selection of the present corpus is that all the mediations are restricted to a homogeneous cultural area in the Western world. Other cultural domains would certainly involve arguments based on different culturally based premises (*endoxa*) and, supposedly, also different rhetorical strategies.

Given these considerations, it would be interesting to move from the results obtained in this research to analyse and evaluate the actualizations and interpretations of mediation in different geographical and cultural environments and in a higher number of cases. In this relation, on the one hand, the analysis of the best practices performed here can be used as an evaluative model to define the canonical way of handling argumentation in mediation.[4] On the other hand, different actualizations and cultural approaches can be expected to bring fresh insights and new directions to the study of mediation.

7.2 Prominent features of argumentation in mediation

I shall now discuss the prominent features that emerged when analysing the structuring of argumentation in dispute mediation in Chapter 6, in particular in relation to the parties' progressive ability to handle their differences of opinion in a reasonable fashion.

7.2.1 A macro-text of argumentative discussions

We could read the mediator's interventions as a series of punctual, locally relevant moves aimed at the parties' own engagement in an argumentative discussion about the resolution of their conflict. This latter discussion, however, is not a single and unitary one. Rather, there is a concatenation of argumentative discussions that is typical of mediation, as it responds to the goals of the various phases of the core resolution process and allows their achievement (see Section 6.2.3). More precisely, when analysing the development of argumentation in mediation on the basis of the model of a critical discussion (van Eemeren & Grootendorst 1992, 2004), one notices the presence of more than a single critical discussion. In fact,

4. The cases I have selected, due to their exemplary status, also present ideal cases of mediator's behaviour. It is certainly to be considered that the mediators' strategic manoeuvring can derail for a number of reasons and their interventions can be less than ideal in many cases. In this relation, including also some *a-contrario* cases in which mediation fails, it would be interesting to understand what argumentative problems can be identified. This methodology has been used, for example, in Jacobs and Aakhus (2002a).

the argumentative exchange can be interpreted as a *multiple dispute in a qualitative sense* (van Eemeren, Houtlosser & Snoeck-Henkemans 2007); namely a discussion in which more than one issue is tackled. In this kind of dispute, the issues are not listed separately, but are seen to have important logical connections. Thus, for example, the resolution of a specific difference of opinion on an issue may reveal that other issues are automatically solved. What happens in general is that the mediator helps the parties reconstruct the confrontation and opening stages of the discussion about their conflict as it happened in the past (see in particular Section 6.2 for a detailed discussion of these results). Once the issues at the origin of the conflict are identified, however, the mediator shifts the discussion on to the options for conflict resolution. In this way, he opens a series of sub-discussions about the possible worlds corresponding to as many components of the parties' solution of the conflict. The sum of these sub-discussions may be viewed as a complex argumentation stage in the parties' general critical discussion about the resolution of their conflict. The concluding stage is ideally represented by the resolution of the conflict itself. In order to stress the unity between these different discussions, which are not simply juxtaposed, but are connected by their responding to the same ultimate pragmatic goal, namely settling the conflict, the term *macro-text* is appropriate. Figure 6.6 in Chapter 6 represents this macro-text visually.

7.2.2 Strategic manoeuvring with topical potential

The mediator's role as a guide and heuristic advisor (Greco Morasso 2007) for the parties to construct their own argumentative discussion is difficult to overestimate. In fact, it is the mediator's work that can explain the parties' change in attitude. In particular, prominent from the argumentative point of view is the mediator's wise management of his *topical potential*. This is true on different levels, concerning the confrontation, opening and argumentation stages of the parties' critical discussion.

It has been shown that the confrontation stage of the disputants' discussion, in which they would be expected to advance standpoints about the resolution of their conflict, to cast doubts or advance objections, is far from being spontaneously generated; on the contrary, it is created by the mediator's strategic manoeuvring with the potential issues. Sometimes the mediator even argues explicitly, at a meta-level, to persuade parties to accept a given issue as a basis for their argumentative discussion. This kind of direct argumentation does not contradict the mediator's neutral stance. On the contrary, it explains how mediators can handle their paradoxical role by exploiting the topical potential of their strategic manoeuvring, which brings them to shape the structure of the parties' discussion while at the same time manifestingly avoiding the role of direct protagonist or antagonist in a critical discussion.[5]

By managing the selection of the parties' discussion issues, the mediator makes them move from an initial status of conflict and interpersonal hostility to the identification of the *real issue* constituted by the difference of opinion that has originated their conflict and that, as any issue, could have been resolved by non-conflictual argumentative means. As emerged in Chapter 6, such an issue is tightly connected to the parties' deep interests, namely to the concerns that worry them. But these concerns also represent the reasons why the conflict can be settled: they constitute the values that the parties do not want to lose, or the goals they want to achieve by their engagement in mediation.

In this sense, the mediator's work, which, as noted, contributes to the construction of a dialectically sound confrontation stage, at the same time constitutes a step-by-step construction of the parties' common ground. In argumentative terms, it turns out to be part of a mediator-guided construction of an *opening stage* of a critical discussion. In particular, part of this work is constituted by the analysis of the *conflict* and, together with it, the story of the relationships shaping the *context* of the dispute. Through this procedure, the parties are given the opportunity to reveal those aspects of their relationship that are endangered by the conflict. In the argumentation stage of their critical discussion, these aspects may become reasons to resolve the conflict or, better, premises of arguments about the resolution of the conflict: if a relationship is valuable, it should not be lost because of a difficulty that could be overcome.

7.2.3 The locus from termination and setting up

The argumentative tool that makes it possible for the parties to reason about endangered relationships is the *locus of termination and setting up* (Rigotti & Greco Morasso 2006b). This locus is frequently employed in dispute mediation and tightly connected with the parties' decision to solve their conflict through the means of mediation. In dispute mediation, the locus from termination and setting up is often applied starting from the maxim "if something is a value, it should not be terminated/interrupted". The use of arguments based on this premise is often solicited or proposed by the mediator. On closer inspection, it appears that such a reasoning scheme is determinant in a process like that of mediation, because it is

5. In Case 6, one of the parties explicitly asks the mediator to formulate his opinion about which solution would be reasonable, and he answers: "S- so (.) Let me just ask you more questions because (.) I think what's more important is (.) what you two find reasonable" (turn 334).

strictly bound to its very nature. In fact, by its very nature, the conflict that parties are experiencing endangers their relationship – be it interpersonal as a friendship, or more institutionalized, as collaboration in a business corporation – and makes them fear that something they care for can be compromised or lost forever. In this sense, reflecting on the value of a relationship that risks being terminated can be the key to the resolution of the conflict itself. Of course, the premise "if something is a value, it should not be terminated/interrupted" is an abstract principle that, in order to become effective, needs to be applied to some form of relationship or value that is *actually* worthwhile for the parties. This could be the parties' friendship, their business relationship, their common values and aspirations, their children's happiness, and so on. During the opening stage, contextual data about what the parties consider worthwhile normally emerge through the mediator's questioning. These data can then be exploited to construct arguments based on the locus from termination and setting up.

Moreover, the use of this locus can be hypothesized to activate specific emotional dynamics in the parties who, from the emotions in which they are locked by the conflict, move to *hope* for a resolution.

7.2.4 Meeting on the ground of interests

In the brief description of the complex structuring of the mediation macro-text of argumentative discussions outlined above, the notion of *interest* has repeatedly emerged at crucial points. The important role of interests in mediation is, indeed, an established acquisition for conflict resolution studies (see Fisher, Ury & Patton 1991). It is well known, in fact, that probably the most important value of mediation resides in the possibility that the parties will consider their deep interests in the design of a solution to their conflict. What was still lacking, however, was the understanding of *how* interests are activated in practice by means of specific communicative moves. In this relation, the present research project has helped elicit how interests that are at the very origin of the parties' engagement in the resolution of their conflict can be solicited by the mediator's argumentative interventions.

The consideration of the parties' interests has emerged as even more crucial than expected. *In fact, interests become the keystones of the parties' opening stage*; in non-metaphorical terms, they represent the ultimate premises that enable parties to reasonably solve their conflict by means of an argumentative discussion.

Furthermore, the results that emerged in Chapter 6 show that the mediator's role in eliciting the parties' interests is even more crucial than expected. The mediator, in fact, takes a risk to evoke the parties' interests, often even anticipating their explicit concessions by means of *presupposition accommodation* (see Greco 2003), i.e. by taking for granted that some compatible interests (in particular the continuation of the parties' relationship) exist, although they have not been declared by the parties themselves. Mediators do so by constructing arguments based on supposedly shared premises (*endoxa*); by evoking such premises, mediators "test" the parties' agreement on them and the correspondence of these premises to their interests. Moreover, mediators equally test and challenge the parties' interests by means of presupposition accommodation when they shift the focus of the discussion from the conflict to its possible solutions, thus taking for granted that it is possible and convenient to find some solution to the conflict, and that what has to be ascertained is only *how* (which solution).

By means of these strategies, all bound to the mediator's management of the topical potential, the conflict resolution principle is realized, which recommends focusing on the parties' *objective interests* rather than on their explicit positions (Fisher, Ury & Patton 1991). In successful cases at least, when the mediator dares to make the strings of objective interests vibrate, the parties resound in sympathy, and the encounter between them becomes possible. In this relation, the parties' deepest interests, at least sometimes, turn out to be associated with some form of *relational happiness*, by which they "discover" that they gain from the other party's feeling comfortable and from the continuation of their relationship.

Presupposition accommodation emerges thus as a linguistic strategy allowing the mediator's selection of the parties' interests within the topical potential. This device, which is often exploited in manipulative uses, is seen in this case to have a virtuous application. In fact, the mediator does not impose unacceptable premises onto the parties, but he leaves them the possibility of accepting or refusing all levels of the presupposed common ground. Letting interests emerge or provoking interests by presupposition accommodation signals a specific way to achieve a successful mediation. In fact, parties can overcome their interpersonal difficulty and become co-arguers by the mutual recognition of their interests, including personal respect and recognition for one another as human beings. The mediator's work, thus, is not that of making parties walk together towards some form of unhappy compromise, which could leave them resentful. It is to make them meet on the ground of finding what is truly and objectively important to them.

7.3 On the study of argumentation in context

This study represents an attempt to study how argumentation is developed in a specific communication context, namely *dispute mediation*. In this study, dispute mediation has been characterized as an *interaction scheme* which moulds its structure on a variety of interaction fields to which it can be applied. From the methodological point of view, the structure of this study could be assumed as a working hypothesis for further investigations into contextualized argumentation. Two aspects are particularly worth retaining.

First, the empirical argumentative analysis of a specific argumentative reality is only the tip of the iceberg within a study of argumentation in context. In fact, a large part of the present volume is devoted to the mapping of mediation as a context for argumentative discussion. This process culminates with the outline of an ontology-oriented conceptual framework of mediation, which also includes the argumentative perspective. Without this conceptual analysis of the context in which argumentation is developed, including the interpersonal and institutional dimensions, it would have been impossible to determine to what extent the establishment of an argumentative discussion favours conflict resolution in mediation. And the analysis of mediation has only been possible by assuming an interdisciplinary attitude, through which the different contributions are critically confronted and their major insights retained.

Second, and conversely, a pure conceptual analysis of a certain communication context which did not include the argumentative analysis of the actual interaction would remain a somewhat incomplete description of the possible interrelation between argumentation and a certain activity type. The argumentative analysis has made the identification possible of *prominent features* of the mediation interaction (see Section 7.2 for a summary), which characterize dispute mediation from the argumentative point of view. I believe that the search for characterizing features of argumentation in specific contexts is to be retained as a crucial component to synthetically describe how argumentation works in a specific context.

In sum, both components, the careful conceptual analysis and the empirical argumentative analysis, are thus required in order to understand how argumentation is determinant to mould communication contexts. If, on the one hand, the specific modalities through which this research path has been realized in this work depend strictly on its specific object of investigation, it seems nonetheless that an analogous approach should prove to be expedient also in the analysis of other interaction contexts. Thus, the methodology elaborated in the present work could contribute to existing and well-founded knowledge of interaction schemes and activity types such as, for example, legal argumentation (Feteris 1999, 2005). But it could also help plough up new ground, for example, in relation to the argumentative instrumentation employed in financial negotiations (see Palmieri 2008 for some first results in this direction).

I would also like to add a brief consideration of the possible professional fall-out of the study of argumentation in context. I maintain that this kind of study may be relevant not only at the scientific but also at the societal level. If we manage to demonstrate how argumentation is relevant to achieve the specific goals of a certain context – for example, a professional practice like dispute mediation – that would constitute an advance also at the level of the professional understanding of that context. In the case of mediation, for example, the introduction of the argumentative perspective could contribute, on a professional level, to an improvement in the design of mediation training courses and to the integration of their communicative instrumentation in relation to argumentation, the importance of which is implicitly acknowledged by conflict resolution studies nowadays.[6]

But mediation is not the only context of human interaction in which humans would need to increase their awareness of sound and unsound uses of argumentative means in order to improve their professional practice. For this reason, the study of argumentation in context could also be seen as a basis for establishing more reasonable and better-founded communicative interactions in different spheres of our society.

6. The present study contributes a contrast to a possible objection to the introduction of argumentation in the professional mediators' curriculum, concerning the suspicion that an argumentative engagement could affect the neutral and facilitative role that mediators must keep. This suspicion, which is fuelled, at least in part, by the polysemy of *argumentation, to argue* and of related terms often associated with a polemical meaning (see the interpretation in Besemer 1993), stems from the interpretation of the argumentative attitude as "directive" and "impositive"; argumentation, in this sense, would clearly be irremediably incompatible with the attitude of an ideal mediator. As the results of this research project show, the mediator's way of arguing is specific and in line with their commitment to favour the parties' discussion without taking a position on possible solutions of the conflict. Even when mediators argue directly, or when they risk suggesting cues to the parties to construct their own arguments on the basis of supposedly shared interests, their argumentative moves are always in line with their function as neutral facilitators. In this context, the careful analysis of the prominent features of the mediators' argumentation, which have emerged in Chapter 6, can be of use to dissipate doubts about the role of the mediator's argumentation in the process of conflict resolution.

References

Aakhus, M. 2003. Neither naïve nor critical reconstruction: dispute mediators, impasse, and the design of argumentation. *Argumentation* 17 (3): 265–290.

Alexander, N. 2003. (ed.). *Global Trends in Mediation*. Köln: Otto Schmidt.

American Arbitration Association (AAA). http://www.adr.org/ [September 1, 2010].

American Arbitration Association. 2007. *Resolving Professional Accounting and Related Services Disputes – A Guide to Alternative Dispute Resolution*. http://www.adr.org/si.asp?id=4134 [September 1, 2010].

Arcidiacono, F. 2007. *Conflitti e interazione in famiglia*. Roma: Carocci.

Arcidiacono, F., C. Pontecorvo & S. Greco Morasso. 2009. Family conversations: The relevance of context in evaluating argumentation. *Studies in Communication Sciences* 9 (2): 79–92.

Argumentum. An e-course of argumentation theory for the human and social sciences. www.argumentum.ch [September 1, 2010].

Argupolis. A doctoral program on argumentation practices in context. www.argupolis.net [September 1, 2010].

Aristotelis *Ars Rhetorica*. English translation by W. Rhys Roberts. 1924. *The Rhetoric of Aristotle*. Oxford: Clarendon Press.

Aristotelis *Topica et Sophistici Elenchi*, ed. W.D. Ross. 1958. Oxford: Oxford University Press. English translation of topics: Pickard-Cambridge, W.A. 2004. *Topics by Aristotle*. University of Adelaide: eBooks@Adelaide, http://etext.library.adelaide.edu.au [September 1, 2010].

Aristotelis *Categoriae et liber de interpretatione*, ed. L. Minio-Paluello. 1949. Oxford: Oxford University Press.

Association for Conflict Resolution. http://acrnet.org/ [September 1, 2010].

Atran, S., & R. Axelrod. 2008. Reframing sacred values. *Negotiation Journal* 24 (3): 221–246.

Austin, J.L. 1969. *How to do things with words*. Oxford: Oxford University Press.

Avruch, K. 2003. Type I and type II errors in culturally sensitive conflict resolution practice. *Conflict Resolution Quarterly* 20 (3): 351–71.

Bailey, J.D., & S.P. Robbins. 2005. Couple empowerment in divorce: A comparison of mediated and nonmediated outcomes. *Conflict Resolution Quarterly* 22 (4): 453–472.

Bailey, S.D. 1985. Non-official mediation in disputes: Reflections on Quaker experience. *International Affairs* 61 (2): 205–222.

Bannink, F.P. 2008. Solution-focused mediation: The future with a difference. *Conflict Resolution Quarterly* 25 (2): 163–183.

Barone-Adesi, G. 2002. The Role of Inside Information. Financial Disclosure and Value Creation. In *Business Journalism, Corporate Communications, and Newsroom Management*, eds. S. Russ-Mohl & S. Fengler, 63–68. Lugano: Università della Svizzera Italiana.

Barrett, J.T., & J.P. Barrett. 2004. *A history of alternative dispute resolution. The story of a political, cultural, and social movement*. San Francisco: Jossey-Bass.

Barth, E.M. & E.C.W. Krabbe. 1982. *From Axiom to Dialogue. A Philosophical Study of Logics and Argumentation*. Berlin/New York: Walter de Gruyter.

Benadava, S. 1989. La mediación de la Santa Sede en el diferendo chileno-argentino sobre la zona Austral. In: *International law at a time of perplexity*, ed. Y. Dinstein & M. Tabory, 33–50. Dordrecht/Boston/London: Martinus Nijhoff Publishers.

Bertoluzzo, M. 2006. Uno "spazio" per il conflitto: l'esperienza del Gruppo Abele a Torino. In *La mediazione come strumento d'intervento sociale. Problemi e prospettive internazionali*, ed. L. Luison, 206–215. Milano: FrancoAngeli.

Bercovitch, J. 1992. The structure and diversity of mediation in international relations. In *Mediation in international relations. Multiple approaches to conflict management*, ed. J. Bercovitch & J.Z. Rubin, 1–29. London: Macmillan Press and New York: St. Martin's Press.

———. 2002. (ed.). *Studies in international mediation. Essays in honor of Jeffrey Z. Rubin*. Houndmislls/Basingstoke/Hampshire/New York: Palgrave Macmillan.

Bercovitch, J., & J.Z. Rubin. 1992. *Mediation in international relations. Multiple approaches to conflict management*. London: Macmillan Press and New York: St. Martin's Press.

Berthoud, A.-C. 2004. Ces obscurs objets du discours. *SAGW-Akademiefortäge* XII: 1–17.

Besemer, C. 1993. *Mediation – Vermittlung in Konflikten*. Baden: Werkstatt für Gewaltfreie Aktion.

Bickmore, K. 2003. Peer mediation training and program implementation in elementary schools: Research results. *Conflict Resolution Quarterly* 20 (2): 137–160.

Bigi, S. 2007. *Keywords* in argumentative texts and their persuasive power. In *Proceedings of the Sixth Conference of the International Society for the Study of Argumentation*, ed. F.H. van Eemeren, J. Anthony Blair, C.A. Willard, & B. Garssen, 129–135. Amsterdam: Sic-Sat.

Bigi S., S. Cigada, G. Gobber, & S. Greco Morasso. 2007. Cosa succede durante una consultazione medica? "Esame obiettivo" di una consultazione medico-paziente. Paper presented at the Conferenza sulla Comunicazione per la Salute del Centro Universitario di Ricerca sugli Aspetti comunicativo-relazionali in medicina (C.U.R.A.), Università degli Studi di Milano, November 10, 2007.

Bingham, L.B. 2004. Employment dispute resolution: The case for mediation. *Conflict Resolution Quarterly* 22 (1–2): 145–174.

Boethii *De topicis differentiis*. English translation in: Stump, E. 2004. (ed.). *Boethius's "De topicis differentiis"*. Ithaca (NY): Cornell University Press.

Breidenbach, S. 1995. *Mediation. Struktur, Chanchen und Risiken von Vermittlung im Konflikt*. Köhln: Otto Schmidt.

Brett, J.M., & S.B. Goldberg. 1983. Grievance mediation in the coal industry: A field experiment. *Industrial and Labor Relations Review* 37 (1): 49–69.

Broome, B.J., & J.S. Murray. 2002. Improving third-party decisions at choice points: A Cyprus case study. *Negotiation Journal* 18 (1): 75–98.

Broussolle, D. 2006. The peace of work agreement: The emergence and enforcement of a Swiss labour market institution. Working Papers of LaRGE (Laboratoire de Recherche en Gestion et Economie) 2006–04, LaRGE, Université Louis Pasteur, Strasbourg (France).

Brown, M.D. 1998. Rush Hospital's medical malpractice mediation program: An ADR success story. *Illinois Bar Journal* 86 (8): 432–440.

I. Buridani *Summulae de dialectica*. English translation by G. Klima. 2002. New Haven: Yale University Press.

Burrell, N.A., C.S. Zirbel, & M. Allen. 2003. Evaluating peer mediation outcomes in educational settings: A meta-analytic review. *Conflict Resolution Quarterly* 21 (1): 7–26.

Burton, J.W. 1969. *Conflict and Communication. The use of controlled communication in international relations.* New York: Free Press.

Bühring-Uhle, C., L. Kirkhoff & G. Scherer. 2006. (2nd ed.). *Arbitration and mediation in international business.* The Hague: Kluwer Law International.

Bush, R.A.B., & J.P. Folger. 1994. *The Promise of Mediation.* San Francisco: Jossey-Bass.

Caffi, C. 2007. *Mitigation.* Amsterdam (etc.): Elsevier.

CAIN. Conflict Archive on the INternet. http://cain.ulst.ac.uk/ [September 1, 2010].

Callister, R.R., & J.A. Wall, Jr. 1997. Japanese community and organizational mediation. *Journal of Conflict Resolution* 41 (2): 311–328.

Callister, R.R., & J.A. Wall, Jr. 2004. Thai and U.S. community mediation. *Journal of Conflict Resolution* 48 (4): 573–97.

Cantoni, L. 2004. La comunicazione interna, fra miti, riti e modelli: un approccio formativo. *FOR – Rivista per la formazione* 61: 49–53.

Cantoni, L. & N. Di Blas. 2006. *Comunicazione: Teoria e pratiche* (2nd edition). Milano: Apogeo.

Cantoni, L., N. Di Blas, S. Rubinelli, & S. Tardini. 2008. *Pensare e comunicare.* Milano: Apogeo.

Carnevale, P.J.D. 1986. Strategic choice in mediation. *Negotiation Journal* 2 (1): 41–56.

Canyameres I Sanahuja, M. 2002. Empresas familiares, conflictos familiares. *Entreprises familiales, conflits familaux.* In: *Médiation en Europe: Echanges sur les pratiques/Master Européen en Médiation*, 99–112. Sion: Institut Universitaire Kurt Bösch.

Castiglioni, M. 1997. *La mediazione linguistico-culturale. Principi, strategie, esperienze.* Milano: FrancoAngeli.

Christopher Guerra, S. 2008. Themen, Thesen und Argumente zur Position des Italienischen in der viersprachigen Schweiz. *Studies in Communication Sciences* 8 (1): 135–159.

M.T. Ciceronis *Topica*, ed. T. Reinhardt. 2003. Oxford: Oxford University Press.

M.T. Ciceronis *De inventione; De optimo genere oratorum; Topica.* With an English translation by H.M. Hubbel. 1976. Cambridge: Cambridge University Press/London: William Heinemman.

Cigada, S. 2006. Connectif et relation entre locuteurs. Application à l'analyse d'un corpus de presse politique sur la question européenne ("Le Monde", 11 mai 1950). In *Sýndesmoi. Connettivi nella realtà dei testi*, ed. G. Gobber, M.C. Gatti, & S. Cigada, 97–173. Milano: Vita e Pensiero.

———. 2007. Past-oriented and future-oriented emotions in argumentation for Europe during the Fifties. In: *Proceedings of the Sixth Conference of the International Society for the Study of Argumentation*, op.cit., 241–245.

———. 2008. *Les émotions dans le discours de la construction européenne.* Milano: ISU.

Cigoli, V., & E. Scabini. 2004. La mediazione familiare: L'orizzonte relazionale-simbolico. In: *Rigenerare i legami: La mediazione nelle relazioni familiari e comunitarie* (2nd edition), eds. E. Scabini & G. Rossi, 19–55. Milano: Vita e Pensiero.

Cisterna Rojas, V. 2007. Pragma-dialectical analysis of two family mediation cases in Chile. In: *Proceedings of the Sixth Conference of the International Society for the Study of Argumentation*, op. cit.: 247–252.

Cohen, C.F. et al. 2006. Managing conflict during an organizational acquisition. *Conflict Resolution Quarterly* 23 (3): 317–331.

Collier, P., & A. Hoeffler. 1998. On economic causes of civil war. *Oxford Economic Papers* 50: 563–573.

———. 2005. Resource rents, governance, and conflict. *Journal of Conflict Resolution* 49 (4): 625–633.

Commission of the European Communities. 2002. Green Paper on alternative dispute resolution in civil and commercial law (presented by the Commission). http://europa.eu/eur-lex/en/com/gpr/2002/com2002_0196en01.pdf [September 20, 2008].

Compton, R. 2002. Discovering the promise of curriculum integration: The National Curriculum Integration Project. *Conflict Resolution Quarterly* 19 (4): 447–464.

Conley Tyler, M., & J. Bornstein. 2006. Accreditation of on-line dispute resolution practitioners. *Conflict Resolution Quarterly* 23 (3): 383–404.

Conley Tyler, M., & S.S. Raines. 2006. The human face of on-line dispute resolution. *Conflict Resolution Quarterly* 23 (3): 333–42.

Conflict Information Consortium (formerly Conflict Research Consortium) at the University of Colorado at Boulder. http://conflict.colorado.edu/ [September 1, 2010].

CRInfo. The conflict resolution information source. http://www.crinfo.org/ [September 1, 2010].

Cutler, D.M., & L.H. Summers. 1988. The cost of conflict resolution and financial distress: evidence from the Texaco-Pennzoil litigation. *The rand journal of economics* 19 (2): 157–172.

Dascal, M. 1989/2003. Controversies as quasi-dialogues. In *Dialoganalyse II, vol.* 1, ed. E. Weigand & F. Hundsnurscher, 147–159. Tübingen: Niemeyer. Reprinted in: *Interpretation and Understanding*, ed. M. Dascal, 280–292. Amsterdam/Philadelphia: John Benjamins.

———. 1998. Types of polemics and types of polemical moves. In *Dialoganalyse VI, vol. 1*, ed. S. Cmejrkova, J. Hoffmannova, O. Mullerova, & J. Svetla, 15–33. Tubingen: Niemeyer.

———. 2008. Dichotomies and types of debate. In *Controversy and Confrontation: Relating Controversy Analysis with Argumentation Theory*, ed. F.H. van Eemeren & B. Garssen, 27–49. Amsterdam: John Benjamins.

Dascal, M., & C. Marras. Forthcoming. The *Republique des lettres*: a republic of quarrels? http://www.tau.ac.il/humanities/philos/dascal/ [September 1, 2010].

Dauer, E.A., & L.J. Marcus. 1997. Adapting mediation to link resolution of medical malpractice disputes with health care quality improvement. *Law and Contemporary Problems* 60 (1): 185–218.

Davidheiser, M. 2006. Harmony, peacemaking, and power: Controlling processes and African mediation. *Conflict Resolution Quarterly* 23 (3): 281–99.

Desivilya, H.S., & R. Gal. 2003. Theory-based training in constructing conflict for trauma relief personnel: The case of Croatia and Bosnia. *Conflict Resolution Quarterly* 21 (2): 155–67.

De Stefani, E. 2007. Regards sur la langue. Les données vidéo dans la recherche linguistique. In *Regards sur la langue. Les données vidéo dans la recherche linguistique*, ed. E. De Stefani, 1–9. *Bulletin VALS-ASLA* 85.

Deutsch, M. 2002. Social psychology's contributions to the study of conflict resolution. *Negotiation Journal* 18 (4): 307–320.

———. 2006. (2nd edition). Cooperation and competition. In *The handbook of conflict resolution. Theory and practice*, ed. M. Deutsch, P.T. Coleman, & E.C. Marcus. San Francisco: Jossey-Bass.

Dumont, M., A.N. Perret-Clermont, & E. Moss. 1995. Influence de la relation d'affinité affective sur le raisonnement moral et la coordination socio-cognitive d'enfants en interaction sur une tache de résolution de problème social. *Cahiers de Psychologie de l'Université de Neuchâtel* 32: 41–66.

Durrer, R. 1917–1921. *Die ältesten Quellen über den seiligen Nikolaus von Flüe, sein Leben und seinen Einfluss*. Sarnen: Regierungsdrückerei.

Duss-von Werdt, J. 2005. *Homo Mediator. Geschichte und Menschenbild der Mediation*. Stuttgart: Klett-Cotta.

Eisenhardt, K. 1989. Agency theory: An assessment and review. *The Academy of Management Review* 14 (1): 57–74.

Van Eemeren, F.H. 2009. (ed.). *Examining argumentation in context: Fifteen studies on strategic manoeuvring.* Amsterdam/Philadelphia: John Benjamins.

———. 2010. *Strategic manoeuvring in argumentative discourse. Extending the pragma-dialectical theory of argumentation.* Amsterdam/Philadelphia: John Benjamins.

Van Eemeren, F.H., & R. Grootendorst. 1984. *Speech acts in argumentative discussions.* Dordrecht/Cinnaminson: Foris.

———. 1992. *Argumentation, communication, and fallacies. A pragma-dialectical perspective.* Hillsdale (NJ) etc: Erlbaum.

———. 1994. Rationale for a pragma-dialectical perspective. In *Studies in Pragma-Dialectics*, ed. F.H. van Eemeren & R. Grootendorst, 11–28. Amsterdam: Sic-Sat.

———. 2004. *A systematic theory of argumentation: The pragma-dialectical account.* Cambridge: Cambridge University Press.

Van Eemeren, F.H., R. Grootendorst, S. Jackson, & S. Jacobs. 1993. *Reconstructing argumentative discourse.* Tuscaloosa/London: The University of Alabama Press.

Van Eemeren, F.H., R. Grootendorst, & A.F. Snoeck-Henkemans. 2002. *Argumentation: Analysis, evaluation, presentation.* Mahwah (NJ)/London: Erlbaum.

Van Eemeren, F.H., & P. Houtlosser. 2002. Strategic Maneuvering: Maintaining a Delicate Balance, in: *Dialectic and rhetoric: The warp and woof of argumentation analysis*, ed. F.H. van Eemeren & P. Houtlosser, 131–159. Dordrecht: Kluwer Academic Publishers.

———. 2005. Theoretical construction and argumentative reality: An analytic model of critical discussion and conventionalised types of argumentative activity. In *The Uses of Argument. Proceedings of a Conference at McMaster University, 18–21 May 2005*, ed. D. Hitchcock & D. Farr, 75–84. Hamilton: Ontario Society for the Study of Argumentation.

———. 2007. Seizing the occasion: Parameters for analysing ways of strategic manoeuvring. In *Proceedings of the Sixth Conference of the International Society for the Study of Argumentation*, op. cit., 375–380.

Van Eemeren, F.H., P. Houtlosser, & A.F. Snoeck-Henkemans. 2007. *Argumentative indicators in discourse. A pragma-dialectical study.* New York: Springer.

van Eemeren, F. H, S. Greco Morasso, M. Grossen, A.-N. Perret-Clermont, & E. Rigotti. 2009. Argupolis: A doctoral program on argumentation practices in different communication contexts. *Studies in Communication sciences* 9 (1): 289–301.

Elia, C. 2007. Vierzig Jahre Presseombudsmann: Wer sind die Leserschaftsanwälte und wie kommunizieren sie? Eine vergleichende Analyse. *Europäische Medienethiken, zfkm, Zentrum für Kommunikations- und Medienwissenschaft* 9 (1): 100–105.

European Union. 2008. *Directive 2008/52/EC of the European Parliament and of the Council of 21 May 2008 on certain aspects of mediation in civil and commercial aspects.* http://eur-lex.europa.eu/LexUriServ/LexUriServ.do?uri=CELEX:32008L0052:EN:NOT [September 1, 2010].

———. 2004. European code of conduct on mediation. http://ec.europa.eu/civiljustice/adr/adr_ec_code_conduct_en.htm [September 1, 2010].

Felstiner, W.L.F., R.L. Abel, & A. Sarat. 1980–81. The emergence and transformation of disputes: naming, blaming, claiming. *Law & Society Review* 15 (3–4): 631–654.

Feteris, E.T. 1987. *The dialectical role of the judge in a legal process. In: Argument and critical practices. Proceedings of the fifth SCA/AFA Conference on Argumentation*, ed. J.W. Wenzer, 335–339. Annandale: Speech Communication Association.

———. 1993. The judge as a critical antagonist in a legal process: a pragma-dialectical perspective. In *Argument and the postmodern challenge, Proceedings of the Eight SCA/AFA Conference on Argumentation*, ed. R.E. McKenow, 476–480. Annandale: Speech Communication Association.

———. 1999. *Fundamentals of legal argumentation: a survey of theories on the justification of judicial decisions*. Dodrecht: Kluwer Academic Publishers.

———. 2005. (ed.). *Schemes and Structures of Legal Argumentation. Argumentation* 19 (4), Special issue.

Filimon, I.A. 2009. Kyosei – An example of cultural keyword argumentatively exploited in corporate reporting discourse. *Studies in Communication Sciences* 9 (2): 131–152.

Filler, E.A. 2006. *Wirtschaftsmediation im Europäischen Vergleich: Erfarungswerte von Unternehmen Mediatoren*. Wien: European Institute for Business Mediation. http://www.europemediation.eu/CSR, [September 1, 2010].

Fillmore, C.J. 1971. Verbs of judging: An exercise in semantic description. In *Studies in Linguistic Semantics*, ed. C.J. Fillmore & D.T Langendoen, 272–289. New York: Holt, Rinehart & Winston.

Fisher, R., W. Ury & B. Patton. 1991. (2nd edition). *Getting to yes. Negotiating agreement without giving in*. New York: Penguin Books.

Folberg, J., & A.L. Milne (1988 eds). *Divorce mediation: theory and practice*. New York/London: The Guilford Press.

Folberg, J., A.L. Milne, & P. Salem. 2004. (eds). *Divorce and family mediation: Models, techniques, and applications*. New York/London: The Guilford Press.

Folger, J.P. & T. Jones. 1994. (eds). *New directions in mediation. Communication research and perspectives*. Thousand Oaks/London/New Delhi: Sage.

Fong, L. 2005. Milan Mediation Model. In *Proceedings of the V International Conference of the World Mediation Forum*, Cransmontana, September 9–11, 2005, 184–189.

Fongmediate.com. Psychology-Mediation-Arbitration-Corporate Consulting. http://www.fongmediate.com [September 1, 2010].

Forester, J. 1994. Lawrence Susskind: Activist mediation and public disputes. In *When talk works: Profiles of mediators*, ed. D.M. Kolb and associates, 309–354. San Francisco: Jossey-Bass.

Foster, M.R. 1998. Effective job analysis methods. In *Handbook of Human Resources Management*, ed. S.E. Condrey, 528–555. San Francisco: Jossey Bass.

Friedman, G.J. 1993. *A guide to divorce mediation. How to reach a fair, legal settlement at a fraction of the cost*. New York: Workman Publishing Company.

Friedman, G.J., & J. Himmelstein. 2007. Metodologia e tecnica di mediazione. Il ruolo del mediatore e il processo di comunicazione. Unpublished notes for the intervention within the SUPSI post-diploma course in Mediazione e utilizzo di tecniche mediative sul posto di lavoro. Ascona, May 30–June 3, 2007.

Garssen, B. 2001. Argument schemes. In *Crucial concepts in argumentation theory*, ed. F.H. van Eeemeren, 81–99. Amsterdam: Sic-Sat.

Gatti, M.C. 2000. *La negazione fra semantica e pragmatica*. Milano: ISU.

———. 2003. Pratiche di analisi semiotica in Jurij M. Lotman e Boris A.Uspenski. In *Semiotica II. Configurazione disciplinare e questioni contemporanee*, ed. G. Bettetini, S. Cigada, S. Raynaud, & E. Rigotti, 141–165. Brescia: La scuola.

Giugliano, A. 2007. Dinamiche della comunicazione tra insegnanti ed alumni alla scuola media. Studio comparativo tra lezioni di matematica ed italiano. Unpublished Ph.D. dissertation, USI-University of Lugano.

Glasl, F. 2004. *Selbsthilfe in Konflikten. Konzepte – Übungen – Praktische Methoden.* Stuttgart/Bern: Freies Geistesleben.

Glenn, Ph., & L. Susskind. 2010. How talk works: Studying negotiation interaction. *Negotiation Journal* 26 (2): 117–123.

Gobber, G. 1999. *Pragmatica delle frasi interrogative. Con applicazioni al Tedesco, al Polacco e al Russo.* Milano: I.S.U.

———. 2007. Some remarks on interrogativity and argumentation. In: *Proceedings of the Sixth Conference of the International Society for the Study of Argumentation*, op. cit., 461–464.

Gobber, G., M.C. Gatti, & S. Cigada. 2006. (eds.). *Sýndesmoi. Connettivi nella realtà dei testi.* Milano: Vita e Pensiero.

Goldberg, S.B. 1989. Grievance mediation. A successful alternative to labor arbitration. *Negotiation Journal* 5 (1): 9–15.

Goldberg, S.B., F.E.A. Sander, N.H. Rogers, & S. Rudolph Cole. 2007. (5th edition). *Dispute resolution: Negotiation, mediation and other processes.* Austin (etc.): Wolters Kluwer.

Goleman, D. 1998. *Working with emotional intelligence.* New York: Bantam.

Graumann, C.F., & W. Kallmeyer. 2002. Perspective and perspectivation in discourse: An introduction. In *Perspective and perspectivation in discourse*, ed. C.F. Graumann & W. Kallmeyer, 1–11. Amsterdam/Philadelphia: John Benjamins.

Greco, S. 2003. When presupposing becomes dangerous. How the procedure of presuppositional accommodation can be exploited in manipulative discourses. *Studies in Communication Sciences* 3 (2): 217–234.

———. 2005a. Der kommunikative Bestandteil der mediatorischen Kompetenz. *Forum Mediation* 8 (2): 4–15.

———. 2005b. The intercultural mediator: Personal qualities and communicative skills. In *Proceedings of the V International Conference of the World Mediation Forum*, Cransmontana, September 9–11, 2005, 195–206.

Greco Morasso, S. 2007. The covert argumentativity of mediation: Developing argumentation through asking questions. In *Proceedings of the Sixth Conference of the International Society for the Study of Argumentation,* op. cit., 513–520.

———. 2008. The ontology of conflict. *Pragmatics & Cognition* 16 (3): 540–567.

———. 2009a. *Argumentative and other communicative strategies of the mediation practice.* Unpublished Ph.D. dissertation, USI-University of Lugano.

———. 2009b. The Argumentum experience. In *Argumentation and education: theoretical foundations and practices*, ed. N. Muller-Mirza & A.-N. Perret-Clermont, 215–235. New York: Springer.

Grossen, M. 1992. Intersubjectivité et negotiation de la demande dans un entretien thérapeutique. In: *L'espace thérapeutique: Cadres et contextes*, ed. M. Grossen & A.-N. Perret-Clermont, 165–191. Neuchâtel/Paris: Delachaux et Niestlé.

———. 2001. La notion de contexte: Quelle définition pour quelle psychologie? Un essai de mise au point. In *Apprentissage, développement et significations*, ed. J.P. Bernié, 59–76. Bordeaux: Presses Universitaires de Bordeaux.

Grossen, M., & A.N. Perret-Clermont. 1992. (eds). *L'espace thérapeutique: Cadres et contextes*, op. cit.

———. 1994. Psychosocial perspective on cognitive development: Construction of adult-child intersubjectivity in logic tasks. In *Sociogenesis re-examined*, ed. W. De Graaf & R. Maier, 243–260. New York: Springer.

Grossi, P. 2003. *Prima lezione di diritto*. Roma/Bari: Laterza.

———. 2007. *L'Europa del diritto*. Roma/Bari: Laterza.

Guy-Ecabert, C. 2002. De la médiation des conflits à la culture de la médiation: L'école face à la violence et aux incivilités. In: *Médiation en Europe: Echanges sur les pratiques/Master Européen en Médiation*, 171–189. Sion: Institut Universitaire Kurt Bösch.

Hamblin, C. 1970. *Fallacies*. London: Methuen.

Harrison, T.R. 2004. What is success in ombuds processes? Evaluation of a university ombudsman. *Conflict Resolution Quarterly* 21 (3): 313–35.

Hatch, M.J. 1997. *Organization Theory. Modern, Symbolic, and Postmodern Perspectives*. Oxford: Oxford University Press.

Haynes, J.M. 1994. *The fundamentals of family mediation*. New York: SUNY.

———. 2004. Vienna speech: Support for human and social growth. In *Mediation: Positive conflict management*, ed. J.M. Haynes, G.L. Haynes & L.S. Fong, 261–69. New York: SUNY.

Haynes, J.M., & G.L. Haynes. 1989. *Mediating divorce. Casebook of strategies for successful family negotiations*. San Francisco: Jossey-Bass.

Haynes, G.L. Haynes & L.S. Fong. 2004. *Mediation: Positive conflict management*, op. cit.

Herberger, M. 1986. *Sprach- und Handlungsmuster in der Rechtsgeschichte der Schlichtung. In Kommunikationstypologie. Handlungsmuster, Textsorten, Situationstypen*, ed. W. Kallmeyer, 227–244. Düsseldorf: Jahrbuch des Instituts für deutsche Sprache 1985.

Herrman, M.S., N. Hollett, J. Gale, & M. Foster. 2001. Defining mediator knowledge and skills. *Negotiation Journal* 17 (2): 139–53.

Herrman, M.S., Hollett, N. & Gale, J. 2006. Mediation from beginning to end: A testable model. In *Handbook of Mediation. Bridging Theory, Research, and Practice*, ed. M.S. Herrman, 19–78. Malden (MA)/ Oxford (UK)/ Victoria (Australia): Blackwell Publishing.

Hicks, T. 2001. Another look at identity-based conflict: The roots of conflict in the psychology of consciousness. *Negotiation Journal* 17 (1): 35–45.

Honeyman, Ch., B.C. Goh, & L. Kelly. 2004. Skill is not enough: seeking connectedness and authority in mediation. *Negotiation Journal* 20 (4): 489–511.

Hopmann, P.T. 1996. *The negotiation process and the resolution of international conflicts*. Columbia: University of South Carolina Press.

Hopper, R., S. Koch, & J. Mandelbaum. 1986. Conversation analysis methods. In *Contemporary issues in language and discourse processes*, ed. D.G. Ellis & W.A. Donohue, 169–186. Hillsdale (N.J.)/ London: Lawrence Erlbaum.

Houston, A. 1999. International conflict management 1945–1995. Official codebook for the International conflict management dataset (1999.DAT). http://www.posc.canterbury.ac.nz/jbercovitch/mediation/1999%20rationale.pdf [October 11, 2008].

Hyman, C.S., & C.B. Schecther. 2006. Mediating medical malpractice lawsuits against hospitals: New York City's pilot project. *Health Affairs* 25 (5): 1394–1399.

INCORE. International Conflict Research. http://www.incore.ulst.ac.uk [September 1, 2010].

Integrated Data for Events Analysis (IDEA). http://www.vranet.com/idea/ [September 1, 2010].

Jackson, S. 1986. Building a case for claims about discourse structure. In *Contemporary issues in language and discourse processes*, op. cit., 129–147.

Jacobs, S. 1986. How to make an argument from example in discourse analysis. In *Contemporary issues in language and discourse processes*, op. cit., 149–167.

———. 1989. Speech acts and arguments. *Argumentation* 3 (4): 345–365.

———. 2002. Maintaining neutrality in dispute mediation: managing disagreement while managing not to disagree. *Journal of Pragmatics* 34 (10–11): 1402–1426.

Jacobs, S., & M. Aakhus. 2002a. How to resolve a conflict: two models of dispute resolution. In *Advances in pragma-dialectics*, ed. F.H. van Eemeren, 29–44. Amsterdam: Sic Sat/ Newport News: Vale Press.

———. 2002b. What mediators do with words: implementing three models of rational discussion in dispute mediation. *Conflict resolution quarterly* 20 (2): 177–203.

Jackendoff, R. 1983. *Semantics and cognition*. Cambridge: MIT Press.

———. 1990. *Semantic structures*. Cambridge: MIT Press.

Jones, T.S. 2004. Conflict resolution education: The field, the findings, and the future. *Conflict Resolution Quarterly* 22 (1–2): 233–267.

———. 2005. (ed.). *Conflict Resolution Quarterly* 22 (4).

Jones, T.S., & A. Bodtker. 2001. Mediating with hearth in mind: Addressing emotion in mediation practice. *Negotiation Journal* 17 (3): 217–244.

Journet, Ch. 1980. *Saint Nicolas de Flue* (4th edition). Fribourg/Paris: Éditions Saint-Paul.

Kelly, J.B. 2004. Family mediation research: Is there empirical support for the field? *Conflict Resolution Quarterly* 22 (1–2): 3–35.

Kerbrat-Orecchioni, C., & V. Traverso. 2007. Introduction. In *Confidence/Confiding: Dévoilement de soi dans l'interaction/Self-disclosure in interaction*, ed. C. Kerbrat-Orecchioni & V. Traverso, 1–34. Tübingen: Niemeyer.

Kim, N.H., J.A. Wall, Jr., D. Sohn, & J.S. Kim. 1993. Community and industrial mediation in South Korea. *Journal of Conflict Resolution* 37 (2): 361–381.

Knight, J. 1992. *Institutions and social conflict*. Cambridge: Cambridge University Press.

Kolb, D.M., and associates. 1994. (ed.). *When talk works: Profiles of mediators*. San Francisco: Jossey-Bass.

Königswieser, R., & A. Exner. 1998. *Systemische Intervention – Architekturen und Designs für Berater und Veränderungsmanager*. Stuttgart: Klett-Cotta.

Königswieser, R., & M. Hillebrand. 2008. (4th edition). *Einführung in die systemische Organisationsberatung*. Heidelberg: Carl-Auer.

Kovach, K.K. 2005. Mediation. In *The handbook of dispute resolution*, ed. M.L. Moffitt & R.C. Bordone, 304–317. San Francisco: Jossey-Bass.

Kressel, K. 1994. Frances Butler: Questions that lead to answers in child custody mediation. In *When talk works: Profiles of mediators*, op. cit., 17–58.

Krivis, J. 2006. *Improvisational negotiation. A mediator's stories of conflict about love, money, anger – and the strategies that resolved them*. San Francisco: Jossey-Bass.

Lall, A. 1966. *Modern international negotiation: Principles and practice*. New York/London: Columbia University Press.

Lawrence, P.R., & J.W. Lorsch. 1967. *Organization and environment. Managing differentiation and integration*. Boston (MA): Harvard Business School Press.

Levine, H. 2005. Mediating the War of olives and pines: Consensus-based land-use planning in a multicultural setting. *Negotiation Journal* 21 (1): 29–69.

Levinson, S.C. 1979/1992. Activity types and language. *Linguistics* 17. Reprinted in *Talk at work*, ed. P. Drew & J. Heritage, 66–100. Cambridge: Cambridge University Press.

Li, C. 2001. Evaluating the various non-litigation processes for resolving disputes: The cost-effectiveness approach. *Journal of International Arbitration* 18 (4): 435–447.

Liebman, C.B., & C.S. Hyman. 2004. A mediation skills model to manage disclosure of errors and adverse events to patients. *Health Affairs* 23 (4): 22–32.

Light, P., & A.N. Perret-Clermont. 1989. Social Context Effects in Learning and Testing. In *Cognition and Social Worlds*, ed. A. Gellatly, D. Rogers & J.A. Sloboda, 99–112. Oxford: Oxford University Press.

Lodder, A.R., & G.A.W. Vreeswijk. 2004. Online arbitration services at a turning point. *ICC International Court of Arbitration Bullettin*: 21–28.

Long, J.J. 2003. Compliance in small claims court: exploring the factors associated with defendants' level of compliance with mediated and adjudicated outcomes. *Conflict Resolution Quarterly* 21 (2): 139–153.

Lotman, J., & B.A. Uspenskij. 1987. *Tipologia della cultura*. Milano: Bompiani.

Lowry, C., & S. Littlejohn. 2006. Dialogue and the discourse of peacebuilding in Maluku, Indonesia. *Conflict Resolution Quarterly* 23 (4): 409–426.

Malhotra, D., & S. Liyanage. 2005. Long-term effects of peace workshops in protracted conflicts. *Journal of Conflict Resolution* 49 (6): 908–424.

Mann, S. 1997. (2nd edition). Agency theory. In *The Blackwell Enclyclopedia of management,* ed. J. Garrett, 1–2. Malden: Blackwell Publishing.

Mann, W.C. 2002. Dialogue macrogame theory. In *Proceedings of the* 3rd *SIGdial workshop on Discourse and dialogue (Philadelphia, Pennsylvania, July 11 and 12, 2002)*, 129–141. http://portal.acm.org/citation.cfm?id=1118139 [September 1, 2010].

Mansfield, E.D., & B. Pollins. 2001. The study of interdependence and conflict. *Journal of Conflict Resolution* 45 (6): 834–859.

March, J.G., & H.A. Simon. 1958. *Organizations*. New York: John Wiley and Sons.

Marinoni, R. 2001. L'analisi dei conflitti organizzativi nella consulenza sistemica alle imprese. *Mediazione familiare sistemica* 1.

Martello, M. 2006. (ed.). *Le A.D.R.: risposta al contenzioso scolastico, risorsa per il progetto formativo della scuola. Atti del convegno nazionale dirigenti scolastici degli istituti statali e non statali*, Milano: Provincia di Milano e Assessorato all'istruzione.

Martini, G., E. Rigotti, & R. Palmieri. 2008. Teoria economica e razionalità. *Atlantide* 14 (2): 73–78.

Marzotto, C. & G. Tamanza. 2004. La mediazione e la cura dei legami familiari. In: *Rigenerare i legami: La mediazione nelle relazioni familiari e comunitarie*, op. cit. 71–103.

Matz, D. 2006. Reconstructing Camp David. *Negotiation Journal* 22 (1): 89–103.

Mediation Matters. http://www.mediationmatters.org [September 1, 2010].

Meierding, N.R. 1993. Does mediation work? A survey of long-term satisfaction and durability rates for privately mediated agreements. *Mediation Quarterly* 11 (2): 157–170.

Mel'čuk, I.A. 1997. *Vers une linguistique sens-texte. Leçon inaugurale (faite le vendredi 10 janvier 1997, Collège de France, Chaire internationale)*. http://www.olst.umontreal.ca/melcuk [September 1, 2010].

———. 2001. *Communicative Organization in Natural Language. The Semantic-Communicative Structure of Sentences*. Amsterdam/Philadelphia: John Benjamins.

Menkel-Meadow, C. 1984. Toward another view of legal negotiation: The structure of problem-solving. *UCLA Law Review* 31: 754–842.

———. 2001. When winning isn't everything: The lawyer as problem-solver. Georgetown Public Law Research Paper No. 258166.

———. 2005. Roots and inspirations. A brief history of the foundations of dispute resolution. In *The handbook of dispute resolution*, op. cit.

Moffitt, M.L. 2006. Before the Big Bang: The making of an ADR pioneer. *Negotiation Journal* 22 (4): 437–443.

Moffitt, M.L., & R.C. Bordone. 2005. Perspectives on dispute resolution. An introduction. In *The handbook of dispute resolution*, 1–12. San *Francisco*: Jossey-Bass.

Mondada, L. 2002. Pratiques de transcription et effets de categorisation. In *Transcrire l'interaction*, ed. B. Bonu, Numero special de *Cahiers de praxématique* 39: 45–75.

———. 2006. Video recording as the preservation of the fundamental features for analysis. In *Video analysis*, ed. H. Knoblauch, J. Raab, H.-G. Soeffner, & B. Schnettler, 51–67. Bern: Peter Lang.

Muller, N., & A.N. Perret-Clermont. 1999. Dimensions institutionnelles, interpersonnelles et culturelles d'un dispositif pour penser et apprendre. *Cahiers de Psychologie de l'Université de Neuchâtel* n. 35: 3–15.

Muller-Mirza, N., & A.N. Perret-Clermont. 2009. *Argumentation and education: Theoretical foundations and practices*, op. cit.

Nader, L., & H.F. Todd. 1978. Introduction. In *The disputing process. Law in ten societies*, ed. L. Nader & H.F. Todd, 1–40. New York: Columbia University Press.

Nobel Foundation. http://nobelprize.org [September 1, 2010].

Noel, B.R., A. Torfin Shoemake, & C.L. Hale. 2006. Conflict resolution in a non-Western context: Conversations with Indonesian scholars and practitioners. *Conflict Resolution Quarterly* 23 (4): 427–446.

Nothdurft, W. 1995a. (ed.). *Schlichtung, Band 1: Streit schlichten. Gesprächsanalytische Untersuchungen zu institutionellen Formen konsensueller Konfliktregelung*. Berlin/New York: Walter de Gruyter.

———. 1995b. Gesprächsanalyse von Schlichtung. Die Geschichte eines Forschungspojekts und die Entwicklung seiner Ergebnisse. In *Schlichtung, Band 1: Streit schlichten…*, op. cit., 1–26.

———. 1997. *Schlichtung. Band 2. Konfliktstoff. Gesprächsanalyse der Konfliktbearbeitung in Schlichtungsgesprächen*. Berlin/New York: Walter de Gruyter.

Nowell, B.L., & D. Salem. 2004. State-level associations: An emerging trend in community mediation. *Conflict Resolution Quarterly* 21 (4): 399–417.

Organisation for Economic Co-operation and Development. 2001. *The DAC guidelines: Helping prevent violent conflict*. http://www.oecd.org/dataoecd/15/54/1886146.pdf [September 1, 2010].

Organization of News Ombudsmen (ONO). http://www.newsombudsmen.org/what.htm [September 1, 2010].

Orr, P.J., K. Emerson, & D.L. Keyes. 2008. Environmental conflict resolution practice and performance: An evaluation framework. *Conflict Resolution Quarterly* 25 (3): 283–301.

Palmieri, R. 2009. Regaining trust through argumentation in the context of the current financial-economic crisis. *Studies in Communication Sciences* 9 (2): 59–78.

Palmieri, R., & E. Rigotti. 2010. Analysing and evaluating complex argumentation in an economic-financial context. In *Dialectics, dialogue and argumentation: An examination of Douglas Walton's theories of reasoning and argument*, ed. C. Reed & C.W. Tindale, 85–99. London: College Publications.

Parkinson, L. 1997. *Family mediation*. London: Sweet & Maxwell.

Patton, B. 2005. Negotiation. In *The handbook of dispute resolution*, op. cit., 279–303.

Pearson d'Estrée, T., L.A. Fast, J.N. Weiss, & M.S. Jakobsen. 2001. Changing the debate about "success" in conflict resolution efforts. *Negotiation Journal* 17 (2): 101–113.

Perret-Clermont, A.N. 2006. Comments on Rigotti and Rocci. In *The Communication sciences as a multidisciplinary enterprise*, ed. M. Colombetti, 181–188. *Studies in Communication Sciences* 6 (2), Anniversary issue.

Perret-Clermont, A.N., F. Carugati, & J. Oates. 2004. A socio-cognitive perspective on learning and cognitive development. In *Cognitive and language development in children*, ed. J. Oates & A. Grayson 305–332. Oxford: Blackwell Publishing.

Petri Hispani *Summulae logicales*, ed. I.M. Bochenski. 1947. Torino: Marietti.

Philips, B. 1999. Reformulating dispute narratives through active listening. *Mediation Quarterly* 17 (2): 161–180.

Pontecorvo, C. & F. Arcidiacono. 2007. *Famiglie all'italiana. Parlare a tavola*. Milano: Raffaello Cortina.

Potok, Ch. 1973. *My name is Asher Lev*. London: Penguin Books. (First edition: William Heinenmann 1972).

Povey, A., K. Cattell, & K. Michell. 2005. Mediation practice in the South African construction industry: The influence of culture, the legislative environment, and the professional institutions. *Negotiation Journal* 21 (4): 481–493.

Princen, T. 1992a. *Intermediaries in international conflict*. Princeton (New Jersey): Princeton University Press.

———. 1992b. Mediation by a transnational organization: The case of the Vatican. In *Mediation in international relations. Multiple approaches to conflict management*, ed. J. Bercovitch & J.Z. Rubin, 149–175. London: Macmillan Press and New York: St. Martin's Press.

Program on Negotiation at Harvard Law School: A university consortium dedicated to developing the theory and practice of negotiation and dispute resolution. http://www.pon.harvard.edu [September 1, 2010].

Reuveny, R. & J.W. Maxwell. 2001. Conflict and renewable resources. *Journal of Conflict Resolution* 45 (6): 719–743.

Van Rees, M.A. 1992. *The use of language in conversation. An introduction to research in conversational analysis*. Amsterdam: Sic-Sat.

———. 2003. Pragma-dialectical analysis and evaluation of problem-solving discussions. *Argumentation* 17 (4): 465–479.

———. 2005. Dissociation: A dialogue technique. In *Argumentation in dialogic interaction*. Special issue of *Studies in Communication Sciences*, ed. M. Dascal, F.H. van Eemeren, E. Rigotti, S. Stati & A. Rocci, 35–49.

Rigotti, E. 1991. L'originarsi del senso nella domanda. *Synesis* 4: 7–14.

———. 1993. La sequenza testuale. *L'analisi linguistica e letteraria* 1: 43–148.

———. 2003. La linguistica tra le scienze della comunicazione. In *Linguistica e nuove professioni*, ed. A. Giacalone Ramat, E. Rigotti & A. Rocci, 21–35. Milano: FrancoAngeli.

———. 2005a. Congruity theory and argumentation. In *Argumentation in dialogic interaction*, op. cit., 75–96.

———. 2005b. Plurilinguismo e unità culturale in Europa. In *Europa plurilingue: Comunicazione e didattica*, ed. B. Cambiaghi, C. Milani e P. Pontani, 307–319. Milano: Vita e Pensiero.

———. 2006. Relevance of context-bound loci to topical potential in the argumentation stage. *Argumentation* 20 (4): 519–540.

———. 2008. Locus a causa finali. In *Proceedings of the IADA Workshop Word meaning in argumentative dialogue. Homage to Sorin Stati*, ed. G. Gobber, S. Cantarini, S. Cigada, M.C. Gatti & S. Gilardoni. Special issue of *L'analisi linguistica e letteraria* XVI 2: 559–576.

———. 2009. Whether and how classical topics can be revived in the contemporary theory of argumentation. In *Pondering on problems of argumentation*, ed. F.H. van Eemeren & B. Garssen, 157–178. New York: Springer.

Rigotti, E., & S. Cigada. 2004. *La comunicazione verbale*. Milano: Apogeo.

Rigotti, E., & S. Greco. 2005. *Introducing argumentation*. Argumentum eLearning module, www.argumentum.ch [September 1, 2010].

Rigotti, E., & S. Greco Morasso. 2006a. Argomentazione nei media: Preliminaries. In E. Rigotti et. al., *Argomentazione nei media*, Argumentum eLearning module, www.argumentum.ch [September 1, 2010].

———. 2006b. Topics: the argument generator. In *Argumentation for financial communication*, E. Rigotti et al., Argumentum eLearning module, www.argumentum.ch [September 1, 2010].

———. 2009a. Argumentation as object of interest and as social and cultural resource. In *Argumentation and education: theoretical foundations and practices*, op. cit., 9–66.

———. 2009b. (eds.). Argumentative processes and communication contexts. Thematic section of *Studies in Communication sciences.*

———. 2010. Comparing the Argumentum Model of Topics to other contemporary approaches to argument schemes: The procedural and material components. *Argumentation* 24 (4): 489–512.

Rigotti, E. & A. Rocci. 2001. Sens – non-sens – contresens. Tentative d'une définition explicative. *Studies in Communication Sciences* 1 (2): 45–80.

Rigotti, E., & A. Rocci. 2006. Towards a definition of communication context. Foundations of an interdisciplinary approach to communication. In *The Communication sciences as a multidisciplinary enterprise*, ed. M. Colombetti, 155–180. *Studies in Communication Sciences* 6 (2), Anniversary issue.

Rigotti, E., A. Rocci, & S. Greco. 2006. The semantics of reasonableness. In *Considering Pragma-Dialectics*, ed. P. Houtlosser & A. van Rees, 257–274. Mahwah, New Jersey/London: Lawrence Erlbaum Associates.

Rocci, A. 2005. *La modalità epistemica tra semantica e argomentazione*. Milano: ISU.

Ross, S.A. 1973. The economic theory of agency: The principal's problem. *The American Economic Review* 63 (2): 134–139.

Ross, W.H., & D.E. Conlon. 2000. Hybrid forms of third-party dispute resolution: Theoretical implications of combining mediation and arbitration. *The Academy of Management Review* 25 (2): 416–427.

Rubin, J.Z., & C. Rubin. 1989. *When Families Fight: How to Handle Conflict With Those You Love.* Boyne City, Michigan: Harbour House.

Rudolph Cole, S., & K.M. Blankley. 2005. Arbitration. In *The handbook of dispute resolution*, op. cit., 318–335.

Sander, F.E.A. 1979. Varieties of dispute processing. In *The Pound Conference: Perspectives on justice in the future. Proceedings of the National conference on the causes of popular dissatisfaction with the administration of justice*, ed. A.L. Levin & R.R. Wheeler, 65–87. St. Paul (Minnesota): West Publishing Co.

Sander, F.E.A., & S.B. Goldberg. 1994. Fitting the forum to the fuss: A user-friendly guide to selecting an ADR procedure. *Negotiation Journal* 10 (1): 49–68.

Saposnek, D. 2004. Commentary: The future of the history of family mediation research. *Conflict Resolution Quarterly* 22 (1–2): 37–53.

Schweingruber, E. 1979. *Friedenspflicht und Konfliktserledigung aufgrund der Gesamtarbeitsverträge in der Schweiz*. Zürich: Juris Druck.

Schrodt, Ph. 2006. TABARI: Textual Analysis by Augmented Replacement Instructions. Version 0.5. http://web.ku.edu/keds/tabari.dir/tabari.manual.060228.pdf [September 1, 2010].

Schrodt, Ph., D.J. Gerner, Ö. Yilmaz, & D. Hermreck. 2005. The CAMEO (Conflict and Mediation Event Observations) Actor Coding Framework. Paper prepared for delivery at the 2005 Annual Meeting of the American Political Science Association, 1 – 4 September 2005.

Schröder, P. 1997. (ed.). *Schlichtung. Band 3. Schlichtungsgespräche. Ein Textband mit einer esemplarischen Analyse*. Berlin/New York: Walter de Gruyter.

Schwarz, B., A.-N. Perret-Clermont, A. Trognon, & P. Marro. 2008. Emergent learning in successive activities: Learning in interaction in a laboratory context. *Pragmatics & Cognition* 16 (1): 57–87.

Searle, J. 1969. *Speech Acts*. Cambridge: Cambridge University Press.
———. 1995. *The construction of social reality*. New York: Free Press.
Seul, J.R. 2005. Litigation as a dispute resolution alternative. In *The handbook of dispute resolution*, op. cit., 336–357.
Seuren, P.A.M. 1988. Lexical meaning and presupposition. In *Understanding the lexicon. Meaning, sense and world knowledge in lexical semantics*, ed. W. Hüllen & S. Schulze, 170–187. Tübingen: Niemeyer.
———. 2000. Presupposition, negation and trivalence. *Journal of Linguistics* 36: 261–297.
Shapiro, D.L. 2002. Negotiating emotions. *Conflict Resolution Quarterly* 20 (1): 67–82.
Singer, J. 2004. *The EU Mediation Atlas: Practice and Regulation*. London: LexisNexis.
Sørli, M.E., N. Petter Gleditsch, & H. Strand. 2005. Why is there so much conflict in the Middle East?. *Journal of Conflict Resolution* 49 (1): 141–165.
Stieber, C. 2000. 57 varieties: Has the ombudsman concept become diluted? *Negotiation Journal* 16 (1): 49–57.
Susskind, L.E. 2000. Confessions of a public dispute mediator. *Negotiation Journal* 16 (2): 129–132.
Susskind, L.E., R.H. Mnookin, B. Fuller, & L. Rozdeiczer. 2003. *Teaching multiparty negotiation: a workbook*. Cambridge (MA): Program On Negotiation. http://www.pon.org/downloads/Teaching%20Multiparty%20Negotiation.pdf [September 1, 2010].
Swiss Banking Ombudsman. http://www.bankingombudsman.ch [September 1, 2010].
Syme, D. 2006. Keeping pace: On-line technology and ADR services. *Conflict Resolution Quarterly* 2003. (3): 343–57.
Tardini, S. 1997. L'entimema nella struttura logica del linguaggio. *L'analisi linguistica e letteraria* 2: 419–40.
The Kansas Event Data System (KEDS) Project Website. http://web.ku.edu/keds/index.html [September 1, 2010].
The National Conference of Commissioners On Uniform State Laws. 2001. UNIFORM MEDIATION ACT of The American Bar Association Section of Dispute Resolution. http://www.nvbar.org/PDF/UniMedAct.PDF [September 1, 2010].
Touval, S., & I.W. Zartman. 1985a. International mediation: Conflict resolution and power politics. *Journal of Social Issues* 41 (2): 27–45.
———. 1985b. Introduction: Mediation in theory. In *International mediation in theory and practice*, ed. S. Touval & I.W. Zartman, 7–17. Boulder/London: Westview Press.
Traverso, V. 1999. *L'analyse des conversations*. Paris: Nathan.
Umbreit, M.S. 2001. *The handbook of victim-offender mediation*. San Francisco: Jossey-Bass.
Umbreit, M.S., R.B. Coates, & B. Vos. 2004. Victim-offender mediation: Three decades of practice and research. *Conflict Resolution Quarterly* 22 (1–2): 279–303.
Ury, W.L., J.M. Brett, & S.B. Goldberg. 1988a. Designing an effective dispute resolution system. *Negotiation Journal* 4 (4): 413–431.
———. 1988b. *Getting disputes resolved: Designing systems to cut the costs of conflict*. San Francisco: Jossey-Bass.
Uspenskij, B.A. 2005. *Il segno della Croce e lo spazio sacro. Perché gli ortodossi si fanno il segno della croce da destra a sinistra mentre i cattolici da sinistra a destra?* Napoli: M. D'Auria Editore.
Uzqueda, A., & P. Frediani. 2002. *La conciliazione. Guida per la soluzione negoziale delle controversie*. Milano: Giuffrè.
Volpe, M.R., & N. Phillips. 2003. Police use of mediation. *Conflict Resolution Quarterly* 21 (2): 263–26.

Volpe, M.R., & S. Strobl. 2005. Restorative justice responses to post-September 11 hate crimes: Potential and challenges. *Conflict Resolution Quarterly* 22 (4): 527–535.

Vraneski, A., & R. Richter. 2003. What's news? Reflections of intractable environmental conflicts in the news: Some promises, many premises. *Conflict Resolution Quarterly* 21 (2): 239–262.

Wall, J.A. Jr. 1981. Mediation. An analysis, review, and proposed research. *Journal of Conflict Resolution* 25 (1): 157–180.

Wall, J.A. Jr., & M. Blum. 1991. Community mediation in the People's Republic of China. *Journal of Conflict Resolution* 35 (1): 3–20.

Wall, J.A. Jr., & R.R. Callister. 1995. Ho'oponopono: Some lessons from Hawaiian mediation. *Negotiation Journal* 11 (1): 45–54.

———. 1999. Malaysian community mediation. *Journal of Conflict Resolution* 43 (3): 343–365.

Wall, J.A., Jr., & A. Lynn. 1993. Mediation: A current review. *Journal of Conflict Resolution* 37 (1): 160–194.

Wall, J.A. Jr., J. Stark & R.L. Standifer. 2001. Mediation: a current review and theory development. *Journal of Conflict Resolution* 45 (3): 370–391.

Walton, D.N. 1998. *The new dialectic: Conversational contexts of argument*. Toronto: University of Toronto Press.

Walton, D.N. 2007. The speech act of clarification in a dialogue model. *Studies in Communication Sciences* 7 (2): 165–197.

Walton, D.N., & A.R. Lodder. 2005. What role can rational argument play in ADR and Online Dispute Resolution? In *Second international ODR Workshop (odrworkshop.info)*, ed. J. Zeleznikow & A.R. Lodder, 69–76. Tilburg: Wolf Legal Publishers.

Walton, D.N., & D.M. Godden. 2006. Persuasion dialogue in online dispute resolution. *Artificial Intelligence and Law* 13 (2): 273–95.

Wegener, Ph. 1885/1991. Untersuchungen über die Grundfragen des Sprachlebens. Halle a.d. Saale: Niemeyer.

Wehr, P. 1979. *Conflict Regulation*. Boulder: Westview Press.

Winslade, J., & G. Monk. 2001. *Narrative Mediation*. San Francisco: Jossey-Bass.

Yarn, D.H. 1999. (ed). *Dictionary of Conflict Resolution*. San Francisco: Jossey-Bass.

Zehr, H. 2004. Commentary: Restorative justice: Beyond victim-offender mediation. *Conflict Resolution Quarterly* 22 (1–2): 305–315.

Zittoun, T., A.N. Perret-Clermont, & F. Carugati. 1997. Note sur la notion de conflit sociocognitif. *Cahiers de Psychologie de l'Université de Neuchâtel* 33: 27–30.

ANNEX

List of interviewed professionals

	Name	Organization-professional role	Prevailing mediation field	Date
1.	Marianne Galli-Widmer	Former President of the Associazione Ticinese per la Mediazione (ATME), Lugano, CH	Family and community mediation	10/05/2004 and 27/05/2008
2.	Maddalena Ermotti-Lepori	Former president of ATME, Lugano, CH	Family and community mediation	10/05/2004
3.	Marina Bernardo	Mediator, Centro delle Mediazioni di Lugano, Lugano, CH	Family and community mediation	18/05/2004
4.	Tamara Erez	Mediation Aargau, CH	Business and family mediation	24/06/2004
5.	Rosa Anaba	AIDS-Hilfe, Basel, CH	Support to migrants concerning health care and other issues. Community mediation.	26/07/2004
6.	Dante Lorenzetti	Director of the school program "Pre-tirocinio di orientamento", Lugano, CH	Informal activity of mediation in the school context	10/12/2005
7.	Filippo Jörg	Responsible of the pre- apprenticeship for integration and orientation of the Professional Education Department of DECS, Lugano, CH	Informal activity of mediation with foreign students in Lugano	20/01/2005
8.	Patricia Hasler-Arana	Project Dime, Bern, CH	Intercultural mediation with Swiss and foreign citizens	07/09/2005
9.	Larry Fong	Larry Fong Mediation, Alberta, Canada	Family, community and business mediation	07/09/2005
10.	Tim Hardy	CMS Cameron McKenna and CEDR, the Centre for Effective Dispute Resolution, London, UK	Commercial mediation	07/09/2005

	Name	Organization-professional role	Prevailing mediation field	Date
11.	Diana De la Rua Eugenio	Respuesta para la paz, Mediación en la comunidad, Buenos Aires, Argentina	Community mediation in the marginal neighbourhoods in Buenos Aires	08/09/2005
12.	Isabella Buzzi	Studio TdL, Milan, Italy	Family mediation	10/06/2008
13.	Radouan Jelassi	Imam, Lugano, CH	Intercultural mediation	03/07/2008
14.	Thomas Flucher	KoMeT Kommunikation-Mediation-Teamentwicklung, Sempach Station, CH	Organizational mediation, business mediation, construction mediation	31/07/2008
15.	Gianfranco Domenighetti	Director of the Sezione Sanitaria del Dipartimento della Sanità e della Socialità del Cantone Ticino, CH	Medical organizations	26/08/2008
16.	Mauro Martinoni	Former head of the Office for University studies of Ticino Canton, Bellinzona, CH	Mediation in institutional contexts	27/08/08

The majority of the interviews were held in face-to-face modality. A few of them were supported by other means (telephone or e-mail).

Index of authors

Index of terms